HISTORY OF
WORLD
WAR II

1939-1945

CLB 4400
This edition published 1994 by
Tiger Books International PLC, Twickenham
© 1994 CLB Publishing, Godalming, Surrey
Printed and bound in South Africa
ISBN 1-85501-603-6

HISTORY OF
WORLD
WAR II

1939 - 1945

IVOR MATANLE

TIGER BOOKS INTERNATIONAL
LONDON

CONTENTS

FOREWORD 7

1 CAUSE AND EFFECT
Versailles to Poland and the Pact of
Steel 8

2 THE WORLD WATCHES AND WAITS
Poland, Finland and the Phoney War 13

3 THE BATTLE FOR NORWAY
And the Fall of Denmark 18

4 THE INVASION OF THE LOW
COUNTRIES
And the Little Ships of Dunkirk 22

5 THE HUMILIATION OF FRANCE
The Avenging of Versailles 26

6 THE SUMMER OF 1940
And the Battle of Britain 30

7 THE BLITZ
The Bombs Rain Down 36

8 NEUTRALITY AS A WEAPON
The USA Takes a Hand 38

9 THE BEGINNINGS OF THE SEA WAR
And the Stalking of the Graf Spee 41

10 GAMBLE IN NORTH AFRICA
Mussolini's Venture – Hitler's
Intervention 46

11 THE BALKANS
Rumania, Greece, Yugoslavia and the
Fall of Crete 50

12 BARBAROSSA
Hitler's Invasion of Russia and
Advance on Moscow 60

13 PEARL HARBOR
The United States Goes to War 66

14 JAPAN TAKES ALL
The Allies Driven from SE Asia 69

15 ROOSEVELT AND CHURCHILL
And their War Leaders 75

16 ROMMEL AND THE DESERT
CAMPAIGN
The Push to Egypt 78

17 THE BATTLE OF THE ATLANTIC
The U-Boat War 85

18 PACIFIC TURNING POINT
The Coral Sea and the Battle of
Midway 90

19 MONTGOMERY AND THE DESERT FOX
Alamein and the Allied Recovery 95

20 OPERATION TORCH
The USA Steps into Africa 99

21 THE EASTERN SUMMER OFFENSIVE
Stalingrad, and the Beginning of the
End 103

22 STALEMATE IN BURMA
Wingate, the Chindits and the Burma
Road 110

23 US COUNTER-ATTACK
Drama in the Pacific – Guadalcanal 113

24 CASABLANCA
Strengthening of the Alliance and the
Balance of Power 116

25 TUNISIA
And the End of the Afrika Korps 120

26 TOEHOLD IN EUROPE
The Assault on Italy 124

27 THE U-BOAT BEATEN
Allied Successes at Sea *130*

28 THE CARDS STACK UP AGAINST JAPAN
New Guinea and the Solomons *133*

29 THE POLITICS OF WAR
Quebec, Cairo and Teheran *139*

30 SOVIET ADVANCES
Kursk, the Counter-attack and the Ukraine *144*

31 THE BATTLES FOR THE ISLANDS
The Gilberts, Marshalls and Philippine Sea *148*

32 THE ADVANCE ON ROME
Anzio, Kesselring and the Struggle in Italy *153*

33 BOMBER OFFENSIVE
The Assault from the Air *158*

34 OVERLORD
The Atlantic Wall and D-day *162*

35 THE BREAKOUT FROM NORMANDY
And the Liberation of France *169*

36 RUSSIA'S INDOMITABLE ADVANCE
Poland and the Approach to Germany *177*

37 BACK IN THE PHILIPPINES
America's Triumph Won with Blood *180*

38 THE GERMAN RETREAT
From the Baltic and the Balkans *187*

39 REVENGE
Hitler's V-weapon Turned on Britain *193*

40 ARNHEM
The Autumn of 1944 in the West *198*

41 THE BATTLE OF THE BULGE
Hitler's Last Offensive *203*

42 THE BATTLE FOR THE RHINE
The Land War Reaches Germany in the West *208*

43 THE RUSSIANS SWEEP INTO GERMANY
The Strike at the Third Reich's Heart *214*

44 DIVIDING THE SPOILS
The Allies Confer at Quebec, Moscow and Yalta *218*

45 THE END IN ITALY
The Net Closes *223*

46 VICTORY IN EUROPE
The End of Hitler's Germany *228*

47 THE FINAL PUSH IN BURMA
The End of Japanese Domination *236*

48 THE LAST OF THE ISLANDS
Iwo Jima and Okinawa *244*

49 FINAL SURRENDER
The Air Offensive – Hiroshima and Nagasaki *247*

50 THE LEGACY OF WAR
And its Post War Impact *253*

FOREWORD

It is a popular fallacy that generals, who achieve fame and significant recognition only through war, are themselves warlike. In the 1914-18 war, a cataclysm which very nearly destroyed the flower of British manhood, my father was a young officer in the trenches in France until he was very badly wounded. After recovering, he returned to the front and served on the staff. These early experiences taught him that it was essential to conduct military operations so that the loss of life was kept to a minimum.

In the Second World War, when my father first commanded the Eighth Army in North Africa, Sicily and Italy, and then the 21st Army Group in North-West Europe, he was able to put into practise what he had both learned in the first conflict, and studied in great detail between the wars. The largest military operation ever undertaken in the history of warfare was the invasion of Normandy in June 1944, when my father commanded all the ground forces of the Allied Armies. Then, as always, the morale of his troops was one of his foremost preoccupations, and he would comment that "there are no bad soldiers, only bad generals". Perhaps it was this characteristic, together with a clear recognition of the efficiency and professional skills of his opponents, that made him one of our last great captains.

In his final message to the troops from Luneburg Heath in May 1945 my father concluded with the words: "We have won the German war. Let us now win the peace". This is the constant lesson of history, and worthy of study by both young and old. To maintain peace in the aftermath of the Second World War, it was essential for the free democratic nations of the Western economic systems to form a strong alliance, and to sustain it against all opposition.

It was this consideration which led to the formation of NATO, which ensured the continuing presence in Europe of the United States of America. The Federal Republic of Germany, once our opponent, has for many years been an important ally, and the alliance has grown with the gradual inclusion of most countries of Western Europe. NATO has given strength through unity, created dialogue between diverse nations, and it is our main hope that peace will prevail.

Viscount Montgomery of Alamein CBE

CAUSE AND EFFECT
VERSAILLES TO POLAND
AND THE PACT OF STEEL

E vents cease to be of our own time, and acquire the perspective of history, suddenly yet unobtrusively. To those who fought against, or suffered under the tyrannies of the Second World War, or who were brought up during those turbulent years, the transition happened quite recently – perhaps during the late Sixties or early Seventies. For those born since the greatest war man has yet known, images and recollections of the Second World War seem quaintly old-fashioned; as much a thread of the tapestry of time as the Black Death or the Spanish Armada. In either case, the sense of detachment that historical perspective provides makes it possible to view both the war itself, and the events that led to its outbreak, with a degree of balanced judgement and impartiality that would have been impossible when the War was still part of the world's immediate experience.

Yet, although the Second World War has undeniably become part of the fabric of history, its effects and consequences shape the very structure of our lives and the politics of the governments under which we live. No previous conflict has had as great an influence upon subsequent events and thought. Most of the wars of history have resolved a dispute, asserted sovereignty, or suppressed rebellion without causing major long-term changes to the course of world history, culture or political thinking. The Second World War was the War that nobody wanted, that everybody expected, and from which only the USSR gained territorial advantage, albeit at huge cost. So how did it happen?

There was no one cause, no one train of events, no single course of political thought that alone brought about the greatest single human tragedy the world has known. The causes of the Second World War are to be found in the combined and coincidental influences of three principal trains of events. The first of these is the political; the consequence of the Great Powers' failure after the First World War to take advantage of the opportunities offered for the creation of a new, stable order. By imposing upon the German people, who never considered that they had lost the war, unrealistic terms under the Treaty of Versailles, they ensured the political and military humiliation of Germany, which with the Weimar Republic's leaders responsibility for its acceptance, was the greatest single plank upon which Hitler built his popular support. The ambivalent attitude of public opinion in Britain and France to the justness of Versailles was, in turn, a powerful argument for inaction by those countries when Hitler's still embryonic army invaded the demilitarised Rhineland in 1936 – and the essentially flabby and indecisive nature of the League of Nations both stifled the individualism and decisiveness of its members, and strengthened the resolve of the Fascist powers to take what they coveted by force. The political structure created after the Great War in a spirit of peace by President Wilson, Clemenceau, Lloyd George and their successors was in fact a blueprint for conflict and disaster.

Even worse, from a political standpoint, were the efforts of the British and French politicians of the mid-Thirties to uphold that structure and maintain the peace at all costs. Paradoxically, by 1938, the only cost at which peace could be maintained was the certainty of subsequent war, and it is clear, with hindsight, that the very weakness displayed by Britain's Neville Chamberlain and Lord Halifax at the time of the Munich Agreement in September 1938 was Hitler's most powerful incentive to march on Czechoslovakia in the Spring of 1939, and to plan the attack on Poland, first for August, then for September. Hitler believed that Britain and France would not go to war in defence of Poland, and that Poland could be defeated in isolation as Czechoslovakia and Austria had been before.

The second stream of events to make a major contribution to the coming of the Second World War was the succession of economic crises of the Twenties and Thirties, and their aftermaths. The willingness of the Weimar government to print money to meet ever-growing demands on its resources caused devastating inflation that ravaged Germany throughout 1922 and 1923 and reduced the value of the mark catastrophically. In 1921, a reasonably stable currency had stood at 75 marks to the dollar. By January 1923, the mark was 18,000 to the dollar; by November one dollar was worth 4 billion marks. The savings and investments of a traditionally thrifty and comparatively wealthy German middle class became worthless. Not surprisingly, they blamed the Weimar government – and their disaffection provided a fertile seedbed for Hitler's later promises of a new German prosperity and industrial might.

Perhaps an even greater economic contribution to the coming of war was made by the financial crisis and subsequent Great Depression of 1929 to 1933. Not only did the spectacle of the great powers writhing in economic disarray provide a credible background to Hitler's assertions of a viable National Socialist alternative in Germany, but the coming of Roosevelt and the New Deal, by galvanising a new self-assertiveness and confidence into American life, greatly increased the power of the American isolationist lobby. To Hitler, watching from afar a succession of Neutrality Acts pass through Congress, it seemed certain that America would never go to war in Europe, and he miscalculated accordingly. Those who campaign in Europe for unilateral nuclear disarmament might pause to consider the lessons in the workings of human nature offered by the Thirties.

The third great course of events that drove the world inexorably to war was the growth of militant totalitarian nationalism. In Russia in 1917, first the February Revolution, which led to the government of Alexander Kerensky, then the Bolshevik October Revolution led by Vladimir Ulyanov, known as Lenin, swept the autocratic Tsarist monarchy from power and established the first of many oligarchic and undemocratic 'democracies' in Europe. Under the Bolsheviks, Russia proselytised the principles of the International. Yet, under Lenin's successor, Josef Stalin, who became General Secretary of the Communist Party in 1922, and achieved supreme power after ousting Trotsky in 1927, Mother Russia became inward-looking, reeling under a scale of tyranny unknown since Torquemada as the Communist government consolidated its hold on the vast confederation of states later known as the USSR, before seeking to extend its horizons.

The success of the Russian revolution in dispensing with the old order inspired Communist revolutionary movements in most of the countries of Western Europe, particularly Germany, Italy, France, Austria and Hungary. Indeed, Communist governments held power briefly in both Budapest and Bavaria after the First World War. It was in the backlash response to these revolutionary pressures that the extreme right-wing Fascist and Nationalist movements were born.

The first was in Italy under Gabriele D'Annunzio, who, in 1919, marched on and took Fiume on the Adriatic, then claimed by Yugoslavia, to the universal approval of the Italian press and the qualified disapproval of the Italian Government. Public adoration of the 'new Garibaldi' was such that another exserviceman's leader, Benito Mussolini, ever one to emulate the success of others, though not always with equal achievement, sought to give Italy the Nationalist government it seemed to want. In 1922, Mussolini 'marched' on Rome at the head of his Fascist Party (in fact he travelled by train), and gained enough support from those in power to be appointed Prime Minister by King Victor Emmanuel.

His success inspired the already active National Socialists in Bavaria, led by Adolf Hitler, to dream of a March on Berlin, an ideal that seemed possible in October 1923. The state government of Bavaria, led by Gustav von Kahr, had declared a State of Emergency in defiance of the Berlin government led by President Ebert and Chancellor Stresemann and seemed ready either to proclaim its independence of Germany, or to support a National Socialist coup in Berlin. Hitler, who in September 1923 had scored a major political triumph by being seen beside General Ludendorff, a disgruntled hero of the Great War, on the platform at a Bavarian rally of the *Deutscher Kampfbund* – the German Fighting Union – had led his followers to believe that the moment of power was at hand. When the situation between von Kahr and the Berlin government became less bellicose at the beginning of November, Hitler feared that von Kahr would opt for Bavarian independence rather than revolution against the central government. He believed that this would deprive the National Socialists of their chance of power, and him of his credibility with his party. The result was the ill-advised and poorly planned Munich beerhall putsch, which earned Hitler nine months of peace in Landsberg Prison to write *Mein Kampf*, gained him national fame for his sensationally effective oratory at his trial in April 1924, and conferred upon the National Socialist party five years of obscurity.

By the end of 1933, the political scene was set for the rise to war and the devastation of Europe. Josef Stalin was subjugating the USSR and speculating on the possibility of expansion westward. Adolf Hitler had finally achieved the Chancellorship of Germany and absolute power, and was dreaming of his advance eastward. Mussolini was the dictator of Italy, nurturing territorial ambitions in Africa and the Balkans. Roosevelt had embarked upon his spectacular first Hundred Days, and had begun the process by which the USA would grow in economic strength and ability to arm, yet would seem to onlookers implacably neutral. In the Far East, Japan had invaded Manchuria, and was turning a baleful eye on China and South-East Asia. Sadly, Britain and France, who should have provided the balancing mechanism and the strength that alone could have averted eventual war, lacked the political direction and will necessary to bring lesser nations to their call and keep the dictators at bay.

Thus began the succession of ever more daring adventures by the Nationalist leaders and by Japan, each countered by little more than admonition and a wish to compromise. In July 1934, Chancellor Dollfuss of Austria was brutally and callously murdered by Austrian Nazis. Mussolini, to his credit, or perhaps because it suited his political needs not to have Hitler baying at his borders, threatened military intervention, and the threat of Nazi takeover was temporarily averted. In March 1935, the German *Luftwaffe* was officially established in flagrant contravention of the Treaty of Versailles and Britain and France did nothing. On October 3rd 1935, Italy invaded Ethiopia. The League of Nations attempted to impose economic sanctions, which were hopelessly ineffective, and in December the Hoare-Laval plan for exchanges of territory between Italy and Ethiopia without reference to the League was leaked, thus weakening forever such influence as the League had ever had, and causing Parliamentary and public outrage in Britain.

In March 1936, Hitler took a massive gamble, and backed his hunch that the signatories to the Treaty of Versailles would do nothing that in any way endangered peace. With hopelessly ill-supported and poorly trained troops, he occupied the Rhineland, specifically declared a demilitarised zone by the Treaty, and awaited developments. None came. Hitler had gained as never before the measure of his opponents.

Other nationalist movements had sprung up around Europe in response to the activities of militant Communist parties. Some, like Sir Oswald Mosley's blackshirts in Britain, very noisy yet ineffective, but, as the political stage was set in the Thirties for the rise to war, a third major Nationalist force arose in Spain under General Franco. In July 1936, Franco led an uprising to unseat the Republican government. Hearing after a performance of one of Wagner's operas at Bayreuth of the outbreak of the Spanish Civil War, Hitler conferred hastily with Goering and von Blomberg, his War Minister, and decided almost on the spur of the moment to support Franco. Germany supplied aircraft, tanks, technicians and money valued at half a billion marks, and detached a large part of the emergent *Luftwaffe* for what amounted to training in active service. Known as the Condor Legion, this German air force killed hundreds of Spaniards when it bombed Guernica, and perfected in Spain the dive bombing and heavy bombing of civilian areas that were to be so significant a feature of later *Blitzkrieg* advances across Europe. After the Civil War, Germany had a corps of battle-trained airmen that no other Western nation possessed, a resource that was to prove of immense value in the training of the world's most powerful air force.

Mussolini was committed to the Spanish Civil War to an even greater degree than Hitler, and, recognising this, one of Hitler's primary objectives in his support of Franco was to keep the war going, hoping thereby to maintain a state of enmity between Mussolini and the politicians of Britain and France. For Hitler knew that, whether or not there was to be war, he needed Mussolini on his side. In October, after a successful visit to Hitler in Berchtesgaden, Count Ciano, Mussolini's son-in-law and Foreign Minister, signed a protocol that set out a common policy for Germany and Italy in the field of foreign affairs. This was the Berlin-Rome Axis, the beginning of the alliance that was to secure Mussolini's downfall.

In the following month, Germany and Japan signed the Anti-Comintern Pact against the Communist International, and, in July 1937, as the Spanish Civil War raged on, the Japanese used the Marco Polo Bridge incident, a skirmish near Peking, as a pretext to invade China. Sensing the way things seemed to be going, Italy joined the Anti-Comintern Pact in November 1937, and the following month the Japanese killed some 150,000 people, mostly civilians, around Nanking.

The following year was a fateful landmark in the progress towards war. On November 5th 1937, Goering and the service chiefs had been told by Hitler in committee that war was inevitable, but that it would come at a time of their choosing. As 1938 began, Hitler took steps to annex Austria, believing, correctly, that once again Britain and France would do nothing. The annexation – *Anschluss* – was completed in a matter of hours on March 13th. Threats against Czechoslovakia arising from Hitler's claim to the Sudetenland, an area of Czechoslovakia inhabited mainly by Germans, led Europe to believe during April and May that it was on the brink of war. After further threats, Hitler secured from Britain's Prime Minister Neville Chamberlain and the French Premier Edouard Daladier at the Munich Conference in September complicity in forcing Czechoslovakia to cede the Sudetenland and some of her most valuable mineral resources to Germany. The willingness of Chamberlain to co-operate in Hitler's territorial ambitions when peace was threatened confirmed Hitler's belief that his military adventures would continue to go unchallenged.

Only six months after guaranteeing in return for the Sudetenland that Czechoslovakia would not be attacked, Hitler's armies entered Prague on March 15th 1939 and annexed Memel, a city of Lithuania inhabited by ethnic Germans, on March 23rd. Once again, Britain and France did nothing, but, at last, Chamberlain spelt out clearly in Parliament British condemnation of Hitler's latest aggression and made it clear that an attack on Poland would not be tolerated. On 30th March, Chamberlain drafted the British guarantee of Poland's independence which was to become the pivot of war. This was accepted by Joseph Beck, Polish Foreign Minister, and consented to, after the event, by France. On April 26th, after Italy seized Albania, Britain reintroduced conscription, a clear indication that, at long last, the British policy of appeasement was being abandoned. Despite this, Hitler was firm in his belief that there would be no retaliation from Britain and France if he attacked Poland.

On May 22nd, Mussolini finally decided to throw in Italy's lot militarily with Germany, and the Pact of Steel was signed, committing each nation to join the other at war. Hitler felt that he had tied up one more loose end, but he was anxious to be sure that Russia would not intervene if Germany attacked Poland. In 1938, the Soviet Union had stopped its aid to the Republicans in Spain, and had thereby secured Franco's victory. Hitler therefore had cause to believe that Stalin wanted no quarrel with Germany, but was concerned at the clear fact that Russia was engaged in protracted negotiations for a treaty with Britain and France. Something had to be done.

In May, after a major speech from Hitler which lacked his usual attacks on 'Bolshevik Jews', Stalin suddenly replaced Litvinov, the Western-orientated Russian Foreign Minister with the tough, uncompromising and seemingly indestructible Molotov. A few days later, a new Russian ambassador arrived in Berlin. Stalin, playing both sides against each other, gave Hitler hope of a treaty without breaking off negotiations with Britain and France, thereby hoping to obtain from Hitler concessions which would enable Russia to occupy the Baltic states of Latvia, Estonia and Lithuania without intervention from Germany. Early in August, the British and French military missions found themselves being delayed in their attempts to conduct talks with Marshal Voroshilov in Moscow, and on August 21st 1939, Stalin announced his intention of signing a Non-Aggression Pact with Germany.

With the signing of this Pact on August 23rd, Hitler's way to Poland seemed open. But, on August 25th, the signing of the Anglo-Polish alliance was announced in London, and Hitler realised that his attempt to isolate Poland had failed. Less than twelve hours before the deadline, the planned German invasion of Poland on the 26th August was halted. On the 27th, Hitler, now less confident about the future of his enterprise, but committed to it, set a new date for the invasion of September 1st. On the 28th, Britain formally rejected Hitler's arrogant and bombastic offer of 'protection' for the British Empire in return for non-intervention of Britain if Poland were attacked, thereby declining to take part in a re-enactment of the fiasco of Munich. But, because Britain also advised Germany that both Britain and Poland were prepared to meet to negotiate, Hitler believed he detected signs of weakness. He thought he saw evidence that Britain would not, after all, act if Poland were attacked. He therefore demanded that a Polish emissary be sent to Berlin with full powers to negotiate and settle. Knowing that this implied a Polish surrender, the Poles refused.

Thus, on September 1st, the German tanks rolled, the guns roared, and the *Wehrmacht* moved forward into Poland. The Second World War was now virtually inevitable. Germany greeted the news with silent resignation; there was no rejoicing as there had been in 1914.

At 9am on September 3rd, Britain's ambassador Sir Neville Henderson in Berlin delivered an ultimatum. Hitler's worst fears were confirmed; this time Chamberlain was not prepared to compromise. The ultimatum said that, unless satisfactory assurances of German action to call off the attack on Poland were received by 11am, a state of war would exist between Britain and Germany. Hitler had gone too far, was too arrogant, too aware of his own political vulnerability to retreat. He did not reply to the ultimatum.

At 11.15am on September 3rd 1939, Neville Chamberlain announced to a hushed nation and an appalled world that Britain was at war with Germany. It was the beginning of the greatest conflict the world has yet seen.

THE WORLD WATCHES AND WAITS

POLAND, FINLAND AND THE PHONEY WAR

By evening on September 3rd 1939, both Britain and France had declared war on Germany. Both countries – indeed most of the world – expected events to gather speed; for a state of war such as had been known a generation earlier in France rapidly to be re-established. Hitler had snatched and held the political initiative for so long that he was expected by almost everybody to seek to retain it in the West, even as his armies subjugated Poland in the East. For, phoney as the war might have seemed in Birmingham or Rouen, in Detroit or Toronto, to the hard-pressed Poles the war was terrifyingly real. By the time France declared war on the evening of 3rd September, the Poles had been in battle for almost three days.

The German technique of *blitzkrieg* – lightning war – was used for the first time in Poland, and proved to be devastatingly effective. At 0430 on 1st September, 48 divisions, six of them armoured, with 1,400 aircraft, invaded on three fronts, from East Germany, East Prussia and Slovakia. The master plan for the invasion, Case White, called for rapid neutralisation of Polish communications, airfields and troop concentrations, and the Junkers 87 'Stuka' dive bomber was used with deadly effect as a form of airborne artillery, taking over the role of harassing enemy positions that had previously been carried out by more vulnerable land based guns. Nonetheless, an early attempt on September 1st to dispose of the Polish Air Force, which had a total of 842 largely obsolete aircraft, only 400 of which were battle-worthy, succeeded only in part, and the Polish airmen fought on heroically and with surprising effectiveness throughout the campaign.

On Sunday, September 3rd, after days of bombing of Warsaw by German He 111 twin-engined bombers, and successful bombing raids by the Poles on German armour in the Radom-Piotrkow area, to the South West of Warsaw, the 1st and 4th *Panzer* divisions crossed the River Warta, and German forces captured Czestochowa. In the North West, the Polish Corridor, which had been a major cause of the dispute between Germany and Poland, was severed. By September 5th, the Germans had broken through to the Vistula and had taken Bydgoszcz in the North West, had destroyed the town of Sulejow by concentrated bombing, and had forced the Polish High Command under Marshal Edward Smigly-Rydz to order a retreat. The advance on Warsaw seemed unstoppable, and on September 5th the Polish Government left Warsaw for Lublin.

By September 8th, the battle of the Bzura, West of Warsaw, had begun in earnest. The 4th *Panzer* Division, which had advanced 225km in 7 days, lost 60 tanks in an attempt to storm the outer defences of the capital. Recognising that they had a tougher fight on their hands than had been anticipated, the *Wehrmacht* moved substantial reinforcements to Poland for the final assault on Warsaw, and by the 15th the capital was surrounded. Despite ultimatums on the 16th and the 25th, mass air attacks on the city and huge fires, the Poles fought on until the 27th, when after a massive indiscriminate artillery bombardment of Warsaw the Polish garrison commander was forced to offer to surrender.

Meanwhile, Russia had invaded Poland from the East on 17th September, advancing 100km with virtually no resistance, and the Polish Government and all surviving Polish aircrews had decamped to Rumania.

So, in Poland, the war was anything but phoney. By the time Hitler arrived for his victory parade in Warsaw on October 5th, 10,572 Germans had died in the fighting and 30,322 had been wounded. Some 217 German tanks and 285 planes had also been destroyed. The Poles had lost about 50,000 dead, some 750,000 prisoners of war to Germany plus about 217,000 to the USSR, and 333 aircraft. Some 105,000 Poles escaped abroad to fight again. Although fast, the German victory was not easy.

Away from the agony of Poland, to those on land there seemed to prevail an uneasy peace. Britain and France had mobilised from September 1st, and the British Expeditionary Force was landed in France during September and October. On September 9th, Marshal Smigly-Rydz had appealed to General Gamelin of France for decisive action in the West to divert some of the force of the German assault away from Poland, but to no avail. The French Army demolished three bridges over the Rhine during minor skirmishes east of the Moselle, but elsewhere the armies waited. Hitler, in his mountain retreat at Berchtesgaden, had at first intended that his attack in the West, on Holland, Belgium and Luxembourg, should be mounted in October 1939, but drew back and deferred the assault until 1940.

The lack of action was not for want of decision on the part of the great powers. The United States, saddled with the Neutrality Acts of the Thirties, had officially announced her neutrality on September 5th, and had established with the Latin American states a Pan American Security Zone by which military operations were forbidden within 1,000km of American shores. But Australia, New Zealand and British India had declared war on the same day as Britain and France. South Africa had declared war on Germany on September 6th; Canada had followed suit on September 10th. But all remained quiet – except at sea.

The seaborne war had begun almost as soon as Chamberlain had risen from his microphone in Downing Street. A single RAF Blenheim aircraft had photographed the German Fleet at Wilhelmshaven on September 3rd, and 29 RAF Blenheims and Wellingtons had attacked the fleet both at Wilhelmshaven and on the Kiel Canal on September 4th, with a loss of 7 aircraft. On September 14th, a German submarine, the U-39, attacked Britain's HMS *Ark Royal*, and was depth charged by accompanying destroyers. Three days later U-29 sank another British aircraft carrier, HMS *Courageous*, and on October 14th the *Kriegsmarine* scored a spectacular success when U-47 penetrated the Royal Navy's 'impregnable' anchorage at Scapa Flow and sank the battleship HMS *Royal Oak*. Two days later, nine of the new Junkers 88 twin-engined fighter bombers, pride of the *Luftwaffe*, dive-bombed Royal Navy warships at Rosyth in the Firth of Forth, and HMS *Southampton* survived only because a bomb that penetrated her decks failed to explode. Next day, a similar raid on Rosyth crippled HMS *Iron Duke*.

In December, the German pocket battleship *Admiral Graf Spee*, which had been tracked by British and French ships all autumn, was brought to battle off the River Plate estuary by the British cruisers *Exeter*, *Ajax* and *Achilles*. The badly damaged HMS *Exeter* was obliged to retire to the Falkland Islands, and was replaced by HMS *Cumberland*, and the three ships lay off the Plate and waited for the *Graf Spee* to emerge. She never came. On Sunday December 17th, her Captain scuttled his ship in the Plate estuary, where the wreck, later bought by the British for a sight of her radar, burned for a week.

Alarming as these events were, they could not be claimed to be the all-out war that had been expected, not least by Hitler's Generals. For, when the 1939 balance of power is studied, Hitler did not have things all his own way.

The Allies had, for a start, considerable naval superiority over Germany. Britain and France between them had 676 ships built or launched; Germany had 130, including 57 U-boats under the command of Admiral Karl Doenitz, eventually to be Hitler's successor. Most of the U-boats were short-range Class 1 and 2 boats, intended for coastal operations, and unsuitable as Atlantic raiders.

In the air, the *Luftwaffe* had considerable superiority. At the beginning of September 1939, Goering could claim, and put in the air, no less than 4,700 aircraft, including a formidable fleet of 552 of the sturdy and reliable Junkers 52 three-engined transports, and nine squadrons of the Ju 87 Stukas. Against this, the Royal Air Force could muster only 3,600 aircraft, of which a great number were obsolescent, or even downright obsolete, a sad situation that resulted from a lack of defence spending by the government of appeasement in the late Thirties. The French had virtually no modern bombers or fighters, and the Poles, although beginning the war with over 800 largely obsolete aircraft, lost most of them in the terrible fighting in their own country.

Comparison of land forces is not so easy. The Germans had 53 divisions in the field at the outbreak of war, every one of them superbly equipped with up-to-date weapons, as one would expect of an army created virtually from nothing in five years. Although the French had 28 divisions, they were, by comparison, poorly equipped with weapons dating mainly from the First World War. The Poles were similarly equipped with rifles and automatic weapons from the Twenties and earlier. The British Army, although professional in outlook, was also sadly ill-equipped, and suffered from too great a belief in the trench warfare tactics which, while they had not won the Great War, could at least be argued not to have lost it.

Why the Allies did not attack Germany in the West when the *Wehrmacht* was preoccupied in Poland has been the subject of much debate, but the answer almost certainly rests in the slowness of French mobilisation, in a mistrust by both the French and British of the principles of the mobile war (later espoused earnestly) and in a correct assessment of the strength of German air power. At the Nuremberg War Trials after the War, General Jodl and Field Marshal Keitel asserted that an attack in the West would have 'encountered only feeble resistance', but this has been questioned by many historians and will doubtless be debated many times yet.

The world's attention was diverted from Hitler's war, or the lack of it, when, at the end of November 1939 the USSR renounced its 1932 Soviet-Finnish Non-Aggression Pact and invaded Finland, with the intention of adding the land of the Finns to its expanding empire. Thus began the Winter War, one of the world's great examples of the triumph of local knowledge and sheer tenacity over brute force.

A redoubtable veteran of 72 years, Field-Marshal Mannerheim, was appointed Defender of Finland and Commander in Chief. He set about defending his country with 400,000 men (9 divisions), 145 aircraft, 2 coastal defence vessels and 5 submarines against Soviet forces amounting to 30 divisions, 1,200 tanks, 696 aircraft, 28 surface warships and 11 submarines. The Russians sought to emulate the Germans' tactics of *Blitzkrieg*, bombing Helsinki repeatedly, believing that, once the Finnish government had been subdued, it would be straightforward to march across Finland to the Gulf of Bothnia. Field-Marshal Mannerheim knew otherwise. Realising that the Finnish winter would inhibit drastically any army's attempt to cross the country North and East of Lake Ladoga, he withdrew the majority of his forces to defend a line drawn across the narrow Karelian Isthmus and across the area to the North of Lake Ladoga. All told, there were five divisions in the Isthmus, two divisions on the other side of the lake, a mere nine battalions covering the considerable area of Central Finland, and four battalions in independent Lappland.

During December, the Soviet Army began to learn the folly of taking on the Finns in an abnormally cold winter. The Soviet 7th Army was stopped dead in the Isthmus; the 8th Army fared no better on the other side of the Lake. Two divisions were utterly destroyed by the Finns at Tolvajarvi on December 12th. The day before, the 163rd Russian division was cut off near Oulu; on the 28th, the 44th Division was ambushed and destroyed. It is estimated that in the first phase of the Winter War, the Russians lost some 27,500 men against Finnish losses of 2,700.

Now the Russians began to recognise their inability to beat the Finns at their own game and changed their tactics. According to Mannerheim, no less than 45 Soviet divisions were deployed on the Finnish front for the second phase of the war at the beginning of 1940, and the tough Marshal Timoshenko was put in command. By mid-February, the Mannerheim Line had been breached, and by early March, as the weather improved and the Finns' natural advantage diminished, Mannerheim had to advise his government to sue for peace. On March 12th, the Russo-Finnish Treaty was signed in Moscow. Finland ceded the Viipuri and Salla districts and a part of Lappland, and was obliged to meet other conditions, but her moral triumph was undiminished. The Soviet position was condemned by the United States, France, Great Britain, Denmark, Norway, Sweden, Belgium, Hungary and Italy. Only Hitler's Germany failed to condemn the attack and remained non-partisan, and, to the fury of Count Ciano, forbade the transport across Germany of arms to be supplied by Italy to the Finns.

On the Western front, however, the winter had passed with only occasional skirmishes and air attacks. Six months after the outbreak of Hitler's war, there remained little war to see. On March 20th, the French Prime Minister Daladier resigned, and was succeeded by Paul Reynaud. On April 3rd, Winston Churchill, who had been appointed First Lord of the Admiralty on September 3rd 1939, became Chairman of the British Government's Military Committee, another step towards the destiny that was to have a profound effect upon the conduct of the war. On April 4th, Neville Chamberlain told a Conservative Party meeting in London that Hitler, by failing to take advantage of his military superiority in September 1939, had 'missed the bus'.

Just five days later, Hitler invaded Norway. The real war had begun.

THE BATTLE FOR NORWAY

AND THE FALL OF DENMARK

Control of Norway was crucially important to Germany's ability to use its sea power effectively against the Allies, particularly Britain. While Norway was at peace, and unoccupied by either of the fighting powers, there was no threat. But the weakness of Norwegian coastal defences, and the inability of her field army to resist effectively a determined invasion by a stronger power were clear. Admiral Raeder had pointed out several times in 1939 the potential danger to Germany of Britain seizing the initiative and launching its own invasion in Scandinavia – if the powerful Royal Navy had bases at Bergen, Narvik and Trondheim, the North Sea would be virtually closed to Germany, and the *Kriegsmarine* would be at risk even in the Baltic.

At the end of 1939, there had been negotiations between Raeder and Vidkun Quisling, the head of the Norwegian Najonal Samling (National Unity) Party, and a plan had been hatched for a takeover of Norway by political bloodless revolution, following which Quisling would have asked Germany for 'protection'. But, because Quisling, whose name has become synonymous with 'traitor', had only around 10,000 Norwegians behind him, that idea was abandoned and, on January 27th, Hitler ordered detailed contingency planning of 'Operation Weser', the taking of Norway. At that stage, there was no commitment to the attack on Norway that was to follow in the spring, but two events moved Hitler to the point of action in April.

The first was the USSR's second, and successful assault on Finland, which threatened to put Russia within striking distance both of Swedish mineral resources and of the Norwegian ports. The second, which finally committed Hitler to action, was the interception by HMS *Cossack*, a British destroyer commanded by Captain Philip Vian, of the German ship *Altmark*, officially the supply ship to the *Graf Spee*, which was carrying 299 British Merchant Navy prisoners back to Germany. When the Norwegians had searched the vessel at Bergen, they had not found the prisoners, who were battened down below decks. But, on the direct orders of Winston Churchill, Captain Vian informed the Norwegians that he was stopping the *Altmark*, boarded the prison ship in Jossing Fjord on February 16th, and released the prisoners, bringing them back to Britain. This made it clear to all concerned that the Norwegians were powerless to act when either power breached international law in Norwegian waters, and emphasised to Hitler the validity of Raeder's fears about a British occupation of Norway. The result was the issuing of two Fuehrer Directives, on February 26th and March 1st, which both appointed a commander for the Norwegian operation, General Nikolaus von Falkenhorst, and made clear that Denmark was to be occupied as part of the same operation.

The invasion of Norway, originally set for March 20th, but postponed to April 9th, was the first major test for the *Kriegsmarine*. The plan required five major naval groups to take part, respectively taking Narvik, Trondheim, Bergen, Kristiansand/Arendal, and Oslo. Most of the *Kriegsmarine's* available warships were actively involved, and the five groups sailed at various times between the 6th and the 8th of April so as to arrive off their targets simultaneously. Two army corps went with them, the 21st for Norway and the 31st for Denmark. Over a thousand German aircraft were committed to the assault. Amazingly, the Norwegian Government had been provided via a friendly Dutch military attache on April 4th with advance warning of the attack, but had not acted upon the information – if they had mobilised in time, history might have been somewhat different.

The assaults on Trondheim and Bergen went well for the Germans, aside from the damaging by shellfire (and subsequent sinking by the British Fleet Air Arm) of the light cruiser *Konigsberg* at Bergen. The *Karlsruhe* was torpedoed and sunk at Kristiansand by a British submarine (the *Truant*). At Stavanger, the paratroops took Sola airfield and the town without difficulty.

Narvik was taken quickly, but not without incident, and largely by treachery. Commodore Paul Bonte's German destroyers demanded the surrender of two Norwegian coastal defence vessels, the *Eidsvold* and the *Norge*. When their commander refused to surrender, his ships were blown out of the water. Almost immediately, Lieutenant-General Dietl led his 3rd *Gebirgsjager* Division into the town, and received its surrender from a Quisling, Colonel Konrad Sundlo.

The assault on Oslo was not so easy. The pocket battleship *Lutzow* was badly damaged by the Norwegian shore batteries in the fjord, and the *Blucher* was sunk by shore-launched torpedoes with the loss of 1,600 lives before the 163rd division managed to capture a large part of Oslo, the arsenal at Horten and the airfield. But for this daring enterprise by Major General Engelbrecht, the battle would have lasted much longer, for it was the ability to land paratroops, in Ju52 aircraft on that airfield, late on April 9th, that determined the course of events in favour of Germany.

Although Norwegian intentions were good, and the willingness of King Haakon, his government and country to fight was evident, Norway's organisation was less than effective and rendered the effort expended on defence largely valueless. General mobilisation was announced only after the invasion had begun. The Commander in Chief was unfit for service, and had to be replaced after the invasion on April 11th by Colonel Otto Ruge, who was hastily promoted to General. The command structure was hopelessly inadequate to deal with a situation as desperately demanding of strong military action. As the evacuation of 24,000 allied troops from Narvik and Harstad was completed two months later, King Haakon and the Norwegian Government were to escape narrowly from Tromso to England aboard HMS *Devonshire* on June 8th and Vidkun Quisling was to proclaim himself the head of the Norwegian Government, saying 'I shall be called the big traitor'. In that at least he was right.

Denmark caused the Germans less difficulty than Norway. King Christian X and his government yielded to the German ultimatum, although there was Danish military resistance at Jutland, and the Royal Guard made a stand at the Amalienborg Palace. The *Luftwaffe* strafed Vaerlose Airfield, headquarters of the

Danish Air Force, destroying many aircraft, but there was little reply. The Danish Navy offered no resistance at all. Denmark seemed to have accepted her fate. Of the 15,450 Danes under arms, only 13 were killed and 23 wounded.

As the German invasion of Norway began, the British were not standing idly by, but the Allies' reaction was appallingly late, disastrously ineffective and disorganised. Admiral Sir Charles Forbes had sailed from Scapa Flow on the evening of the 7th, three days after news of the invasion had been leaked to the Allies. His force of two battleships, one battle-cruiser, four cruisers and 21 destroyers headed for Norway to provide cover for minelaying operations, but with orders that suggested the threatened invasion might be a blind for a breakout of the blockaded German fleet to the Atlantic. On April 8th, one of the destroyers, HMS *Glowworm*, met the *Hipper* and was severely damaged. With tremendous courage, her captain used his doomed ship to ram the *Hipper*, radioing as he did so that the German Fleet was at sea.

As a result, the British Admiralty did exactly what the Germans hoped it would do by instructing Admiral Forbes not to follow the German fleet into Trondheim, which would have been tactically sound, but to intercept the *Scharnhorst* and *Gneisenau*, which were operating as an independent battle squadron, and were in fact functioning as bait to keep the Royal Navy away from the landings in Norway. By the evening of April 9th, Germany was in control of the most important strategic positions in Norway and Denmark, and Hitler had achieved his easiest bridgehead yet. In Britain, Prime Minister Neville Chamberlain, who only days earlier had announced that Hitler had missed the bus, was in deep trouble.

Britain now joined battle in earnest. On April 10th, the First Battle of Narvik brought five British destroyers into conflict with 10 German destroyers, and cost each side two destroyers and one senior commander. The Royal Navy also sank eight German merchant ships and the ammunition carrier *Rauenfels*. On the 11th, the RAF attacked Sola airfield, Stavanger, and lost one Wellington out of six. On the 13th came the Second Battle of Narvik, and a significant victory for the Royal Navy. HMS *Warspite* and nine destroyers attacked eight German destroyers and sank or disabled all of them. By the 14th, the British North Western Expeditionary Force had begun to land at Harstad, the 24th Guards Brigade arriving on the island of Hinnoy, near Harstad, some 96km from Narvik, and separated from the port by a sea channel and snow-covered mountains, on the 15th. On the 16th, the 146th Infantry Brigade landed at Namsos, and on the 17th the 148th landed at Andalsnes. The Germans were now isolated in Narvik, although with plenty of captured Norwegian weapons in addition to their own, and with a 'Mountain Marine' unit of 2,600 men, survivors of the annihilated destroyer fleet, to use the Norwegian rifles and machine guns. This force was ordered to 'hold out for as long as possible'. Each day, the RAF attacked German military installations, and the sea war continued with losses on both sides.

The traitor Quisling, meanwhile, had been ousted on April 15th, and replaced by an 'Administrative Council' of Norwegian bureaucrats and lawyers. Suddenly and belatedly, this government, on April 18th, declared war on Germany. On the 19th, the British 146th Infantry Brigade, advancing South from Namsos, reached Verdal, 80km from Trondheim, and the French *Chasseurs Alpins* – fully trained mountain troops – landed at Namsos. The plan was that these forces would advance on Trondheim and link up with the Norwegian forces retreating northwards, but the arrival of substantial reinforcements for General von Falkenhorst's army, despite the attempt at a blockade of German shipping by

Allied submarines in the Skaggerak, made the Allies look again at the weaknesses of their position.

The British troops in Norway were not properly equipped or trained for the position in which they found themselves. Because of the poor organisation of their embarkation, they had not even their full complement of stores and equipment. The German army was well-organised, well-trained and recently reinforced. It quickly became clear that the British plan to retake the centre of Norway could not work and, as if to emphasise the point, on April 26th the German 196th Division, on the right of the 21st Corps, succeeded in joining up with the 181st Division on the left, south of Trondheim.

All Allied efforts were now concentrated on Narvik, and the blocking of the vital route for iron resources through the port. British and French troops withdrew from Andalsnes and Namsos, King Haakon and General Ruge (and the Norwegian gold reserves) headed for Tromso, and the final phase of the Norwegian battle began on April 26th. It lasted effectively until May 28th, when the French 13th Foreign Legion Demi-Brigade finally recaptured Narvik, although by then other events in the Low Countries and France had captured the news. The Germans expected the Allies to try to make their stay in Narvik permanent – but on June 7th the French and British departed, having covered the evacuation of the Allied armies from Norway. Norway and Denmark were totally in German hands.

The pull back to Narvik on April 26th had also marked the beginning of the final phase of Neville Chamberlain's career as British Prime Minister. A motion of censure in the House of Commons debated on may 7th and 8th brought about his resignation, and on May 10th 1940, Winston Churchill, one of the greatest of Englishmen, became Prime Minister. On that same fateful day, Hitler unleashed his long-awaited *Blitzkrieg* in the West, and the attention of the world shifted from Scandinavia to Holland, Belgium and France.

INVASION OF THE LOW COUNTRIES

AND THE LITTLE SHIPS OF DUNKIRK

O n May 10th 1940, when the much-postponed and frequently amended *Fall Gelb* (Case Yellow) plan for the invasion of Holland, Belgium and France was put into effect, the land forces of Germany totalled 157 divisions, 49 more than there had been when Poland had been attacked at the beginning of September 1939. Seven were fighting in Norway, one was occupying Denmark, ten were keeping watch between the Carpathians and the Baltic. Three more were still training in Germany. The remaining 136 were committed to the great offensive in the West that was to prove to be France's greatest humiliation.

The *Luftwaffe* remained dominant in the air, being able to put into action 3,634 front line aircraft, of which 1,016 were fighters and the rest, 1,562, bombers. The latest French fighter aircraft – the sleek, fast Dewoitine 520 and the Bloch 151 – were both too few and too late to be effective in the battle, and most of the fighters of RAF Fighter Command were at home awaiting the inevitable attack on Britain – there were in fact 130 RAF fighters and 160 British bombers in Europe, many of them hopelessly out of date and outclassed by the modern aircraft of the *Luftwaffe*.

Allied land forces totalled 135 divisions against the 136 fielded by the Germans – 94 French, 10 British, 22 Belgian and 9 Dutch – but, according to military observers of the time, many of the French divisions were made up of poorly trained, ill-disciplined and unwilling conscripts. Thus the balance of power was not as the figures suggest. France had, at that time, mobilised one man in eight. Britain, by contrast, had mobilised one in forty-eight, but her army was more effective, professional in outlook and prepared to fight.

At dawn on May 10th, General Kurt Student's 7th Airborne Division, General Albert Kesselring's *Luftflotte II*, and General Graf von Sponeck's 22nd Infantry Division began the mighty attack that was to complete the subjugation of continental Europe and humiliate France. The *Luftwaffe* raided airfields and towns in Holland, Belgium and Northern France, and Student's airborne troops took the important Moerdijk bridges across the Maas estuary to prevent their destruction, the banks of the Maas at Dordrecht and parts of Rotterdam. The airborne troops also succeeded in capturing Waalhaven airport.

General Von Sponeck's 22nd Infantry Division was given the task of taking The Hague and securing the co-operation, or the person, of Queen Wilhelmina or both. It is said that the General was so confident that he set out in full dress uniform, so that he would be properly dressed for his audience with the Queen. In the event, things did not go too well for him. His troops encountered the Dutch

I Corps, who put up a fierce fight, recapturing the airfields earlier taken by the paratroops of the 22nd Infantry Division as part of the plan to encircle the capital. Von Sponeck was wounded, 1,000 of his men were shipped off to England as prisoners that evening, and he never did get to meet the Queen.

The most sensational event of May 10th and May 11th was the capture by glider-borne paratroops of the fort at Eben-Emael on the junction of the Albert Canal and the Meuse. Regarded as impregnable, Fort Eben-Emael was defended by 1,200 well trained men who had been taught to expect a traditional attack at ground level. The paratroops instead landed on the roof in gliders, and systematically fought their way down through the building, which was not designed to enable its defenders to cope with such an assault. The outcome was that eighty men under the command of a sergeant silenced the mightiest guns on the Meuse, and made possible the capture of the 1,200-strong garrison, all within thirty hours.

Three *Panzer* Corps, Heinz Guderian's 19th, Reinhardt's 41st and Hoth's 20th, attacked at lightning speed through the Ardennes forest in South Belgium and Luxembourg, heading for the Meuse and the battle with France. The Belgian forces withdrew from the Ardennes in the face of this assault to a position behind the Meuse, leaving two infantry companies with the thankless task of holding up Guderian's 1st *Panzer* Division with road blocks.

The Anglo-French Army Group 1, of which the British Expeditionary Force formed part, crossed with a strength of 32 divisions into Belgium, thus putting into action the French C-in-C General Gamelin's brainchild, the Dyle Plan. From his HQ at Vincennes – which, incredibly, had no radio transmitter – Gamelin sought to launch an Allied counter offensive between the Ardennes and the Moselle. Sadly, not all his subordinates had sufficient confidence in the plan to do as they were bidden, and, in any event, Gamelin had neither the quality nor the quantity among his French troops for the plan to work. The German success at Eban-Emael had already taken the Albert Canal and key points on the Meuse. It would take more than the Allied Army Group 1 to do any more than defend. Even that proved difficult.

Although the French 7th Army had reached Breda on May 11th, by the 12th it was in retreat under pressure from Guderian's *Panzers*. Later that day the *Panzer* units reached the Meuse along a 130km front, from Dinant to Sedan. They had advanced 120km in three days. The French 7th Army fell back to Antwerp.

Next day, the Battle of the Meuse began. The three *Panzer* Corps established bridgeheads over the Meuse at Sedan, Montherme and Dinant, destroying the French 9th Army and opening an 80km gap in the Allied line. At Tirlemont, the French 2nd and 3rd Light Mechanised Divisions fought fiercely all day against 16th *Panzer* Corps, but were forced to fall back. On the 14th, Guderian's 1st *Panzer* Division crossed the Meuse at Sedan in force, and by nightfall the next day the French Army was in full retreat.

In Holland, fierce resistance around and in Rotterdam angered the Germans sufficiently for Hitler to order on May 14th the reprisal bombing of the city. Despite the fact that the garrison had already agreed to surrender, 100 Heinkel 111 bombers were not turned back, and the bombing went ahead. Tremendous fires in the fats and margarine stores of the port caused enormous destruction, nearly 1,000 people were killed and 78,000 were made homeless. The next day the Dutch Army formally surrendered, although isolated units held out until the 17th. The Dutch Army had lost 2,890 dead, 6,889 wounded. Some 2,500 Dutch civilians had lost their lives. Many more would follow during the grim days of occupation.

Friday May 17th saw the entry of the Germans into Brussels. At Montcornet, Colonel, later General, de Gaulle's 4th Armoured Division attacked Guderian's 19th *Panzer* Corps fiercely but was driven back, and later that day the 16th and 33rd *Panzer* Corps were detached from the German 6th Army in Belgium and sent to join the forces on the Meuse. Next day, Guderian's *Panzers* reached Peronne on the Somme. Disaster was clearly in the air for the Allies and, on Sunday May 20th, General Gamelin was dismissed and replaced by General Weygand. Colonel de Gaulle seemed almost to celebrate by having another go at Guderian, this time almost taking the General's Headquarters before being driven back by Stuka attacks from the air.

Next day, Guderian raced for the Channel coast along the Somme, and despite fierce resistance from the British 12th and 23rd (Territorial) Divisions, the 1st *Panzer* Division captured Amiens at midday, and the 2nd Division reached Abbeville and Noyelles at the mouth of the river by evening. They had advanced 386km in only 11 days.

By Wednesday May 22nd, Guderian was striking north to attack the encircled British troops at Boulogne, Calais and Dunkirk, and by the next day, as the Germans crossed the River Scheldt at Oudenarde and the British Expeditionary Force in Belgium was put on half rations, the forces on the Channel beaches were hemmed in. At Boulogne, six British destroyers evacuated 4,400 troops under heavy fire, and the French destroyers *Jaguar* and *Orage* were sunk. The situation was desperate.

Then, on Friday May 24th, there occurred one of the strangest events of the war. Hitler and Field-Marshal Gerd von Rundstedt, to the intense frustration of the *Panzer* generals, ordered the *Panzer* Divisions to halt at Gravelines, South West of Dunkirk. Why this order was given remains the subject of intense speculation, but, whatever the reason, it resulted in what has become known as 'The Miracle of Dunkirk'. At Boulogne, the British were less fortunate – 5,000 British and French troops were captured on Sunday 25th May. At Calais, the British garrison rejected a call to surrender and repulsed attack after attack.

All through Sunday 25th, massive preparations had been under way along the British coast to mount one of the strangest and greatest seaborne rescues of all time. On Monday 26th, and for the next week, every vessel that could cross the English Channel to collect men did so – fishing boats, pleasure boats, small sailing boats, even the Thames paddle steamer *Gracie Fields*. Many small vessels, and all the naval ships that survived the fierce bombardment to which the flotilla was subjected returned several times, braving the most appalling conditions to rescue the British and French soldiers marooned on the beaches.

When Hitler and von Rundstedt realised what was afoot, on the 26th, the *Panzer* Divisions were given the order to attack, but the respite had provided the stricken Allies with the opportunity to mount a ring of artillery around the besieged army, and the *Panzers* were unable to penetrate to the beaches and prevent the evacuation. Between the 26th and June 4th, 338,226 men, including some 120,000 French and Belgians, were evacuated from Dunkirk by a total of 861 ships and private craft. Sadly 243 vessels were sunk. The *Luftwaffe* lost more than 130 aircraft, the RAF 106, with 87 pilots either dead or captured. When the Germans took Dunkirk on June 4th, they captured large quantities of abandoned British and French equipment and vehicles – 2,472 guns, 84,427 vehicles and 657,000 tons of ammunition and stores.

Meanwhile, on May 28th, King Leopold of the Belgians had announced the surrender of the Belgian Army against the wishes of his cabinet and many of his people. On Friday May 31st, the French 1st Army surrendered near Lille after a four-day siege.

Dunkirk marked for the people of Britain an end and, in a different way, a beginning. But for France the agony continued. The Battle of France was about to begin.

THE HUMILIATION OF FRANCE

THE AVENGING OF VERSAILLES

The army that had been at the end of the First World War indisputably the greatest in the world, and which had started the Second World War as Germany's most feared opponent, had come to a sorry pass. Badly led, ill-trained, the victim of endless political crises which had stifled military planning throughout the Thirties, the French Army had been inflated to unmanageable ill-disciplined proportions by over-hasty mobilisation. The largely amateur colossus that sought to bestride the most professional mechanised army the world had seen seemed to know its deficiencies; to know it could not win; it seemed almost to be committed to losing even before its leaders urged it to successes it could not achieve. Low morale is the most pernicious of diseases in an army open to infection.

In fact, the French Government was on the way to overcoming many of the underlying problems of supply from which the French armed forces – notably the *Armee de l'Air* – suffered. Nationalised in 1936/37, the French aircraft industry had designed new aircraft but had produced few of them before 1940. Nonetheless, between January and June 1940, production increased to an extraordinary extent. By June 1940, the Dewoitine D.520, the French competitor to the Spitfire and a worthy opponent for the Messerchmitt 109, was being produced at the remarkable rate of one per hour, but there were too few pilots to fly them. The situation was too far gone. France must still be the only power in history to have emerged from losing a campaign with more aircraft than she had had when she started it.

With Dunkirk taken, the German Army turned its attention to the capture of the remainder of France – Operation Red. General Weygand, Allied C-in-C, had 66 divisions available to him – 65 French and one British – and found them facing a reinforced German army of 120 divisions in the line with a further 23 in reserve. Hitler and the OKW staff moved to a temporary headquarters in the Belgian village of Bruly-de-Pesche, and a new plan was devised to enable the predominantly armoured Army Group to make the best use of the terrain. The mass *Panzer* assault was to be made across the plains of Picardy, XV *Panzer* Corps from Longpre, and Kleist's *Panzergruppe* from Amiens and Peronne.

On June 5th, the Battle for France began, and the Germans found that, despite their numerical superiority, they made little progress and suffered considerable losses. By nightfall on the first day, General Erwin Rommel, later to be known as the charismatic 'Desert Fox', and at this time in command of the 7th *Panzer* Division, was only 13km South of the Somme. For days, although some progress was made, the French managed to contain the German forces and inflict great damage upon them. Weygand's army was well dug-in, defending every street corner and hedgerow, and fighting with great tenacity and spirit. Somehow the spirit of Verdun had returned.

On June 6th, Rommel broke through West of Amiens, despite the fierce resistance, and advanced 32km. On June 7th he reached Forges-les-Eaux, near Rouen; on the 8th he advanced 72km and arrived at the Seine. Meanwhile, on the left of the German front, the German 9th Army had made progress across the wooded country of the Chemin des Dames, and on the right the 15th *Panzer* Corps had broken through the French 10th Army. Numerical strength was beginning to show dividends. The progress of the Germans forced General Besson to order General Frere to pull back the 7th Army to create a cohesive line with the 6th and the 10th, thus yielding a great deal of territory and sacrificing both men and weapons. Meanwhile, Rommel had swung back to the Channel at Fecamp, trapping General Ihler's IX Corps. On 12th June, Ihler was forced to surrender, and 46,000 French and British troops became prisoners.

On June 9th, Field-Marshal von Rundstedt's Army Group A had entered the campaign, against the French 4th Army and units of the French VII Corps. Seven French divisions fought gallantly against twice their numbers of fresh troops, inflicting heavy losses, and maintained high morale despite mounting odds. Their demeanour, skill and appetite for the fight could not have been more different from that of the earlier battles on the Somme. Throughout June 9th and 10th, the Germans made little progress, and were admiring of the quality of the French soldiers in their diaries and despatches. Then, inevitably, VII Corps' stand collapsed, and Guderian's *Panzers* crossed the Aisne and made South. On the evening of June 12th, he reached Chalons-sur-Marne.

By this time Weygand had only 27 divisions left in the field, Kleist's *Panzergruppe* had broken through from Peronne and Amiens, and the position was becoming irrecoverable without strategic withdrawal. On June 12th Weygand ordered a retreat to a line from Geneva to Caen; a far longer line to defend with 27 divisions than he had been defending only a week before with 66. On the 14th, the Germans entered Paris and found it almost empty. Only 700,000 people remained of a population of five million. The remainder had taken to the roads. Recognising the seriousness of the situation, and anxious to retain every soldier possible for the next crucial battle, Churchill ordered the immediate evacuation of all remaining British troops in France.

The French Government, which had earlier moved to Tours, now moved again for Bordeaux. Premier Paul Reynaud made a desperate appeal to President Roosevelt to declare war on Germany and come to the rescue of France, but this plea fell on ears that, one suspects, would have liked to have heard but could not. In his reply on June 15th, President Roosevelt promised every aid short of military intervention. On June 15th, as 30,600 British troops were evacuated from Cherbourg, and the Germans captured Verdun, the French Army GHQ moved to Vichy. The next day, Guderian captured Besancon, and it became clear that events were moving swiftly towards an inevitable conclusion. Premier Paul Reynaud resigned, and the veteran Marshal Petain, the hero of Verdun in the Great War, formed a new government. The next day, June 17th, Petain asked the Germans and Italians (Mussolini having declared war on Britain and France on June 10th) for terms for an armistice. On the 18th, Rommel captured Cherbourg, and the 5th *Panzer* Division took Brest. The last RAF squadrons left France. All towns of more than 20,000 inhabitants were declared 'open' and were ordered to surrender without resistance. Most, but not all, did just that. At Saumur, 2,300 cadets of the Cavalry School put up an epic fight under the command of Colonel Michon, and prevented the German 1st Cavalry Division from crossing the Loire for 48 hours. 200 cadets died. The 220,000 French troops holding the Maginot Line, the great fortification stretching from the Swiss border at Basle to Luxembourg, and which had been built to protect France from Germany, held out until June 25th. Sadly, the French governments of the Thirties had never found the budget or the political will in respect of Belgian and Dutch political sensibilities to extend the Maginot Line to the Channel, and the German armies, by taking Holland and Belgium before France, simply went round it.

During the period when British and French troops that could escape to Britain were being evacuated from the Atlantic and Channel ports, every worthwhile warship or supply vessel that was unable to put to sea was scuttled and put beyond service for the German invader. Five submarines, the destroyer *Cyclone*, tankers and fleet auxiliaries, and many smaller vessels that might have helped the enemy were ruthlessly put out of commission by the French. The battleships *Paris* and the *Courbet*, seven submarines, four destroyers, six torpedo boats and thirteen gunboats managed to reach Britain. The newly completed battleship *Richelieu* escaped from Brest and sailed to Dakar; the incomplete *Jean Bart*, after a breathtaking escape from St Nazaire under heavy Stuka attack, and fuelling at sea under fire, ran the gauntlet of the U-boats in the Bay of Biscay and reached Casablanca. They were not all so lucky. The French troopship *Champlain* was seriously damaged by a mine in the Bay of Biscay, and was subsequently finished off by U-65 on June 21st.

While tragedy without equal in the long and glorious history of France was unfolding in the North, one French General was succeeding in his objective far to the South. General Olry, commanding the French 14th and 15th Corps, was facing invasion by the Italians. Mussolini, who customarily waited until the horses were in the home straight before placing his bets, ordered the Prince of Piedmont, who had until that moment been under orders to conduct a defensive strategy, to attack in the Alpine region between Mont Blanc and the Mediterranean. Despite protests from Marshal Badoglio, Mussolini insisted, and the Italian 1st and 4th Armies, some 450,000 men, attacked the 185,000-strong Army commanded by General Olry on 20th June. During the next five days before the Government of Marshal Petain concluded an armistice with the Italians at Villa Inchesa, near Rome, on the 25th, the Italians made little progress against the magnificently trained and disciplined French Army of the Alps. The Italian 1st Army reached Menton, some two miles beyond the French initial line, but only by vast superiority of numbers. Once in Menton, the Italians became bogged down. At the Little St Bernard, the *Alpini* Corps failed even to take the French advanced positions. In the Maurienne Valley, after taking two villages, the Italian 1st Corps ground to a halt before French 75mm guns. On the Col de Mont Genevre, the 4th Corps made minimal progress, but took the Chenaillet redoubt, described by Mussolini with soaring hyperbole as one of the key positions in 'the Maginot system of the Alps'. He omitted to mention that the French artillery had inflicted appalling damage on the Italian fort at Chaberton. The Italian armour never managed to get into action. It was General Olry's victory. Despite the Armistice and Petain's capitulation, Olry's stand saved South-East France from Axis occupation. Remarkably, despite being outnumbered two to one, his forces had lost only 37 killed, 42 wounded and 150 missing. The Italians lost 631 killed, 2,631 wounded and 616 missing. Their performance did not please Adolf Hitler.

Nonetheless, France had fallen. The impossible had happened. As German formations completed the task of subjugating the French nation, de Gaulle broadcast to his country from London, where he was establishing the Free French forces to fight on. Churchill broadcast to Britain a message of indomitable courage and touching simplicity:

'Let us so bear ourselves that, if the British Commonwealth and Empire last for a thousand years, men will say, "This was their finest hour!"'

As Britain braced itself for the ordeal that was to come, Hitler planned the final humiliation for France, and his vengeance for the terms and manner of the Treaty of Versailles. For the signing of the Armistice on June 22nd, he had the original railway carriage in which the 1918 Armistice had been signed brought from the museum in Paris to the Forest of Compiegne, and set up exactly as it had been in 1918. And there he made General Huntziger sign with General Keitel the armistice that gave two thirds of France over to German occupation and disarmed and demobilised the proud French army. The final stroke was the requirement that France pay the costs of the German army of occupation.

The real cost to France was incalculable. The Battle of France had cost between 82,000 and 94,000 French lives and about a quarter of a million wounded. Almost 2 million French soldiers were prisoners of war. The British had lost 3,475 dead and 15,850 wounded since the invasion on May 10th, plus many thousands more to German prisoner of war camps. Germany had suffered the loss of 27,074 dead and 111,034 wounded.

Now Britain waited for invasion. On a clear day, the Germans could see Dover from Calais across the 22-mile-wide straits. How long would it be before they crossed?

THE SUMMER OF 1940

AND THE BATTLE OF BRITAIN

Europe basked in almost continuously magnificent summer weather as the temporary lull in large-scale hostilities caused all the combatant nations to take stock, regroup, redefine their priorities and discuss what the other side would do next. In France on July 1st, the French Government moved once again, this time to the town that was to become synonymous with French collaboration with Hitler – Vichy. Nine days later, on the 10th, the French National Assembly at Vichy gave Petain full powers to govern by a massive majority of 569 votes to 80 with only 17 abstentions. The next day, President Lebrun resigned, and Petain proclaimed himself 'Head of the French State', abolished the 1875 constitution and dismissed the Senate and the Chamber of Deputies.

On July 3rd came the 'Mers-el-Kebir affair'. Believing with some justification that Hitler's and Mussolini's guarantees of the neutrality of the French fleet, given as part of the Armistice agreements, were not to be relied upon, Churchill ordered Royal Navy 'Force H' under Vice-Admiral Sir James Somerville to se-cure for the Allies the naval squadron of Admiral Gensoul, currently at Mers-el-Kebir in Algeria, or sink them. After protracted negotiations, the French Admiral refused to join the British fleet, and, at 1656 hrs, the British ships opened fire. The French battleship *Bretagne* was sunk, with the loss of 977 lives, and the *Dunkerque* was badly damaged with 210 lives lost. *Provence* ran aground; *Mogador* was badly damaged. Only the battleship *Strasbourg* escaped to Toulon.

A similar tragedy could have happened at Alexandria, but for the good sense and co-operation of the two admirals concerned, Cunningham of the British Royal Navy, and Godfroy of the French. Despite his orders from Churchill to achieve results by nightfall on July 3rd, Cunningham held his fire and continued to negotiate. Godfroy, despite the appalling news from Mers-el-Kebir, did the same. On July 4th, agreement was reached. Godfroy's eleven ships were to be immobilised in Alexandria Harbour and land their fuel stocks, and the breech blocks of their guns and the detonators of their torpedoes were to be handed over to the French Consulate in Alexandria.

Nearer home for Churchill and England, French ships in British ports were seized on July 3rd, with some fighting on board the giant submarine *Surcouf* and the destroyer *Mistral*. Nor surprisingly, the Vichy government in France was not happy, and on July 5th Petain broke off diplomatic relations with Britain. On the same day, as a reprisal for the Mers-el-Kebir incident, Vichy French warships captured three British merchant ships.

The U-boat offensive was beginning to bite. On June 20th, the British cargo liner *Avelona Star* was sunk by U-43. On July 2nd, another British liner, the *Arandora Star*, carrying 1,500 Italian and German internees and POWs to Canada, was sunk by the U-47 off Ireland with the loss of 670 lives. Three days later, HMS *Whirlwind*, a destroyer, was sunk by U-34 South West of Ireland, and the soon-to-be famous U Boat base at Lorient received its first boat, the U-30. Then, between July 6th and August 2nd came a series of devastating blows to the Royal Navy. No less than five British submarines were sunk off Norway – the *Shark, Salmon, Thames, Narwhal*, and *Spearfish*. In August, British submarine operations in the area were temporarily suspended.

Germany moved to occupy its first and, it proved, only British territory of the war. On Sunday June 30th, German troops landed on Guernsey in the Channel Islands, and, on the following day, occupied Jersey and the remaining principal inhabited islands. To assert German power and establish a suitable fear of the Fatherland, the Germans had bombed and strafed both Jersey and Guernsey on June 28th, killing 33 people and injuring 40.

Meanwhile, on June 27th 1940, Britain had announced a general blockade of the European coastline from the Bay of Biscay to the North Cape of Norway. In the air, the Allies had scored some successes, balanced by some devastating failures. Sunderland flying boats of the RAF, between 27th and 29th June, worked with destroyers of the Royal Navy to sink four Italian submarines and damage three more in the Eastern Mediterranean. On July 1st, Guy Gibson, later to become famous as the leader of the attack by 617 Squadron RAF on the Ruhr dams, dropped a 2,000lb bomb near the *Scharnhorst*, and his companions hit *Prinz Eugen* with two small bombs. The next week, on the 9th, a small force of 12 RAF Blenheims made a heroic attack on Stavanger airfield in Norway, from which not one returned unscathed. Seven aircraft were lost, five were damaged.

The Battle of Britain Begins
The comparative hush that had descended upon Europe with the Fall of France was not to last long. Hitler was already planning Operation Sealion, the invasion of Britain, and was studying closely the entirely new set of strategic considerations that such an assault made necessary. Comparisons between Hitler's career and that of Napoleon Bonaparte are both inevitable and, perhaps, hackneyed, but there can be little doubt that, when approaching the problem of invading England, both recognised the same difficulties, each attempted to solve them, and both failed.

For both, a successful invasion of Britain could be achieved only if mastery of the English Channel and the North Sea could be attained. In 1940, that implied mastery of the skies, as well as of the seas, and Hitler had to weigh the comparative strengths and strategic ability to fight of both his own *Kriegsmarine* and the Royal Navy on the one hand, and of the *Luftwaffe* and the Royal Air Force on the other. At sea, Hitler lacked the comparative strength that Napoleon had been able to claim in 1805. The crippling naval losses of the operations in Norway had brought the German Navy to a low ebb, with only one pocket battleship, four cruisers and a dozen destroyers. The Home Fleet, based at Scapa Flow, was enormously superior, but already had bitter experience of the strength of the German U-Boat fleet as an adversary, and of the devastating effectiveness of *Luftwaffe* dive bombing against slow-moving ships. Hitler knew that it was very unlikely that the Admiralty would risk its big ships in the Channel, where manoeuvrability would be limited and vulnerability high.

Hence, he reasoned, the matter would be decided by air power. The *Luftwaffe* remained the finest air force in the world. Goering, always a powerful influence upon Hitler in matters concerning air power, believed it to be invincible, and promised Hitler that the *Luftwaffe* would not be beaten. On paper, it seemed likely that that prediction would be fulfilled. Hitler therefore resolved to pit the *Luftwaffe* against the Royal Air Force to secure mastery of the Channel for the invasion of England, set at this stage for shortly after August 25th.

The date of the beginning of the Battle of Britain is a matter of some debate. To the Germans, August 13th was designated *Adlertag* – the Day of the Eagle. Historically, that date marked the beginning of the Battle. And yet the availability of aircraft, the morale and tenor of the crews, was determined on both sides by air operations against England that began on July 10th. On that Wednesday, *Luftwaffe* raids on the British mainland began in earnest, with 60 Junkers 88 twin-engined fighter bombers attacking the ports of Falmouth and Swansea, the Pembrey Royal Ordnance factory in South Wales, where 30 people were killed, and Martlesham airfield near Ipswich. On the same day, 25 Dornier 17 twin-engined bombers attacked a convoy near Dover, which produced the loss of one ship. Two days later, on Friday July 12th, night raids on Aberdeen caused 60 casualties, and Cardiff was bombed.

Amidst the growing threat, the recently arrived Poles and French pilots who had escaped from the German invasions of their countries began to form the Free Polish and Free French squadrons of the Royal Air Force. The first Free Polish Squadron, No. 302, was formed on July 13th, equipped with Hurricanes, and was rapidly to be drawn into the battle. Having experienced the terrors of Nazi invasion at first hand, the Poles particularly were fearless, dedicated, almost fanatical in their opposition to the *Luftwaffe*. Many had lost their families, their homes, everything to the German invasion, and had but one wish – to kill Germans. This made the Polish squadrons magnificently brave to the point of recklessness, but almost uncontrollable in battle, drowning conventional RT procedure with Polish language broadcasts on what they regarded as the dubious parentage of their opponents.

On July 18th, RAF Bomber Command struck back for the bombing raids on United Kingdom targets with night raids on the Krupp armament works at Essen, on targets at Bremen and on the Hamm marshalling yards. The next night, Dornier 17 bombers hit the Rolls Royce aero engine factory at Glasgow. Each day, air raids by each side on shipping and land targets continued, and the pressure on the aircrews mounted. In late July, Goering formed the *Luftwaffe's* first night fighter squadron with Messerschmitt 110 twin-engined fighters, and claimed the first night fighter 'kill' of the war – an RAF Whitley bomber over North West Germany. On July 22nd, only two days later, the RAF night fighters claimed their first night 'kill', a Dornier 17 near Brighton, shot down by a Blenheim using the new AI radar.

By July 28th, the battle was warming up. The South African fighter ace 'Sailor' Malan, based at Biggin Hill, shot and wounded Germany's top fighter pilot Molders, who crash-landed (and survived) in France. At the end of July 1940, Germany had lost 139 aircraft during the month; the RAF had lost only 52.

By August 1st, Hitler's provisional date for the invasion of Britain had been put back one month to September 15th. During the first two weeks of August, the pattern of air attacks on convoys at sea, attacks by night on primarily military targets, and occasional skirmishes between rival fighter formations continued. Then, on August 13th came the beginning of Goering's mighty thrust to destroy

RAF Fighter Command, and clear the skies over the Channel for the invasion of Britain. The Battle of Britain had begun in deadly earnest.

In fact, Goering's much-vaunted assault that was to destroy the Royal Air Force in four days began more with a whimper than a roar. The early morning raids on Britain that were to launch the attack were cancelled, and the only enemy action to disturb the English forenoon that Tuesday was the arrival of 70 unescorted Dornier bombers that dropped their load on Eastchurch airfield near the Thames. A squadron of Junkers 88 fighter bombers that were scheduled to dispense high explosive medicine to Farnborough failed to find their target.

By afternoon, the *Luftwaffe* was beginning to get its act together, and another raid made up of Junkers 88 aircraft started a number of fires in Southampton Docks, but a Spitfire squadron claimed nine Stukas over Hampshire, thereby leaving the RAF with the day's honours. In fact, on the first day, the German air force lost 42 aircraft, the Royal Air Force 13 fighters. The ratio of losses was even more in the RAF's favour on the following day 19 German to four British aircraft destroyed.

On August 15th came the first major show of strength by the *Luftwaffe* over Britain. *Luftflotten* 2, 3 and 5 arrived in force to attack airfields from the South Coast to the Tyne, in North-East England. *Luftflotte* 5, coming from Scandinavia to the Northern parts of the country, was soundly defeated by the RAF, but in the South of England much damage was done. One of Goering's elite units, *Erpr. Gr. 210*, bombed Croydon Airport with considerable effect, killing 62 people. My mother, who lived nearby at the time, recalled watching from her bedroom window as the German aircraft approached, and realising with stark amazement that the objects falling from them were bombs. Despite the damage done, even this first-class Group lost six Messerschmitt 110 aircraft and its commanding officer during the raid. Total *Luftwaffe* losses on August 15th were not the 144 aircraft gleefully claimed by Britain's most vocal newspaper, the *Daily Mirror*, but 76. The Royal Air Force had had a bad day, with 50 aircraft destroyed.

Next day, RAF Tangmere in West Sussex, in the extreme South of England, and seven other RAF stations were bombed. Captured records show that the Luftwaffe Command Staff estimated the RAF to be down to 300 aircraft by this stage, probably because each destroyed RAF aircraft was being claimed by the gunners of several different German aircraft. In fact, the RAF had some 700 fighters still in active service, and most of them were in the air again on Sunday August 18th when the *Luftwaffe* once more launched fierce raids on Air Force bases and various other targets in South East England. Again the *Luftwaffe* came a poor second when the cost was counted, for they lost 19 Stukas, eight out of an escort of 50 Messerschmitt 109 aircraft, and many others. By evening, 62 German aircraft had failed to return to their bases, and 34 British planes had been lost.

After a summer that had so far been almost unremittingly dry, sunny and clear for the deadly business of war, the few days from August 19th to 23rd were wet and dismal, with plentiful low cloud. Although there were intermittent raids, the pilots of the RAF were able to take some desperately needed rest. Ground crews worked feverishly to repair damaged aircraft and equipment, runways were patched, grass airfields were levelled and the craters filled. In Germany, Goering fumed at the wasted time.

By Saturday August 24th, the respite was over, the sun shone, and the *Luftwaffe* resumed its assault with massive raids on airfields across the South East of England, the area designated for Field-Marshal von Rundstedt's forces to land when the invasion began. RAF Manston in Kent had to be evacuated.

Hornchurch, across the Thames in Essex, was badly damaged. Residential areas in coastal towns Portsmouth and Ramsgate were bombed. Most significantly, London was hit by incendiary attacks from a group of aircraft who were targetted to attack the Short flying boat factory at Rochester, but became lost because of British radio countermeasures. The consequences of this single mistake can be argued to have lost Germany the Battle of Britain, and ultimately the war. For the implications of the swell of public and government anger that followed the accidental bombing of London, and of all the events that followed, were immense.

Winston Churchill, incensed at the attack on non-military targets in London ordered the RAF to bomb Berlin, a hazardous long-range task for the aircraft then available. Of the 81 twin-engined bombers that took off for the raid on the night of August 25th, only 29 reached the German capital, (the remainder got lost on the way) and the actual damage done was comparatively slight when compared with the loss of the eight RAF men who were killed and the 29 that were wounded. But Hitler, who had been specifically promised by Goering that no enemy would bomb Berlin, was put into a towering rage, and made the first of many emotional and ill-conceived strategic decisions that were against Germany's military interests. Forgetting the strategy of concentrating all *Luftwaffe* effort on the annihilation of RAF Fighter Command, he ordered that London be subjected to airborne *blitzkrieg*, as Warsaw and Rotterdam had been before. The preparation for this campaign of terror bombing, and the raids themselves, which began on September 7th and continued for 57 appalling days and nights, dispersed *Luftwaffe* effort, and took the pressure off RAF Fighter Command.

In fact, after a bad start during the August 13th-17th period, when Germany lost 255 aircraft, the *Luftwaffe* had been set to win the battle from the 24th onwards. Although more German aircraft than British were being lost daily, the *Luftwaffe* had started from a better base (1,137 fighters against 620 Hurricanes and Spitfires), and many of the planes that were being lost were bombers. Hence, the fighter strength of the *Luftwaffe* by comparison with the RAF was becoming greater as the 1,000 pilots with which the RAF was left by the end of the third week of August became progressively more tired. For as long as Goering could keep up the pressure on the airfields of the South East corner of England, there was little doubt that the RAF would go under eventually. Air Chief Marshal Sir Hugh Dowding, head of Fighter Command, accepted that this was the case, and was on record as informing Churchill of the fact. Perhaps this contributed to his being relieved of his command shortly after his pilots had won their heroic battle.

Hypothesise as one will as to what might have happened had Hitler maintained his original strategy, the facts are that he did not, and that the diverting of resources to the London Blitz enabled Fighter Command to gain the upper hand in the battle for mastery of the Channel airspace. In the last days of August there were daylight raids by the *Luftwaffe* on airfields across the South, around London and in Essex, air battles overhead to entertain the population every day, and a gradual increase in German night raids on civilian targets. Birmingham, Coventry and Plymouth were bombed on August 26th/27th, Liverpool on August 28th, Liverpool and Merseyside again on August 31st/September 1st. The crews and aircraft of RAF Bomber Command were not idle, and bombed Berlin again on the 28th, the 30th and the 31st.

September opened with another major assault on Fighter Command bases, with Biggin Hill in Kent badly damaged on September 1st, and Detling, Eastchurch, and Biggin Hill again hit on September 2nd. The RAF celebrated the first anniversary of the start of the war on September 3rd with the first of nine raids during the month on Berlin. On the same day, Hitler postponed the invasion of Britain from September 15th to September 21st. The 4th and 5th saw heavy and successful German attacks on the Vickers aircraft factory at Brooklands in Surrey, stopping production of Wellington bombers for four days, and again on Biggin Hill and Detling. The 6th brought the bombers to the Hawker aircraft factory at Weybridge in Surrey.

Then, on the 7th September, the London Blitz began, and the daylight raids on the airfields and military installations slowed markedly. But there was to be one last major assault before the *Luftwaffe* acknowledged that the Battle of Britain was lost. On 14th September, the *Luftwaffe* had considerable success with daylight raids on Southern England, and met with comparatively weak resistance. Encouraged, Goering decided to launch an all-out offensive on Sunday, September 15th, the nearest Sunday to which is now commemorated each year in Britain as 'Battle of Britain Day'. Two major raids in daylight on London were massacred by the RAF fighters, which claimed in its enthusiasm 185 aircraft shot down, although the actual number was 53, with 16 damaged. The RAF lost 26 planes and 13 pilots. Bombs fell all over London; even Buckingham Palace was hit on September 13th.

The next day was strangely quiet in the RAF control rooms. Little happened. On the 17th, it seemed that the pressure might be on again, as large formations of Messerschmitt 109 aircraft carried out sweeps over Kent. But as the day turned to evening, and the 18th came and went without the massive attacks that RAF personnel had come to regard as normal, everybody realised that the men of Fighter Command whom Winston Churchill had called 'The Few' had indeed won a great victory and vanquished a mighty enemy.

On that same day, Hitler put off Operation Sealion indefinitely. The postponement was a historic decision of considerable magnitude and far-reaching consequences. The invasion of England was the only amphibious invasion that Hitler planned, and the only invasion that he planned and did not execute. By failing to take England, and therefore failing to complete his domination of Western Europe before turning East, he committed Germany to war on several fronts. By failing to quash the spirit of defiance that had sustained England through its ordeal, he unwittingly inspired the world, particularly the USA, to recognise that he could, and would, be defeated.

The Battle of Britain was the first setback for Hitler as assuredly as the Battle of Midway was later to prove the first setback for the Japanese in the Pacific. As the summer of 1940 became autumn, the world waited anxiously to see what would happen next.

THE BLITZ
THE BOMBS RAIN DOWN

On 30th August 1940, the German News Bureau announced to London 'The attacks of our *Luftwaffe* are only a prelude. The decisive blow is about to fall.'

For once, the German propaganda machine spoke the truth. At 4.56pm on the fine, late summer afternoon of Saturday September 7th, London's air-raid sirens, later to be known less than affectionately as 'Moaning Minnies', announced the arrival of 375 German bombers and supporting fighters. They came up the Thames to London from the sea and set the London docks ablaze. As darkness fell, the fires burnt fiercely all over East London, and illuminated the efforts of a London Fire Brigade that was to have no rest for almost two months. This was the beginning of the London Blitz, and the only mass daylight raid of a campaign of terror that was characterised by the undaunted spirit of the civilian population. Although the daylight bombers were gone by 6pm that evening, the fires were still burning fiercely when the night raiders arrived to inflict more damage at 8.10pm.

The raid lasted until 4.30am. Seemingly endless sticks of incendiary bombs and high explosive rained down. By dawn London had nine major conflagrations: huge spreading areas of flame, nineteen fires that would normally have called for thirty pumps or more, forty ten-pump fires, and nearly a thousand lesser fires, any one of which would have made the front pages in peace time. Thousands of houses in the inner suburbs along the Thames were destroyed or damaged in one night. Some 430 men, women and children were killed and 1,600 were seriously injured.

The next night, the German bombers came again, this time attacking the ancient square mile of the City of London, financial capital of the world, as well as the London docks. For nine and a half hours, 200 bombers droned overhead, causing no less than twelve conflagrations, putting the railway network to the South of London out of action and destroying hundreds of houses. A further 412 civilians were killed, and 747 were seriously injured.

On Monday night, 370 were killed and 1,400 injured. On Tuesday a similarly frightening trail of destruction was left by another mighty raid. But on Wednesday London began to fight back, as the anti-aircraft batteries in the middle of the great sprawling city opened up with their reassuring racket. No aircraft were destroyed, but casualties were fewer and damage reduced.

Every single night for the rest of September the bombers came, the fires burned, and the death toll mounted. By the end of the month, 5,730 people had been killed and nearly 10,000 badly injured. Roads were cratered, telephone systems crippled, gas mains fractured, electricity supplies destroyed. Hospitals all over Greater London were damaged, some severely.

October seemed to produce a lessening of the scale of the attack. On the 6th, only one bomb fell. But still the bombers came every night, people died, and homes burned. The 15th's full moon was to prove hard on Londoners who had already endured almost six weeks of continuous bombing. Over 400 bombers arrived and dropped more than a thousand bombs: 430 were killed, 900 badly hurt. The pattern, the grisly monotony, continued until the nightly raiders left after their attack on the night of November 2nd, the 57th consecutive night of the Blitz. Wearily, London fought its fires, sought its dead, picked through the rubble and waited for nightfall to bring the next lot. But miraculously the raiders did not come. The spell was broken.

There were, in fact, only three nights in November when London was not bombed. Once again, the German crews celebrated the time around full moon with the biggest raid of the month, on the 15th, but, on the previous night, another terrifying raid had been directed, not against the capital but against Coventry, an attractive Midlands city in the industrial heartland of England. We now know that Churchill had been told in advance of this raid, because the secret intelligence centre at Bletchley Park had been able to decode monitored *Luftwaffe* orders with its captured German 'Enigma' coding machine. Despite this terrible knowledge, Churchill had been unable to increase Coventry's defences or give warning, lest the Germans discovered that the Allies were able to decode their signals. The priceless secret of 'Ultra', as the decoding operation was known, was somehow preserved, not only until the end of the war, but for decades after it. Few intelligence operations in history have been so successful, or have yielded so much strategically valuable information. But that was no comfort to the people of devastated Coventry, who, on 14th/15th November 1940, lost their cathedral, their homes, and, in many cases, members of their families.

By the end of November 1940, 12,696 civilians in the London area had died, about 20,000 had been seriously injured, and approximately 36,000 bombs had fallen on England's capital. After November, the German Command realised that the strategy of total destruction and the crushing of Britain's will simply could not work, and the pattern of bombing became more widespread, though no less destructive. There were great fire raids on the City of London in December, and more raids in January 1941, but the force of the London Blitz was for the time being spent. Across Britain, the raids continued until May 1941, by which time 40,000 British civilians had been killed, 46,000 had been seriously injured, and over a million homes had been destroyed or damaged. In the Battle of Britain and the Blitz combined, the *Luftwaffe* had lost 2,400 aircraft, without achieving any of its objectives.

NEUTRALITY AS A WEAPON

THE U.S.A. TAKES A HAND

Although by spring 1941, as the Blitz in London passed its peak, the USA was still neutral, President Roosevelt's administration, usually but not always with the consent of Congress, was taking an increasingly active role in Britain's lone struggle to resist the onslaught of Nazism in Europe. His doing so was, in traditionally neutral America, something of a political hot potato. To understand the events of the time, it is necessary to look back a little at the nature of America's view of European conflict.

The involvement of the United States in the First World War had been a major psychological trauma for a nation reared and developed on the concept of isolationism. Then, far more than now, the United States was a nation of immigrants, still retaining close nationalistic ties with their homelands. When the Great War began in 1914, and throughout 1915, thousands of Americans left their now-native shores to return to Europe and fight for the Kaiser. Nonetheless, the nation as a whole wished wholeheartedly to remain neutral; to keep clear of a conflict that could benefit them nothing, but damage them greatly. Despite this wish, Americans could not restrain their anger at the reports of German brutality in Belgium and France which repeatedly reached the press in the USA, probably with assistance from (and exaggeration by) the Allied propaganda machine.

Despite clear preference for the British and French cause expressed almost daily by some, though not all, members of the US administration, and in American newspapers, the US government, for reasons that are now not easy to understand, expected Germany to honour American unilaterally declared neutrality. The Wilson administration was incensed when Germany announced unrestricted submarine warfare, and its anger made it inevitable that the USA would enter the war, despite Woodrow Wilson's avowed intention to keep his country out of it.

After the Great War, public opinion in the USA could not forget that the US involvement in the conflict had been the result of political mismanagement (from the isolationist standpoint). There was great pressure on Congress progressively to define in far greater detail than hitherto the nature of US neutrality. In 1935, Congress enacted a law which authorised the President to prevent the shipment of arms and prohibit US citizens from travelling on foreign ships, except at their own risk. As the European political situation drifted towards war, and the US became nervous of the alliance between Japan and Germany, a Neutrality Act of November 1939 repealed the arms embargo element of the earlier legislation and instituted what became known as the 'cash and carry' arms system, designed to help friendly nations who were attacked by the tyrannies of Europe while keeping American out of the battle.

The USA was now beginning to show signs of the same philosophy that had caused the problems in 1916: the wish to help one side in a war while remaining neutral. Despite protests from midwestern isolationists and right wing senators, America began to sell arms to Britain and France. By so doing, Roosevelt made American neutrality wholly dependent upon the Axis powers' acceptance of the principle that a neutral power had the right to sell arms to Axis enemies. Clearly, it was a position that was tenable only for as long as Hitler and his Axis allies wished it to be.

By the time Nazi Germany had taken Norway, Denmark, the Low Countries and France, Roosevelt was advising the American nation to 'have done with fears and illusion'. In the year following the May 1940 German invasion of North West Europe, Congress appropriated $37,000,000,000, more than the total US expenditure on the Great War, for rearmament and aid to the Allies.

Public opinion in the USA was sharply divided. On the one hand William Allen White's Committee to Defend America by Aiding the Allies urged that the USA should become Britain's non-belligerent ally. On the other, the America First Committee, whose policy was one of pacifism, isolationism, anti-Semitism and dislike of almost anything British gained the strong support of many public figures, including Charles A. Lindbergh. Because Germany and Russia were signatories to a Non-aggression Pact, following the August 1939 agreement, pro-Nazis and pro-Communists joined in an unlikely alliance to keep the USA out of the war.

On June 10th 1940, Roosevelt, in a famous speech at Charlottesville, Virginia, warned the US people that they could not risk becoming 'a lone island in a world dominated by the philosophy of force', and promised to 'extend to the opponents of force the material resources of this nation'. At the end of July, by the Act of Havana, the USA announced its protection of Latin America, and thereby prevented Germany from taking control of French and Dutch colonies. Then in September, as America reeled with shock at Britain's struggle in the Battle of Britain, Roosevelt declared a State of Emergency on September 8th, instituted the draft and called up 800,000 men.

In August, after some delay and somewhat contentious negotiation (see next chapter), the USA had provided Britain with 50 desperately needed destroyers, all but three of which were of First World War vintage. Roosevelt had called this 'an epochal and far-reaching' act of preparation for continental defence in the face of danger, because he had been able to justify the action politically by securing in exchange 99-year leases on seven British bases from Guiana to Newfoundland.

Now the country prepared openly for war, retooling the factories and retraining the workers for the production of munitions. An Office of Production was established to co-ordinate defence output and do everything possible to expedite aid to Britain ('short of war'). The USA had now become what Roosevelt was to call at the end of the year 'The Arsenal of Democracy', and the Presidential election of November 1940 was fought against the background of the world crisis, with Roosevelt running for a third term on the grounds that the crisis demanded it. His campaign platform remained one of support for Britain but non-participation in foreign conflicts. Elected once more to the Presidency, Roosevelt found himself leading a country whose mood was changing fast. Americans had grown to admire Britain's desperate stand; to detest the tyranny of the jackboot.

Sensing that the time was right to extend more help to Britain, Roosevelt proposed in January 1941 the Lend-Lease programme.

Lend-Lease came as a replacement for the 'cash-and-carry' arms policy just in time for Britain, whose reserves of gold, dollars and US investment were almost exhausted by the cost of the war. When the bill, with the curiously patriotic designation HR-1776, became law in March, Roosevelt had been given the greatest discretionary authority ever given to an American President. An initial appropriation of $7,000,000,000 was authorised by Congress, and arms, ships, and aircraft began to cross the Atlantic with the least possible red tape and official hold-up. RAF pilots were sent to the USA to train. American warships began convoy escort duties, and inevitably became involved in actions against U-Boats. As a neutral nation, America now lacked a certain credibility. As an ally in the battle against Nazism, she was a prize without price.

Meanwhile, the USA had become increasingly the principal obstacle to Japan's expansionist aims. All through the Thirties, as Japan first invaded Manchuria, then attacked China, then became Hitler's ally, the relationship between the USA and Japan had become progressively more strained. In the summer of 1940, as support for Britain's war effort was stepped up, sales of strategic materials to Japan were banned. On September 27th 1940, Japan joined Italy and Germany in a tripartite pact that required each to come to the others' aid should the USA enter the war, and, the following April, Japan signed a Neutrality Pact with Russia, who was, it should be remembered, still a party to a non-aggression pact with Germany.

The tightening stranglehold on trade with Japan, and the increasingly evident readiness to fight displayed by the USA, put pressure on Japan to expand and find new resources by colonial acquisition. On July 2nd 1941, 50,000 Japanese troops occupied Indo-China, until then administered by the Vichy French government; Britain and the USA froze all Japanese investment assets, and the slide towards war in the Asian theatre had begun. In July of 1941, as German armies fought their way across Russia, President Roosevelt's envoy Harry Hopkins flew to Britain to see Churchill, and flew in a PBY Catalina to Moscow. He took to Stalin a letter from Roosevelt offering assistance to Russia 'in its magnificent resistance to the treacherous aggression by Hitlerite Germany'. This resulted in a protocol signed on October 1st by Averell Harriman, US lease-lend representative, Britain's Lord Beaverbrook and the Russian Foreign Minister Molotov, by which it was agreed that a huge volume of supplies would be sent to Russia.

Meanwhile, on August 9th-12th, Roosevelt had conferred with Churchill at Argentia Bay, Newfoundland, exchanging visits aboard their warships *Prince of Wales* and *Augusta*. This conference produced a remarkable document that will be a part of history for centuries to come – the Atlantic Charter. Essentially a statement of the principles for which the war was being fought, and of the shape of the world that they hoped would emerge from the war, the Charter was drafted by Churchill, and amended and developed by the two statesmen together. Subsequently incorporated into a Declaration of the United Nations, the Atlantic Charter is, in its way, as historic as Magna Carta, or the American Declaration of Independence. It was also an act of true friendship between men and between nations.

Thus the USA, without declaring war, without going to war, became deeply implicated in the greatest war man had yet known. The stage was set.

THE BEGINNINGS OF THE SEA WAR

AND THE STALKING OF THE GRAF SPEE

We have already, in this book, noted some of the events of the war at sea in the context of other episodes and battles that took place before the end of 1940. It now seems right to take a brief yet detailed look at the course of the sea war from September 1939.

For the first three weeks of hostilities, the German Navy was kept tightly in check. Commanders were ordered to follow the rules of the London Convention of 1936 to the letter – and that meant that attacking passenger ships or French vessels was outlawed. Hitler was anxious not to repeat the mistakes of the First World War, when the sinking of the *Lusitania* in 1915 had become a significant factor in the entry of the United States into the conflict, although the British liner SS *Athenia* was torpedoed and sunk by U-30 on 3rd September 1939 with the loss of 112 lives. On September 24th, Nazi Germany's unaccustomed pretence of adhering to the rules was abandoned, and the ban on attacks on French ships was lifted. By the end of the month, the pocket battleships *Graf Spee* and *Deutschland* had sailed to their holding positions in the Atlantic, and the Allies awaited developments.

Most of the significant naval attacks of the period September – December 1939 have been mentioned earlier; suffice it to say that, despite the considerable naval inferiority in terms of both ships and training of the German Navy, they finished 1939 only marginally the loser. German U-Boats had sunk 114 Allied and neutral merchant ships, and would have sunk many more but for the reintroduction of the convoy system, which had saved many ships and lives in the First World War, and for the extraordinarily inefficient magnetic trigger mechanisms of the German torpedoes. But for these defective triggers, the aircraft carrier *Ark Royal*, later to be 'sunk' so many times by Goebbels' propaganda, would actually have gone to the bottom on September 17th. Similarly, on October 30th, the battleship *Nelson* was hit three times by torpedoes, none of which exploded.

The British (and later the Americans) started with the clear advantage of having Asdic, the submarine detection equipment that the US Navy called Sonar. The Germans had no equipment like it, and U-boats were frequently located, although in the early stages rarely destroyed, by British ships uttering the pinging signal of the Asdic transmitter. Nonetheless, nine U-boats were sunk during 1939, six of them ocean-going vessels.

Hitler had placed great reliance upon the big guns, vast fuel capacity and enormous range of his pocket battleships, and had frequently expressed the belief that their value as ocean raiders would give Germany command of the seas and the ability to enforce a blockade. In practice, the pocket battleships were a disappointment. The *Deutschland*, renamed *Lutzow* after her first cruise of the war because of Hitler's deep-seated fear of a ship named 'Germany' being sunk, disposed of only 7,000 tons of small-scale shipping in her two months at sea from August 24th to November 1st.

On November 23rd, the *Scharnhorst* and the *Gneisenau*, ordered to lay on a show of force in the North Atlantic to draw some of the attention of the Allied Navy from the *Graf Spee* in the South, had surprised and overwhelmed the armed merchantman *Rawalpindi*, which sank with considerable loss of life. Among the dead was her commander Captain Kennedy, the father of Britain's well-known author and TV personality Ludovic Kennedy. But even this was a lone incident in an otherwise inglorious career for the pocket battleships.

The *Graf Spee* had more success in her first couple of months. Ordered to commence hostilities against Allied shipping while off Brazil on September 27th, she sank over 50,000 tons of shipping before meeting her Waterloo in the form of Commodore Harwood's Royal Navy South Atlantic cruiser squadron, near the estuary of the River Plate, at dawn on December 13th, an action mentioned in an earlier chapter of this book.

Commodore Harwood's force consisted of the cruisers *Exeter*, *Ajax* and *Achilles*, whose 8-inch and 6-inch guns were hopelessly outclassed by the six 11-inch guns of *Graf Spee*. The German ship was also better armoured, and was equipped with radar, which Commodore Harwood did not have on any of his ships. Despite these disadvantages, Harwood went straight into action, sending the *Exeter* in for a head-on confrontation, while *Ajax* and *Achilles* skirted the battle to attack on the flank. Before *Ajax* and *Achilles* could bring their guns to bear, Captain Hans Langsdorff of the *Graff Spee* had brought the full force of the 11-inch guns down on the *Exeter*, knocking out all her guns, holing the hull and making the ship largely unmanoeuvrable. Even with this terrible damage, the captain and crew of the *Exeter* maintained the attack by firing torpedoes right to the last moment, but had to break away and limp smoking out of range at 7.15am.

Ajax and *Achilles* kept fighting as best they could with their light guns, but in the effort to get close enough to do some damage, *Ajax* had most of her guns knocked out, so Commodore Harwood decided that discretion was the better part of valour, and retired to an honourable distance. On board the *Graf Spee*, 36 men had died, and 59 were wounded. The ship was not at risk, but was quite seriously damaged superficially, and Langsdorff decided, perhaps over-cautiously, not to attempt the home run through the northern seas in winter, but to put in to Montevideo, in neutral Uruguay, for repairs.

The Uruguayan Government was less than enthusiastic about the appearance of a German armed raider in the River Plate, and allowed Langsdorff only the 72 hours' grace that the strict letter of international law permitted. This was not long enough for the repair work to be carried out, and on December 17th, Langsdorff sailed from Montevideo. Believing entirely unfounded rumours that Britain's battle cruiser *Renown* and the aircraft carrier *Ark Royal* were waiting for *Graf Spee* out in the Atlantic, Langsdorff scuttled his ship in the Plate estuary. Perhaps because he felt unable to face the fury of Hitler, or possibly as a result of the humiliation he had suffered, he shot himself on December 20th.

A more serious hazard to Allied and neutral shipping in the early stages of the war was the magnetic mine, a massive semi-submerged or submerged bomb detonated by the magnetic field of a ship passing over it. Germany laid thousands of these mines from aircraft and U-boats, and sank 59 Allied and neutral ships with them before the end of 1939.

The salvation of the Allies' shipping came in the form of a magnetic mine washed up at Shoeburyness, on England's Thames estuary, on the night of November 22nd/23rd. Defusing this unexploded monster was a daunting and extremely dangerous task, for the techniques of coping with unexploded bombs were still in their infancy by comparison with the level of expertise a year or two later. Nonetheless, Commander J.G.D. Ouvry, Royal Navy, tackled the job and succeeded. As a result, scientists were able to understand how the mines operated, and devised a countermeasure known as degaussing. An electric cable carrying a current was passed around the ship, effectively neutralising the vessel's magnetic field. By March 1940, most Allied ships had been degaussed, and the peril of the magnetic mine was largely past.

In the first quarter of 1940, the Allies were more or less in control of the situation at sea. There were as yet relatively few ocean-going U-boats, the terror of the magnetic mine had been overcome, and the convoy system was proving reasonably effective in protecting merchant ships from those submarines that were at sea. Nonetheless, 108 merchantmen were sunk between January 1st and March 31st 1940, almost 350,000 tons in the three months, at a time when British shipbuilders were constructing new ships at the rate of 200,000 tons every month. Naval convoy escorts sank eight U-boats during the same period, and the British and French navies felt they had matters well in hand.

The German invasion of Norway in April 1940 took most of Admiral Doenitz's U-boats out of the Atlantic raiding business for two months, and the merchant convoys had eight weeks of comparative respite. During that time only 20 Allied merchant ships totalling about 88,000 tons were sunk. Defective torpedo detonators continued to dog the efforts of the German submarine commanders, and Doenitz is on record as having said that the magnetic trigger problem spared an entire Royal Navy battle squadron – the battleship *Warspite*, seven cruisers, seven destroyers and five transports. Meanwhile, six U-boats were sunk in the North Sea between April 10th and May 31st.

June brought a wave of appalling destruction to the merchant fleets, as the U-boats were released after Germany's victory in Norway, and returned to the task of sinking merchant ships. Fifty-eight vessels were sunk by U-boats in one month, and the *Luftwaffe*, from their newly-acquired bases in Holland, Belgium and Northern France, claimed forty-four more. More than half a million tons of Allied shipping – 144 separate ships – were sunk by the end of the month.

Now the balance of naval power shifted sharply in Germany's favour as the Italian Navy entered the war on Germany's side, and the French Navy was effectively put out of the fight by the fall of France. Maintaining the pressure on the Italian fleet in the Mediterranean, formerly a problem left to the French, was now entirely in the hands of Admiral Somerville's Force 'H', based at Gibraltar. The Royal navy had only a limited choice of bases in Britain and elsewhere, whereas the Germans had the facilities of every Atlantic port between Tromso and St Jeande-Luz. Britain had a naval base outside the British Isles only because, on May 10th 1940, following the German occupation of Denmark, Britain had occupied Iceland and the Faeroe Islands, until then Danish territory. Thus, although the Royal Navy could no longer blockade the North Sea between Scapa Flow and Norway, it was able still to maintain coverage of a line from the Orkneys and Shetlands, through the Faeroes to Greenland.

The reinforcement of naval strength as a result of German conquest did not all flow Germany's way. A thousand ships of the Norwegian merchant fleet, totalling four million tons, and much of the Dutch and Belgian merchant marine had escaped the clutches of the Germans, and had been put at the disposal of Britain after May 1940. This additional tonnage was considerable – equivalent to some 34 per cent of the total British merchant marine in September 1939. As a result, Britain was able to face the Battle of the Atlantic with almost 30 million tons of shipping.

Admiral Karl Doenitz was not slow to seize for his U-boat fleet the benefits of the new bases that were available to the German Navy. As early as July 7th, the port of Lorient received its first U-boat for refuelling and rearming, and by August, when Doenitz established the headquarters of the U-boat fleet at Kernevel, just outside Lorient, work on refitting the port with the most up-to-date equipment in the world was well under way.

The subsequent successes of the German submarine flet owed much to the dedication with which German scientists had pursued advanced radio technology, and to the readiness of the German Navy to accept what were then new scientific ideas. German radio direction finding had become very sophisticated by mid-1940, and the new installation at Lorient was capable of establishing a position from the briefest of transmissions by a convoy at considerable range. German codebreaking was also very effective, and the records suggest that Doenitz's team were usually able to decipher signals to convoys from British Western Approaches Command. Most important of all, the development for the *Wehrmacht* of what was for the period an immensely powerful radio that enabled whole tank formations to be controlled in a cohesive manner – something that the Allies could not yet do – made is possible for the Lorient U-boat headquarters to be provided with radio transmitters able to communicate directly with U-boat commanders at great range, and direct several submarines on to the same target. This was the origin of the infamous 'Wolf Pack', that was to wreak such terrible havoc on Allied convoys.

As the new Lorient HQ was brought into commission, the U-boat fleet was still not large – 57 boats in September 1940. In the first year of war, the Germans had lost 28 submarines, and had commissioned exactly the same number. Because the training of a submarine crew took (and still takes) a long time, Doenitz was rarely able at this time to put more than nine U-boats into the Atlantic West of Ireland. That his hand-picked and dedicated commanders managed to maintain an average of 920 tons of shipping sunk per U-boat, per day, during October 1940 is an indication of just how effective his crews and his organisation were.

In the face of this efficient offensive force, Britain was desperately short of convoy protection and anti-submarine vessels. Until the destroyers and corvettes ordered during 1939 and 1940 were available, Britain needed more ships, and fast. In May 1940, Churchill had asked President Roosevelt for help in the form of some 50 American destroyers built at the end of the First World War. By July, having heard nothing and with an ever-more pressing need, Churchill tried again, with a further request on July 11th. Although a majority of American public opinion was in favour of helping Britain, and was sympathetic towards both the magnitude of her problems, and the fortitude with which she withstood them, there was great concern about the possible reprisals that such help might exact from Germany and Italy. Fears were expressed that the USA would be dragged into a war for which its industrial production facilities were as yet ill-prepared.

Roosevelt sought a compromise by offering Churchill an alternative deal that would have a direct benefit to US security. In return for the 50 destroyers, proposed Roosevelt, the USA would be allowed to establish bases in Guiana, the

Antilles, Bermuda, the Bahamas and, given the agreement of Canada, in New-foundland, for 99 years. London accepted these terms, but objected sharply when Roosevelt attempted to make a further condition that the British Government declare that Britain's fleet would be sailed to America if it could not be maintained in Home waters. Churchill curtly pointed out that the risk of having to scuttle or surrender the Fleet was one to which the German navy, or what was left of it, was more subject than the British.

Thus Britain approached the sea war of 1941 and 1942 with growing strength, but little effective means to fight the menace to merchant convoys posed by the U-boat. The terror of the wolf-pack was to prove one of the most fearsome chapters of the war. But, for the moment, let us return to the land-based war, and the warmer waters of the Mediterranean.

GAMBLE IN NORTH AFRICA
MUSSOLINI'S VENTURE – HITLER'S INTERVENTION

In June 1940, when Mussolini at last cast his hand for war, Italy had already in North Africa some 236,000 troops, over 1,800 guns, 150 aircraft and some 340 light tanks. These were divided as the Italian 5th Army to the West of Libya, and the 10th Army to the East, the two together amounting to a total of 14 Italian divisions. Ranged against them, but not yet in action, were eight French and five British divisions, the British under the command of General Sir Archibald Wavell. Of the 100,000 British troops, only 36,000 were in Egypt and ready to fight if their positions were attacked. The remainder were to the rear.

The armistice with the French at the end of June altered the balance significantly, taking the French army out of the calculation, and, on the other side of the coin, destroying the Italian commander Marshal Balbo's hopes of taking the Tunisian port of Bizerta to simplify his line of supply. To keep the Italians at a disadvantage, the British 7th Armoured Division began to make daily armoured raids across the Libyan frontier, the success of which, although in fact due to superior British training and discipline, was interpreted by the Italian Army as being the result of the inferiority of Italian weapons.

On June 28th, when it became clear that French North Africa would remain loyal to the Vichy government of Marshal Petain, the Italian Supreme Command ordered Balbo to invade Egypt. On the same day, having not received the order, Balbo suffered a fate that justified the Germans' worst fears about their tempestuous allies – he was shot out of the air over Tobruk by his own anti-aircraft gunners and killed. This was neither the first time nor the last that the Italian forces employed the 'own goal' as a technique in warfare, but it was the only occasion when they used it to dispose of their own Commander in Chief.

Balbo's command was assumed by Marshal Rodolfo Graziani, and the date for the invasion was set for July 15th, 1940. The difficulties presented by the enterprise were formidable. There was but one supply route available across the desert from the Libyan frontier to Alexandria, and that route included two British bases, Sidi Barrani and Mersa Matruh. Graziani, sensibly, decided he was not prepared to begin the advance until he had sufficient trucks and water transport to keep his forces supplied. He asked approval to defer the assault until October 1940. Mussolini, predictably, refused to countenance such a practical suggestion. Knowing that Hitler intended to invade Britain on the 15th September, he was determined that Italy should take Egypt from Britain on the same day. Throughout July and August there were fierce disputes, inflammatory telegrams and endless problems between Mussolini and the Supreme Command, and between Mussolini and Graziani.

Eventually, still ill-prepared, Graziani was obliged to launch the might of Fascist Italy's 10th Army on the pitifully small British defending force on September 13th. Four divisions and an armoured group under General Bergonzoli advanced slowly across a hostile landscape in temperatures of up to 122 degrees Fahrenheit (50 degrees Celsius), succeeding in covering only some 12 miles a day. On September 16th, the crack '23rd of March' Blackshirt Division occupied Sidi Barrani, the 7th Armoured Division having been ordered to fall back before the advance. The Italians were now 60 miles into their 315-mile journey to their objective, Alexandria. Mersa Matruh lay 75 miles ahead.

To Mussolini's intense chagrin, Graziani, who was a veteran of desert operations, decided to pause, repair the damage done by the retreating British Army, set up a fresh water pipeline and stock Sidi Barrani so that it could be effective as a forward supply base. Wavell, like Mussolini, was disappointed, although for different reasons. He had hoped to see the Italians overextend their line of supply. Graziani knew that his equipment was inadequate, that he had too few men for the assault with which he had been entrusted, and that unless he ensured adequate support, his army would stand no chance at all in the latter stages of the advance. Had Mussolini not retained in Italy for his forthcoming assault on Greece most of the troops that had recently been in action in the Alps, things might have been very different.

Graziani's pause lasted into October. At the Brenner Pass Conference on October 4th, at which Hitler, Mussolini, Ribbentrop and Count Ciano met to discuss strategy, the possibility of eventually sending a German armed detachment to North Africa was discussed, but Mussolini made it quite clear that Italy could handle North Africa alone for the time being without German assistance. In Mussolini's opinion, German *Panzer* support would be required only when the third stage of his conquest of Egypt was reached, the advance from Mersa Matruh to Alexandria. By October 21st, Mussolini was warning Graziani in some exasperation that, if the march on Mersa Matruh did not commence shortly, Graziani's resignation from his command would not come amiss. Graziani, who had been waiting for the arrival of three motorised battalions, armoured cars and additional water trucks, was not disposed to put his troops at risk. Because of the imminent Italian campaign in the Balkans, there was little prospect of either of those reinforcements arriving, or of the request for Graziani's resignation being enforced. Mussolini had other things on his mind.

In fact, the blame for the defeat at Sidi Barrani that was inflicted by Wavell on December 9th should not be laid entirely at Mussolini's door. The Italian 10th Army was deployed, in a manner that had obvious and exploitable weaknesses, in two separate groups fifteen miles apart with an undefended gap between. Two Libyan native divisions under Graziani's command were holding positions along the coast, and the 4th Blackshirt Division was to the rear of Sidi Barrani.

The British plan for the attack was daring. Lieutenant-General Sir Richard O'Connor's Western Desert Force was to penetrate the gap between the two halves of the 10th Army, and attack the coastal units from the rear, while the British 7th Armoured Division would advance towards Buqbuq to cut Italian communications and prevent reinforcements reaching the army under attack. An additional secondary brigade-strength attack under Brigadier Selby was to keep the coastal camp at Maktila busy. All told, only 36,000 British troops were taking on a force of almost five times as many men.

The attack on December 9th came as a surprise to the Italians, who had wrongly interpreted aerial reconnaissance information that British troops were on the move as evidence of a weary army being relieved. The 4th Indian Division, and the Matilda tank battalion, together part of O'Connor's force, attacked Nibeiwa, and took 2,000 prisoners for the loss of 56 men. The 7th Armoured division reached the sea by evening, and cut off the retreat of the 2nd Libyan Division. Graziani ordered XXI Corps to withdraw to the frontier, and one division made it without difficulty. The other, the 'Catanzaro' Division, was less fortunate, and was almost annihilated. In a few short hours the Italian army had lost 38,000 prisoners, 237 guns and 73 tanks, against British losses of 624 dead.

At this crucial stage, General O'Connor had the victorious 4th Indian Division taken from his command for action against the Italians in Eritrea, and was awarded the 6th Australian Division as a replacement. He decided not to wait, and instead gave chase to the disorganised and humiliated Italians. On December 14th, O'Connor crossed the Libyan frontier at Capuzzo, swung north and attacked Bardia, defended by 45,000 Italian troops and 430 guns. On the 18th December, General Mackay and the Australian 6th Division arrived, ready for a fight. They celebrated the New Year with another victory. Bardia was captured on January 5th. The Italians lost a further 45,000 men as prisoners, and saw another 130 of their tanks captured.

By now Hitler was becoming increasingly worried at the antics of Mussolini, who had during the autumn launched his ill-prepared armies upon Greece without first advising Germany of his intentions, and was now about to improve British morale and ruin the image of the all-victorious Axis with a devastating defeat in North Africa. In preparation for German intervention, *Luftwaffe X Fliegerkorps* was sent to Sicily at the end of December 1940, and by February 6th, after the fall of Tobruk to O'Connor's all-conquering 7th Armoured Division, General Erwin Rommel was being briefed by Field Marshal von Brauchitsch to command the *Afrika Korps*, scheduled to land in North Africa by mid-February.

In Libya, O'Connor had, even before the fall of Bardia at the beginning of the month, detached the 7th Armoured Division to cut the communications of Tobruk, a vital deep-water port capable of providing a far more efficient means of landing supplies for the Allied force than the long overland route from Alexandria. At dawn on the 21st of January, a full-scale-attack on Tobruk was mounted by the 6th Australian Division, who, because they were down to only 12 Matilda tanks, put captured Italian M-13/40 light tanks into action against their former owners. By the following afternoon, 22nd January, O'Connor was embarrassed with a further 25,000 Italian prisoners and had added 208 guns, 23 medium tanks and 200 trucks to his growing arsenal of alien equipment. Because of the speed of the advance, the Allies captured the vital sea-water distillation plant intact, and the port installation was sufficiently little damaged to be operating again within four days. In addition to the port of Tobruk, the victory brought the bonus of the airfield at El Adem, another vital link in the supply chain which, like Tobruk, was to be in the news more than once in the months to come.

Graziani now set about a half-hearted defence of, and retreat from, Cyrenaica, the desert area that lay between O'Connor's forces and Benghazi, the next target that would be on the Allies' shopping list. Despite Mussolini's instruction to defend it, Graziani was more concerned to fall back to what he considered to be a defensible position. By January 27th, the 7th Armoured Division was at Mechili, some 140 miles from Beda Fomm, near the Gulf of Sirte, South of

Benghazi. In appalling conditions, as the Italians retreated along the much lengthier but better coast road, the *Via Balbia*, the 7th Armoured cut straight across the desert towards the coast. By 3pm on February 4th, the 11th Hussars were at Msus, some 60 miles from the *Via Balbia*, and at noon on the 5th they reached Beda Fomm, half an hour before the Italians retreating from Benghazi down the *Via Balbia*. By February 7th, Generals Cona and Babini had been captured, General Tellera was dead, and O'Connor had another 20,000 Italians to look after. The British had also reached El Agheila at the foot of the Gulf of Sirte, a position commanding the 15-mile-wide access to the sea from the desert. The British were poised to invade Tripolitania. And Rommel was about to arrive in North Africa.

THE BALKANS
RUMANIA, GREECE, YUGOSLAVIA AND CRETE

The fall of France in June 1940 had brought to the surface a dispute which had smouldered for years and which, although not in itself directly connected with the war between the great powers, was about to exert a major influence upon it. This was the territorial disagreement between Hungary and Rumania, which arose from the Treaty of Trianon in 1920. This Treaty had, following the defeat of Austria-Hungary in the Great War, caused Hungary to cede Transylvania, beloved of all followers of Dracula, to Rumania – a not unreasonable boundary change in most respects, since the majority of the inhabitants of Transylvania were, in any case, of Rumanian origin.

There were however, within Transylvania, some two million people of the Magyar race, known as the Sicules, who had no wish to be Rumanian, and who persistently refused to accept their change of nationality. When France fell, the Hungarian Government made approaches to King Carol II of Rumania, but it soon became apparent that Rumania was immoveable on the issue. War seemed inevitable, but Hitler, whose reliance upon the oil wells at Ploesti caused him to put a high priority upon the maintenance of access to Rumania, intervened. Hungary, whose government had a sympathetic ear in Italy, agreed, if Rumania was also agreeable, to submit to Axis arbitration on the dispute. As a result, Ciano and Ribbentrop presided over arbitration proceedings in Vienna in August 1940. Their verdict was that Transylvania should be partitioned, the west going to Rumania. Hungary was to gain the area occupied by the Sicules, plus the extension of her 1920 frontier to the Moldavian Carpathians. This had the effect of putting three million Rumanians into Hungary, a neat reversal of the previous position.

The Rumanians resented their government's acceptance of this proposal deeply, and General Antonescu, appointed Premier by King Carol II on September 4th, rapidly forced King Carol to abdicate and established Carol's son Prince Michael on the throne. Antonescu asked Hitler to provide military assistance to Rumania, and on October 7th the 13th German Motorised Division began to arrive in Bucharest.

Mussolini was indignant at the occupation, particularly since his allies had not told him of it before it took place. He resolved to reward Germany in kind, and to the horror of his Generals, who had, only three weeks before, demobilised 600,000 men on the Duce's orders, instructed them to prepare to invade Greece on October 26th. Count Ciano, Mussolini's son-in-law and Foreign Minister, believed that neither Yugoslavia nor Turkey would come to the aid of Greece, to whom they were allied by the Balkan Pact, and that Bulgaria would approve of Italy's actions. Lieutenant-General Jacomoni, in command in Albania, told the planning conference on 14th October 1940 that everyone in Albania was anxious to settle the account with Greece. Faced with universal approval of Mussolini's scheme, Marshal Badoglio, who had severe doubts as to its military practicality, gave way and agreed, subject to an extension of the deadline for the attack for two days to October 28th.

On the morning of that day, having been warned by the German Ambassador that Italy was about to invade Greece, Hitler travelled to Florence to try and prevent the rash act that was to extend the Axis front and create new potential for defeat. He was greeted by a Mussolini wreathed in smiles, who obviously expected Hitler to be equally happy at his master stroke. 'Führer' he is reported to have said, 'we are on the march! At dawn this morning our Italian troops victoriously crossed the Albanian-Greek frontier'.

Early in the Italian campaign, it became clear that many of Ciano's political bases for the strategy were hopelessly wrong. Above all, the Italians had misjudged totally both their own standing with the Greek people, and the Greeks' patriotism and preparedness to fight. The plain fact was that the Greeks loathed Mussolini, his regime, his army and his ideas. They had seen the cruelty of Fascism, and they wanted none of it.

As soon as the invasion took place, the Greek Prime Minister, General Metaxas, ordered general mobilisation, which provided the commander of the Greek forces, General Alexandros Pagagos, with 15 infantry divisions, 4 infantry brigades and a cavalry division, which together were assembled as five Army Corps. Although a head count gave the Italians the advantage, the mountainous terrain, the determination of the Greeks, the essentially flabby nature of the Italian troops and and the communications advantage enjoyed by the Greek army fighting on its own ground gave the defenders the edge. The Greeks also benefited from the extremely wet weather, which slowed down the invasion from the start, and made it virtually impossible for the Italian Air Force to give effective cover.

On the left of General Visconti-Prasca's invading army, the Alpine Division managed by November 2nd to break through the advanced Greek positions and take the village of Vovoussa, some 25 miles from the border, but a Greek counterattack on the following day drove them back whence they came in considerable disarray. In the centre, the armour and infantry that were headed for Yanina were held up totally. On the right, the Siena Division took Filiates and Paramithia, and looked able to take Yanina. But the weather raged on, the Italian Air Force was unable to prevent the Greeks from completing their mobilisation and concentration, and General Papagos made the most of the situation. By November 12th, Papagos could claim 100 battalions ranged in mountainous country they knew well, against 50 Italian battalions who wished they were elsewhere. He decided that the time had come to counterattack.

On November 14th, five days after the Italian command passed from General Visconti-Prasca to General Ubaldo Soddu, the Greeks attacked along the entire front, from the Ionian Sea to Lake Prespa.

Almost immediately, the Greek 5th Corps under General Tzolakoglou broke the Italian line at Mount Morova. Eight days after commencing the attack, Tzolakoglou crushed the Italian 9th Army at Koritsa, taking 2,000 prisoners, 80 field guns, 55 anti-tank guns, and 300 machine guns from the 'Tridentina' Mountain Division and two infantry divisions.

November 21st saw the Greek 2nd Corps under General Papadopoulos cross the Albanian frontier to take Erseke and Leskovik. On December 4th, the 3rd Corps occupied Pograde, and the following day the 2nd took Permet, 23 miles inside Albania. The 1st Corps under General Kosmas meanwhile chased the Italian 11th Army down the Dhrin valley, and were greeted delightedly by the very Albanian people upon whose loyalty the Italians believed they could count totally. The 1st had also taken Sarande.

Now the weather, and the almost total lack of Greek armour, began to take a hand in the campaign. While the Greeks were able to fight in the hills they could win. Once on the plains they were no match for Italian tanks. Eight new Italian divisions had been sent to Albania between the end of October and December 31st, but the Greeks had no reinforcements, either from their own or British sources. The weather was bitterly cold, and the troops of both sides were suffering from a shortage of adequate winter equipment and of food. For a time there was virtual stalemate.

The Implications of Taranto

It is necessary at this stage to take a look at the Mediterranean sea war, for the highly successful torpedo bomber attack on the Italian fleet in its base at Taranto by Admiral Cunningham's Mediterranean Fleet had a profound influence upon the Italian campaign in the Balkans. In the latter part of October, Cunningham and Rear-Admiral Lyster, commander of the Royal Navy's aircraft carrier force in the Mediterranean, had planned an attack on the Italian fleet, which was showing a marked disinclination to come out and fight. On November 11th, air reconnaissance established that all six Italian battleships were in port at Taranto, and 21 obsolete Swordfish biplanes armed with torpedoes (eleven aircraft) and bombs (the other 10) took off from the *Illustrious* to attack in two waves. Fortune was to some extent favouring the attack – the protective balloon barrage around the anchorage had been damaged by storms, and the Italian torpedo nets extended only 26 feet down into the water, whereas British torpedoes ran at 30 feet depth. Nonetheless it was a daring attack, carried out in slow-moving aircraft in the face of 21 batteries of 100mm guns and 200 light anti-aircraft guns, plus the guns of the ships they were attacking. Six torpedoes scored hits, putting *Littorio* and *Duilio* out of action for six months and sinking the *Cavour*. The Royal Navy lost only two aircraft, with one crewman dead and three prisoners, despite the Italians having fired no less than 8,500 shells.

The Italians responded to the Greeks' successes in the Balkans, and to the loss of half their capital ships at Taranto, with an orgy of blame and recrimination, refusing as always to accept that the true cause of the disaster was the incompetence, mismanagement and sheer vanity of Mussolini. Badoglio, who had warned against the militarily unsound Balkans attack in the first place, was pilloried in the press and on the radio, and resigned in disgust on November 26th. In his place, General Cavallero became Chief of Staff or *Comando Supremo*.

Meanwhile Hitler, who had been preoccupied with plans for 'Operation Felix' to take Gibraltar, destined to come to nothing because Spain's General Franco refused to throw in his lot with the Axis, had decided that Germany could not stand by and watch Mussolini and his compatriots annihilated. If he allowed the Balkan campaign to go to the Allies, the Rumanian oil fields would be threatened. Something had to be done. A date of March 15th was therefore set for a German invasion of Greece.

On December 29th, Cavallero arrived in Albania to take over personal command of operations from General Soddu. He had orders to go onto the offensive, and to prove that German intervention in Albania would be unnecessary. To achieve this he had 16 divisions spread across a largely mountainous front of 156 miles, made up of troops in poor health, with inadequate equipment and an over-extended supply line. The Greeks had roughly 13 divisions, and were on the offensive, although on a strictly limited-objective basis, taking a position here and a position there, with occasional dramatic success. An example was their defeat of the 'Wolves of Tuscany' division at Klisura. Nonetheless, Cavallero meant business, and between December 29th and March 26th, brought in reinforcements of 10 divisions and 4 machine gun battalions, plus 3 legions and 17 battalions of Blackshirts from Italy. The Greeks' inability to fight offensively became more and more apparent as the weather improved, as the Italian Air Force was increasingly brought into action, and as the lack of Greek armour made any form of modern attack impossible.

With his reinforcements in place, and much of his supply problem rectified, Cavallero went on to the offensive on March 9th with an attack on three divisions of General Papadopoulos' 2nd Corps between the rivers Apsos in the North East, and the Aoos in the South West. Against them beneath the Trebesina mountains were ranged no less than eleven divisions of Italian infantry and the 'Centauro' armoured division. After two days of fighting, with well dug in Greek artillery using their ammunition sparingly yet tellingly, the Italians had failed to break through, despite their great superiority of numbers, and were losing a great many men. General Papagos managed to reach Papadopoulos' Corps and reinforce his force with a further two divisions, and by the 15th March the Italians were no further towards their objective than they had been on the 9th.

Finally, on the 15th, Mussolini, who had watched the sorry affair of the Trebesina offensive in person with Cavallero, called off the attack and returned to Rome. The Italian Army had lost 12,000 dead and wounded for no very obvious gain. Meanwhile the tough and uncompromising General Metaxas had died in January, and had been replaced as Greek Prime Minister by Petros Koryzis. The British, approached by him to aid the Greeks in their fight against the Axis, consulted General Wavell, Air Chief Marshal Longmore and Admiral Cunningham, who all expressed doubts as to the capability of the RAF to hold Salonikan airspace against the *Luftwaffe*, if, as expected. Germany entered the Balkan struggle. At a conference in Athens on February 22nd 1941, attended by King George of Greece, British Foreign Secretary Anthony Eden, Prime Minister Koryzis and Generals Dill and Wavell, there was extensive discussion as to the expected attitude of still neutral Yugoslavia to the anticipated German offensive, and of the reaction of Yugoslavia if the Greeks were obliged to withdraw from Salonika. Eventually the conference made the dangerous decision to attempt to reestablish a British presence in Europe by sending an expeditionary force to Athens should the Germans take action in the Balkans.

On March 1st 1941, Bulgaria belatedly allied herself with Germany, whereupon the German 12th Army crossed the Danube and triggered the plan for the British landings in Greece. From March 7th onwards the force, commanded by General Sir Henry Maitland Wilson, landed at Piraeus and Volos. Some 57,000 men and 100 tanks were put ashore, a force made up of the 6th Australian Division, the 2nd New Zealand Division and the 1st Armoured Brigade. By the end of March, Maitland Wilson's formations were established and had acquired, after protracted negotiations, three Greek divisions. But his forces were seriously under strength, mainly because he had been allotted the 7th Australian Division and the 1st Polish Brigade, neither of which was actually sent to Greece.

Germany attacks Yugoslavia

The establishment of German garrisons in Bulgaria gave Yugoslavia problems. No less than three countries were making claims upon Yugoslav territory; Italy, Hungary and Bulgaria. If Yugoslavia did not now agree to join the Tripartite Pact, and ally herself with Germany, the probability was that Germany and Italy would see to it that the country was divided among their allies. Since Hitler had given assurances that German armies would not pass through Yugoslavia to invade Greece, it seemed inescapably opportune that she should now give in and join. On March 25th, the Regent, Prince Paul, and his Prime Minister did just that. This capitulation set in motion a military plot which, on March 27th, overthrew Paul and his government, proclaimed the young King Peter's majority and put General Simovic in power. Yet, despite this sudden action, the new government did nothing to anger the Third Reich, nothing to change policy in any significant way. This provided Germany with the opportunity to do what Germany was best at – seizing the initiative by force of arms.

A massive force of two Armies plus General Kleist's *Panzer* Group was detailed for the assault, which took just twelve days to defeat Yugoslavia. On April 6th 1941, the *Luftwaffe* hit Belgrade with massive bombing raids, while Kleist's *Panzers* began the attack on the ground. By April 13th, Kleist and General von Wietresheim's 14th Motorised Corps, which had advanced 312 miles in seven days, met General Reinhardt's 41st *Panzer* Corps in Belgrade. Now the 46th *Panzer* Corps under General von Vietinghof captured by surprise a vital bridge over the River Drava at Barcs, and opened the way to the rendezvous with the Italians at Karlovac, Sarajevo was occupied on the 15th April, and on the 17th the Yugoslav army surrendered, at which time 6,028 officers and 337,684 NCOs and men became prisoners of war. But some 300,000 men escaped and took to the mountains, where they continued to fight and harry the Germans throughout their uncomfortable stay in Yugoslavia.

Tito's Partisans

The principal architect of the *Wehrmacht's* considerable discomfort in Yugoslavia was Josip Broz, known as Tito, a Croatian communist who narrowly escaped German arrest when he left Zagreb, his accustomed political base, in May 1941. Tito was a revolutionary leader of long standing who believed passionately in the Comintern and already led a substantial body of communist sympathisers before the German invasion of Yugoslavia.

By the end of May, Tito, by this time in Belgrade, believed that the Germans were about to invade the Soviet Union, and saw in this and the already complete German occupation of his country a potential opportunity for power. The three German divisions plus one regiment, commanded by Field Marshal von Weichs, which had remained in Yugoslavia after the capitulation, were removed late in April and early in May and were replaced by three divisions of older men more suited to occupation than to battle. Tito's belief that trouble for Stalin was afoot was turned into certainty by intelligence, gained by a White Russian from a German officer, that Russia was 'about to be liberated'.

The announcement of the German invasion of the Soviet Union on 22nd June 1941 brought celebration among Yugoslav communists, for it released them from the Comintern ban on military action imposed as a result of the Soviet/German non-aggression pact of August 1939. On 3rd July, Stalin issued an appeal for guerilla activities by all those behind the German lines, and Tito's Comintern controller Dimitrov issued more specific orders.

'The peoples of Yugoslavia now have the opportunity to create a general liberation struggle against the German invader. It is a vital necessity to undertake all actions to assist and facilitate the just war of the Soviet people .... Remember that at present it is a question of liberation from Fascist domination, and not a question of Socialist revolution'.

Tito issued a proclamation, printed on the Yugoslav party's already established secret press, and on 27th June 1941 set up a General Headquarters of National Liberation Partisans' Detachments. Individual acts of sabotage began to take place throughout the country, as yet largely uncoordinated and boosted by another major proclamation from Tito on 12th July. On 7th July, a Yugoslav veteran of the Spanish Civil War, Zikica Jovanovic, urged a crowd in the village of Bela Crkva, in Serbia, to resistance, shot two policemen and escaped. This incident marked the beginning of the great uprising.

Tito's most able and trusted lieutenants were sent to each of the regions to organise revolt under Tito's control. Some party groups, notably in Montenegro, did not accept that their role was solely to fight Germans rather than create a Socialist revolution, and for some weeks Tito had problems in establishing control. From his Belgrade headquarters, nonetheless, Tito controlled a rapidly expanding field army of small Partisan detachments, mostly living in the hills and keeping Tito's Intelligence Chief, Alexander Ranković, supplied with detailed information on Axis troop movements and concentrations. In return, Tito organised the capture and distribution of arms and ammunition and provided a headquarters training operation. Ranković's career was, in fact, almost brought to an early end in July, when he was arrested by the Gestapo as he planned to blow up Radio Belgrade. However, on 29th July, forty Partisans armed with revolvers and grenades freed him from a hospital where he was being held, without any of his rescuers being killed. Ranković went to the party headquarters in Western Serbia, and Tito himself had to leave Belgrade on 16th September. He was not to return until October 1944.

Within the six months between July and the end of 1941, Tito created an army of 80,000 men under arms, the nucleus of a force that was later to be estimated by the Germans, in late 1943, to total 111,000 men. His policy was to set out to clear the Axis troops from specific areas of the country, to call those areas 'liberated territories' and to use them both as operational bases and as footholds for eventual Communist power. By the end of August 1941, the Serbian insurrection, organised by Tito, had cleared the German army from almost two thirds of the Serbian countryside and the Germans had begun to re-think their attitude to the Partisans. Although the Partisans subsequently lost much of that initial territorial gain as the three long years of guerilla warfare got under way, the Germans were never again to believe that holding Yugoslavia would be easy. At its peak, the Partisan Army was to tie down more than twenty Axis divisions in the retention of a country which Germany had expected to occupy comparatively peacefully.

The Četniks

In organising resistance against the Axis invaders, Tito did not initially appear to have things all his own way. As early as April 1941, officers and men of the defeated Royalist army had begun to live and fight in the woods of Serbia under various leaders. But from them emerged Colonel Dragoljub Mihailović, who went to Western Bosnia when Yugoslavia capitulated and was in mid-Serbia by the middle of May 1941.

Intensely pro-Serb and anti-Croat, like many army officers, Mihailović was not a communist and had a low opinion of Tito, regarding him as (perhaps justifiably at the time) no more than an upstart Croat revolutionary. Mihailović resisted German domination purely for reasons of pride and Serbian nationalism. By the end of September 1941, there were 5,000 Četniks. As Tito sought aid, arms and ammunition from the Soviet Union, so Mihailović looked for help from Britain. Initially, little came from either source to either leader and, at talks between Mihailović and Tito in October 1941, it became apparent that the Četniks were more opposed to communist domination under a Croatian leader than they were to the German occupation.

By the beginning of November, the Četniks were attacking Tito's Partisan positions, although without conspicuous success, for Mihailović had significantly underestimated the military capability of Tito's forces. Nonetheless, at this stage in events, the British, influenced by their commitment to the Yugoslav Royalist government in exile, seemed genuinely to believe Mihailović's assertions that Tito was a fraud who did not represent the Yugoslav people, and on 15th November had the BBC announce that Mihailović had been made 'Commander-in-Chief of Yugoslav forces in the Fatherland'. Less than a week earlier, Mihailović had received his first parachuted supplies from the British, and on 12th November had been on the verge of losing his headquarters to the Partisans, who came within one mile of Ravna Gora, where the Četniks prepared for hasty evacuation.

At the height of this drama, Mihailović was at a meeting with German officers proposing joint operations against the Partisans, in return for which Serbia would be returned to the control of the Četniks. He assured the Germans that his main aim was to save the majority of his people from annihilation. The Germans did not fully trust him, and did not at this stage enter into an agreement, recognising that he was not the power he claimed to be and that Tito and his Partisans were far more dangerous.

While Mihailović was discussing terms with the Germans, two of his officers were holding talks with the Partisans, and reached a nine-point agreement to end hostilities. At the end of November, when major German response to earlier Partisan successes in Serbia had pushed the Partisans into retreat, Mihailović refused an offer from Tito of joint leadership and operations, stating that he was the only recognised leader of Yugoslav resistance. By the end of 1941, Mihailović had decided to make agreements with the occupiers and fight only against the communists. Only then did the British government realise something of the true situation and begin to think of Mihailović as being more of a master of compromise and prevarication than a Resistance leader.

Nonetheless, it was not until early 1944 that the British government, committed by its agreement with the Yugoslav Royalist government in exile to support of the Četniks, finally lost patience with Mihailović and withdrew the British liaison officers who had been seconded to the Četniks throughout the period when Tito's Partisan Army had been doing battle with the Axis. Not until mid-1943 was significant, though qualified, Allied support given to Tito, and not until the summer of 1944, only months before his victory in Yugoslavia, was the Partisan Army fully recognised by the Allies. Tito's cool, resourceful leadership and considerable grasp of military strategy and tactics enabled him to keep an

Axis force more than three times the size of his Partisan Army busy for more than three years.

Greece Invaded by Germany
When the Greeks heard of the Yugoslav signing of the Tripartite Pact on March 25th, General Papagos had ordered withdrawal from Salonika, but he changed his mind and issued orders to stand firm when news of the overthrow of Regent Paul on the 27th reached him. On the night of April 4th/5th, he conferred with Britain's Anthony Eden, General Dill and the Yugoslav General Jankovic on the border between Greece and Yugoslavia. Papagos tried to persuade Jankovic to defend with the Greeks the short front necessary to prevent the Germans advancing to Greece if they entered Yugoslavia. Jankovic would have none of it. On April 6th, Papagos, knowing that the German invasion was imminent and that the defence of the full frontier was impossible, ordered the demolition of installations between the Bulgarian border and the forward Greek positions.

At 5.15am on the 6th, as *Panzer* Group Kleist entered Yugoslavia, Field-Marshal List crossed the border between Bulgaria and Greece with five divisions from the German XXX Corps in the East and the XVIII Mountain Corps in the West. Overhead, Stukas of the *Luftwaffe* attacked the fortified Metaxas line, receiving as they did so a nasty surprise, for alone among such fortifications in Europe, the Metaxas Line had 37mm guns, which did a great deal of harm to the Ju87 aircraft. The Greeks held out with enormous courage and no little success. The Germans suffered substantial losses at the Nevrokop Basin, and in the Rupel Pass, and at no point found their advance easy. The Greeks were a tougher opponent than most that Germany had encountered. Nonetheless, sheer force of numbers and armaments ensured that the Germans advanced towards their objective, and gradually the Greek units began to surrender when they could do nothing more.

On April 8th, Lieutenant-General Vieil and his 2nd *Panzer* Division, after a lightning advance through Yugoslavia, crossed the border into Greece and dashed 56 miles in the day to occupy Salonika. General Bakopoulos was surrounded and, without communications, was forced to surrender. His 70,000 men were taken prisoner. By April 11th, the Yugoslav army having collapsed, the German 12th Army found itself in contact with General Sir Henry Maitland Wilson's Anglo-Greek formation. The British 1st Armoured Brigade had only 100 largely obsolete tanks to field against Field-Marshal List's 500-plus, and was unable to hold its position. The 2nd New Zealand Division, fighting every inch of the way, had to withdraw, thereby enabling German units to get between the British Expeditionary Force and the Greeks retreating from Albania.

On April 21st, the crack SS Division *Leibstandarte Adolf Hitler* captured Yanina to the rear of the Greeks. Going against orders from his government in Athens, the Greek commander General Tzolakoglou negotiated with the Germans, and surrendered sixteen Greek Divisions, the instrument of surrender being signed at Larisa by a representative of the Greek Parliament and Field-Marshal List.

Mussolini was not pleased, and felt that he should have been present to gloat over the surrender, despite his army's almost total failure to contribute to the victory that made it possible. To gratify his ally's ludicrous vanity, Hitler therefore ordered a further signing ceremony to be set up for April 24th, and at that entirely bogus ceremony Mussolini attended the demise of the independent Greek state. On April 19th it was decided that the British Expeditionary Force must be evacuated from mainland Greece. Rear-Admiral Baillie-Grohman, entrusted with this hazardous task, managed on April 25th to get almost 51,000 British, Australian and New Zealand troops out despite the efforts of German paratroops landing along the Corinth canal and the arrival of the *Leibstandarte Adolf Hitler* on all sides. This near-miraculous escape, more daring than Dunkirk, and at the time almost as valuable in terms of resources saved, was pulled off with the loss of only four transport vessels and two destroyers. It stands as one of the major achievements of the Second World War.

The Expeditionary Force had lost 12,712 men either killed, wounded or taken prisoner, and had no military advantage, although the political benefits of their brave attempt to save Greece from occupation were to be felt when Britain's involvement in the resolution of the Greek Civil War (1944-45) and the return of the Government was accepted by the Greek people. Militarily, the Greek adventure was a disaster for Britain at a time when it could not afford setbacks of any kind.

The Invasion of Crete

Now, to prevent the RAF from having an easy base to attack his oil resources in Rumania during the invasion of Russia that was about to commence, Hitler turned his attention to Crete. On April 25th 1941, General Kurt Student, mastermind of the German paratroop forces, was given the task of planning the invasion of the little island in the Mediterranean that was so strategically placed.

Student planned a predominantly airborne invasion by the 7th Paratroop Division, reinforced by three infantry regiments, and backed by the air support of 228 bombers, 205 dive bombers, 233 fighters and 50 reconnaissance aircraft. The airborne units were to be dropped from 493 three-engined Ju52 transports, although some were to make a glider-borne landing in a force of 72 gliders. A force of 63 small ships was hastily requisitioned to ferry the infantry units, and the Italian Navy provided a destroyer and 12 torpedo boats to escort them.

The Allies, because of their secret ability to decode Enigma signals, were well aware of the plan to attack Crete, and resolved to hold the island if at all possible. There were 42,500 men already in position, of whom 10,300 were Greeks. There were 6,540 Australian and 7,700 New Zealand troops who had been evacuated from Greece, but these units were very short of vehicles, arms and supplies because of the haste of their departure. Thus the force was far less formidable than it seemed on paper.

The RAF had 35 operational aircraft on the island on May 1st, but the heavy bombardment by the *Luftwaffe* during the run up to the attack left only four Hurricanes and three Gladiators in a fit condition to take off and fly to Egypt on the 19th May.

The British forces were commanded by General Freyberg, an able and brave commander, but one who had arrived on the island only on April 30th, three weeks before the German attack came on May 20th. Throughout that day, the German 7th Airborne were dropped at Maleme, west of Canea, and around Heraklion and Rethimnon. There was bitter fighting, and the Germans had an unlucky day for losses of commanders – at Maleme, General Meindl was seriously wounded and had to hand over his command to Colonel Ramcke; at Rethimnon the Germans arrived without a commander at all, for General Sussman had been in a glider that had crashed en route.

The key to the battle lay with the Navy's effort to destroy the flotilla of small ships that was bringing the infantry reinforcements to the island. In this Cunningham's fleet was less than successful, losing in quick succession two cruisers and four destroyers, among them HMS *Kelly*, commanded by Lord Louis Mountbatten, and seeing *Warspite* and *Formidable* so seriously damaged that they had to be taken out the action. Although much pressure was applied from London, Cunningham knew when he was beaten, and pulled back. On the 25th, the German infantry under Lieutenant-General Ringel succeeded in breaking out from the Maleme perimeter, and General Freyberg decided on the 27th that the time had come to evacuate the Allied troops from the island and asked the Mediterranean Fleet to take them off. The evacuation through the little port of Sphakia took every minute of the time from the night of May 28/29th to dawn on June 2nd. The anti-aircraft cruiser *Calcutta* and two destroyers, *Hereward* and *Imperial* were lost, and 260 men were killed and 280 wounded on board *Orion* by a German bomb.

When the losses of the Crete operation were added up, the Commonwealth forces had lost 1,800 dead, and about 12,000 captured out of 32,000. The Royal Navy lost 1,828 killed and 183 wounded. But 18,000 troops were successfully evacuated. The Germans lost almost 4,000 killed and roughly 2,500 wounded, all of them fully trained top-quality combat troops, and most of them hard-to-replace paratroops. Neither side had found Crete easy.

BARBAROSSA
– HITLER'S INVASION OF RUSSIA AND
ADVANCE ON MOSCOW

From September 1939 until June 1941, the Second World War was, like the First, essentially a European war. Unlike the Great War of 1914-18, it was also a war founded on opposing concepts of politics, moral values and even religious outlook. The armies of both sides were not just patriotic and willing – they fought with a strong moral conviction.

Since 1924, when he dictated *Mein Kampf* to Rudolf Hess while imprisoned at Landsberg Prison, Hitler had made no secret of his loathing of Communism, and of his wish to annihilate the 'Bolshevik Jews'. By 1937, the principle of *Lebensraum*, of finding new 'living space' to the East, was well established in Nazi philosophy, and it was generally assumed that this implied a threat to Soviet Russia – hence Churchill's reference to the signing of the Non-aggression Pact between Russia and Germany on August 23rd 1939 as 'this unnatural act'. The Pact seemed to indicate an uncharacteristic change of heart by Hitler – and yet it is clear that, when Britain was on the verge of defeat in 1940, Hitler hoped for an alliance with Britain against the Bolsheviks. As early as July 29th 1940, Colonel-General Alfred Jodl, chief of Operations, had announced to an assembly of staff officers that Hitler had decided to attack the USSR in the spring of 1941. On July 31st, Hitler himself said at a briefing 'Wiping out the very power to exist of Russia! That is the goal!'

The simple truth was that the Non-Aggression Pact was no more than a device to buy time to defeat the Western democracies before turning East. It had always been Hitler's intention to attack Russia once all in the West had gone to plan. Now, in the summer of 1941, the whole of continental Europe with the exception of the neutrals (Sweden, Switzerland, Spain, Portugal) was either occupied or ceded to a puppet government – as was the case with Vichy France. Only Britain remained undefeated.

It seems likely that Hitler greatly underestimated both Britain's ability to recover from the military defeats she had suffered, and the extent to which the USA, even as a neutral, was prepared to supply arms and munitions. He also miscalculated totally the likelihood of the USA entering the war as a combatant, largely because his Japanese allies were not prepared to brief him in advance on their intentions.

Certainly, Hitler thought, at the end of 1940, when his Directive No. 21 – Barbarossa – was issued to the High Command, that he could expect to remain in control of the war despite opening a new front, that the British were now largely a spent force, and that there was no reason to expect an expansion of the geographical compass of the war beyond his own attack on his allies in Russia.

In fact, as we now know, 1941 was the year when the essentially European nature of the Second World War evaporated, and it became a genuinely world-wide conflict. The year was to see Asia, America and Africa plunged into war, and the first signs of the Axis being pointed inexorably towards defeat. It was also the year when much wider polarisation of beliefs and cultures entered into the conflict; the Communist versus the Fascist; the Oriental opposing the Occidental.

At the beginning of the year Hitler was at the pinnacle of his power; the architect of the greatest conquest the world had ever known; personally respons-ible for strategic decisions that his generals had said would be disastrous, and which had instead been outstandingly successful. When he said that Russia would be taken by Autumn 1941, there was, although logic was not on the side of his assertion, little reason for disbelieving him.

Yet, despite Hitler's long stated hatred of Bolshevism, Josef Stalin showed no sign of apprehension. Stalin had on May 7th 1941 added to his Secretaryship of the Communist Party of the USSR the Chairmanship of the Council of People's Com-missars, a job he took over from Molotov, and evidently had no inkling of the likelihood of attack by Germany, then only six weeks ahead. Winston Churchill recalled in his *The Second World War* that intelligence reports from the Balkans and Germany had convinced him by March 1941 that Hitler intended to attack Russia, and that by May he was certain of it. Churchill tried, with a short, sharp telegram, to warn Stalin, but the Kremlin responded with a communique dictated to *Tass*, the Russian News Agency, accusing Britain of spreading ugly rumours about Ger-many, and doing everything possible to appease Hitler. Stalin did not wish to be confused with facts, an act of stubbornness that was to cost the USSR a large part of the Soviet Air Force, destroyed on the ground in the first wave of the attack.

June 22nd 1941

Thus, when the fateful day of Barbarossa dawned, the Soviet armed forces were prepared neither for the fury of the treacherous attack launched upon them, nor for the barbarity of the treatment meted out by the German forces to Russian civilians and prisoners of war on the direct orders of Hitler, who instructed his armies to regard their Russian enemy as less than human. The assault brought into conflict 3,400,000 Germans and 4,700,000 Russian troops. The sheer scale both of the ar-mies involved, and of their appalling losses, has no equal in any war in history.

Barbarossa began at 3.15am on that June morning along a front of no less than 2,900 kilometres, from the Baltic to the Black Sea. Into the attack went 153 divi-sions of the 208 that Germany had available, 120 of the 153 being thrown into the actual assault, the remainder being held in reserve. There were 29 *Panzer* and motorised divisions, with a total of 3,090 tanks. Four air fleets of the *Luftwaffe* were deployed on the new Eastern Front, bringing with them 1,945 aircraft.

By comparison, the Red Army, still unconcernedly engaged upon its summer manoeuvres when the blow fell, was sadly inadequate. Stalin had, since 1937, remorselessly 'eliminated' any major military figure who showed initiative, dis-agreed with his policies or attempted to wield influence. He had thus encour-aged mediocrity, and brought to high command mainly incompetent sycophants who knew little other than when to keep their mouths shut. There were excep-tions, whose names ring forth from the history of the Russian War – notably Malinovsky, Konev and Zhukov. But, in the opening weeks of the campaign, the military ineptitude of the majority of the Russian High Command killed almost as many Russian soldiers as did the fighting proficiency of the *Wehrmacht*.

Numerically, the Russian forces were not at any severe disadvantage. In terms of training, equipment, and, above all, quality of military leadership, they were no match for the might of the world's most experienced and efficient fighting machine. Only in July 1940 had previous resistance to the use of large scale tank formations been reversed, and mechanised and armoured divisions been formed. Many of the inexperienced tank units were annihilated during the first few weeks of the campaign, and only those equipped with the new T-34 medium tank, and the KV-2 and T-35 heavy tanks were able to give the Germans any show of real resistance. These tanks were, in fact, the strongest features of the Soviet military profile – they were actually better than anything the Germans could put in the field. The T-34 in particular has been likened to Britain's Spitfire fighter in its importance to Allied success against Germany. With its 33 mph speed, 7.62cm gun, low fire risk from its 500 hp diesel engine and cleverly shaped armour that was impenetrable to current German anti-tank weapons, the T-34 tank was to remain a major problem to the German army throughout the campaign and the war – but, although 1,225 had been produced by the time Barbarossa began, the T-34 was not actually fielded against the German armies until they reached Smolensk. On the debit side of the account was the fact that, in June 1941, only 29 per cent of Russia's tanks were in a fit condition to fight. Incompetent organisation had ensured that spares for the older tanks were in short supply and that maintenance had been inadequate.

The tremendous speed with which the German armour advanced into Russia is not therefore as remarkable as it first seems. By the evening of the first day, Colonel-General Guderian's *Panzer* divisions in the 'Army Group Centre' area had reached Kobrin and Pruzhany, almost 50 miles into Russia. Colonel-General Hoth's *Panzer* divisions were 59 miles from their starting point, and had taken the bridges over the important River Niemen intact. In the North, Field-Marshal von Leeb's *Panzergruppe IV* under Colonel-General Hoeppner had also progressed 50 miles and had successfully taken the viaduct across the Doubissa gorges at Airogala.

Successful German bombing raids had destroyed a large proportion of the Soviet Air Force on the ground during the first hour of Barbarossa, and those that were left gave the *Luftwaffe* little trouble. Field-Marshal Albert Kesselring, commanding the *Luftwaffe* on the Eastern Front, reported that the Russian pilots were 'innocents to the slaughter', and his pilots had an easy campaign in the early stages, despite the Russians having 3,000 aircraft in the frontier regions on the day before Barbarossa began. The success of the initial bombing raids destroyed some 2,500 aircraft, and many more were shot down in combat on the first day. By June 23rd, resistance in the air was minimal.

Because Russian communications were almost non-existent, the High Command had no means of appreciating what was happening in such a modern, high-speed war. Their already inadequate grasp of tactics was rendered utterly useless by this lack of effective radio. Thus each Russian commander was taking separate, independent and often conflicting decisions against an enemy that was under the total and effective control of its High Command. Inevitably, gaps in the defensive line opened of their own accord for the Germans to sweep through; vital positions, bridges, installations were not destroyed before the Russians were forced to retreat.

The lightning advance continued. By June 25th, Guderian had reached Baranovichi, and Hoth was in Molodechno. The next day, the two *Panzergruppen* made contact and pushed on to Minsk, where, on the 29th they closed with a pincer movement behind the unfortunate defenders. By July 8th, General Halder was noting in his diary that 32 of the 43 divisions of the Soviet 3rd, 4th and 10th armies had been virtually annihilated. The Germans had taken nearly 290,000 prisoners; captured 2,585 tanks, 1,449 guns, 246 aircraft.

July 11th saw the German armour cross the Dnieper, and Army Group South approaching Kiev. Not until mid-July, when a second pincer movement by *Panzergruppen* 2 and 3 brought massive forces to bear at Smolensk, did the Germans encounter any really successful resistance. The Russians trapped by the pincer fought furiously and well to break out, while, from the outside, Marshal Timoshenko and Lieutenant-General Eremenko fought hard to break in and relieve the besieged army. The battle went on until August 8th, when Marshal Timoshenko was defeated at Roslavl. Guderian took 38,000 prisoners, 300 tanks and 300 guns. Almost immediately, Smolensk fell, and German Army High Command (OKH) announced the taking of 310,000 prisoners, the capture or destruction of over 3,000 armoured vehicles, and 3,000 artillery pieces.

German armour at Elnia was now only 200 miles from Moscow. German casualties at August 13th had reached, since the beginning of the campaign, 389,924 officers and men, of whom 98,600 were killed or missing. Compare that with comparable German figures for the whole war to May 31st 1941 – 218,109 casualties, of whom 97,000 were killed. It had been a devastating seven weeks for the cream of German manhood, as well as for Russia. The pace of the advance, the appalling roads and rough country conditions, and the abrasive dust were having a serious effect on the mechanical condition of the German armour. Try as they might, the Germans were slowing down.

Now Hitler took a personal hand in the campaign in his role as military tactician, a pursuit for which he was fast proving himself manifestly unsuited. His Directive No. 34 of August 12th 1941 changed the whole strategic plan of Barbarossa by insisting on what he saw as a tactical move to take Leningrad and the North, plus the Crimea and the Donets coal and industrial basin before winter. In vain did Field Marshal Brauchitsch, and Generals Halder and Guderian express their belief that the army should continue its advance and take Moscow. Hitler was adamant. As usual, the Generals bowed to his will. From that time on, the campaign in Russia was doomed. Not one but two factors brought about the change of fortune. Barbarossa had been scheduled originally for May 1941, but Hitler had postponed it for more than a month because of the Balkan campaign. Even then Brauchitsch had predicted disaster in Russia when winter came. Now, Hitler's diversion of the attack wasted more of the vital summer weather.

But the effect was not immediate. In late August, Field-Marshal von Rundstedt's 11th, 17th and 6th Armies established four bridgeheads on the left bank of the Dnieper and on September 11th, Kleist linked up with Guderian at Kremenchug. In the South, Marshal Budenny requested permission to evacuate the Kiev pocket. Stalin rejected his request. By the 17th, when the armies were at last given permission to withdraw, they were encircled and could go nowhere. On the 18th, Kiev fell, and the commander, General Kirponos, was killed. Vast numbers of men and machines were captured. The numbers are still the subject of dispute, but it is reasonably certain that over half a million men, more than 750 tanks and some 3,500 guns were captured. By the end of September, Russian losses since June amounted to 2,500,000 men, 22,000 guns, 18,000 tanks and 14,000 aircraft.

In the north, Leeb's Army Group North had reached the shores of Lake Ladoga, east of Leningrad, on September 8th, and had begun the siege that was intended to realise Hitler's intention of taking Leningrad for the winter. To the West of their positions, Marshal Mannerheim's Finns were recapturing the positions they had lost in the Winter War of 1940, and were in control of the Karelian Isthmus, but refused to assist Germany in the expected final assault on Leningrad. On September 11th, Stalin moved General Zhukov to take over the defence of Leningrad from the inscrutably mediocre Marshal Voroshilov, and, not for the last time, Zhukov pulled a garrison together, regenerated the Russians' morale and self discipline, and began the erection of stronger defences. By the 16th September, Hitler had ordered a major artillery and *Luftwaffe* bombing offensive against Leningrad and the nearby naval base in Kronstadt harbour, and over the next few days one Russian battleship was sunk, and 2 battleships and 2 cruisers were seriously damaged at Kronstadt.

By the 30th September, the siege of Leningrad had claimed 4,409 civilian lives, an appalling death toll resulting from 200 artillery bombardments and 23 air raids in one month. Still the city did not surrender. As winter closed in famine gripped the city, and the citizens of Leningrad ate their pets, their wallpaper, their hair oil – anything that promised to sustain life. Not until January 1943 were the Russians able to open a rail link to the city, and not until January 1944 did the German bombing and shelling of the city finally stop. More than a million civilians died in what must surely be the most vicious siege in history. But they never surrendered.

As the German advance in the other sectors slowed, the Red Army began, despite its losses, to regroup, and to reassemble artillery, rockets and new infantry weapons. Belated reorganisation of the command structure began, and some semblance of morale and resurgent military discipline gave the Russian troops new heart. During the first two weeks of October, a massive offensive was launched by the Germans to take Moscow, and by October 20th, Bock was within forty miles of the capital. A massive evacuation of the government, foreign diplomats and much of the civilian population was under way; only Stalin and his military command remained in the Kremlin. On the night of October 14th-15th, it seemed to the Russian defenders that the crunch had come, as German armour attacked with great force, breaking through the perimeter of Moscow at one point, and coming within sight of Moscow's famous Khimke water tower.

At this crucial moment, Stalin replaced Timoshenko with Zhukov, who had revitalised the defence of Leningrad. An able tactician, Zhukov recognised the German army's vulnerability to the cruel Russian winter, and contented himself with holding the line until the snow, which was already falling, took hold and bogged down the *Wehrmacht* in a misery of perpetual wet boots and temperatures far below zero. As the snow alternated with torrential rain, the German army became virtually immoveable. Judging his moment to a nicety, Zhukov chose December 6th to go on to the offensive. From now on, the Germans would never again be truly in the ascendant on the Eastern Front.

The Russians Fight Back

Throughout the great German offensive into Russia, the *Wehrmacht* had seemed invincible; better equipped, infinitely better led, better trained, more experienced in every field of conflict. But that was in summer and autumn. So confident had Hitler been that his mighty army would subdue Russia by October, that millions of German soldiers and airmen had gone to the East Front with only summer kit. Now, in December, the temperature fell to twenty, sometimes more than thirty, degrees below zero. With little shelter, inadequate food and nil achievement since winter came, the morale of the *Wehrmacht* sank lower than ever before.

By contrast, the Red Army had regrouped, using the comparative lull in the campaign to bring up artillery, armour and reserve manpower. The coming of

Zhukov had an effect on the defenders of beleaguered Moscow not unlike that later to be seen when General Montgomery took command of the British Eighth Army – morale was boosted for no very logical or explicable reason other than the sheer magnetism of the commander and the respect his troops held for him. Above all, the Russian soldiers were properly equipped with warm quilted winter coats, waterproof boots and clothing designed to minimise wind chill.

German morale was not helped by Hitler's adamant refusal to permit tactical withdrawal. Hitler ordered that not an inch of ground be given. His commanders were bitter about this decision, believing that tens of thousands of German lives might have been saved if a limited withdrawal to positions affording some shelter had been permitted. Ultimately, this decision was to prove one of the principal reasons for the failure of Hitler's Russian campaign. Frozen almost, and in some cases actually, to death, his troops were no match physically or mentally for the counteroffensive when it came. And come it did, on December 6th.

Initially, the ferocious onslaught of Zhukov's offensive set the German army reeling, although it fought bravely, as always, and just managed to hold its line. The Russians were now, entirely unexpectedly to the Germans, able to field 160 Divisions against Bock's 68, and were to go on to reinforce their strength with a further 60 divisions in the first six months of 1942. Production of the new tanks was now outstripping the rate at which the Germans were able to destroy them, and by the time the Battle of Moscow began, 1,853 T-34 tanks had been delivered to the Red Army. On December 20th, aware that without the opportunity to make a tactical withdrawal, eventual defeat was certain, Colonel-General Guderian left for Hitler's Eastern headquarters at Rastenburg, in East Prussia, to try and obtain the Fuehrer's agreement to a retreat. No permission was forthcoming. Hitler insisted on an attack that was manifestly beyond the army's capability.

Now, at what was already their worst hour, the Germans began to suffer an appalling loss of experienced commanders. On the 16th December, Field-Marshal von Bock asked to resign – a decision made necessary by a combination of ill-health and inability to agree with Hitler – and was succeeded by Kluge. On December 19th, Field-Marshal von Brauchitsch, who had had a heart attack in November, left the Army High Command (OKH), and Hitler took the opportunity of assuming his role as Commander in Chief of the Army. Then, on December 26th, Guderian was relieved of his command, being replaced by General Schmidt, and, at the beginning of January, Colonel-General Hoeppner was disgraced for ordering the *4th Panzerarmee* to disengage, and was replaced by Colonel-General Hoth. On January 18th, Field-Marshal von Reichenau suddenly died – and Bock was brought back to active service against his wishes, with the luckless General Paulus being ordered to take over the Sixth Army. In the North, Field-Marshal von Leeb requested permission to retire, and was replaced as commander of Army Group North by Colonel-General von Kuchler.

To stiffen the German line, which at the beginning of 1942 showed every sign of breaking, Hitler began to bring in 22 infantry divisions from France and Germany in the first three months of 1942, but the Russians forestalled their arrival with further orders to Generals Konev and Zhukov, commanding the Kalinin and West Fronts, to attack and annihilate German Army Group Centre, which had so recently expected to celebrate Christmas in Red Square.

Thus began, on January 9th and 10th 1942, the offensive that was to lead to the appalling defeat of Stalingrad, and ultimately to the subjugation of Eastern Europe. The Bear had awakened.

PEARL HARBOR

THE UNITED STATES GOES TO WAR

If Hitler's assault on Russia had, in mid 1941, taken the Second World War beyond its European boundaries, then it was the infamous attack by Japan upon the US naval base at Pearl Harbor, on Oahu in the Hawaiian Islands, that finally made the war global in scale. For the devastating Japanese raid was the first roll of the dice in a mighty strategy which encompassed the whole of South-East Asia, and which almost succeeded.

The background to Japan's assault upon Pearl Harbor and the Pacific stretched back into the Thirties to the beginning of her protracted war with China. In that conflict, her troops had gained experience, her pilots had seen active service, her aircraft had gained in reliability. As Germany launched the Second World War in Europe, with a not dissimilar background of experience in the Spanish Civil War behind her, Japan saw clearly the triumphs that could be won by sheer brute force and military skill allied with audacity, surprise and speed. The lesson of *Blitzkrieg* was not lost on the subjects of Hirohito. Suddenly the world of the East seemed open to Japan, and she resolved to take her opportunity, and the wealth it could bring. Only the United States of America stood in the way, for America was neutral, and, unlike Britain, was not already irrevocably locked in European combat. Even Russia did not count as a threat for, although Russia had the manpower to fight on several fronts, Japan and Russia had signed a mutual non-aggression pact which, uncharacteristically, both Japan and Russia honoured until the very last days of the war.

The plan was first to destroy the American Fleet, then, while the USA was unable to put to sea with its armies, to overrun the whole of South-East Asia at a pace reminiscent of German *Blitzrieg*, seizing in concurrent assaults Thailand, Burma, Malaya and Singapore, plus the Philippines and Dutch East Indies archipelagoes. Once the Pacific and Indian Ocean nations between Burma in the West, New Guinea in the South, and the Aleutians and the Gilbert Islands in the North and East were under the Rising Sun, Japan planned to throw a defensive perimeter around the newly-won territories, and exploit the mineral, natural and human resources of a vast area of the earth upon which the rest of the world had until then relied heavily. This ambitious programme was ratified by the Japanese government at a Supreme War Council held on September 6th 1941, not eleven months after the near-murder of Prime Minister Prince Funimaro Konoye, who had urged restraint and compromise with the USA. Konoye resigned on 16th October 1941, and was replaced by the warlike General Hideki Tojo, who was bent on war as a means for Japanese expansion.

In April 1941, five months before the Japanese made their irrevocable decision to wage war, an allied plan known as ABC-1 for the defence of South-East Asia had been agreed between the British and the Americans in Washington. Believing that the recently appointed Far East Commander, General Douglas MacArthur, would be able to retain control of the Philippines in the event of an attack by the Japanese, the planners agreed on a concentration of force against Germany, and a relatively low-key holding operation against Japan. Despite the fact that, as early as January 1941, US Ambassador Joseph Grew had reported from Tokyo the belief that the Japanese might attempt a surprise attack on Pearl Harbor, no allowance was made in the plan for an attack on the US Navy in the Hawaiian Islands. As late as November 1941, American aircraft were still parked undispersed and wing to wing on Hawaiian airfields, a perfect target for bombers.

The detailed plan for the attack from the air that was to give the world its first truly global war was worked out by a naval staff under the gifted Admiral Isoroku Yamamoto, Commander in Chief of the Japanese Navy. He had six aircraft carriers, with a strong force of 14 protective surface ships and three submarines, plus a total of 432 bombers, torpedo bombers and fighter aircraft with which to carry out the surprise assault. In November, Yamamoto announced the plan to his assembled officers on board the old 30,000 ton battleship *Nagato*. He told them not to underestimate the American armed services, and assured them that Japan needed a great victory if she was to be seen as a great power. Soon after, on November 25th, the task force under Vice-Admiral Nagumo left the Kurile Islands, and on December 2nd the signal 'Climb Mount Niitaka' gave the fleet the irreversible order to proceed with the attack; Operational Order No.1 was to be put into effect.

Incredible as it seems to us now with the benefit of hindsight, Admiral Kimmel and General Short, the US commanders at Hawaii, were warned of the likelihood of imminent war on November 27th, but did virtually nothing to improve the security of the fleet, most of which was at anchor in Pearl Harbor, nor to protect the aircraft parked undispersed on the ground. There was a total failure to accept or recognise the possibility that an attack might be directed against Hawaii. Maybe it just seemed too nice a place.

When, at just before eight o'clock on the morning on December 7th, the 214 aircraft of the first of two waves came speeding in from the Pacific to the attack, the entire establishment was enjoying a typical peacetime Sunday. The formation of aircraft had been spotted at 7.15am on radar, but the young Air Force officer to whom it was reported did nothing with the report because he was expecting a formation of B17 Flying Fortresses at the same time and place. If he had raised the alarm, the eight battleships and the other 86 vessels around them in Pearl Harbor would have had half an hour to recover their crews from their weekend ashore. As it was, they had only their watches on board. The aircraft were not armed. Even the anti-aircraft guns were not fully manned; their ammunition boxes were locked; the crews did not have the keys.

The next two hours were mayhem. Although the defenders reached their posts as quickly as they could in the circumstances, and put up a good fight, the damage was already done. A 1,760 pound bomb blew up the forward magazine of the USS *Arizona*, which quickly sank with 1,106 of her crew plus Rear-Admiral Isaac C. Kidd, and is still on the bottom of Pearl Harbor today. The *Nevada* was hit by two bombs and a torpedo, but maintained a magnificent fight despite being in desperate straits. *Oklahoma* capsized after being hit by five torpedoes, trapping within the hull 415 of her crew. Some of them were still alive, though doomed to die, seventeen days later on Christmas Eve. *West Virginia* and *California* were also hit, as were *Tennessee* and *Maryland*, although these last two were far less severely damaged. Three cruisers and three destroyers were also partially disabled by the ferocity of the first attack.

One hour after the first wave, giving almost no opportunity for the defenders of Pearl Harbor to regroup, the second wave of aircraft attacked. The 54 bombers, 80 divebombers and 36 fighters continued the destruction of the pride of the US Navy, then turned on the air force bases at Wheeler and Hickham Fields, the flying boat station at Kaneohe and the naval installations on Ford Island. A total of 65 aircraft were destroyed.

By 10am the attack was over. In all, 2,403 Americans had died, and 1,178 had been wounded. The Japanese had lost just 29 aircraft and 55 airmen, a relatively small price for inflicting a significant blow on the ability of the US Navy to strike back. It would, however, be unwise to adopt the view, often set out in books discussing the attack on Pearl Harbor, that the damage to the US fleet and its strategic capability was as significant as Yamamoto had hoped. The plain fact is that the loss of two battleships, and the disabling of six others, did not leave the US Navy without teeth. The fleet's three aircraft carriers had not been in port and were intact. Experience was to show that their destruction would have been infinitely more beneficial to the Japanese strategy. No less than 20 cruisers and 65 destroyers were undamaged and ready to fight. Almost as, or perhaps even more, important was the failure of the Japanese to attack the oil storage depots on the Hawaiian Islands, without which the US Navy would have been immobilised for months.

Interestingly, Admiral Chester Nimitz offered in his postwar memoirs an analysis of the losses of Pearl Harbor which actually argued that the element of surprise had worked to the advantage of the USA. He wrote:

'No one regrets more than I our 3,000 dead .... But if Admiral Husband Kimmel ... had had information of the attack 24 hours in advance, he would have sent off all our forces to meet the Japanese.'

'We had not one aircraft carrier capable of opposing Admiral Nagumo's aircraft carrier formation, and the Japanese would have sunk all our ships on the High Seas. We would have lost 6,000 men and almost all our Pacific fleet.'

The greatest single effect of the Pearl Harbor incident was the almost total polarisation of world opinion that it brought about, the consequences of which were colossal. The United States formally declared war on Japan on December 8th, and on the same day Britain honoured Churchill's pledge to join the USA in war with Japan if the USA were obliged to declare it. Germany and Italy rashly declared war on the United States on December 11th, thereby signing the death warrant of the Axis in Europe. Throughout the next week, nation after nation fell into place on one side or the other; virtually all of Latin America fell in behind the United States and declared war on, or broke off diplomatic relations with, Japan. Before Christmas, thirty-eight nations of the world, representing half the population of the earth, were at war.

This more than any other factor made the attack on Pearl Harbor, while a military success, a strategic blunder. More than any other single event of the war, it mobilised opinion and diverted effort to the defeat of the Axis.

JAPAN TAKES ALL
THE ALLIES DRIVEN FROM S.E. ASIA

In the early stages of the Pacific and Far East war, between December 7th 1941 and June 1942, the great Japanese strategy was outstandingly and, for the Allies, ruinously successful in a purely military sense, although, as we have seen, the political effect of Pearl Harbour was in no way to the advantage of Japan or of her Axis partners. The Japanese inflicted an appalling series of defeats upon the USA and Britain, and seemed unstoppable. It was not until the reverse for Japan of the Battle of Midway, in June 1942, that it seemed possible for Nipponese might to be beaten, and not until the Battle of Guadalcanal in August that the USA showed signs of achieving the miracle. But the fight back across the Pacific was to prove long, arduous and bloody.

Japan brought to her war approximately 1,400,000 men as 51 divisions, one million of whom (40 divisions) were in China, Korea and Manchuria. She had 2,400 aircraft of which 1,540 were earmarked for the Pacific, 11 aircraft carriers, 41 cruisers, 129 destroyers and 67 submarines. At the same time, the USA was able to field 1,643,477 men as 34 divisions, of whom 31,000 were in the Philippines; about 2,846 aircraft; 17 battleships (of which 9 were in the Pacific, and six were put out by Pearl Harbor); 6 aircraft carriers (3 in the Pacific); 37 cruisers (24 in the Pacific); 171 destroyers (80 in the Pacific) and 114 submarines (56 of which were in the Pacific).

Hostilities were not long delayed following Pearl Harbor. Later the same day, the Japanese struck at British territory for the first time by bombing Singapore and landing at Kota Bharu in Malaya. Further landings took place at two points in Thailand, Sangora and Patani, and the next day, December 8th, the Battle for Hong Kong began, as the Japanese 38th Infantry Division attacked the 12,000 strong British, Canadian and Indian garrison. That same day, the Japanese landed on Bataan Island, South of Formosa, now Taiwan, and destroyed more than 100 American aircraft in raids on the Philippines.

Hearing the news of the Japanese landing at Singora, not far from the Malayan border, Britain's Admiral Sir Tom Phillips, recently appointed C.-in-C. of the Royal Navy's presence in Singapore, weighed anchor and sailed with *Prince of Wales* and *Repulse*, escorted by three destroyers, to try and surprise the enemy while the Japanese were landing men and supplies. Although he asked for fighters as air cover, he was told that none was available. On the 9th, the arrival of Japanese aircraft over his small force caused him (erroneously) to believe that the element of surprise was lost, and, learning that, in any event, no fighter cover could be provided for an attack at Singora, he turned to Kuantan to investigate reports of enemy landings. But, although the aircraft he had spotted had not blown his cover, a Japanese submarine had. Japan's Rear-Admiral Matsunaga despatched 11 reconnaissance planes, 52 torpedo planes and 34 bombers from Saigon to attack the squadron at sea.

The encounter came at 11am on December 10th, some 322 kilometres North-East of Singapore after Admiral Phillips had established that nothing was amiss at Kuantan and had turned back for Singapore. With no RAF aircraft to deter the aim of the Japanese pilots, the crossfire of torpedoes was unavoidable. First *Repulse*, then *Prince of Wales* was sunk, taking with them 840 officers and men, including Admiral Phillips and Captain Leach of the *Prince of Wales*. Ironically, even as the rescue operation was under way to pick up the 2,081 survivors, the RAF appeared to provide the cover that might have saved the ships.

The elimination of these two formidable battleships at a stroke was of tremendous benefit to the Japanese Navy, which had the task of protecting the Japanese armies that were about to conquer the Philippines, Malaya and Singapore. Their loss by the failure to provide air cover was a major blunder.

The Philippines Invaded

The Japanese landings in the Philippines on December 10th found the Americans considerably outnumbered and outgunned. General MacArthur's forces numbered some 31,000, of whom about 19,000 were American, whereas General Homma's 14th Army totalled two divisions. MacArthur's air power numbered 350 aircraft, rapidly reduced by the bombing of Clark Field, which eliminated almost half of the US B-17 Flying Fortress fleet of 36 aircraft based in the Philippines. The Japanese were able to put 750 aircraft in the air. In this, as in all the opening battles of the campaign, the many myths about the inferiority of Japanese aircraft and their pilots were swiftly shown to be false.

When, on December 10th, General Homma established his first beach-head at Aparri, in the North of Luzon, his plan was to keep the defenders busy while a second landing was made at the bay of Lingayen with the intention of encircling and destroying the American force. General MacArthur was not fooled, and ordered a swift and effective withdrawal in a manner that was quite unexpected by the Japanese. For, instead of falling back, as expected, to defend Manila, the capital, MacArthur moved swiftly West to prearranged defensive positions on the peninsula of Bataan. There his army dug itself in and defended its positions bravely and well for some five months.

At the same time as Homma was discovering MacArthur to be a tougher opponent than expected in the Philippines, General Sakai and the Japanese 23rd Army were attacking Hong Kong, defended by Britain's Major-General Maltby and 12,000 men. During the night of December 9th to 10th, the Japanese attacked the mainland peninsula of Kowloon, and, after three days of fierce resistance, the British were forced to withdraw to the island of Victoria. Five days later, again at night, the Japanese crossed to the island, and General Maltby found himself hopelessly outnumbered. Nonetheless, his force held on bravely until Christmas Day 1941, when they were forced to surrender.

Singapore

The balance of forces in the Japanese attack on Singapore favoured the Japanese far less than in their other operations. General Tomoyuki Yamashita was given the task of taking Singapore before the 100th day of the campaign to capture South-East Asia – which gave him until March 16th 1942. He began with three divisions, and was later reinforced with one more, but even so his army was only slightly larger than that of the British defenders. However, the Japanese regarded Singapore as a plum target, and had given Yamashita's 25th Army both the best troops and the most up to date air cover. In the end, the effectiveness of the air cover, plus the celebrated fact that Singapore's defensive guns could not be pointed inland, were to win the day for Japan. For the air attacks were so effective, and became so frequent, that the British forces were unable to regroup and counterattack.

Yamashita, although a vicious and cruel man hanged after the war for his crimes, was a capable general and a cunning tactician. Known as 'the Rommel of the Jungle' he was every bit as wily as his namesake, as he showed when he advanced on Singapore by a series of rapid flanking attacks which kept Lieutenant-General A.E. Percival's troops constantly on the retreat. Yamashita had picked commando groups to infiltrate the British lines and harry the retreating units, thereby maintaining the impression that his army was invincible and that the British were surrounded. By the end of December Yamashita's army was, if anything, ahead of schedule. He had taken Kota Bharu, half way up the East coast of the Malay Peninsula, and was well placed for the final push to take Singapore.

The problem of defending the Malay Peninsula, which fell to Lieutenant-General Percival in his role as GOC Malaya, was demanding and difficult. He had two Indian divisions and one Australian division to hold a country almost entirely covered by dense jungle. Percival deployed his troops to cover forward airfields, and to hold the few main roads of the peninsula, bringing up reinforcements as they arrived to assist in his army's plight – four brigades arrived during January. But the Japanese troops were trained to jungle conditions, were tough and well disciplined, and moved South through the jungle, constantly outflanking the British positions.

On January 1st 1942, the Japanese had reached Kuantan, roughly halfway down the East coast from Kota Bharu to Singapore. On the West side of the peninsula, Kuala Lumpur fell on the 11th, and Percival decided by the end of the month that his best chance of holding off the Japanese was to conserve his army by falling back to the supposedly impregnable 'fortress' of Singapore. On January 30th the causeway joining the island to the mainland was blown up. Now the almost total lack of defences against attack from the mainland became appallingly clear. In his *Second World War*, Winston Churchill said that 'the possibility of Singapore having no landward defences no more entered my mind than that of a battleship being launched without a bottom.'

It took only a week for Yamashita to prepare. The night of February 8th/9th saw his troops cross the Strait of Johore and establish a beach-head North-East of the city. On the 9th, the airfield at Tengah fell, and with it the reservoirs that provided Singapore with water. By the 15th General Percival had no alternative but to surrender.

The Malayan campaign cost the Japanese 3,507 dead and 6,150 wounded. The Allies lost almost 9,000 dead, and 130,000 as prisoners of war, most of whom were treated with appalling cruelty and inhumanity by their captors, who, applying Japanese traditional standards to their Western prisoners, regarded the Allied troops as unworthy of honourable treatment because they had chosen surrender rather than death.

The Islands, Borneo, Java, Sumatra
Meanwhile, the Japanese invasions and successes had proceeded apace all over South East Asia. As early as December 10th, the American island of Guam, isolated among other islands of the Marianas, which were legitimately Japanese

following the Treaty of Versailles, surrendered when its commander found himself in a totally indefensible position. Wake Island was able to put up a better show, and the US forces there managed to inflict some psychologically important reverses upon the Japanese before the island fell. A squadron of Grumman Wildcat aircraft had arrived on Wake Island on December 4th, just before Pearl Harbor, and the Japanese received a considerable surprise when they attacked, losing two destroyers and a large number of men. The garrison fought on, but the all-conquering Japanese Zero fighter, with its 332 mph maximum speed, was too much for the Wildcats which, although only slightly slower, were less manoeuvrable and not so well armed. On December 21st, the last Wildcat was shot down, and on the 23rd, with the defensive batteries bombed and destroyed, the garrison was forced to surrender.

The Celebes and the Moluccas fell in January and February 1942, and as each new island territory was added to the Japanese Empire, the Japanese Navy and air force units gained new bases, new superiority. The first landing on Borneo came on December 16th, the invasion of Sumatra on February 14th, and that of Timor on the 20th. As General Wavell, commanding the American, British, Dutch and Australian forces in South East Asia was ordered to move his headquarters to Ceylon – now Sri Lanka – on February 25th, news came of the imminent invasion by the Japanese 16th Army of Java, defended by only 30,000 troops under the Dutch General ter Poorten. To try and head off the invasion convoy, Rear-Admiral Karel Doorman of the Royal Dutch Navy was despatched with a fleet consisting of two heavy cruisers (the British *Exeter* and the American *Houston*; three light cruisers, the Dutch *De Ruyter* and *Java* and the Australian *Perth*; and nine destroyers – three British, four American and two Dutch. Theirs was to be the disaster of the Battle of the Java Sea.

At 4.15pm on February 27th, the fleet began firing on the Japanese convoy, the stopping of which represented the Allies' only real hope of gaining control over the Japanese assault on Java. The Japanese stood off as far as possible, and conducted the battle at extreme range – 13 miles – which gave their ships the advantage because they had more 8-inch guns. The Allied fleet had no air cover, and had poorly co-ordinated communications, so was unable to make effective use of its fire power. Shortly after 5pm, HMS *Exeter* was hit in her engine room and had to retreat out of range. The Dutch destroyer *Kortenaer* was hit by a torpedo, exploded and sank. The British *Electra* was set ablaze by gunfire. Later, the Allied fleet inadvertently crossed a minefield, and the British destroyer *Jupiter* was blown up. As matters became worse for the Allied fleet, the Japanese ships *Nachi* and *Haguro* moved in and sank both *De Ruyter* and *Java*, the former taking Rear-Admiral Doorman with it to the bottom.

Perth and *Houston* broke off the battle and returned to Batavia, from where they were ordered to retire Southwards through the Sunda Strait. Here they ran into another Japanese convoy and, after a fierce battle which cost the Japanese four ships, both were sunk. The final disaster came when *Exeter* and the US destroyer *Pope* were sunk trying to run the Sunda Strait on March 1st.

The defeat of the Java Sea ensured that Java would fall to Japan. On March 5th, the Dutch were obliged to evacuate Batavia, which was declared an 'open city', and on March 9th the Dutch and Allied forces in Java surrendered.

The Philippines
While all these events were causing the British, Australians and Dutch grave problems, General MacArthur and his Americans were making a determined

stand against General Homma's 14th Army in the Bataan Peninsula. A demand from the Japanese for surrender on January 10th was ignored, and the fierce attack that followed made it necessary for the US forces to fall back to their secondary defensive line. From this, Homma could not budge them, and had to call for reinforcements, something no Japanese General ever did willingly.

On February 22nd, as the US troops, now getting desperately short of food and medical supplies, still held their line, MacArthur was ordered by Washington to leave for Australia. He politely declined and kept fighting. By March 10th Roosevelt was adamant, and it became clear that even General MacArthur had to do what he was told sometimes. He reluctantly handed over his command to General Wainwright, and left with his family and staff in four PT boats from the island of Corregidor. After a hazardous and eventful journey, they made it to Mindanao, from where they were flown to Australia by B-17. There General Douglas MacArthur made his most famous, and entirely accurate, pronouncement. 'I shall return!'

Meanwhile, in Bataan, General King and the US troops were in serious trouble. Lack of food, dysentery, almost exhausted medical supplies, and sheer exhaustion were telling on morale and the ability to fight. A further demand for surrender from General Homma on April 1st was ignored by Wainwright as studiedly as previous similar demands. But this time the Japanese were able to break through, and on Thursday April 9th it became clear that the end of the brave stand had come. The numerically largest surrender in US history was signed on the 10th, and 12,000 American troops and 64,000 Filipinos, including a great many civilians, were taken prisoner. Although their long battle was at an end, their sufferings were far from over.

For, having taken their prisoners, the Japanese ruthlessly imposed upon thousands of men already ravaged by hunger, disease and exhaustion the terrible 55-mile 'Death March' from Mariveles to the railhead at San Fernando. No less than 2,330 Americans and over 7,000 Filipinos died during that ordeal, and General Homma was tried and executed after the war for the suffering he thus inflicted.

With the fall of Bataan, only the island of Corregidor and some islets nearby remained in US hands, but these last possessions were of vital importance because they controlled the approaches to Manila harbour. A tremendous assault was mounted by the Japanese at the beginning of May 1942, and a large force was landed on the island on May 4th under cover of a barrage of 16,000 shells. Wainwright was in a hopeless position, commanding 15,000 men, most of whom were not in a fit state to fight. The Japanese called for a surrender, insisting that it must encompass not only Corregidor, but also all other US forces in the Philippines archipelago – which implied their taking Mindanao and a number of islands without a fight. Both MacArthur from afar, and Wainwright's subordinates on the spot, tried to prevent him surrendering, but on May 6th, Wainwright agreed to sign and all US resistance in the Philippines came to an end.

Siam and Burma

Of all the assaults by which Japan began its conquest of South East Asia in December 1941, Siam – now Thailand – caused her armies the least trouble. General Iida met virtually no resistance as his 15th Army marched through to Burma, his way smoothed at every major obstacle by a Quisling government. When his army reached the borders of Burma, important to the Japanese for its oil and natural resources, but strategically vital because it offered control of the 'Burma

Road' by which US arms and supplies were reaching Chiang Kai-shek's Nationalist army, he encountered stiff resistance. The recently appointed British commander in chief, Major-General T.J. Hutton, was poorly equipped for the fight, with roughly one division of mixed British, Burmese and Indian troops, reinforced in late January with most of the 17th Indian Division. His air power was virtually non-existent; four Blenheims and 24 obsolete Brewster Buffalo fighters.

On January 18th, as the Japanese took Tavoy in the South and moved on to Moulmein, which fell on the 31st, the British were attempting to round up infiltrators, collaborators and spies, and arrested the appropriately named Prime Minister U Saw among many others. Early in February, the Japanese pushed on towards the Sittang River, held by the 17th Indian Division under Major-General J. Smyth, VC. Sadly, the Allied forces blew prematurely the bridge they planned to use while they were still on the wrong side of the river, thereby creating their own disaster. Two thirds of the division, all its guns and most of its transport was surrendered on February 22nd, and the future for Burma looked grim.

The remnants of the 17th Division fell back to defend the capital, Rangoon, and the 1st Burma Division was in action to the North. But the lack of manpower in both caused a gap to open between them, through which the Japanese were able to push. On March 5th 1942, General Sir Harold Alexander had arrived in Burma to take over from Hutton, but had rapidly realised the appalling gravity of the situation. His first view was that Rangoon must be held at all costs, but he quickly came to agree with Hutton that the Japanese were too strong, and the Allied force numerically too weak for this to be feasible. He therefore ordered a retreat to the North, and abandoned Rangoon on March 7th. At this point, as the British retreated up the Irawaddy valley, reinforcements arrived in the shape of the British 7th Armoured Brigade, infantry battalions, and more air support. The whole was regrouped under the command of Lieutenant-General William Slim.

The strategic objective now was to prevent the Japanese gaining control of the Yenangyaung oilfields. To the battle came the Chinese 5th and 6th armies under the command of American Lieutenant-General Stilwell – known as 'Vinegar Joe'. But the Japanese army had also been reinforced, and had two additional divisions and many more aircraft. The Allied line South of Mandalay proved unable to contain the pressure of the Japanese advance, and the oilfields fell in mid-April, although not before the Allies had sabotaged the oil-wells and put them out of action. On the 29th April, the Chinese were driven back over the border into China, and General Alexander was obliged to evacuate Mandalay and retreat to India via the Irawaddy and Chindwin rivers.

Thus Burma fell too, and Japan, by mid 1942, had achieved virtually all her initial objectives. But retribution was not to be long in coming.

ROOSEVELT AND CHURCHILL

AND THEIR WAR LEADERS

Franklin D. Roosevelt was a politician and a statesman, but never a soldier. He was a man of consistent and balanced views, with a strong sense of moral purpose and a desire to serve his people. Winston Churchill was at once a patrician and a rebel; a soldier in his youth, a politician in his prime and a statesman in his maturity. Churchill was a man of action, an inspired leader. Roosevelt was a creature of reason. That the two achieved such close understanding and coincidence of purpose was in many ways remarkable, for they were in almost every respect quite different men.

Roosevelt brought to the strategy of the Second World War exactly that quality of balance, compromise and political opportunism that was needed to steer the rocky course between Stalin and Churchill; between conflicting ideologies and viewpoints. His was a contribution that, it might be argued, no soldier could have made. For Roosevelt recognised that the great weakness of the Axis was its inability to take and follow joint decisions that were mutually beneficial and jointly acceptable.

Both Roosevelt and Churchill reasoned that the greatest potential strength of the Allies rested in true international strength and command, and both worked ceaselessly to achieve the unity and consistency of policy that, contrasting with the grotesque disharmony of the Axis commands, did so much to hasten the end of the war. Yet it was Churchill's pugnacious inability to compromise, which had brought him long periods in the political wilderness before the war, that made him unwilling to accept anything less than what he saw to be right, and which, ultimately steered the Allies towards total victory. For much of Europe, Churchill's determination was the pivot of freedom.

Nonetheless, it fell to Roosevelt to seek the middle course that would preserve the unity of the alliance with the Soviet Union, and thus make it possible to win the war. He saw that Stalin wanted the British and Americans to open 'The Second Front' in France in 1942. He recognised that Churchill was correct in his view that the Allies were not ready – but proposed instead that the USA should join in prosecuting a new offensive in North Africa and thereby appease Stalin. He knew that there was a powerful groundswell of public opinion that demanded an all-out effort to defeat the Japanese as a higher priority than the conquering of Germany, but saw that the Allied strategy of 'Germany first' must be preserved if world peace was to be achieved. His was a rare ability among men of politics, for he was able to compromise without being seen to deviate from an agreed policy.

These, then, were the men who led the USA and Britain to war. Whom did they choose to help steer their ships of state?

The strength of Roosevelt's team rested in men of his own kind, the civilians mainly from the Eastern states with a predominance of Harvard graduates, the military an immensely able group of commanders, each capable of seeing and valuing others' points of view. General George C. Marshall was Army Chief of Staff, a man who later demonstrated great political ability during the postwar period. Admiral Ernest J. King was Chief of Naval Operations, General Henry H. Arnold the head of the Air Corps. All were far more than just military leaders, for they were the backbone of wartime government in the USA. Alongside them worked men of the calibre of Henry L. Stimson, Secretary of War; Edward R. Stettinius, who first ran Lend Lease, then became Secretary of State in 1944, and Joseph C. Grew, who as US Ambassador in Tokyo had foreseen the risk to Pearl Harbor and Hawaii and was now senior adviser on Asian matters.

Add to these and other men of stature – Cordell Hull, Sumner Welles, Frank Knox, James Forrestal – the extraordinary Harry Hopkins, son of an Iowa harness maker – and one cannot but recognise the unique nature of the team. Hopkins was the fast-moving, fast-talking go-between who did much to fashion Roosevelt's working relationships with Churchill and Stalin and to whom Roosevelt turned more than to any other. Few actually liked him, but all respected him.

In Britain, Churchill had assembled men whose integrity, drive, ability and determination almost matched his own. Impelled by the events of April and May 1940 and the fall of his own party leader Neville Chamberlain to create a coalition government of national unity, he turned a political situation which most party politicians would have regarded as a disaster into a source of strength. Instead of being constrained by party loyalties to appoint to great office only parliamentarians of his own Conservative party, Churchill was able to select the finest talents in the land. He began with the service ministries. From the Labour Party he drew A.V. Alexander, later first Earl of Hillsborough, to become First Lord of the Admiralty. From the Liberal party came Sir Archibald Sinclair as Secretary of State for Air. From the Conservative Party he appointed, as Secretary of State for War, Anthony Eden, who as Foreign Secretary had resigned from Chamberlain's government because of his opposition to Chamberlain's appeasement of the dictators.

In addition to his role as Prime Minister, Churchill also created for himself the position of Minister of Defence. He resisted immense political pressure in 1940 to remove from office as Foreign Secretary the greatly experienced Lord Halifax, and retained at that time even Neville Chamberlain in the post of Lord President of the Council, setting the value of experience above considerations of politics. Halifax was eventually replaced as Foreign Secretary in December 1940 by Anthony Eden, Viscount Halifax becoming Britain's Ambassador in Washington, and David Margesson replacing Eden as Secretary of State for War.

Continuing the all-party policy, Churchill appointed Labour's extremely able Ernest Bevin as Minister of Labour, the leader of the Labour Party, Clement Attlee, as Lord Privy Seal and Herbert Morrison as Minister of Supply. The charismatic Canadian newspaper publisher Lord Beaverbrook became Minister of Aircraft Production, his success as a non-politician in that role providing a curious parallel to that of Germany's Albert Speer, an architect by profession and an immense success as Reich Minister for Armaments Production. Brendan Bracken, Churchill's Parliamentary Private Secretary and an unfailing support during his wilderness years, was appointed a Privy Councillor, despite initial opposition from King George VI.

Churchill's Chiefs of Staff were, like their American counterparts, both able and successful as a team. Admiral of the Fleet Sir Dudley Pound was First Sea Lord and Chief of Naval Staff until his death in 1943, when he was succeeded by Admiral of the Fleet Andrew Cunningham, later Viscount Cunningham of Hyndhope. Chief of the Air Staff, appointed in October 1940, was Air Vice Marshal (at that time) Sir Charles Portal, and in the key role of Chief of the Imperial General Staff was General Alan Brooke, later to be Field Marshal Lord Alanbrooke, more than any other Churchill's friend and military confidant. Another vital figure, acting as principal intermediary between the Chiefs of Staff and Churchill in his role as Minister of Defence, was Major-General (later General Lord) Hastings Ismay, Secretary of the Imperial Defence Committee.

The Allies had good cause to be grateful for the immense ability of the men both Roosevelt and Churchill gathered around them. For their quality was such that, on both sides of the Atlantic, virtually no cabinet or Chief of Staff changes were necessary throughout the war other than where caused by ill health or death. Rarely in history has there been such a consistent and unanimous sense of purpose felt by the great men of nations at war.

ROMMEL AND THE DESERT CAMPAIGN
THE PUSH TO EGYPT

At this point, this book must go back in time – a manoeuvre that all writers tackling a subject as vast as the Second World War seem unable to avoid. We must return to North Africa, and to March 1941. General O'Connor and his two divisions, who had on December 9th 1940 set out on what was intended as a nine-day raid, had instead advanced 560 miles across the desert to Tobruk and Benghazi, destroying nine Italian divisions, capturing 130,000 men (including 22 Generals and an Admiral), and eliminating 845 guns and 380 tanks, all for the loss of 500 dead, 1,373 wounded and 56 missing. The Italians were humiliated, Hitler was angry, and Lieutenant-General Erwin Rommel was summoned by Field Marshal Brauchitsch to take command of a new offensive.

Rommel arrived in Tripoli on February 12th, and presented himself to the Italian General Gariboldi, who had just taken over from Graziani. During the eighteen months from March 1941 to September 1942, Rommel was to prove himself one of the most able field commanders of military history; a man capable of leading an army from a major defeat at Tobruk to almost total victory at the gates of Alexandria; a man whose name and ability were respected on both sides of the battle he so nearly won. He was also to prove infuriatingly blinkered and single-minded to his army command colleagues, whose understanding and appreciation of the overall strategy of the war was usually greater than his, and who resented bitterly Rommel's purloining *Luftwaffe* resources intended for the capture of Malta and the relief of the fierce Allied campaign against Italian merchant ships in the Mediterranean. First Cavallero, then Kesselring became exasperated with Rommel's insistence on ever-greater support, and with Hitler's acceptance of his arguments.

The new German offensive was to be launched by the 15th *Panzer* Division and the 5th Light Division, and advance units were sent to Tripoli from Italy during February. It was expected that the whole 5th Light Division would be ready in North Africa by mid-April, and that the last of 15th *Panzer* would have arrived by the end of May. The first attack on Agedabia was therefore scheduled by the German High Command for May, and General Wavell, in command of the Allied force, knowing that extensive German forces and armour had perforce to be shipped to North Africa, believed that no counter attack was likely before then. Thus, there was not undue concern that many of O'Connor's hard pressed tanks had to be withdrawn from Tobruk for maintenance because the speed of O'Connor's unscheduled advance had left the maintenance facilities far behind.

Rommel, who had been awarded Benghazi as his spring campaign objective, was not pleased with the conservative approach of the High Command, and sensed that the Allies were less well prepared for a fight than their success against the Italians suggested. He resolved to test their strength, and at dawn on March 24th, the 5th Light Division attacked El Agheila. The British defenders fell back without a fight to stronger positions at Marsa Brega, with the Gulf of Sirte on one side, and a salt marsh that tanks could not cross on the other. Rommel's orders now required that he wait for the remainder of the 15th *Panzer* Division to arrive before exploiting his initial advantage, but he was unwilling to allow the Allies time to regroup and bring up more armour. So, on March 31st he attacked again, and, despite putting up a stiff fight, the British defenders were dislodged from what would have become an excellent defensive position.

By the end of April 2nd, Rommel and his German forces, backed by two Italian divisions, had occupied the Agedabia area almost two months sooner than the German High Command had envisaged. The Rommel legend was in the making. So also was trouble with the High Command. For not only did nobody know what Rommel was up to, but neither General von Rintelen nor Gariboldi was able to answer Mussolini's questions as to what he would do next. They soon found out. On the night of April 3rd/4th, as Gariboldi chased after Rommel to stop his impetuous habit of winning battles, the reconnaissance unit of the 5th Light Division took Benghazi, and swept on towards Mechili. Berlin, recognising that success was at hand, whether intended or not, applauded Rommel's adventures, and Gariboldi was obliged to retire and leave Germany's one-man success story to his desert *Blitzkrieg*.

The Allies sought to reorganise their command structure before it was too late, and Wavell decided to put O'Connor, whose own version of *Blitzkrieg* had rivalled Rommel's, in charge of a counter attack. But O'Connor had the ill-luck to be captured by a German patrol while driving with General Neame to a staff conference. The apocryphal story goes that, on arrival at Rommel's desert Headquarters, O'Connor barked 'Anybody here speak English?'. 'I do, sir' replied a German officer, snapping to attention. 'Well, get lost.' retorted O'Connor. It was, regrettably, his last shot in North Africa.

The *Afrika Korps* thrust onward, from Mechili to Derna and the Gulf of Bomba. Recognising the O'Connor tactic of Beda Fomm being performed in reverse, the Allies escaped the net and retreated to Tobruk. There it was decided by Wavell, Air Chief Marshal Longmore and Admiral Cunningham that the line would be held. To stop Rommel, the garrison consisted of the 9th Australian Division, a brigade of the 7th, an armoured regiment equipped with armoured cars and an anti aircraft brigade – some 36,000 men all told, commanded by the immensely tough and experienced General Leslie Morshead, who had commanded a battalion in the Great War at the age of 20.

The initial German attack on April 10th by a motorised detachment of the 15th *Panzer* Division was repulsed, with the loss of General von Prittwitz, who was killed by a shell. Three days later, a battalion of the 5th Light Division found its way through the minefield but was destroyed by the ferocious Australian defence. The Italians attacked, and were repulsed. But, while Tobruk was besieged, Rommel's units were re-taking other major positions – Halfaya, Sollum and Capuzzo – and were thus back on the Egyptian border.

Nonetheless, the continued success of the German campaign in North Africa depended on the capture of Tobruk, and General Halder and Field Marshal Brauchitsch at German Army High Command saw in the stalemate on the Tobruk perimeter complete justification for their distrust of Rommel and his methods. But Hitler remained convinced that Rommel could provide Germany with much needed victory, and, over the next two months, changed the command structure such that the North African command came under OKW (Armed Forces High Command) rather than OKH (Army High Command).

In mid-May, a beleaguered Allied convoy managed successfully to unload much needed aircraft and tanks for Wavell's army at Alexandria, and Wavell was ordered by the British War Cabinet to attack and relieve Tobruk. This was attempted as an encircling movement to Halfaya Pass, but went badly wrong, partly because the units of the 15th *Panzer* Division at Halfaya Pass fought exceptionally well, but also because the German 88mm gun was capable of knocking out the British tanks before they had the German armour within range of their 40mm guns. The defence at Halfaya gave Rommel the time to bring his full force to bear, and the battle developed by mid-June into an ugly and expensive stalemate.

A lesser General would have breathed a sigh of relief. Rommel saw the respite as an opportunity. He went on to the attack, and fought his way rapidly South, then East, attempting to encircle the main British force, which saw the threat and managed to escape. But to do so they had to retreat. Once more, Rommel had the initiative.

The British War Cabinet now attempted to improve matters by replacing Wavell with General Sir Claude Auchinleck, known as 'The Auk'. Auchinleck infuriated Churchill by demanding three months of preparation time and three or four extra divisions before he would be ready to launch his offensive, and a protracted argument developed, with Auchinleck summoned to London to explain himself to Churchill. Meanwhile, the battle lines in the desert were comparatively quiet as the battle around Malta raged in the Mediterranean, and the Russian campaign preoccupied the German High Command. Auchinleck's offensive was first put off until September, then, to Churchill's great displeasure, until November 1st. To satisfy Australian public opinion, the Australian 9th Division in Tobruk was relieved by sea, and replaced with the British 70th Division and the Polish 1st Carpathian Division. Finally, to cap all the other delays, the late arrival in Egypt of the 22nd Armoured Brigade caused the Allied attack to be postponed once again, to November 18th.

Rommel had plans too, and, like those of the Allies, his schemes were being postponed because of military priorities elsewhere. The considerable Allied successes against Italian convoys in the Mediterranean were preoccupying the *Luftwaffe*, and reducing the flow of supplies to the *Afrika Korps* to such an extent that Rommel's planned campaign to take Tobruk was put off again and again. Not until November 4th was he able to present his proposals to Marshal Cavallero in Rome, when he outlined his intention to attack when the moon was full, between November 20th and December 4th. He planned that, on the day before that set for the attack, the Italian *Brescia* Division would make a diversionary attack from the South-West, to lessen resistance to his own attack with the *Afrika Korps* and the Italian XXI Corps from the South-East. He and his staff officers took pains to emphasise to the Italians their 'belief' that there was no imminent Allied attack planned, and no build-up of Allied strength, although it is now known (since Rommel's intelligence chief Major von Mellenthin's memoirs were published in 1955) that Rommel knew full well that Auchinleck was almost ready to strike. Clearly, his faith in his Italian allies was minimal.

Meanwhile, Auckinleck had created the Eighth Army by combining the reinforcements he had received with the battle hardened troops that remaining from Wavell's campaign. This was under the command of Lieutenant-General Sir Alan Cunningham, brother of Admiral Sir Andrew Cunningham who commanded the fleet giving support from the seaward side of Tobruk. Because the

C-in-C of the Royal Air Force in the desert was, coincidentally, Air Vice Marshal H. Coningham, the troops referred to their commanders as 'Cunningham, Cunningham and Coningham'. All told, the Allies had six divisions.

In August, Rommel had been elevated to the command of *Panzegruppe Afrika*, of which his *Afrika Korps* was but one corps, now under the command of General Cruewell. The 5th Light Division, reinforced with new armour, became the 15th *Panzer* Division, and there were other units of German armour. The Italian XX and XXI Corps completed Axis forces totalling ten divisions on paper, although the worsening supplies position and manpower shortage in the Italian formations meant that the Axis forces were actually appreciably less powerful than the figures suggest.

The Allies attacked on November 18th, expecting that their appearance in strength would draw Rommel's forces out to fight at Gabr Saleh. Instead, Rommel, who was preparing his own attack, decided that the Allied effort was no more than a large scale reconnaissance, and stayed put in his defensive position near the coast at Gambut. This first failure of British planning was compounded by the German capture on the 19th of the Eighth Army's operational orders, and by the failure of the 22nd Armoured Brigade to take Bir-el-Gubi. The problems mounted for the Allies as the British XXX Corps was defeated at Sidi Rezegh on November 22nd, with massive tank losses, and the 5th South African brigade was similarly devastated on the 23rd. It looked as if the Axis would annihilate XXX Corps entirely, as would certainly have happened if the initial success had been pressed home. Instead, Rommel showed his skill as a tactician by using the confusion created as an opportunity to take personal command of the 15th and 21st *Panzer* Divisions, and to set out across the desert to the Mediterranean via Sidi Omar to attack the already vulnerable Allied troops from the rear.

Auchinleck refused to be rattled, although Cunningham was clearly pessimistic about the situation. In a lightning move which restored morale and stiffened British resolve, Auchinleck replaced Cunningham on November 24th with Major-General Neil Methuen Ritchie, and moved himself firmly into the driving seat. By November 27th, the New Zealand division had made contact with the Tobruk garrison, which had broken out at El Duda, and Rommel, now back at *Panzer* Group headquarters, was failing still to take Tobruk despite frequent attacks. On December 5th, realising that his supplies were desperately stretched with little potential for new arrivals of ammunition, food and fuel before the second half of December, Rommel began his withdrawal from Tobruk, pursued by the Allied forces under Ritchie, who reached Benghazi on Christmas Day.

The pursuit continued, but Rommel's retreat was as skilful as his advance and the British armour did not succeed in engaging the Axis formations before they reached their planned defensive position at El Agheila, 340 tanks down on the strength they had enjoyed when the Allied attack began on November 18th. On January 17th came the final act of Auchinleck's successful 'Operation Crusader', when the Italian *Savona* Division, left behind by the retreating Rommel with the thankless task of defending the Bardia/Sollum/Halfaya area, surrendered to the 2nd South African Division. In two months, the Eighth Army had taken 32,000 prisoners, for the loss of 18,000 men, variously killed, wounded or taken prisoner.

It seemed on the face of it that the Allies could now launch their long awaited Operation 'Acrobat' to advance to Morocco and Algeria. But events at sea in the Mediterranean had been going disastrously wrong for the Allies at the end of 1941 and at the turn of the year, and the balance of power at sea changed dramatically the extent to which Germany was able to re-equip and resupply Rommel's forces for their next offensive. On November 13th, the *Ark Royal*, Britain's finest aircraft carrier, had been sunk by U-81. This was rapidly followed by the loss of the battleship *Barham* and the light cruiser *Galatea*. Force K, based on Malta, and the greatest hazard of all to the Axis convoys, was virtually annihilated. Hitler saw his advantage developing, and both reinforced the *Luftwaffe* in the Mediterranean theatre by withdrawing *II Fliegerkorps* from the Eastern Front, and also changed the command structure by instituting a 'Supreme Commander South' in the person of the likeable, yet ruthlessly effective Field-Marshal Kesselring, once an artilleryman, now one of the architects of the *Luftwaffe* (and, incidentally, an accomplished pilot and aerial photographer.)

At the same time, reinforcements that had been earmarked for Auchinleck and 'Operation Acrobat', the planned 8th Army push to the frontier of Tunisia, and four squadrons of Hurricanes intended for Air Chief Marshal Tedder's Middle East Air Force were diverted to Singapore and to the new war against Japan. As the Allied position weakened, so Rommel's was greatly enhanced by the arrival of large numbers of new tanks and vehicles, huge quantities of fuel and new guns of improved performance. In mid-January he decided to counter-attack, telling neither the German High Command nor the Italians of his intentions until the attack had begun on the grounds that 'the Italian Headquarters cannot keep things to themselves.' As a result, the Axis forces achieved almost total surprise.

Rommel's Lightning Advance

Moving against the British 1st Armoured Division, which was new to Africa and had a mere 150 tanks, the advance of the Italian Mobile Corps on the coast and the *Afrika Korps* inland was made easier by the splitting of the British Division into three separate forces, each of which was too small to be self-supporting. To make matters worse for the Allies, the experienced 4th Indian Division was stuck at Benghazi, and the 7th Armoured Division had been sent back to Tobruk. Within two days, Rommel was at Agedabia, and on the 27th January almost succeeded in cutting off the 4th Indian Division in Benghazi. Mussolini had issued orders personally to Rommel that he was to retreat back to his former positions. Rommel simply ignored the Duce. By February 3rd, the *Afrika Korps* had skirted around Derna, reached the Gulf of Bomba and ground to a halt at the British positions at Gazala. This was *Blitzkrieg* in the grand manner, and General Ritchie, having lost almost 1,400 men, 72 tanks and 80 guns was not in a strong position. Rommel had pushed 375 miles back towards Egypt in defiance of his orders, yet, despite his insubordination, was rewarded with a promotion to Colonel-General.

The effects of the Axis advance reached well beyond North Africa. The island of Malta was still being defended against ever increasing German and Italian air attacks, and needed desperately the air support that the mainland Middle East Air Force could provide from Benghazi and Derna. With those forward positions lost, air support became impossible because Malta was out of range from Tobruk. Add to that the ability of Rommel's forces to harass the Malta convoys from Cyrenaica, and it can be seen that Admiral Cunningham's problems in attempting to supply Malta were made much greater. Only endless disputes throughout the spring of 1942 between the German and Italian High Commands, and between the individual members of those commands prevented 'Operation Hercules' to take Malta and Gozo being mounted. Kesselring believed that, if 'Hercules' had gone ahead, it would have succeeded. That belief was based on the positions of the 8th Army and the *Afrika Korps* after Rommel's advance.

Meanwhile, Auchinleck's failure to go on to the offensive against the Axis forces was galling Winston Churchill. Since February he had been demanding action, but Auchinleck and Tedder agreed that no offensive launched before June could succeed. Attempts to persuade them otherwise by sending Lieutenant-General Nye and Sir Stafford Cripps to Cairo resulted in the visitors being converted to Auchinleck's viewpoint. By mid-May there was still no British offensive, but a Churchill ultimatum to Auckinleck finally secured action and planning. By then it was too late. Rommel was ready, and attacked first. Once more the Eighth Army had been caught on the wrong foot, albeit for the best of reasons. Current British tanks, aircraft and anti-tank guns available in North Africa were all outclassed by their Axis equivalents. Auchinleck was right to judge that trouble lay ahead.

The Axis forces attacked in two principal groups; on the one hand the Italian XXI and X Corps plus some German reinforcement were to launch, under General Cruewell, a frontal assault on the Eighth Army to 'keep them busy' and prevent them manoeuvring for advantage. On the other, Rommel himself took command of the mobile and armoured units – the Italian XX Corps and the divisions that made up the *Afrika Korps*, the 15th and 21st *Panzer* plus the 90th Light Division. In the evening of May 26th, Rommel moved from the positions he had held for so long to outflank his enemy by passing both North and South of Bir Hakeim, thereby putting his tanks to the rear of the Eighth Army. Thus, on May 27th, the British forces found themselves attacked on both sides, yet, after a confused battle in which both sides could claim some success, the Allies had not fared badly. The two Italian divisions of the XX Corps, the 'Trieste' and the 'Ariete', were virtually routed, and lost many tanks. Although the 15th and 21st *Panzer* Divisions did great damage to the 4th Indian and 7th Armoured Divisions, their armour was somewhat dented, and many German tanks were badly damaged. By the end of the 27th, the Eighth Army's communications remained intact, and the Axis forces were already short of fuel – Rommel's perennial problem. Two days later, General Cruewell was captured after a forced landing behind the British lines.

Rommel was, however, not to be daunted by a few reverses. Having sent advance parties to improve communications with the Italians, and clear a narrow path through the minefield that lay between his forces and the British XIII Corps, he attacked the strongpoint at Got el Oualeb, while the Italian 10th Corps attacked from the West. By June 2nd he had a victory. The British 150th Infantry Brigade and the 1st Army Tank Brigade surrendered, and 3,000 men, 124 guns and 101 armoured vehicles of all descriptions fell into Axis hands. Now Rommel was able to move reunited Axis forces through the minefield and close in around Bir Hakeim. British communications were as bad as those of the Axis forces were good. Probably because of this, General Ritchie failed to exploit any of the opportunities for counter-offensive with which the overstretched Axis forces provided him, and by the time XIII and XXX Corps attacked the German forces, the Germans had laid effective minefield defences. The Axis assault now centred on the battlefield known as 'Knightsbridge' – little more, in fact, than a convergence of sand tracks across the desert which led to Sidi Muftah, Gazala and Bir Hakeim. As the two British corps, which were too thinly spread across the desert with poor communications and control, fell back before the German attack, 4,000 more prisoners fell into German hands, and the 32nd Tank Brigade lost more than half its tanks.

Now Bir Hakeim was surrounded, with no hope of relief. General Koenig, commanding the 1st Free French Brigade, politely declined to surrender, and held on valiantly for eight days, falling back to the British lines only when directly ordered to do so on June 10th. By the 13th, Ritchie was in danger of being encircled and attempted to fall back to Tobruk, but his greatly depleted tank force was outflanked and cut off. The way was now open for Rommel to attack Tobruk.

Thus, at dawn on June 20th, the 15th and 21st *Panzer* Divisions and the Italian XX Corps made their final assault from the South-East, supported by Ju87 'Stuka' dive bombers. Progress was rapid. By 8am, the anti-tank ditch was breached; by nightfall the forts at Solaro and Pilastrino had fallen. The next morning, June 21st, Major-General Klopper surrendered the garrison to General Navarrini. Another 33,000 men fell into Axis hands, but the greatest windfall for Rommel was the huge quantity of gasoline and supplies that he had captured – some 2,200,000 gallons of fuel for which the German armour was desperate.

Now Rommel was set for the advance to Egypt, but the agreement between the German and Italian High Commands to embark upon 'Operation Hercules', the attack on Malta, stood in the way. Substantial sections of his *Panzerarmee* were due to be withdrawn for the assault on Malta, and Rommel knew he could not hope to advance further in North Africa without them. He appealed to Hitler to abandon 'Hercules' in favour of an advance to Egypt, and the Fuehrer, probably seeing the potential for a link-up of Axis forces in the Middle East following a successful summer offensive in Russia, agreed. The assault on Malta was abandoned, and Rommel, who had just been promoted Field-Marshal on the strength of his successes, was given the authority to proceed. As always, he had not waited for permission, and was already beyond Sidi Barrani and heading for Mersa Matruh, where General Ritchie was preparing for a last ditch stand.

At this crucial point, Auchinleck took over command on the spot from Ritchie and saw the acute danger that X Corps might be trapped at Mersa Matruh. Auchinleck's speedy response to the situation enabled the Corps, and in particular Major-General Freyberg's New Zealand Division to retreat back to defensible positions at El Alamein, between the Mediterranean and the Qattara Depression, an impassable area of salt marshes. There they were joined by the 9th Australian Division brought in from Syria, and the 4th Indian Division from Cyprus.

Having advanced 644 kilometres – over 400 miles – in 36 days, Rommel was badly overstretched. His total forces facing the British positions on July 1st amounted only to 6,400 men, 41 tanks and 71 guns. He should have stopped, dug in, held his line and waited for reinforcements in strength. But an almost Messianic belief in the invincibility of speed and thrust drove him on to attack immediately. The assault, to become known as the First Battle of El Alamein, was a disaster, and by July 17th, despite having been reinforced during the preceding two weeks to a nominal strength of 30 battalions, his four armoured divisions were reduced to having only 58 tanks between them, and he could call on fewer than 5,000 infantry. Now, in a fit of depression, Rommel contemplated retreat, but, once his customary verve was restored, he recognised the situation for what it was and prepared defensive positions to await supplies, further reinforcements and developments. Meanwhile the Axis powers, anticipating that the halt in Rommel's advance represented only a temporary lull, promised Egypt, whose borders were almost in sight of Rommel's army, complete independence and national sovereignty.

There we leave North Africa and turn to the war at sea. But we shall return in Chapter 19 to the Desert and to the Allies' triumphant reversal of their position.

THE BATTLE OF THE ATLANTIC

THE U-BOAT WAR

Once more, this book must step back a little in time, to March 1941. You may remember from Chapter 9 that, following the fall of France, Admiral Doenitz had established the headquarters of the U-Boat fleet at Lorient, and had prepared for the mighty offensive against the Atlantic sea routes that were so crucial to supplies of both food and war materials from the USA and Canada. The British success in countering the effectiveness of the magnetic mine had pinned German hopes for an Atlantic victory firmly upon the submarine fleet, to which was now added the strength of the *Luftwaffe's* latest acquisition, the four-engined long range *Focke-Wulf* Fw200 Condor bomber, which proved very effective against merchant ships at sea.

In March 1941, Churchill established in London a Committee to meet daily and marshal the resources required to 'defeat the attempt to strangle our food supplies and our connection with the United States'. This group recognised the fact that *Luftwaffe* attacks on the British ports were every bit as serious a threat to the convoys across the Atlantic as the U-Boat attacks themselves, and set about strengthening the anti-aircraft defences of the principal docks and ship repair facilities around the British coast. They did not have long to wait.

As soon as March 13th and 14th, the *Luftwaffe* attacked the docks along the River Clyde in Scotland with great force, putting some of them out of action until the summer and even into the autumn. At the beginning of May, the attack hit the docks of Liverpool and the Mersey, which were pounded remorselessly for seven consecutive nights. Sixty-nine of the 144 available mooring bays were eliminated, and some 3,000 people were killed or injured. Then, just as it seemed that a pattern of airborne offensive against the docks was becoming established, the *Luftwaffe* raids ceased as suddenly as they had begun. Churchill was of the opinion that, had the assault on the ports continued, the war might well have been lost.

Now RAF Coastal Command, whose aircraft searched the seas, reported enemy shipping movements, attacked enemy ships, laid mines and hunted surface raiders was placed under the command of the Admiralty from April 1941. The fitting of better anti-aircraft defences to merchant ships was given a high priority. Britain had, in the summer of 1941, a total of 695 vessels deployed for the defence of the Western Approaches, but of these only 248 were destroyers, of which 59 were being refitted and were out of action. There were 99 of the little corvettes that were to prove so effective against the U-Boats, and 48 sloops. The biggest trump card that Admiral Sir Percy Noble, C-in-C Western Approaches, had was the presence on most of the escort vessels of radar, which effectively prevented the U-Boat fleet attacking on the surface after dark. Radar was also gradually added to the armament of RAF Coastal Command aircraft.

Strangely, the British did not take the opportunity of destroying the U-Boat pens as they were built along the French Atlantic coast at Brest, Lorient, and Bordeaux. Had they done so, the course of the Battle of the Atlantic might have been different. Once the pens were completed, their 12 feet thick concrete walls proved capable of withstanding all the bombs then available, and many fine pilots lost their lives attempting to rescue the strategists from their earlier mistakes.

The course of the Battle of the Atlantic in 1941 can best be viewed in the light of a comparison between shipping sunk and new shipping built – which in turn highlights one of the principal reasons why the battle swung in the Allies favour in 1942. British official records show that in 1941, shipping losses were some 340,000 tons (240 ships) higher than in 1940, with a total tonnage sunk of 4,328,558 tons, a total of 1,299 ships. Losses of Allied ships to submarines were down in 1941; losses to air attack were up. Total Allied shipbuilding in 1941 came to just over 1.5 million tons. Thus, in the year, the available shipping tonnage to bring arms and food across the Atlantic was reduced by around 2.8 million tons. By the end of 1941, the USA was officially in the war – and that brought American shipbuilding capacity of some five million tons per annum into the equation, which redressed the balance in the Allies' favour.

The Battle did not go entirely Germany's way in the early stages, despite the fact that her strategic objectives were being achieved. Although 41 British and Allied ships totalling 243,000 tons were sunk by U-Boats in March 1941, five U-Boats were lost by the Germans, three of them commanded by 'ace' captains whom Doenitz could ill afford to lose. On March 7th, Gunther Prien, famed for his attack on the *Royal Oak* in Scapa Flow, was located by the destroyer HMS *Wolverine* using radar, and was blown up while attacking convoy OB.293. Nine days later on March 16th 1941, Captain Donald Macintyre, commanding the escort to HX.112, scored heavily after the U-Boats had claimed five ships from his convoy, with considerable loss of life. The destroyer *Vanoc* rammed and destroyed U-100, crushing to death her famous commander Joachim Schepke in the collision, and Captain Macintyre's own HMS *Walker* depth-charged U-99, capturing the far more famous Otto Kretschmer, darling of the U-Boat fleet, who had sunk a total of 44 ships.

The worst month of the campaign for the Allies was May 1941, when 58 ships were lost to the German attacks. Totalling 325,492 tons, the lost ships took to the bottom many fine sailors and thousands of tons of supplies and arms that were vital to the Allied war effort. At the same time, the adventures in the Balkans and Greece were costing many more ships, and putting the two together one sees a pattern emerging that must have been very satisfying to the German strategic planners – total Allied losses in April and May 1941 of over 1.1 million tons.

The second half of 1941 was far less damaging to the Allies. The part of the Atlantic between Iceland and Eastern Newfoundland was now in the US Security Zone announced by President Roosevelt, and this and the posting of US naval forces near Greenland and Iceland released Royal Navy vessels for escort duties in the main battle zone. Moreover, from September 11th, US ships in the Atlantic were authorised to shoot on sight. But German policy was also working against continued success in the Battle of the Atlantic. Hitler had ordered the detachment of four U-Boats to the Arctic Ocean as soon as the attack on the USSR began, and, although they were recalled, they were deployed next to defend the

Norwegian coast against British attack. Six more U-Boats were detached from the Atlantic fleet in the summer of 1941 to the Mediterranean, where they did a great deal of damage, but that was small consolation to Doenitz, who believed (probably correctly) that to win the Battle of the Atlantic before the USA entered the conflict was to win the War.

By the turn of the year, there were no less than 23 U-Boats in the Mediterranean, where they were virtually trapped, since currents through the Straits of Gibraltar prevented them leaving through the Straits underwater, and Royal Navy defences effectively prevented their leaving on the surface. Doenitz now had 55 U-boats under his command for the continuation of the Battle of the Atlantic into 1942. Had Goering recognised the full potential of co-operation between the new Condor bombers and the U-Boats, and had the servicing of the Condors been more effective and capable of keeping more than two airworthy at a time, the utilisation of the U-Boat fleet might have been far more damaging to the Allies.

Perhaps more to the point, 60 per cent of the German Atlantic U-Boat fleet was unserviceable at the end of 1941 because the vital maintenance resources had been diverted during the year to the prestige projects of repairing the *Scharnhorst, Gneisenau* and *Prinz Eugen*, all of which had been damaged by air attack during the middle four months of the year.

However, it would be wrong to underestimate the extent to which the Royal Navy was improving in its counter-submarine measures. Larger escort forces, better radar, improved use of ASDIC and the benefit of hard-won experience were making the Navy escorts tough opponents for the U-Boat crews. A much-quoted example of this is the experience of Convoy HG.76, which conducted a running battle with a pack of U-Boats from Gibraltar to Ushant in December 1941. The escort force consisted of an escort carrier, three destroyers, four sloops and ten corvettes, which between them protected 32 merchant ships. After one of the toughest nine days of the Atlantic battle, the Royal Navy had lost the escort carrier *Audacity* and the destroyer *Stanley* plus two merchantmen. Against that, the *Kriegsmarine* had lost five of the ten submarines that took part in the battle, including U-567 commanded by Leutenant Endrass, another of Germany's U-Boat aces. These sinkings brought total U-Boat losses in 1941 to 35, of which 27 had gone in the Battle of the Atlantic. Nonetheless, Doenitz ended the year with more submarines than he had had at the beginning – no less than 198 new U-Boats had been built during 1941.

The Battleships – and the Hunt for the *Bismarck*

The preoccupation with the U-Boats, both then and now, has a way of obscuring the very important events that took place in the declining arena of surface sea power. Germany was heavily committed to major surface ships, as has been mentioned briefly in an earlier chapter, and during 1941 had also developed the concept of the armed offensive merchantman. These surface vessels between them destroyed the considerable total of 427,000 tons of Allied merchant shipping in 1941. The warships also performed the less obvious but tactically vital task of tying down Allied surface vessels that might otherwise have been used for convoy escort duties.

The sister ship of the *Admiral Graf Spee*, the 12,000 ton pocket battleship *Admiral Scheer*, sank some 99,000 tons in the first three months of 1941 before evading the watching British warships to dock at Kiel. The 14,000 ton cruiser *Admiral Hipper* had had remarkable success in February, sinking no less than seven merchant ships in 90 minutes with her torpedoes and 8-inch guns, and returning to Kiel in triumph ahead of the *Admiral Scheer*. Meanwhile, the heavily armed battle-cruisers *Scharnhorst* and *Gneisenau*, at 32,000 tons apiece, had managed to slip out of Kiel in January with orders from Admiral Raeder not to engage any ship with 15-inch guns. After failing to engage Convoy HX.106 because the venerable 29,000 ton battleship *Ramillies*, completed in 1917, was leading the escort, they sank three merchant ships and two tankers off Newfoundland, then headed South-East across the Atlantic towards the North African coast.

Off the Canary Islands they again failed to attack a convoy, this time because the even older (1916) battleship *Malaya*, again with 15-inch guns, was leading the escort, following which they headed back North-West and played havoc with a convoy from Halifax, Nova Scotia. By the time the two ships reached Brest, successfully evading the Royal Navy, they had sunk 22 ships, but had run their turbines into the ground. Repairs were scheduled to take weeks, and neither ship was ready to accompany the *Bismarck* and the *Prinz Eugen* on their marauding foray into the Atlantic, which began on May 20th 1941.

Bismarck was not hampered by the restriction on attacking capital ships that had prevented the previous squadron doing more damage. At 41,700 tons, with eight 15-inch guns in four turrets plus a new range-finding radar, the *Bismarck* was one of the finest ships afloat. Her captain and crew were similarly out of the top drawer. She was a formidable opponent. The heavy cruiser *Prinz Eugen*, although much smaller at 13,900 tons, was also brand new (1940) with eight 8-inch guns and a top speed of 32 knots.

The day after the squadron put out from Kiel, they were photographed by aerial reconnaissance in Korsfjord, south of Bergen. Vice-Admiral Holland of the Royal Navy was ordered from Scapa Flow towards Norway with his squadron – the battle-cruiser *Hood*, the battleship *Prince of Wales* and six destroyers – and the squadron sailed taking with them some civilian workmen who were still working on the newly installed 14-inch gun turrets of *Prince of Wales*. By the next day, it was apparent that the two German raiders had eluded reconnaissance and had vanished from their fjord. So Admiral Tovey sailed with the main fleet to intercept.

During the evening of May 23rd, the *Bismarck* was spotted on radar by the Kent class cruiser HMS *Suffolk*, who called up the cruiser *Norfolk*. Jointly they stalked *Bismarck*, reporting her position so that Holland's squadron was able to intercept early the next morning. Although Admiral Holland's initial position was ideal, and enabled him to bring virtually all his squadron's guns to bear, he turned to a less favourable position before attacking, a manoeuvre that has been the subject of debate ever since. The likely explanation is that he did it to get as close as possible as rapidly as possible, so as to get the lightly armoured and ageing 41,000 ton *Hood*, which first entered service in 1920, inside the range at which enemy shells would plunge down on the battle-cruiser's relatively thin deck, and gain the benefit of a flatter trajectory, which presented armour almost four times as thick to the enemy.

After half an hour, Holland opened fire, believing he was aimed at *Bismarck* when he was actually attacking *Prinz Eugen*. *Prince of Wales* rectified the error in part by attacking *Bismarck*. Ten minutes later, the British squadron turned, and the *Hood* prepared to fire on the *Bismarck*. A 15-inch salvo from the German flagship got to *Hood* first, and in what must have been one of the mightiest non-nuclear explosions of the war, the *Hood* blew up, killing all but three of her total crew of 95 officers and 1,324 men. Without pausing, the German ships bore down on *Prince of Wales*, landing seven shells on the ship, and killing all on the bridge except Captain Leach and a signaller. Several of *Prince of Wales'* turrets were now out of action, and she broke off the battle.

Although *Bismarck* had clearly achieved major success, one of *Prince of Wales'* shells had damaged a fuel bunker and her fuel was becoming contaminated with sea water. An oil slick behind the ship was also a clear hazard to its security. So Admiral Lutjens advised his High Command that he was making for St Nazaire. There followed a remarkable chase across a broad stretch of the Atlantic by Vice-Admiral Wake-Walker, who took under his command *Prince of Wales* and the rest of Holland's battle-cruiser squadron, and Admiral Sir John Tovey with *King George V* and the Home Fleet. An epic attack by Swordfish biplanes from HMS *Victorious* succeeded in hitting the *Bismarck* with a torpedo but did little actual damage. Gradually, all Tovey's ships had to break off for refuelling until only *Prince of Wales* was left on the trail of the German ship – *Prinz Eugen* having been ordered to break away and continue her mission independently of *Bismarck*. Contact with the damaged German ship had been lost, but, on May 26th, a Coastal Command Catalina (PBY) spotted the ship and reported her position.

Now Force H, which had been diverted to the hunt from near Gibraltar, took a hand, and launched an attack with Swordfish biplanes from *Ark Royal*. The first attempt almost sank HMS *Sheffield* – a rather nasty case of mistaken identity – but the second attack took 15 aircraft through a wall of fire to score two hits, the second of which disabled *Bismarck's* steering gear. Admiral Lutjens knew he could not now make port, and sent a signal saying he would fight to the last shell. Shortly after, the *Bismarck* ran into a force of five destroyers commanded by Captain Vian, who decided to attack, but achieved only two inconclusive hits because of the devastating accuracy of *Bismarck's* fire and the need for constant evasive action. Next morning, *King George V, Rodney and Norfolk* arrived, and sent a hail of 16-inch and 14-inch shells crashing on to the German ship. Although the *Bismarck's* superstructure was almost destroyed, none of these shells pierced the ship's armour, and she remained afloat. At 10.36am, two torpedoes from the *Dorsetshire* holed and sank her. Sir John Tovey concluded in his report.

'*Bismarck* fought an extremely courageous battle against greatly superior forces; in the best tradition of the old Imperial Navy, she went down with her colours flying.'

PACIFIC TURNING POINT

THE CORAL SEA AND THE BATTLE OF MIDWAY

In the earlier chapter of this book covering the initial Japanese conquests in South-East Asia following their surprise attack on Pearl Harbor, the Japanese strategy was defined as being first the neutralisation of the US fleet, then the rapid concurrent conquest of all key areas of South-East Asia, followed by the establishment of a defensive perimeter around those conquests. We have seen that, to a large extent, Japan succeeded in putting that strategy into effect.

Nonetheless, success was not total, and the USA and her allies survived to fight, and ultimately to win. Foremost among initial Japanese miscalculations was the belief that the attack on Pearl Harbor could be expected to immobilise the US Pacific fleet. What it actually did was to force naval warfare firmly into the 20th century. For, although the capital ships that were the pride of the US Navy were either disabled or sunk, neither the aircraft carriers nor the bulk of the Navy's destroyers were in Pearl Harbor when the attack came. Entrusted with the task of holding a line from Alaska to Midway Atoll in the Pacific, and from Midway to Australia, the newly promoted Admiral Chester Nimitz, Roosevelt's personal choice as C-in-C Pacific Fleet, had little choice but to think in terms of using air power.

Thus, as the Commander in Chief of the Imperial Japanese Navy, Admiral Yammamoto, argued with his colleagues and with Japanese High Command about the rights and wrongs of invading Oahu and taking Pearl Harbor, and of the potential for an assault on Australia to prevent its eventual use as a base for Allied counter-offensive, Nimitz was calling up reserves and reorganising the fleet for the battle he knew had to come. From the Atlantic, the 20,000 ton carrier *Yorktown* was ordered through the Panama Canal to join her sister ship *Enterprise*, already with the 33,000 ton sister carriers *Lexington* and *Saratoga*, together with the smaller 19,800 ton *Hornet* in the Pacific – although the *Saratoga* was in fact out of action until May 1942 following a contretemps with a torpedo on the 11th of January 1942. Nimitz also had, in addition to the carriers, 16 cruisers, 44 destroyers and 16 submarines.

In February, carrier groups under Vice-Admiral Halsey and Rear-Admiral Fletcher each launched raids on Japanese held positions in the Marshall Islands and the Gilbert archipelago, and Wake Island and Marcus Island were bombed at the end of the month. These comparatively minor adventures, which nonetheless brought the war to within little more than a thousand miles of Tokyo, reinforced Yamamoto's unwavering opinion that the US Pacific Fleet had to be finally and irrevocably crushed. At the beginning of April, Yamamoto submitted his plan for an attack on the Midway Atoll, with a diversionary assault on the Aleutian Islands to draw off some of the power of the US Fleet. The ostensible reason for the attack was to gain control of the forward airfield on Midway and deny it to the US forces. The actual reason was that Yamamoto intended to smash the US Navy once and for all.

Because the arguments within Japan's High Command about strategy were still raging, Yamamoto's plan might well have been put on ice or simply turned down. But in the third week of April came the Doolittle Raid, a daring attack on the Japanese mainland that, although militarily and strategically unimportant, was extremely effective as an exercise in propaganda. Lieutenant-Colonel James H. Doolittle of the Air Corps, already 45 years old and a veteran of World War 1, had conceived the idea of launching a force of fully laden twin-engined Mitchell B-25 bombers against Tokyo from an aircraft carrier. Doubt had been expressed whether this was possible; nobody had ever flown such large or heavy aircraft from a ship before. Practising in Florida, Doolittle's pilots proved they could get their lumbering B-25s off the ground in the 750 feet run that was available to them. Getting them back down again was another matter – that simply could not be done. So a plan was devised by which the aircraft would be brought within 500 miles of Tokyo aboard the carrier *Hornet*, launched on their raid, and then landed in friendly Nationalist China.

On April 18th, after the *Hornet* had unexpectedly encountered an enemy patrol while still 700 miles out from Japan, it was decided that, as secrecy could no longer be guaranteed for the force, the B-25s should be launched. All 16 aircraft made successful take-offs despite rough seas and high winds, and arrived over the Japanese cities of Tokyo, Nagoya, Osaka and Kobe, and over the Yokosuka naval base, at treetop height with almost nil warning.

The Japanese people, who had been assured that US aircraft could not reach the shores of Japan, were first terrified, then appalled. Where had the bombers come from that now climbed to 1,500 feet, dropped their 500 pound bombs and then turned out to sea at wavetop height? Enjoying the discomfiture of the Japanese military enormously, Roosevelt suggested they had come from Shangri-La, the mythical mountain kingdom of Hilton's *Lost Horizon*.

Because of their premature launch, the brave pilots of the Doolittle raid did not fare well. Doolittle himself crash-landed in China, unhurt; one aircraft was seized after landing at Vladivostock airfield; the crew of another was executed after crash-landing in Japanese-held territory. None other than the Vladivostock arrival landed normally.

The damage to the all-important Japanese self-esteem was immeasurable, and Yamamoto now had no difficulty in securing approval for his plan to attack Midway. On May 5th the order was given for the attack to have been mounted by June 20th. Meanwhile, although the views of those in the Japanese High Command who believed that Australia should be attacked were not gaining support, the potential of Australia as an Allied base was taken seriously. The Japanese 4th Fleet, reinforced with three aircraft carriers and two heavy cruisers, was therefore despatched to take Port Moresby on the southern coast of New Guinea, and to occupy Tulagi in the Solomon Islands, as a preliminary to seizing New Caledonia and Fiji.

Earlier in the year, the US backroom boys in Washington had secured one of the most important victories of the Pacific War by breaking the Japanese Naval code. Thus Admiral Chester Nimitz knew of the 4th Fleet's orders almost as soon as they did, and was able to act on the recently concluded Anglo-American agreement by which the USA took responsibility for the Pacific defences of Australia and New Zealand. Rear-Admiral Fletcher's Task Force 17, with the carriers *Yorktown* and *Lexington* was sent to Port Moresby, and was joined en route by an Australian cruiser force under Rear-Admiral Crace. The actions that followed from May 6th to May 8th are remembered as the Battle of the Coral Sea.

There is no doubt that the Battle of the Coral Sea was something new in naval warfare. For the first time in history an entire sea battle was fought without a ship's guns being brought to bear or a single salvo fired. From start to finish, the battle was fought by carriers and aircraft. But the Battle of the Coral Sea was also a strategic milestone. Although the Battle of Midway that followed it is regarded as the great reverse for the Japanese, and is remembered as the turning point of the Pacific War, the Coral Sea was in fact the first significant failure of the Japanese Navy, and the first occasion when a Japanese force was obliged to retreat. For, although the action resulted in the sad loss of the US carrier *Lexington*, and of an oiler mistaken by the Japanese for another carrier, the Japanese themselves lost the elderly 7,500 ton light carrier *Shoho*, a destroyer, a minelayer and three minesweepers, and, more important, were left with the new 26,000 ton carrier *Shokaku* severely damaged and her sister carrier *Zuikaku* virtually without aircraft. Because of the severely depleted carrier force, Admiral Inouye gave up the idea of landing at Port Moresby, and New Guinea was spared the pleasure of his company. Moreover, the task forces charged with the assaults on Midway and the Aleutians found themselves significantly depleted.

The Battle of Midway

The plan with which Admiral Yamamoto approached the set piece Battle of Midway made sweeping assumptions which were not realised on the day. The first was that the diversionary attack on the Aleutian Islands would cause Admiral Nimitz to split up the US Fleet and weaken his defences. The second was that the intended bombardment of Midway Atoll on June 4th would cause Nimitz to commit his fleet to a major sea battle on June 7th or 8th, giving Yamamoto time to reassemble his five separate task forces into one cohesive battle group. The third was that the Japanese submarine force which, since the Twenties had been built and trained on the assumption that the right and proper function of a submarine was scouting and reconnaissance, would be able to detect all US movements to the Midway area as they developed.

Yamamoto did not know, of course, that the US Fleet was well aware of his intentions and battle plan, and had even proved to its own satisfaction that the target was Midway by planting some false information for Japanese listening posts to report back to High Command. He did not know that Nimitz had the *Yorktown* – Japanese intelligence had assured him, quite erroneously, that an 800lb bomb that had hit the carrier during the Battle of the Coral Sea had sent her to the bottom. He assumed, with dangerously cavalier arrogance, that his carriers would be enough and that he could keep his other ships in reserve – in the event, the nine battleships, 11 cruisers and 32 destroyers that Yamamoto had available were not allowed near the battle, and did not fire a single shot. On Midway Atoll itself, the small (and understandably nervous) US garrison had been built up to more than 3,000 men and 115 aircraft, and was bristling with anti-aircraft guns.

When Yamamoto's submarines reached their stations to report the expected movements of US ships after the 'surprise' attack, the birds had already flown. Yamamoto thus had no information on the size and disposition of the US forces, and could do little else but rely upon his already dangerously inaccurate intelligence. On June 3rd, a US Navy Catalina spotted the invasion fleet approaching, and called up a force of B-17 four engined bombers to attack the Japanese. By dawn on the 4th, the Japanese fleet was 280 miles off Midway, and launched 108 aircraft to the attack. The fighters put up by the US defenders on Midway had a bad day against the greatly superior Japanese Zeros, and 17 of the 26 aircraft that took off to meet the first assault were shot down. Despite this, the Japanese, acting on ill-considered advice from the commander of the Japanese air attack, launched a largely unnecessary second wave of fighters against Midway, with the result that, when the US Fleet was spotted only 240 miles away and approaching rapidly, Admiral Nagumo had no fighters available to cover his dive bombers if they were sent to attack the US ships. He therefore waited for the fighters' return.

Meanwhile the approaching US force under Admirals Fletcher and Spruance had decided to launch their attack at the earliest possible moment, and by sheer good fortune caught the carriers *Akagi* and *Kaga* at their most vulnerable, just as the fighters returned. The first two waves of US torpedo bombers were TBD Devastators from USS *Hornet*, an obsolescent slow type of aircraft quite incapable of defending itself against the Zero, which, with the British Spitfire was one of the world's two finest fighter aircraft. The returning Zeros made mincemeat of them, destroying all fifteen of the first wave, with a loss of 29 of the 30 crewmen, and 20 of the 26 of the second wave. But the Zeros were so busy demolishing the Devastators and their luckless crews that they failed to notice the arrival of a squadron of Douglas Dauntlesses, the latest and fastest US dive-bomber, capable of carrying a 1,000lb bomb at a maximum speed of over 250mph. The Dauntlesses attacked the Japanese carriers from just short of 20,000 feet, and, in moments, the 36,500 ton *Akagi* was holed and burning. The 38,200 ton *Kaga* had also been hit and was burning fiercely with immense loss of life. The older 18,800 ton *Soryu* had lost her rudder and engines to the Dauntlesses, and was unable to manoeuvre. Only the 20,000 ton *Hiryu* remained in action, and she despatched an attack to wreak vengeance upon the US carrier *Yorktown*. American fighters despatched 12 of the 18 Japanese attackers, but the *Yorktown* was hit, first with bombs, then with torpedoes, and had to be abandoned because of the danger of capsizing. That evening, Admiral Spruance had his revenge. Twenty four Dauntlesses under Lieutenant-Commander Clarence W. McClusky hit *Hiryu* with four bombs and disabled her. The next day Yamamoto ordered his fleet to finish off *Hiryu* and *Akagi* with torpedoes. The entire Japanese carrier force had been lost.

Admiral Nimitz's policy of concentrating his defence and attacking forces early had caught Yamamoto's forces still widely scattered. On June 5th, there was nothing Yamamoto could do to recover the situation, and he ordered the abandonment of the assault on Midway. But his fleet's troubles were not yet over. Two of his cruisers collided with each other during the night; the *Mogami*, badly damaged, was unable to defend herself properly against air attack, and was so badly damaged as to be out of action until mid-1943. The other cruiser, *Mikuma*, sank on June 6th.

The Americans, too, had their problems. Later the same day a Japanese submarine came upon the disabled *Yorktown*, under tow for Pearl Harbor, and sank both her and the destroyer *Hammann*.

The final tally for the Battle of Midway was the loss by the Americans of one carrier, 307 men and 147 aircraft. The Japanese lost four carriers, 3,500 men and

332 aircraft. The battle proved that the Japanese could be beaten, and gave the Allies hope that they would be vanquished. The sole ray of brightness for the Japanese was their success in the Aleutians. They had expected the USA to defend them heavily – instead, because Nimitz concentrated on Midway, the Aleutians were undefended. The Japanese occupied them on June 6th and 7th.

MONTGOMERY AND THE DESERT FOX

ALAMEIN AND THE ALLIED RECOVERY

We left the British Eighth Army and Rommel's much-depleted *Panzerarmee Afrika* in mid-July 1942 facing each other at El Alamein, 60 miles from Alexandria. Rommel was badly overstretched; short of men, supplies, equipment and fuel. The Eighth Army had been severely demoralised by Rommel's lightning advance after the fall of Tobruk in June, had been heartened by their comparative success in the first Battle of Alamein, and now awaited badly needed reinforcements and some more positive leadership than that provided thus far by General Auchinleck and Lieutenant-General Ritchie.

On hearing of the fall of Tobruk, President Roosevelt and General Marshall had arranged, almost without asking Churchill, to re-equip the Eighth Army with the new 30 ton M4 Sherman tank, whose superior turret, 75mm gun and greater off-road speed than the M3 Grant made it approximately the equal of the German PzKpfw IV. The USA also supplied 100 self-propelled guns, and the combination of the American guns and tanks potentially changed the balance of power in North Africa. But the most potent of weapons is inadequate without the inspiration of great commanders, and Churchill, impetuous as always, yet understanding of the psychological need of an army to taste success, grew increasingly impatient of Auchlinleck's failure to capitalise on his recent success against Rommel's attempt to push on to Egypt.

Anglo-American planning was already well-advanced for Operation Torch, the Allied landings in French North Africa, scheduled for November 1942, and General Sir Harold Alexander had been appointed as General Eisenhower's deputy for that operation, in command of the British 1st Army.

Churchill decided, at the beginning of August 1942, to see for himself the Eighth Army, its command structure and the position in which it found itself, and on August 4th arrived in Cairo. He found that the Cairo GHQ favoured a wait at least until September for an attack on Rommel's positions, in order to assemble reinforcements, regroup and plan its offensive. He was not pleased, and on August 6th asked the Chief of the Imperial General Staff, General Sir Alan Brooke (later Field-Marshal Lord Alanbrooke) to assume command in the Middle East, with General Auchinleck taking only the Iraq and Iran theatres. Brooke felt that he was of more service in his existing role, and tactfully refused, whereupon Churchill asked the Americans to accept that General Alexander be released from his responsibilities to Operation Torch to take over in the Western Desert. For the command of the Eighth Army, Alexander and Churchill initially selected Lieutenant-General W.H.E. Gott, but he was killed in an air crash days afterwards. Their choice then fell on General Bernard Law Montgomery, who had been intended as Alexander's replacement as commander of the British 1st Army for 'Torch', and now moved to the desert, leaving Eisenhower wondering why Churchill kept taking his deputies away from him. The arrival of Montgomery in Cairo was historic. Arrogant, less than totally lovable, yet an inspiration to all who served with and under him, he was destined to become one of the best known figures of the Second World War. His was the fire that was to drive the Eighth Army forward and the *Afrika Korps* back, not only to Rommel's starting point, but far beyond to Tripoli, in less than a year.

There was much to do. Montgomery launched himself upon the task of strengthening the defences of the El Alamein position and, knowing that the *Panzerarmee Afrika* was now heavily reinforced, made the assumption that it could not be long before Rommel attacked. The presence and virtual impassability of the Qattara depression, the height of the Alam el Halfa ridge, and the proximity of the sea made it unlikely that Rommel could execute one of the outflanking manoeuvres that he had made peculiarly his own. Montgomery therefore decided that Rommel would attack where he was least expected, and would try to 'tease' out the tanks of the Eighth Army to be destroyed by the superior German anti-tank guns. Acting on this hunch, the British commander ordered the 44th Division and two brigades of the 10th Armoured to reinforce the defences of the Alam el Halfa ridge, and ordered the tanks to dig in and act defensively rather than adopt a mobile offensive role.

The German attack expected at full moon on August 26th did not materialise. The British generals (Horrocks and de Guingand), under Montgomery's direction, used the interlude to indulge in a little deception which had almost the qualities of comic opera, but which was nonetheless effective in misleading the Germans and giving the British army the edge in the battle that followed. They produced a map which gave a highly inaccurate yet detailed picture of the Allied minefields and the natural hazards of the desert, and then arranged for it to be abandoned after an armoured car 'broke down' in no man's land. The Germans took the bait. When the attack finally came in the early hours of August 31st, the progress of the 15th and 21st *Panzer* Divisions was slow; they were hampered by unexpected minefields and by an enemy who seemed to know exactly where to shell and attack from the air. In the melee, the commanders of both *Panzer* Divisions were put out of the action – Major-General von Bismarck of the 21st, killed by a mine, and Lieutenant-General Nehring of the 15th, severely injured by air attack.

Air power and a defensive use of artillery were, in fact, the deciding factors in the Battle of Alam el Halfa. The Germans and Italians were repulsed at every turn, and were losing men and armour to little effect. The enormously long line of supply back to Benghazi began to tell once more, and, on September 3rd, Rommel called off the attack.

Alexander and Montgomery, despite this considerable success, decided still to remain on the defensive until such time as they had been reinforced to a level of men and equipment that they knew could and would defeat their enemy. Shortly after the battle of Alam el Halfa, in the early part of September, President Roosevelt's gift of 300 Sherman tanks and 100 self-propelled guns began to arrive in Egypt, and the improvement in Allied sea and air power in the Mediterranean (British submarines were able to use Malta again from July) was ensuring an ever greater volume of supplies for the Allies. The reverse was, for the same reason, true for the Axis, and the German and Italian forces now experienced a considerable reduction in supplies of fuel and arms to reinforce the *Panzerarmee Afrika*.

Allied air power was built up impressively. The lessons of Hitler's *Blitzkrieg* had been well learnt, and long-range bombers became an important part of the tactical planning for the coming desert offensive. The crews of newly arrived American B-25 Mitchells and British Wellingtons began training in desert conditions, and a full-scale ground training programme initiated British crews into the mysteries of the Sherman tank.

Deception began once more to take a hand in the planning of the great Battle of Alamein, which was such a mighty undertaking that it was not to come until October's full moon. Montgomery made the assumption that Rommel would expect him to follow, as had previous commanders of the Eighth Army, the established British approach to tactical planning. Given that assumption, Montgomery reasoned, Rommel would expect him to attack from the South and try to drive the Axis forces into the sea, and to attack the armour first, expecting to mop up the German and Italian infantry later. The British plan was therefore based upon exactly the opposite procedure – an assault from the seabound North; a massive artillery barrage being followed by an infantry advance, the objective being to cut off the German armour, separate it from its supporting infantry and eliminate it piecemeal.

If Rommel was not to learn of this plan, the massive movements of British troops northward from the southern positions had to be concealed. Montgomery's mastermind of 'Operation Bertram' was Major Charles Richardson, who hit upon the idea of replacing every vehicle that stole away in the night with an inflatable rubber replica, realistic enough to fool aerial reconnaissance and long distance observers. A fake pipeline was built, and was deliberately constructed slowly so that the Germans would believe the attack to be scheduled for November rather than October. False radio traffic was used to make the Axis listening posts believe that a third Armoured Division was in position to the South, between the Qattara Depression and Ruweisat Ridge. Camouflage assumed a new importance as the vast dumps of fuel and stores near the coast were concealed from prying Axis eyes.

Meanwhile the 7th Armoured Division and XXX Corps had new commanders – Major-General Harding and Lieutenant-General Sir Oliver Leese respectively – and a far tougher intensive training programme than they had previously experienced. A third Corps – X Corps – had been formed under Lieutenant-General Lumsden with the specific brief to pursue the enemy once the artillery and infantry had created a breach in the line. By mid-October, the Allies were ready. But what of Rommel?

He had in fact left the front because of poor health, and handed over command of *Panzerarmee Afrika* to General Georg Stumme, albeit with strict instructions to his successor to follow the agreed plan of campaign without undue display of initiative. The Axis had not been idle during the previous six weeks, and almost half a million German mines now lay between the Allied attackers and their enemy. The German and Italian Armoured Divisions had been withdrawn to the rear, and six divisions of infantry, including one Airborne, held the line. The 21st *Panzer* and the Italian 'Ariete' Division were in the northern sector. The 15th *Panzer* and the 'Littorio' Tank Division were stationed in the South.

The Greatest Bombardment in History

When Montgomery's surprise attack came at 9.40 in the evening of October 23rd 1942, the Axis were totally unprepared for its force, and had no inkling of the appointed date or hour. Rommel was still away from his Command, and two of the Italian commanders were on leave in Italy. A total of 592 Allied guns opened up simultaneously along a front from the Mediterranean to the Qattara Depression, the vast bulk of them – 456 – in the northern sector. For 15 minutes this enormous fire power hammered at the Axis positions, cutting communications, detonating many mines, disorientating the German and Italian defenders. As soon as the barrage ended, sappers and mine detectors – new devices at the time – and specially adapted tanks called 'Scorpions' with flails to detonate mines advanced into the minefields, with the infantry close behind. In the southern sector General Horrocks' XIII Corps staged a successful but costly diversion which succeeded in its objective of preventing the 'Ariete' Division reinforcing the armour to the north.

Although the British divisions made considerable progress, they had by the 26th, when Rommel returned to his command, two days after his deputy Stumme had died of a heart attack in the field, failed to punch their way through to the Axis' rear, as Montgomery's plan demanded. The British armour was therefore held up and relatively ineffectual, although in fact the Axis forces had taken heavy losses, and had few tanks, widely dispersed. Rommel's first move was to concentrate the armour and, as always, lead from the front, taking a powerful tank force to attack Montgomery's forward positions. But he reckoned without the formidably increased air power of Tedder's Desert Air Force, which now had a total of 1,200 aircraft, several times the available *Luftwaffe* resources.

The RAF bombers killed large numbers of troops and disabled tanks by the score, as did the new 6-pounder anti-tank gun that was newly arrived in North Africa. As Rommel fell back, the Allied armoured formations began to cut through their opponents' positions and fan out. By the 31st of October, Rommel was in a desperate position but was holding the line by bringing up his last reserves. There had in fact been a reduction in the ferocity of Montgomery's assault, and a withdrawal of Allied troops into reserve. This tactic reportedly caused Churchill much disquiet, and he had to be calmed by the ever-present Sir Alan Brooke. In fact, Montgomery was setting up the final assault that would set the Eighth Army on the road to Tunis – 'Operation Supercharge'.

On November 2nd, Major-General Freyberg's New Zealand Division led 'Supercharge' and encountered some of the closest in-fighting of the war – tank battles at ranges of only 20 and 30 yards were reported. Despite enormous Allied losses, the attack gradually wore down the *Afrika Korps*, which by November 3rd had only some 35 tanks left. On the 4th, the German line was breached, and X Corps almost wiped out the 'Ariete' Division and captured General von Thoma, the commander of the *Afrika Korps*.

The remains of *Panzerarmee Afrika* was now in full retreat westward, but much of the Italian infantry strength was surrounded and captured. The Battle of Alamein was over. Montgomery and Tedder had shown that Rommel was not invincible, but the cost had been considerable. The Allies had lost 13,560 men, of whom 4,610 were killed or missing. The Axis had fared far worse – they had lost 25,000 killed and wounded, and 30,000 prisoners including nine Generals.

Rommel was never again to hold the initiative or win a major victory in North Africa. His path to Tunis and defeat was clear. Despite orders from 'Commando Supremo', he made no attempt to stand and counter attack at El Agheila. He had met his match.

OPERATION TORCH
THE U.S.A. STEPS INTO AFRICA

The invasion of French North Africa by an Allied force in November 1942 had as its objective the seizure of Morocco, Algeria and Tunisia, and the creation, with the British and Empire armies in the Western Desert, of a giant pincer within which to crush the Axis forces under Rommel. Militarily desirable as the operation was, it nonetheless had a firm basis in politics. This is not, however, to restate the old and inaccurate claim that Roosevelt set up Operation Torch to corner a greater Democratic vote in the 1944 Presidential election. The politics were of a higher order.

In January 1942, the so-called 'Arcadia' conference between Churchill and Roosevelt, immediately following America's entry into the war, had confirmed the policy of 'Germany First' that had been tacitly agreed long before the USA had been officially part of the conflict. As the Russians fought back after their appalling 1941 losses, Stalin put great pressure upon both Roosevelt and Churchill to open a second front against Germany – by which Stalin meant an invasion of France. Churchill knew that there was no way in which such an invasion could be possible before 1943 at the earliest, with or without the complicity of America, but there was substantial, and slightly naive, pressure from both public and military opinion in the USA for an invasion of the European mainland in 1942. Among the generals wanting to hit Germany where it hurt was Dwight D. Eisenhower. He and other generals outlined a proposal to build up US forces and arms in Britain – a plan which became known as 'Bolero' – prior to a limited attack on France in 1943 to seize a bridghead in the area of Cherbourg. This latter operation was to be known as 'Sledgehammer'. This in turn was to be followed by a full scale invasion across the Channel, also in 1943, to be known as 'Roundup'.

Roosevelt doubted the short term practicality of this scheme, whatever its emotional desirability, since the USA had the potential for little more than three combat divisions ready for action in 1942. He therefore sent Harry Hopkins, his adviser and confidant, and General Marshall to London to discuss the whole issue with Churchill and his military staff. The outcome of this meeting was that 'Bolero' was agreed for initial action, with Eisenhower as its commander, but the second front remained a matter of contention. Marshall wanted the 'Sledgehammer' plan agreed as a means of reducing military pressure upon and political pressure from the USSR. Churchill wanted an operation in North Africa to provide evidence of political will to the USSR and evidence of active US involvement in the 'European' war, without the peril of an invasion of Europe that was ill-prepared.

Eventually, following Churchill's visit to Washington in June, and a further visit by the American team to London in July, all prospect of a full-scale invasion of Europe being launched in 1942 was vetoed by Churchill, but it was agreed that the experimental 'mini-invasion' at Dieppe, which had been in the detailed planning stage for months, should go ahead under the recently (November 1941) appointed Chief of Combined Operations, Rear-Admiral Lord Louis Mountbatten. It was intended that this landing, which took place on August 19th 1942, should test on a small scale whether it was realistically possible to mount a cross-Channel invasion on the scale necessary to open the Second Front in Europe. In the event, the raid was a disaster, not least because the defending Germans were aware that it was coming. The Canadian 2nd Division lost 882 killed of the 4,963 men who took part, with 597 wounded. The British Commandos of Nos 3 and 4 Commando lost 275 killed, wounded or taken prisoner. But the raid nonetheless proved that a cross-Channel invasion was feasible, and pointed the way to the training and equipment requirements that needed to be met if the eventual invasion of France was to be successful.

However, to the Soviet leaders, operations like the Dieppe Raid were a sideshow, and to maintain credibility with the USSR 'Operation Torch', the invasion of North Africa, was agreed upon. Because of French susceptibilities following the events of 1940, it was felt to be advisable that, although 'Operation Torch' was to be demonstrably a joint Allied operation, with, in fact, more British troops than American, the actual invasion force should appear to be almost entirely American, and should have an American ground commander. This job fell to the colourful, aggressive and World War I experienced Major-General George C. Patton. As Deputy Commander-in-Chief, Eisenhower chose Major-General Mark Clark, who was to prove an able commander in his own right. The British troops, who were to land soon after the Americans, were to be commanded by Lieutenant-General Kenneth Anderson.

After much discussion based upon fears of Axis countermeasures from nearby Sicily, a plan for 'Torch' was agreed upon which called for three separate US landings, two on the Mediterranean coast of North Africa, at Oran and near Algiers, and one on the Atlantic coast at Casablanca. Once the American landings were established, the British 1st Army was to go ashore at Algiers and, having established a bridgehead, turn East for an attack on Tunis. 'Torch', at 60,000 men, was the largest combat force ever to have been shipped from the United States, and Norfolk, Virginia, its embarkation point, was absurdly stretched to cope. Training was at a frantic pace, command structures were fragile because of constant changes of personnel, and many of Patton's officers despaired of ever getting the force together as a cohesive whole.

In Britain, from where the Centre and Eastern Task forces were to begin their voyage, similar stresses prevailed and confusion reigned. The US Army had not attempted any feat of organisation quite so large before, and problems arising from inexperience and mismanagement were everywhere. Despite it all, the US 1st Armoured Division, and the 1st and 34th Infantry Divisions were embarked in Liverpool and Glasgow late in September and headed in convoy for the Straits of Gibraltar and the Mediterranean, traversing the Straits on the night of November 5th to 6th.

The Western Taskforce of the invasion, consisting of more than 100 ships, also managed to arrive off the coast of Morocco on schedule after a rendezvous at sea and an encounter with a U-Boat on the way across the Atlantic. On the night of November 7th 1942, the Western Taskforce split into three attack groups and, early in the morning of the 8th, went ashore by landing craft. Their initial objective was to capture the heavily defended city of Casablanca and its airport. The group given the airport landed at Mehdia, the others either side of the city at Safi and Fedala.

The Mehdia landing group under Major-General Lucien Truscott, which consisted of some 9,000 men from the 2nd Armoured and 9th Divisions, ran into heavy resistance from the Vichy French defending forces, and having had reinforcements delayed by French shelling of the fleet, was in a decidedly tricky position by the evening of the 8th. The arrival of reinforcements from the fleet on the 9th enabled them to fight on and capture the airport on the 10th, but not before 79 Americans had been killed and many more injured.

At Safi, to the South of Casablanca, Major-General Ernest Harmon, commander of the 2nd Armoured Division took 6,500 men of the 2nd Armoured and 9th Divisions ashore, again encountering tough opposition, and established the necessary beach-head. On the 9th November, Harmon's force encountered a French infantry force at Bou Guedra, and the resulting battle held up their advance until the next day when he was once again able to advance towards Casablanca. Harmon took Mazagan on the morning of the 11th and was on the road to Casablanca when he, like the other commanders, heard news of a ceasefire arranged with the complicity of Admiral Darlan, second in command to Marshal Petain in Vichy France, who was coincidentally in North Africa when the invasion took place.

The northernmost landing group of the Western Taskforce landed against similarly stiff opposition at Fedala under Major-General Jonathan Anderson, who had the largest force of the three – 16,500 men, mainly of General Anderson's own 3rd Division. They had almost reached Casablanca, and were about to turn their artillery loose on the city when news of the ceasefire reached them.

The Centre Taskforce, whose objective was the capture of Oran in Algeria, was the only one of the three taskforces to be able to claim a concluded military victory. The 22,000 men of the force attacked at several points, the 1st Infantry Division being allotted the task of encircling the city from East and West, and the 1st Armoured the job of pushing inland to come back upon the city from the South. Initial resistance was weaker than expected because the attack came as an almost total surprise to the defenders, but November 9th brought heavy fighting. On the 10th a US armoured thrust penetrated the city, and the French authorities surrendered at midday. The fighting in Oran cost the American force some 600 killed or wounded.

By far the most crucial job fell to the Eastern Taskforce, whose assault was upon Algiers, the centre of all French government in North Africa and the jumping-off point for the planned assault on Tunis. Landings on both sides of the city by three separate parts of the taskforce met comparatively little resistance – the westernmost landing party at Castiglione found that the local French defenders claimed to have been ordered not to resist at all. Only a small assault group of 650 Americans, plus some British officers in American uniforms, ran into heavy resistance when they atempted a frontal assault on the harbour at Algiers, a bold venture that enabled them to capture their initial objectives only to be forced to surrender when their position became hopeless.

In the afternoon of the 8th, Admiral Darlan recognised that the French position was hopeless, and that he had a choice between surrender without further bloodshed and defeat with a great deal of bloodletting on both sides. After consultations by radio with Petain, Darlan and General Juin agreed to a ceasefire in

Algiers, but not, at this stage, elsewhere in North Africa. On the 9th November, General Mark Clark arrived in Algiers to negotiate a ceasefire for the whole of French North Africa, and agreement was reached late the following day.

Meanwhile, General Anderson's British 1st Army was on its way over rocky roads to Tunisia, almost 400 miles to the East. Prompted by the Allied invasion, German and Italian troops were already arriving at Bizerta and Tunis by sea and air to secure Tunisia and the rear of *Panzerarmee Afrika*, and the French forces between the newly arrived Germans and the advancing Allies lacked the orders or the clear moral guidance that was necessary if they were to resist the Axis landings – quite simply, they were not sure for whom they were supposed to be fighting. Thus the German and Italian invaders rapidly established defensive positions in Tunisia, which were contained by French troops from mid-November once the French had clear guidance as to which side they were on. Although Anderson made contact with his enemy on November 20th, the momentum had gone, the Axis forces were too strong to be shifted quickly, and no amount of reinforcements and fighting could alter the position of stalemate. On Christmas Eve, as Darlan was assassinated by a young French monarchist, Eisenhower had reluctantly to abandon the idea of a swift capture of Tunis and Bizerta. Roughly 110,000 troops had taken part in 'Torch' which, as improvisations go, was outstandingly successful, and laid the ground for the final defeat of the Axis in North Africa.

Although American soldiers had experienced battle in the 'Torch' landings, they had yet to discover just how tough a foe the Germans could be. The bitter experience of the Battle of Kasserine Pass in 1943 would teach them that. Thus far, the US land forces had fought only the Vichy French army, whose loyalties were in any case divided, and who had been relatively easily overcome. The US Navy and the British Royal Navy had, however, not had quite such an easy time off North Africa.

The Vichy French Navy had joined battle in earnest with the escort vessels of the US taskforces, and had sustained heavy losses, including the cruiser *Primauguet*, 10 destroyers and 13 submarines. At Casablanca, the USS *Massachusetts* fought a brisk battle with the still incomplete French battleship *Jean Bart* and was fired upon from the shore. Attempts to send British naval sloops into Algiers harbour early in the battle for the French seat of North African government had resulted in the *Walney*, the *Hartland* and the *Broke* being lost, and the *Malcolm* making a hair's breadth escape.

Nonetheless, the overall picture was one of Allied success, not only in the objective of strategically occupying French North Africa, but also in its being the first large-scale Allied combined operation, and the first major Allied amphibious invasion. It was the taste of things to come.

THE EASTERN OFFENSIVE

STALINGRAD, AND THE BEGINNING OF THE END

For Germany, and for Hitler in particular, the Eastern front was of dominating importance during 1941 and 1942. The sheer scale of the task that the Third Reich had undertaken in attempting to overrun Russia, and the overwhelming proportion of the German armed forces that were committed to the task, made it inevitable that its successful completion should be at the forefront of Hitler's thinking.

The winter of 1941/42 had, as we have seen, inflicted appalling suffering upon an ill-prepared German army that lacked proper winter clothing, and which was subjected to a ferocious counter-attack by Zhukov's Russian forces in December. Morale had reached a desperately low state. Generals had asked for and had been refused permission to retreat. Yet, somehow, the superbly trained and experienced German army had held its line despite the hardships inflicted upon it. The Hitler magic was still there. The decay of the conquering spirit of the Third Reich had not yet eaten into the fabric of the world's greatest fighting machine.

Thus, by April, when Hitler issued his Directive No. 41 for the 1942 summer offensive and beyond on the Eastern Front, the Fuehrer was able to claim with some truth that 'Thanks to the extraordinary bravery and spirit of sacrifice displayed by our troops, the defensive battle on the Eastern Front is proving a most striking success for German arms'. The Directive went on to define the objectives for the *Wehrmacht* in Russia, and the means by which it was to achieve them. In summary, the objectives were to capture or destroy the remaining Russian armed forces – Hitler believed on the basis of faulty intelligence that the Russian army was so depleted as to be near defeat – and to capture the rich sources of raw materials that the southern USSR had to offer.

To achieve this, Hitler directed, the entire force of the *Wehrmacht* on the Eastern Front, with the exception of those engaged in the siege of Leningrad, was to be concentrated in the southern sector in a drive to the Don, and to the oilfields and mountains of the Caucasus. Beyond the Caucasus lay Turkey and the Middle East – and Hitler confidently expected that 1942 would also see the Axis conquest of Egypt and an assault on the British protected territories beyond, making it theoretically possible for the Axis forces to link in a mighty circle from Libya almost to the Arctic. While there is no firm evidence that Hitler actually planned such a vast operation, there is written proof that it was discussed (and rejected) by his generals, notably by Halder. On a more limited canvas, the generals were, in any case, less than enthusiastic about Hitler's planned offensive, believing that there was more than a danger of the Russians having greater reserves than German intelligence indicated, and that the commitment of greater resources to the Russian adventure would further weaken the ability of Germany to sustain its position on other fronts.

To the final defeat of what Hitler believed was a severely depleted Russian enemy, the *Wehrmacht* brought 18 more infantry divisions than had been available in Russia in 1941, but virtually no increase in the available armoured and motorised divisions – a factor that was to prove important to the coming campaign. On paper, the equivalent of 215 German divisions were massed against Russia for the summer offensive, of which 31 were 'Satellite' (Rumanian, Hungarian and Slovak) divisions. These in fact numbered 46, but were marked down in value by a third by cautious German planners doubtful of their actual capability in the field.

The assault by the augmented Army Group South was code-named 'Operation Blue', and was to be preceded by attacks designed to retake the positions around Izyum captured by the Russians during their December offensive, and to mop up the remaining Russian defence of the Crimea. Beginning on May 8th 1942, nine Axis divisions, three of them Rumanian, attacked 17 Russian divisions. The German formations, despite their numerical inferiority, made rapid progress, largely because of their superiority in the air. Colonel-General Lohr's *Luftflotte IV* provided constant dive-bombing and strafing support, and reduced the effectiveness of the Soviet Air Force in harrying the advancing German columns. By May 9th, the day after the attack began, the Germans had broken through the Russian lines and were fanning out. By May 11th, eight Russian divisions had been driven back to the Sea of Azov; on May 20th what was left of the Russian forces in the northern part of the Crimea retreated across the narrow Strait between the Black Sea and the Sea of Azov, losing in the process 170,000 prisoners, 258 tanks and 1,138 guns.

On the Izyum salient, things did not go so easily for the Germans. Bock had decided to attack on the 18th May, but the Russians attacked first, advancing on General Paulus' Sixth Army around Kharkov with great ferocity. As if from nowhere, the Russians under Marshal Timoshenko produced a major force of some 36 divisions with plenty of modern armour, advancing as a two-pronged attack. The northern attack was checked comparatively quickly, and held by the Germans, but in the South the Russians advanced inexorably until the 16th, virtually routing a Hungarian division and a German 'Security' Division. The German commanders, somewhat rattled, revised their plan intended for the 18th, and launched their armoured assault under Kleist on the 17th, whose *Panzergruppe* advanced rapidly with *Luftwaffe* support to the Donets.

At this point Timoshenko appealed to Stalin to allow a retreat from Kharkov, but was ordered to hold his position, vulnerable as it was to encirclement. He did not have to wait long. General Mackensen's 3rd *Panzerkorps* moved swiftly up the right bank of the Donets river, pushed the rear positions of the Russian army aside, and made contact with General von Seydlitz-Kurzbach's Corps, thereby sealing off the Russians in the Izyum pocket. Fight as they might, the Russian forces could not break out, and by the 28th, when the end came, the German Sixth Army had crushed the Russian army, which lost 1,246 tanks, 2,026 guns and an incredible 214,000 prisoners. General Gorodnyansky was killed in the closing stages of the fighting.

By failing to allow Timoshenko to pull Gorodnyansky's army back, Stalin had temporarily lost much of his ability to restrain the German advance in that part of Russia. Paulus was quick to seize the advantage that this offered, and the German Sixth Army pushed onward and eastward to the River Volga, meeting comparatively little resistance by comparison with its recent experiences.

Meanwhile, in the South of the Crimea, Colonel-General Erich von Manstein, probably Germany's greatest military strategist of the war, was preparing to take Sebastopol. With the Russians gone from the North of the peninsula, he was able to devote all his forces to the attack on the besieged Russians, which began on June 7th. Reinforced with massive siege artillery and large numbers of the comparatively new *Nebelwerfer* rocket launchers, and supported as ever by the strafing and dive-bombing attacks of the *Luftwaffe*, against which the Russians had no effective remedy, Manstein's task looked straightforward. That it was not, and became a protracted and bloody battle, was entirely due to the tactical skill and bravery of the Russian commander, General Petrov, and of his eight divisions plus three brigades of Marines. Not until July 9th, five days after Hitler promoted von Manstein Field-Marshal, did the last defenders of Sebastopol surrender. Even then, their capitulation was due only to total exhaustion of their ammunition and water supplies. For the loss of just over 24,000 German dead, the invaders had captured 95,000 prisoners and 467 guns.

The Push to the Caucasus and Stalingrad

Throughout June and the first half of July, the 1st and 4th *Panzerarmee* under Colonel-Generals von Kleist and Hoth respectively maintained their advance towards the Caucasus, and General von Paulus' Sixth Army continued towards Stalingrad, as set out in Hitler's Directive for the summer offensive. But, in late July, Hitler's Directive No. 45 meddled with the original plan, and against the judgment of Halder, Hoth and Kleist, swung the *Panzer* armies South-East, away from their eastward course. General Paulus and his Sixth Army continued, in accordance with the original plan, towards Stalingrad, but without the support of the *Panzer* armies. This made his position progressively weaker as his supply line became more extended and his rear more vulnerable. By 15th August, four weeks later, after a slow advance hampered by lack of fuel and poor supplies of food, ammunition and medical supplies, General Paulus was close enough to Stalingrad to issue his orders for an attack upon the city.

The German assault on 15th August was in two waves. The 14th *Panzer* Division attacked the North of the city, defended by General Gordov, and by the 22nd of August was ensconced in the northern suburbs. On August 23rd, the 79th *Panzergrenadier* Regiment announced by radio that it was in the suburb of Spartanovka, on the Volga, commanding a view South over the southern suburbs. Stalin was not pleased, and for the next few crucial days took tactical command of operations himself, drawing to do so on his detailed personal knowledge of the city. When the Germans failed to make rapid progress in the southern part of Stalingrad, the *Luftwaffe* was called up to deliver a demoralising blow to the defenders, and *Luftflotte VIII* bombed both residential and commercial areas with a devastating rain of high explosive.

Once more, defective German intelligence hampered German planning and assisted the Russian defenders. The sheer size of Stalingrad had not been appreciated by the Germans, and their tactical plans had not taken account of the fact that the city extended 20 miles along the banks of the Volga. Perhaps more to the point, the assumption was made that the Russians were a demoralised and almost beaten enemy. In fact, Stalin was as determined to prevent Hitler taking Stalingrad as Hitler was determined to capture it, and massive reinforcements were poured in as the battle for the South of the city wore on. Everywhere, the Soviet troops displayed a toughness and a skill in street fighting that was quite unexpected by the Germans. The battle for Stalingrad stretched on through September and the Autumn and into the Winter, and by its nature deprived the Germans of their principal strengths – air support and skill in tank warfare. Reduced to street by street clearance of the Russian troops, the Germans found the Soviet army difficult to beat.

To the South, Army Group A's advance on the Caucasus had begun to peter out after the fall of Rostov, and Hitler had become enraged at the failure to make the rapid, searing progress that he had envisaged for the assault. After sending General Jodl to check on Field Marshal List's plans and strategy and receiving a report from Jodl that he agreed entirely with what List was doing and planning, Hitler dismissed Field Marshal List and, extraordinarily, took command for himself of Army Group A, in addition to his roles as Commander in Chief of OKW (Armed Forces High Command) and Commander in Chief of OKH (Army High Command). Hitler was now personally directing the attack on the Caucasus, and, to cap his other changes, dismissed General Halder from his position as Chief of Staff at OKW and appointed in his place the relatively inexperienced General Kurt Zeitzler, whose principal qualification for the task was that he could be relied upon not to disagree with the Fuehrer.

Defending the southern areas of Stalingrad, General Chuikov made the maximum use of the resistance to artillery fire offered by modern concrete commercial buildings, of which there were many in the city, and of the guerilla tactics of sniper fire and Molotov cocktails. More than 1,000 armed workers fought alongside the Russian troops in the defence of the city. At the end of August, on the 27th, Stalin reinforced the Russian armies around Stalingrad by sending Zhukov and the 24th, 66th and 1st Guards Armies to attack the Germans to the North of the City. After some initial failures, Zhukov launched a fierce offensive, supported by heavy bombing by General Golovanov's heavy bombers, but had to report to Stalin that he could not make sufficient headway against the 14th *Panzer* Division to be able to link up with the Russian defenders in the South of the city.

General Paulus' army was taking severe losses, but Hitler was determined to have Stalingrad. On September 12th, three *Panzer* Divisions and 11 infantry divisions were added to the German strength in the South of the city. Colonel-General Hoth's *panzers* had penetrated the southern suburb of Kuporosnoye, (thereby dividing the Russian armies) and had taken the high Mamaya Kurgan, which provided a commanding view of the city, but lost it again to the Russian 13th Guards in fierce hand to hand fighting on the 14th. Every day throughout September the Stukas dive-bombed, the shelling continued, and the bloodiest battles ebbed and flowed through the streets of Stalingrad.

At the beginning of October 1942, Paulus was ordered to take the city at any cost, and was supplied with five battalions of sappers to reinforce his efforts. Even this was not enough to ensure results, for the Russian forces continued to be reinforced nightly, as they had been in September, via ferry boats from the other side of the broad River Volga. For every new German that appeared at Stalingrad, there were several new Russians.

The suffering on both sides during the battle of Stalingrad was appalling. Bombing attacks reduced large areas of the city to rubble. German tanks climbed over that rubble to the attack and, not infrequently fell victim to snipers with anti-tank rifles, able to get a good shot while the tank was relatively immobile.

Civilians had either left and become homeless refugees on the other side of the Volga, or were being killed and maimed in the fighting. The Russian soldiers were being bombed, strafed, shot at and beleaguered from all sides. Yet still they held on.

Both sides planned massive attacks for 7th October. In the event the German assault started first, with two divisions attacking Chuikov's forces on Paulus' direct orders. They stood little chance of success and the attack resulted in enormous slaughter of German troops – almost four battalions were killed and dozens of tanks were destroyed. It has been said that this and other suicidal missions ordered by Paulus had their origin in Paulus' personal ambition to be promoted Field-Marshal once successful at Stalingrad, but it seems more likely that the Germans continued to underestimate the strength of the Russian forces, and their superiority in a street fighting environment.

On October 14th, a massive German push by two *Panzer* Divisions – the 14th and 24th – and two infantry divisions wrought appalling damage on the two major industrial areas of Stalingrad, known as 'Barricades' and 'Dzerzinsky', but, despite inflicting crushing damage, failed to make much headway. Not until a month later did the Germans succeed in penetrating the area of 'Barricades', and cutting off its defenders from the rest of the Russian 62nd Army. But even then, on November 11th, they were unable to press home the final force of their attack. For their men and machines were in a sad state – the two *Panzer* Divisions had fewer than 200 tanks between them, and the German infantry were at less than half strength. Every man was exhausted, most had minor wounds. All were hungry.

Stalingrad's Russian defenders were in a similarly poor state, but the German attacks of November 11th proved to be the last, and Chuikov at last had time to breathe again, albeit for a very short time. Winter was setting in, the ice was forming on the Volga, and once again the Russians planned a winter counter-offensive to take advantage of the Germans' poorer winter equipment and ability to withstand the cold. General Chuikov had only to hold his ground for a little longer.

Away from Stalingrad, Colonel-General von Kleist's 1st *Panzerarmee* had been ground to a halt only some 50 miles from the Groznyy oilfields, and had been unable to reach them. The German forces in the foothills of the Caucasus had been unable to complete the encircling movement that Hitler's Directive required of them. The German advance had come to an end.

The Sixth Army Forced to Surrender

On October 14th, Hitler had issued a Directive ordering all *Wehrmacht* Eastern Front offensives other than in Stalingrad and the Caucasus, to cease. The German forces in Russia were ordered to prepare for winter defence, and it was announced that the Red Army would be destroyed in 1943. He and Zeitzler had decided, again apparently on the basis of intelligence that the Soviet armies had little in reserve, that no Russian offensive would be possible this winter. All the *Wehrmacht* had to do was wait for spring.

In fact, Stalin and Zhukov had spent a large part of October planning alternative versions of a major offensive. The offensive in the North, on the River Don, was to be very similar in concept to that which, in August 1942, Hitler had himself warned could occur – foresight which he seemed to have abandoned by November. Codenamed 'Saturn', the northern offensive was to break through the German line and retake a line from Rostov to Milerovo. The alternative plan for a southerly offensive, known as 'Uranus', sought to break through at two points simultaneously North and South of the German Sixth Army some sixty miles West of Stalingrad, and encircle the much weakened German forces in the battle-torn city.

Stalin, Vasilievsky and Zhukov opted for 'Uranus', and, on 19th November, ten days after the 'Torch' landings in North Africa, the carefully planned offensive was launched after weeks of personal briefings by Zhukov and his colleagues of all the commanders in the field. To the operation the Russians brought 1,000,500 men, 13,541 guns, 894 tanks and 1,115 aircraft. Bad weather hampered routine German reconnaissance, and the Germans had little or no idea of what was about to hit them. It has been suggested that 'Uranus' was the greatest surprise the *Wehrmacht* ever received.

The initial attack was to the North of Stalingrad. After an artillery barrage through freezing fog, Russian infantry poured down upon Rumanian Axis troops, who fought vigorously to defend their positions. Unclear as to exactly what was happening, Hitler sent orders from his HQ at Vinnitsa that General Heim's 48th *Panzerkorps* should attack towards Kletskaya. This did not work because the enemy was somewhere else, and the unfortunate Heim lost valuable time and tactical advantage. Instead he found himself facing General Romanenko's 5th Tank Army in the snow, which caused panic among the Rumanian infantry. The 1st Rumanian Armoured Division was virtually annihilated, and the breakthrough in the North was achieved. Late on the 19th, Hitler ordered Paulus to deal with the gap in his defences to the North, not knowing that the next morning would see even bigger events to the South of the line.

Next morning, General Eremenko's southern offensive began with an artillery barrage at 10am, again in freezing fog. The Rumanian 6th Corps surrendered, and what was left of the 4th *Panzerarmee* had to withdraw at considerable speed to avoid being encircled and trapped. Two days later, General Volsky's advance over-ran the positions of the German headquarters, and by November 23rd, the Russian forces of the northern and southern attacks had met at the village of Sovetsky to complete the encirclement of the Axis forces in Stalingrad.

To the utter amazement of the unfortunate General Paulus, Hitler sent a telegram commanding him to 'adopt a hedgehog position' and await relief 'when it was convenient'. Paulus swiftly sent a signal back to Hitler telling him that the situation was desperate, that ammunition and petrol supplies were running out, and that the only available course of action was to break out by delivering a knockout blow to the encircling Russians. Colonel-General Weichs, who was still in contact with Paulus, supported this view. He told Hitler that it would be impossible to supply an army of 22 divisions from the air, and that an offensive to relieve Stalingrad could not possibly be launched until December 10th, by which time the 6th Army's position would be desperate in the extreme. Hitler replied, after some hours, with a new order to Paulus to hold Stalingrad at all costs, apparently based on boastful and groundless assurances from Hermann Goering that 500 tons of supplies per day would be dropped to the besieged army by the *Luftwaffe*.

In fact, as winter set in, and the much improved Soviet Air Force took its toll of *Luftwaffe* supply aircraft, the average drop of supplies reaching Stalingrad from December 1st to 12th was only 97.3 tons per day. In the second half of December the figure rose to just over 135 tons per day, then it fell again as the winter weather and the worsening military position made the airlift more difficult. The deficiency of supplies by comparison with Goering's estimate was 81% over the whole 70 days of the airlift, and the Germans lost 488 aircraft, including 266 valuable Ju52 transports.

Besieged within the city and immediately around it, Paulus had 278,000 men and their equipment. The task of relieving the city and making possible the rescue of the 6th Army was given to Field Marshal Erich von Manstein, who had just been given the command, in the third week of November, of a new Army Group, to be called 'Army Group Don'. On November 27th, his command was reinforced by the arrival of the first units of the 6th *Panzer* Division, assigned to him from France. Once the whole division had arrived, it added 160 tanks, 42 self-propelled guns and a battalion of half-tracks to his much depleted strength – by now the 4th *Panzerarmee* amounted to little more than one Corps. The 23rd *Panzer* Division, imported from the Caucasus, had only 20 tanks, and the 17th had only 30.

On December 12th-13th, the Germans succeeded in crossing the Aksai River, and, by December 16th were within 30 miles of Stalingrad after battling 50 miles in eight days. But they were not to succeed, for the Russians launched an attack under Zhukov to destroy the Rumanian 3rd Army and the Italian 8th Army, and thereby open the way for an advance to Rostov. Manstein's plan to bring the 48th *Panzer* Corps across the Don to reinforce the advance on Stalingrad had to be abandoned, and that in turn made it necessary to call the 6th *Panzer* Corps back across the Don to counter the Russian offensive. The attempt to relieve Stalingrad was effectively over.

As the New Year came and went, the situation of the Sixth Army became more desperate, and the extent of the criminal disregard of reality by Hitler and Goering in asserting that they could be supplied from the air became clearer. As the Russians advanced towards Rostov, the *Luftwaffe* was obliged to retreat to new bases, which lengthened its flights to the besieged city. General Paulus and his men were starving, virtually without fuel and ammunition, victims of Hitler's megalomaniacal zeal for unattainable victory. On January 8th, the Russians offered Paulus surrender terms under flag of truce. Paulus made no reply. Two days later, the Russians attacked the half-starved German army around Stalingrad with 7,000 guns and mortars. Gradually the Russians closed in, capturing on January 17th the airfield at Gumrak, the last at which German aircraft could land to bring supplies to Paulus' army. On January 26th, after Hitler had ignored Paulus' appeal to be allowed to surrender, the Russians drove a wedge between two halves of the 6th Army, separating the 71st, 113th, 297th and Rumanian 20th Divisions from Paulus' command. All were obliged to surrender. Finally, on the 31st January 1943, Paulus, newly and cynically promoted Field-Marshal by Hitler, apparently on grounds of superstition because Hitler had noted that no German Field-Marshal had ever surrendered, decided that the end had come. Honourably and with dignity, he surrendered to the Russian General Shumilov. But even that was not the end of the Stalingrad tragedy. General Strecker, commanding the northern pocket of the besieged army, held out until February 2nd. He and his men were the last of the betrayed to surrender.

STALEMATE IN BURMA

WINGATE, THE CHINDITS, AND THE BURMA ROAD

An earlier chapter has described, as a part of the story of Japan's whirlwind conquest of South East Asia, the series of events that culminated in the Japanese occupation of Burma, and the Allies' departure to India. As a prelude to subsequent events in this theatre of the war, it is worth taking a look at the reasons why Japan bothered to capture Burma in the first place, and at why she did not then go on to attack India.

The events of 1942 to 1945 in Burma had their origins in Japan's struggle with China, which had begun with the Japanese occupation of Manchuria in 1931 following a faked bomb outrage against Japanese possessions, and their creation of the puppet state of Manchukuo. The League of Nations, to which China had protested, had ineffectually urged Japan to desist from her occupation of Chinese territory, and had been totally ignored. Since, as was always the case, no member of the League was prepared to do more than express displeasure, however grave the crime, it seemed that there was no country prepared to stand up to Japan.

The United States, a neutral and an isolationist power, was not a member of the League of Nations, had a close relationship with China, and was disturbed that another major Pacific power was acting aggressively, so warned Japan that their sovereignty over territory seized by force would not be recognised. Although this achieved little at the time, the gesture strengthened the ties between the USA and China, and created permanent US distrust of Japanese intentions. By 1937, when Japan invaded the Chinese mainland in force, Japan had signed the Anti-Comintern Pact with Hitler, had made her belief in the destiny of Japan to rule South East Asia clear to those who would listen, and was becoming a formidable military power. By 1939, after a protracted and bloody war, the North and the Eastern coastal strip of China were largely occupied by Japan, but the West and South-West were held by Chinese troops under General Chiang Kai-shek, who continued to fight bravely and well and to contain further Japanese advances. But Chiang Kai-shek had an enemy within as well as the enemy without. Mao Tse-Tung and his Communist revolution sought to dislodge Chiang's hold on China for other reasons, and the USSR, then as now, had every reason to support the revolution that might enable a Communist government to seize power.

Thus a complex situation existed in which the Russians were concerned lest the Japanese should capture China, inhibit Mao's revolution and knock at the Eastern door of the Soviet Union; the USA was worried lest the Japanese should over-run their Chinese friends, and the British were concerned that a Japanese victory would position an aggressive Japan just North and East of British possessions. The key to the exercise, Britain and America agreed, rested in maintaining supplies to Chiang Kai-shek via the Burma Road, which ran through the mountains from Lashio, in northern Burma to Chungking, Chiang Kai-shek's capital, and along which vital supplies of arms, fuel and food could be convoyed through incredibly rugged terrain.

When France fell to Germany in June 1940, and Britain was hard-pressed at home, the Japanese applied pressure to Britain to close the road, implying that not to do so would result in severe Japanese reprisals. In the circumstances Britain could do little else but accept the situation, and cut off supplies to Chiang. So, in October 1940, Chiang asked the USA for a fleet of aircraft and pilots to fly his supplies over what became known as the 'hump' – the Eastern Himalayas – from Assam to China. Roosevelt agreed, and in November 1941 the American Volunteer Group was formed with 100 aircraft and pilots under Colonel Claire Chennault, a former US Army Air Force officer. US Lend Lease was now supplying war materials to the Allies in considerable quantities, so far larger supplies of arms began to be flown to Chiang Kai-shek than had been envisaged originally – and there was always the nagging doubt in American minds that Chiang was using the arms more to hold back Mao's Chinese communists than to fight the Japanese. Therefore, Roosevelt sent General Stilwell to act as Chiang's military adviser, and mastermind the training of the Chinese to give the Japanese a hard time.

By April 1942 the Japanese had taken Burma, primarily to close the Burma Road and remove the possibility of Chiang being supplied by road. Because the existing Burma Road started so far to the North-East, at Lashio, Stilwell and Britain's General Wavell, now Commander in Chief in India following his replacement in the Middle East, decided they would set as their objective the recapture of central Burma and the building of a new road, from Ledo to Kunming. Stilwell therefore began the task of training and re-equipping as many Chinese divisions as he could, and Wavell seized upon a brilliant idea originally conceived by the highly individualistic, academically inclined and even slightly eccentric Brigadier-General Orde Wingate. The idea was the formation of a long-range penetration group, to prove Wingate's belief that victory in South-East Asia could be achieved only by an army prepared to fight in the jungle, away from the confines of the few vulnerable roads and rivers, and willing to accept the hazards of being supplied from the air when necessary. His group became known as the Chindits.

The Chindits were a small force of highly-trained, immensely fit, lightly equipped guerilla marauders who were dropped from the air far behind Japanese lines to harass and disorientate the Japanese troops in the jungle. They were supplied entirely from the air, and their support team was equipped with a remarkable American short take-off and landing aircraft known as the L1, which enabled them to get Chindit wounded out to base hospitals from relatively small clearings and narrow river banks. The attitude of the Chindits was summarised by Wingate's famous telegram – 'The impossible we do in a day. Miracles take a little longer.'

In February 1943, 3,000 Chindits embarked on their first operation, a four-month excursion into Burma to attack the Japanese from behind. In several senses, the operation was a success. It proved conclusively that Wingate's basic contention, backed by General Wavell, was correct. A small, highly mobile force could survive for months in the jungle, doing a great deal of a damage to its enemy, while being totally dependent on radio communication and supply from the air. The operation showed that well-trained guerilla troops could cross the heavily defended River Chindwin, despite the all-conquering Japanese presence. It demonstrated to the Japanese that they could not expect the land war to go their way for ever.

Nonetheless, the first Chindit operation cost many lives. Of the 3,000 men who went in by glider and on foot, only 2,200 returned to be the nucleus of the second and far more ambitious Chindit raid. This did not take place until the beginning of 1944, when, over five days from March 5th, a considerable fleet of Allied aircraft transported 9,000 of the Long Range Penetration Group to air strips that had been prepared earlier by smaller Chindit groups, 161 kilometres behind the Japanese lines at Indaw. Later that same month, Orde Wingate, now a Major-General, was killed at the age of 41 in an air crash in Burma. His loss was a sad blow to the Allies.

During the long period from mid 1942, when the Japanese were consolidating their hold on Burma, to the winter of 1943/44, the Burma front was almost entirely stalemated. The Japanese, having cut the Burma Road, seemed disinclined to devote more effort to the capture of territory in the Indian subcontinent, and the Allies lacked the resources to do more than contain the Japanese in their current positions. General Wavell's attempt in the Spring of 1943 to recapture Akyab, on the west coast of the Arakan peninsula, failed for lack of amphibious support from the sea – the landing craft had been appropriated for operations against the Vichy French in Madagascar – and achieved little. But during the 1943/44 winter, both sides began to brew some action for early 1944. The Japanese had recognised that, although the Burma Road was not available for Chiang Kai-shek's supply line, the US Air Force was achieving significant successes with their airlift of supplies over the 'hump', and resolved to close the air route. To do this, they decided to attack and cut the Bengal-Assam railway, which connected the port of Calcutta with the India railhead used for Chiang's supplies.

The Allies meanwhile, by now under the command of Admiral Lord Louis Mountbatten with Stilwell as his deputy, had resolved to launch attacks by General Stilwell's by now well-trained Chinese forces towards Myitkyina, by the British 14th Army towards Indaw, and by Chiang Kai-shek's army westward across the Salween River from China. The 14th Army was also to take Akyab.

In the event, the Japanese offensive began first, and in the early stages made strong progress through the Arakan hills to outflank the forward units of the 14th Army. But the commander of the 14th Army was one of the truly remarkable Generals of the Second World War – General (later Field Marshal) Sir William Slim. Keeping cool, and assessing that the principal strength of the Japanese lay in their skill in jungle warfare, and that their main weakness was in open battle, Slim withdrew to two highly defensible positions at Imphal and Kohima. There he made his stand, and wrought a defeat that was the beginning of the end for the Japanese in Burma.

U.S. COUNTER-ATTACK

DRAMA IN THE PACIFIC – GUADALCANAL

The Battle of Midway had brought harsh realisation to Japan that they had not wrought at Pearl Harbor the devastation of the US Pacific Fleet that they had intended, even believed, and that they now had little hope of bringing about the destruction of the fleet at sea. The easternmost line of the Japanese Empire seemed stationary at the point where Midway had stopped it – from the Aleutians in the North, past Wake Island to the Gilbert Islands.

In the West, Japan had wisely decided not to emulate Hitler's Napoleonic dreams of conquering Russia, and had advanced no further than her prewar positions along the coastal strip of eastern China and in Manchuria. In Burma, Japan had stopped short of pushing South into India. There was only one place left into which Japan might profitably and with some prospect of success attempt to expand – the southern part of New Guinea and the southern Solomon Islands. From airfields there, the Japanese would be able to bomb and disrupt the vital Allied shipping routes between the USA and Australia, where General MacArthur was building the Allied forces for a counter-attack. Despite the Allied policy of defeating Germany first, a large proportion of the Allied reinforcements that were available for all theatres were being diverted to Australia – for every American soldier sent to Europe in the first half of 1942, four were sent to the Pacific theatre, and Australian units in the Middle East were withdrawn to defend the homeland.

In July 1942, US Intelligence became aware that the Japanese were building an air base on the island of Guadalcanal, at almost the extreme southern tip of the Solomon Islands. The threat was clear and immediate. A plan that had already been agreed and briefed to senior commanders for an amphibious invasion in the Solomon Islands was put into effect. At dawn on August 7th, eight months to the day after the Japanese attack on Pearl Harbor, a massive bombardment from the sea heralded the arrival of the first major seaborne invasion fleet of the Second World War off Guadalcanal and its nearby smaller islands, all of them heavily defended by the Japanese.

Three hours after the Navy's bombardment began, the gunfire ceased and the US Marines under Major-General Vandegrift landed with an initial deceptive lack of opposition. They captured the airfield that was still under construction, fought out a few short sharp engagements on the surrounding islands, and then paused, wondering when the trouble would start. They were not left wondering for long. Two days after the initial landings, a Japanese Naval force struck suddenly at the US Navy off Guadalcanal and sank four ships, one of them Australian, before disappearing as suddenly as it had come, without attacking the many vulnerable transport vessels that were sitting duck targets.

Over the next two months, with periodic harassment from the Japanese, the US Marines built up their presence on the island until more than 17,000 troops were on the exposed area around the airfield. Japanese naval vessels bombarded the US troops and their supply ships at increasingly short intervals, and detachments of Japanese troops were sent by sea from Rabaul. Two and a half months after the original August landings, in late October, the Japanese chanced their arm on a major carrier sea battle, sending a task force that included four of their aircraft carriers to the area of the Pacific North of the island. Two US Navy aircraft carrier forces went out to meet them, one led by the *Hornet*, the other by the *Enterprise*, the whole operation being under the command of Admiral Thomas Kinkaid.

The fierce naval gunnery and air battle that followed, known as the Battle of the Santa Cruz Islands, resulted in the Japanese losing two destroyers, and having two carriers and two battleships badly damaged. Japanese dive bombers inflicted severe damage on the USS *Hornet*, which was subsequently sunk by Japanese naval gunfire with considerable loss of life. But the battle did nothing to conclude the matter of Guadalcanal. Just over two weeks later, the Japanese Navy once again attempted to re-establish its dominance on Guadalcanal and repel the American invasion. A large Imperial Navy task force carrying troops to reinforce the Japanese forces still on Guadalcanal arrived during the night of November 13th, and the two battleships and many smaller warships of the Japanese fleet began furiously to shell the American fleet. In the darkness a considerable melee developed, and the Japanese, in what can only be described as the naval equivalent of close hand-to-hand fighting, lost a battleship. The US Navy lost two cruisers, one of them, the *Juneau*, with 700 men aboard, including a family of five brothers named Sullivan. Two other US ships were damaged, but the US emerged from the first night of the Naval Battle of Guadalcanal bloody but unbowed.

The next night aircraft from the USS *Enterprise* did severe damage to another smaller Japanese squadron, but the major turning point came when US aircraft from the captured airfield on Guadalcanal, now known as Henderson Field, scored a major victory by sinking seven and damaging the remaining four of a force of eleven transport vessels bringing Japanese troops to the island. Now the Japanese gathered up their remaining naval resources in the area for a last try at getting a significant force of reinforcements ashore. A battleship and four cruisers approached Guadalcanal at high speed along the infamous channel between the islands known as 'The Slot'. As they came from one direction, Admiral Willis A. Lee and a US Navy flotilla approached from the other. Lee hurled his force precipitately but effectively into the battle, and claimed another battleship sunk and two more cruisers damaged. By the next day, the Japanese knew they had lost another round, and with it the naval battle of Guadalcanal, for they simply did not have sufficient naval forces remaining in the area to pursue the attack.

Now the Japanese land forces in the densely overgrown jungle of Guadalcanal were on their own without potential for reinforcement, and the young and, until now, almost entirely inexperienced US Marines began the task of flushing out skilled Japanese jungle-trained troops from what was virtually their natural environment. Tackling this task amid heat, discomfort, decomposing vegetation and the risks of poisonous reptiles and insects, often racked with dysentery, malaria and a host of minor ills, the Marines, whose average age was only nineteen years, also had to face the even greater risk of encountering suicidally motivated Japanese snipers. Despite these privations, they methodically fought their way across the island, winkling out pockets of Japanese soldiers from caves and dugouts as they went.

During the first week of February 1943, the Japanese decided that they had little chance of success on Guadalcanal, and sent in the Imperial Navy at night to evacuate the remaining Japanese troops, some 12,000 of them, from Cape Esperance on the North-Western corner of the island. Their evacuation was almost totally successful. At last, Guadalcanal was in American hands, the Japanese had been defeated on land for the first time, and American morale shot sky-high. Now the Marine Corps, having earned a brief respite, built and equipped a rest and retraining centre among the palm trees of Guadalcanal. In the months that followed it was to be sorely needed, for Tokyo, the ultimate goal of the US island hopping campaign across the Pacific, was still 3,000 miles away.

The US forces had lost 1,600 dead during the campaign for Guadalcanal, with just over 4,700 wounded. The Japanese losses were astronomical. No less than 24,000 Japanese soldiers died. The Japanese Navy lost 1 aircraft carrier, 2 battleships, 4 cruisers, 11 destroyers, 6 submarines (including their semi-experimental giant I-1 sub) and 16 transport vessels. The US Navy lost 2 carriers, 8 cruisers, 17 destroyers, 6 MTBs and 4 transports. It had been an expensive but, from the Allies' standpoint, necessary campaign.

CASABLANCA
STRENGTHENING OF THE ALLIANCE AND THE BALANCE OF POWER

After a year of America's participation in the war, the extent of the political manoeuvre and counter-manoeuvre between the Allied leaders seemed to be increasing rather than decreasing as 1943 began. The previous year had seen endless discussion between Roosevelt and Churchill and their respective political advisers and generals on the strategic objectives that the Allies should adopt. 'Bolero', the building and training of a potential invasion force for the opening of a second front on continental Europe, had been agreed as a policy early in 1942, and put into effect. 'Sledgehammer', the creation of a limited bridgehead in Europe, was still in the discussion stage. 'Roundup', the full scale invasion of Europe from the United Kingdom, for which General Dwight D. Eisenhower had been campaigning, had been abandoned as a short term objective in July/ August 1942, much to the displeasure of Josef Stalin, who raged at Churchill and accused Britain of cowardice when Britain's Prime Minister went to Moscow to discuss strategy in August. Instead of 'Roundup', which Churchill knew was far beyond the Allies' state of preparedness in 1942, Operation Torch had been mounted against French North Africa, and had been successful.

The second Battle of Alamein had changed the character of the war in North Africa, and it was clear that the days of domination of the Western Desert by the Axis were past. In the Pacific, the year that had begun so catastrophically with Japan's sweep through the islands; with Corregidor; with Singapore; had suddenly become the year of Midway and Guadalcanal and the dawning of the realisation that the Japanese could be and would be defeated. The year had ended with the Germans encircled at Stalingrad, and faltering on their drive to the Caucasus. There were undoubtedly more successes to the Allies' credit than they might have dared to hope just a few months earlier. As Winston Churchill said in a speech at the Mansion House in the City of London; 'This must not be taken as the end; it may possibly be the beginning of the end; but it is certainly the end of the beginning'.

The political discussions at the end of 1942 had extended even to lengthy arguments about who should be allowed to take part in the discussions. Roosevelt and Churchill agreed that a conference was necessary to determine future policy, but Churchill, who showed a frank dislike and mistrust of Stalin, wanted to meet Roosevelt and agree a common strategic policy for the future conduct of the war with which jointly to confront Stalin. Roosevelt disagreed, believing that to be seen to conspire against Stalin would be intensely damaging to the future of the alliance with Russia. In the event, Stalin resolved that particular conundrum by pointedly declining to attend the Casablanca conference on the grounds that his army was busy defeating Germany at Stalingrad, and he had better things to do.

Thus the conference that assembled in two luxurious rented villas high in the hills behind Casablanca between January 14th and 23rd 1943 consisted only of Roosevelt and Churchill and their chiefs of staff, with their entourages and aides housed in a nearby hotel. Essentially, the conference was faced with deciding two major, fundamental and interdependent issues. The first was the balance of war resources to be allotted to the European war on the one hand, and to the Pacific war on the other. The second was the question of whether the Allied invasion of Europe should be from the Mediterranean during 1943, or across the Channel from Britain, probably rather later.

The British team, often subsequently accused of railroading the US delegation to accepting their viewpoint, certainly came better equipped with a closely argued case than did their US counterparts. The fact that Churchill was now Britain's Minister of Defence as well as her Prime Minister, and his effective role as Commander in Chief and pivot of all policy, ensured that the facts and figures presented in support of the British contention that Europe should be invaded from the Mediterranean were almost incontrovertible. Churchill had in fact argued strongly before the conference for the original 'Roundup' plan for a cross-channel invasion during 1943 following the success of Operation Torch, but had eventually been dissuaded by his service chiefs on the basis of the sheer weight of evidence that showed such a plan not to be practical. That the Allies agreed that the defeat of Germany must be given a higher priority than the humbling of Japan was already settled – the only question was one of degree.

General George C. Marshall and the US military staff argued strongly that the resources allocated to the Pacific should be sufficient to permit offensive action against the Japanese and to prevent them being able to choose their times and places for battle. The US planners proposed Pacific offensives from the Solomons and New Guinea to New Britain and Rabaul, through the Gilbert, the Marshall and the Caroline Islands to the Japanese naval base at Truk, and against Japanese positions in the Aleutians to regain the islands of Kiska and Agattu. In Burma, the Americans postulated, the time had come for a land based offensive to re-open the Burma Road, and for a seaborne invasion of Burma, both with the objective of making Chiang Kai-shek's forces better supplied and more available as an effective ally – an asset of whose value the British were by now somewhat doubtful. The American viewpoint on the European invasion remained, as it had been a year earlier, strongly in favour of a head-on cross-channel confrontation with the German Army. The US military staff believed that the war would and could be shortened by a cross-channel invasion in 1943.

The British position was more circumspect in its approach. In the first place, great stress was laid upon the necessity of winning the Battle of the Atlantic and defeating the U-Boat menace. If the convoys did not get through from the USA to Europe and from Britain to the USSR, the war with Germany might well be lost. The British military staff, with memories of the huge and bloody stalemate of the trenches of 1914-18, did not believe in the advisability of a full-scale confrontation with the German Army until the Allied armies were stronger, and the German armies were weaker. Since the scale of the German defeat at Stalingrad, and the probability of further major disasters for Germany in the East, suggested that time would certainly weaken the might of the Third Reich, Britain favoured a waiting game. Nevertheless, to hasten the weakening of Germany's resources,

Britain proposed an increased bombing offensive to damage further German armaments production and her ability to supply her armies and air force, and an invasion of Italy from the Mediterranean. In the Pacific, the British position was that no more than the offensives from the Solomons and New Guinea, and limited operations in Burma to open road communication to Chiang Kai-shek and, possibly, to recapture Akyab, were desirable or feasible in 1943 given the available budget.

Not surprisingly, after four days of wearisome conference discussion, the two sides were poles apart in their proposals. General Sir Alan Brooke, the British Chief of the Imperial General Staff, argued for many hours with General Marshall over the issue of the cross-channel invasion, making the point that Germany could, in 1943, mass 44 divisions in France without withdrawing any from Russia, and that it was strategically sounder to invade Italy and force Italy out of the war. This, he argued, would oblige Germany to find troops to replace the Italian garrisons in the Balkans, would deprive Germany of the Italian troops currently fighting in Russia, and would improve the Allies' position in North Africa if that were still a problem at the time of the Italians' defeat.

Gradually, Marshall's colleagues were forced to recognise the merits of other aspects of the British case. It was agreed that an invasion of Italy would disperse German air power, and make effective bombing of German industry more possible. Admiral King came to support a landing in Sicily. Eventually General Marshall came round to accepting the Mediterranean concept, and a Memorandum on the Conduct of the War in 1943 was drawn up for signature. Essentially this allocated the greater part of Allied resources to the defeat of Germany in 1943, but allocated 'adequate forces ... to the Pacific and Far Eastern theatres'. A 'full scale offensive against Japan by the United Nations' was promised 'as soon as Germany is defeated'. The Mediterranean was to be the principal area of Allied effort, and Sicily the first target. The 'defeat of the U-boats remains first charge on resources' the Memorandum stated, and it went on that 'Russia must be sustained by greatest volume of supplies ... without prohibitive cost in shipping'.

Having reached agreement on policy, the Casablanca conference now tackled the task of planning how to achieve the agreed objectives. The conference agreed that the bombing of the yards where U-boats were built and maintained should be stepped up; that the shortage of escort vessels for Atlantic convoys must be rectified. The strategic bombing offensive against German industry was agreed in detail, including what proved to be the immensely costly and relatively ineffective US precision daylight bombing by unescorted formations. The invasion of Sicily – Operation Husky – was scheduled for the end of August, and it was agreed that the build-up of US forces in Britain for the eventual cross-Channel invasion should be continued.

Perhaps the most significant outcome of the Casablanca conference was the decision to accept nothing less than total surrender from Germany and Japan – the so-called 'total surrender policy'. Although arguably a propaganda-inspired decision to appease Stalin's scathing view of his (as he saw it) weak-kneed allies, a view that could be expected to become still more disparaging when he learned that there was to be no cross-Channel invasion early in 1943, the 'total surrender policy' was also a reflection of the realisation that much of the cause of the Second World War lay in the inconclusive ending of the first. Germany had been left with a feeling of 'unfinished business' as well as her sense of betrayal at the terms of Versailles. The Allies did not intend that the Second World War should end with an undefeated Germany or Japan hungering for a chance to start the third.

The Casablanca conference was one of the most significant meetings of the war, and represented the point at which the US and British conflicts of viewpoint were finally reconciled into a cohesive joint policy that was followed by both sides of the alliance. Had the nations of the Axis been as successful in meeting, reconciling their opposing viewpoints and putting common policies into action, the war may have followed a different course. Rarely in history has unity been such a source of strength.

TUNISIA

AND THE END OF THE AFRIKA CORPS

The autumn of 1942 had brought major Allied successes in North Africa. Having been roundly defeated by the British 8th Army at El Alamein, Field Marshal Rommel was, during November, retreating as fast as he could to Tunisia, in the hope that he would be able to inflict there a crushing defeat on the recently arrived American and British forces under General Eisenhower. Because the agreed plan for Operation Torch had precluded any landing where fighter air cover was not available, there had been no Allied landings East of Algiers, some 400 miles from Tunis. Rommel knew that, if he could get to Tunis soon enough, the potential was there for inflicting considerable damage on the British 1st Army formation under Lieutenant-General Anderson.

The German and Italian High Commands, not for the first time, saw things rather differently. Hitler ordered Rommel to hold and defend the position at Marsa el Brega, which General Montgomery and the Eighth Army approached on December 13th 1942. The Italians had earlier ordered him to hold the Sollum-Halfaya line, a patent impossibility given the great superiority of equipment that Montgomery's army had after Alamein, and Rommel had treated the Italian command with the contempt it deserved. However, the Fuehrer's order to hold Marsa el Brega, on the extreme western edge of Cyrenaica, was not entirely without merit. Field Marshal Kesselring, no mean tactician, believed that Montgomery's advance could have been delayed for weeks or even months if he had been made to fight for the 700 miles between Marsa el Brega and Gabes, a town in Tunisia on the western side of the great gulf that forms the Libyan coast. Rommel nonetheless resolved to retreat from Libya as rapidly as possible, believing that if the remains of *Panzerarmee Afrika* made a stand, it would achieve little, and that by strategic withdrawal to Tunis and Bizerta, the veterans of the *Afrika Korps* could first take part in the battle in Tunisia, and then, if that went badly, as Rommel believed it would, be repatriated safely to Europe to continue the war.

In fact, although by his retreat he envisaged lending the weight of his army to the Axis defence of Tunisia, he also assisted the Allied assault on Tunisia by bringing Montgomery's 8th Army to bear on the South-East of the country as Eisenhower's forces, including the British 1st Army under General Anderson, attacked in the North-West. Throughout the latter part of November and December, the build-up of German forces in Tunisia under Colonel-General Hans-Jurgen von Arnim had continued. After December 8th, these were known as the 5th *Panzerarmee*, and by December 31st, von Arnim was in command of 47,000

German troops and more than 17,000 Italians, a battalion of Tiger tanks and the 10th *Panzer* Division, brought in from a comparatively peaceful existence in France. The *Luftwaffe* in North Africa, under the energetic overseeing eye of Kesselring, had been extensively re-equipped and had during December regained effective control of Tunisian airspace, thereby limiting drastically the availability of photo-reconnaissance information to the Allies, and wreaking destruction on Allied supply convoys and troop movements.

Since the negotiated armistice with the French forces in North Africa following Operation Torch in November, substantial French formations had become available to Eisenhower, and the resourceful Frenchmen had miraculously 'rediscovered' large stocks of pre-war vintage arms that had been concealed from the Armistice Commission after the fall of France in June 1940. The French 19th Corps in particular was well dug into defensive positions on the Eastern Dorsale, a mountainous area overlooking the coastal plain of Tunisia, in the vicinity of the holy city of Kairouan and the coastal ports of Sousse and Sfax, and the Barre Group was similarly dug in along the Medjerda River. Their task was to cover the US forces entering the front line between Gafsa and the Mediterranean, along the western edge of Tunisia.

On January 18th 1943, a German force of infantry and tanks attacked and surprised the Barre Group, completely outclassing their outdated French guns with the latest Tiger tanks. Von Arnim followed up this success at the Medjerda River with a push south, but was repulsed by a counter attack by the US Army II Corps. The inability of the French troops, equipped as they were, to fight the German formations on equal terms lent support to changes in the command structure brought about by the Casablanca conference, which took place in Morocco at the same time as these events were occurring. From the beginning of 1943, the French troops were absorbed directly into the British 1st Army. General Juin, who had commanded the French forces in North Africa, was given the task of creating and training the French Expeditionary Corps, later to play an important part in the battle of Monte Cassino.

At the end of January, Rommel finally withdrew from Tripoli and into Tunisia, and viewed with some scepticism the arrival in Tunisia of General Giovanni Messe to command the new Italian 1st Army, made up of the German and Italian Axis forces pulled back from Tripoli. Rommel's view of Italian military achievement was never enthusiastic, and the idea of handing over his command to an Italian General did not appeal to him at all. However, since he was organising the defences along the Mareth line, and had not been recalled as expected by OKW, Rommel decided to make use of the unexpectedly long time that Montgomery was taking to move up to the attack. He embarked upon an assault against the US Army II Corps, which was comparatively close to his forces, in the mountainous area to the West of his positions. Rommel knew that, by virtue of his own position between Montgomery and the Americans, there was little likelihood of the British 8th Army being able to assist their Allies, and reinforcements for his army were arriving steadily, although he was still very short of tanks and artillery. Leaving two Italian Corps and the German 90th and 164th Light Divisions at the Mareth line to keep Montgomery busy, he pulled together at Sfax the 10th and 21st *Panzer* Divisions under Lieutenant-General Ziegler, and the Italian 'Centauro' Armoured Division and his own *Afrika Korps* under his own command. Ziegler's formation was given the task of a surprise attack against Major-General Orlando Ward's 1st US Armoured Division at Faid Pass, while Rommel's force was to head South-West to Gafsa. Once they had succeeded in their initial objectives, the two formations were to join at Sbeitla and attack the Allied position in the Grande Dorsale.

Ziegler's surprise attack at Faid on February 14th was entirely successful, and disorganised the thinly-spread American defending force so much that II Corps withdrew entirely into the Grande Dorsale. Next day Rommel, in the confusion, took Gafsa without a shot being fired, and the two German columns merged for their assault upon the Grande Dorsale. At this point, Rommel, whose position thus far in the command structure had been somewhat vague, was belatedly appointed to the command of a new 'Army Group Africa', perhaps to try and bring him under control. Undeterred by his regained authority, Rommel pressed on, and, after an initial reverse when the French 19th Corps repulsed the 21st *Panzer* Division at Shiba Pass, the 19th *Panzer* Division broke through the Kasserine Pass and headed for Tebessa over the Algerian border, an important supply centre for the Allies. Rommel wanted to push on quickly, as he had done so often before, and take not only Tebessa but also Bone, thereby cutting the British 1st Army's communications and greatly delaying the expected Allied offensive.

Rommel's success rattled the command structures of both the Allies and the Axis. The Allies saw the probability of Rommel attacking Tebessa and argued about the steps to take if he did. The Axis split three ways – von Arnim wanting to hold the assault at Kasserine, Kesselring supporting Rommel's plan and the Italian *Comando Supremo* overriding all of them with an order to turn North-West and attack along a line from Thala to Le Kef, right into the positions of the greatest Allied strength. Rommel was appalled at the order – but did as he was told, meeting fierce and well-organised resistance from the British 6th Armoured Division. Not surprisingly, with his supplies running low, Rommel's attack failed. But the ten days of actions had cost the Americans over 4,000 prisoners, almost 3,000 dead and substantial losses of equipment.

Now Rommel turned South again with his 10th and 21st *Panzer* Divisions to join Messe and Ziegler in tackling Montgomery's impending attack at the Mareth Line – an assault by the German armour from the mountains to Medenine and the Gulf of Gabes, designed to surprise Montgomery's army in the rear, while the Italian 1st Army attacked the British head-on from the front. Typically, the cautious yet intuitive Montgomery guessed what the Axis plan was likely to be, and prepared a welcome for when the attack came on March 6th. A precision artillery barrage pinned down the German attack with deadly effect. The Germans lost 52 tanks; the British just one Sherman.

This misguided offensive, which Rommel knew could not succeed, was the last of Rommel's battles in Africa. He received orders to return to Germany, and Colonel-General von Arnim became the commander of Army Group Africa. But von Arnim faced an impossible task. His supply lines were being harassed on land, and the shipping that brought his reinforcements, his fuel and his replacement vehicles was being decimated by the ever more effective Allied Mediterranean fleet. Knowing that the Axis forces were gradually being hemmed in, the Allied commanders formulated a plan to bring the Tunisian campaign to a successful end in time for the landings in Sicily to go ahead in July, as decided at the Casablanca conference.

On March 20th, the 8th Army's final push northwards from Mareth to Tunis began. The initial frontal assault by Montgomery's artillery was followed by an attack by XXX Corps on the coast, and the plan called for a dash for the Gabes gap and the plain beyond, but appalling weather, swollen rivers and effective resistance bogged down the assault. Not until March 26th did the attack finally break out at El Hamma, assisted by fierce and constant air support from the Desert Air Force. The bulk of the Italian defending army was able to withdraw to Wadi Akarit, but the Allied advance was at last under way. On April 5th/6th the XXX Corps again attacked Messe's positions and, after initial reverses, the British force found its enemy in retreat. It later proved that Messe had wanted to hold his position, but that von Arnim, knowing that the fearsome General Patton was approaching the Italian Army's right, had decided to pull Messe's force back to regroup for what promised to be a major battle.

The tough, uncompromising General Patton had in fact been having a successful few weeks after revitalising the morale of II Corps, and had taken Gafsa on March 17th, and El Guettar, Maknassy and Sbeitla before the end of March. Now he was ready to join up with the British 8th Army, which he did on April 8th, a link which created a unified arc of Allied forces from the US II Corps to the British 1st Army, through the French 19th Corps to the 8th Army. The scene was almost set for the final Allied victory in Africa.

To meet the requirements of General Alexander's plan finally to push the Axis forces back to Tunis and Bizerta, the US II Corps was moved the following week to the right of the 1st Army, to the centre of the attack, and, as this was taking place, lost their charismatic commander. General Patton had a new task – the organisation of the US participation in the forthcoming landings in Sicily. The task of taking the US Army to Bizerta fell to General Omar Bradley, Patton's second in command.

Through the last week of April and the first of May, the attack spearheaded by the British 1st Army under Lieutenant-General Anderson, and the US II Corps under General Bradley went ahead, advancing slowly, losing some of its encounters but winning most. On May 5th, General Bradley's masterly grasp of tactics enabled his 1st Armoured Division to descend from the high ground it had been holding above Mateur and seize the vital Tunis to Bizerta railway line, which the Axis was using for supplies. Gradually the armies closed in, and on May 7th the first units of the British 7th Armoured Division entered Tunis, the US 9th Division reached Bizerta, and the 1st Armoured Division linked up with the 7th. On May 9th, the commander of the Axis troops in the northern part of Tunisia, General Vaerst, asked for an armistice.

On May 12th, the southern forces were surrounded and forced to surrender, General von Arnim being among the men captured after fierce fighting. Virtually the entire Axis army was captured; only a few hundred escaped to Italy to continue their war. Almost a quarter of a million prisoners were taken.

Thus ended the battle for North Africa, the reign of the Desert Fox, and one of the fastest moving campaigns of the Second World War. Almost 50,000 Allied soldiers were killed or wounded in the seven months' campaign for Tunisia. Eisenhower's, Alexander's, Montgomery's and Patton's success was not without price, but final victory could not have been achieved without it.

TOEHOLD IN EUROPE
THE ASSAULT ON ITALY

The defeat of the Axis in North Africa made possible the next stage of the strategy agreed at Casablanca, and reinforced by a meeting between Churchill, Generals Marshall, Eisenhower, Alexander and Ismay, Air Chief Marshal Tedder and Admiral Cunningham in Algeria in May 1943. At this meeting it was agreed that the first objective should be the securing of the Mediterranean sea lanes by the conquest of Sicily. If that went well, the next was to be the increase of pressure on Germany by an invasion of Italy, the elimination of Italy as a combatant, and the establishment of the first Allied permanent presence in mainland Europe since 1940.

Italy had suffered huge losses of men and equipment since her entry into Germany's war, and Mussolini had compounded those losses by his unnecessary and ill-conceived adventures in Albania, North Africa and, more recently, Russia. Of the 95 divisions that the Italians had had at, or had raised since, the start of the war, a third had been annihilated by death or capture, more than another third were distributed about the Axis Empire doing Hitler's bidding, and the remainder, nominally 30 divisions but in fact rather less, were available for the defence of the homeland. With a victorious, battle-hardened and ever better-equipped Allied army poised just across the Mediterranean, it was clear that that defence was about to be necessary.

The Italian Air Force and Navy were in no less difficulty. The Italian fleet had lost approaching half of its strength, and those vessels that remained, particularly the overworked destroyers and escort vessels, were becoming ill-maintained and unreliable. The air force lacked aircraft that were in any way a match for the latest Allied fighters and bombers, and was extremely vulnerable to losses in combat. To add to all these problems, all three services were desperately short of fuel, a situation which seemed likely only to become worse.

Recognising the inability of the Italian forces effectively to resist invasion, Mussolini appealed to Hitler for more assistance, particularly with aircraft and anti-aircraft defences. It was in some ways an unrealistic appeal, for already the *Luftwaffe* was in severe difficulties. Losses of aircraft and crews in Russia were mounting, the fuel shortage was every bit as desperate for the Germans as it was for the Italians, and the demands of Hitler's over-extended position in the Soviet Union were becoming greater every day. Nonetheless, Hitler and Kesselring had maintained considerable land forces in Italy, on the premise that they were better off defending Germany in Italy than defending Germany in Germany, and had allocated two German divisions – the 15th *Panzergrenadier* and the 'Hermann

Goering' *Panzer* Divisions – to the defence of Sicily, albeit with greatly reduced armament, and considerably under strength. They joined the Italian 6th Army under General Guzzoni, which had some 230,000 men and 1,500 guns, few motor vehicles, and quite impossibly large areas of Sicily to defend.

It was, however, by no means accepted in the Axis High Commands that Sicily would be the initial target. A substantial body of opinion that the first invasion would occur in Greece had been created by British Naval Intelligence, who had on 30th April 1943 planted in the sea to drift ashore in Spain the body of a man who had died of pneumonia (and therefore had fluid in his lungs not unlike that expected of someone who had drowned). Dressed in the uniform of a Royal Marines officer, the body, 'Major Martin', carried letters from the Imperial General Staff to Generals Eisenhower and Alexander and to Admiral Cunningham, which referred to 'the imminent landings in Greece'. While treated with reserve, the ruse was taken seriously enough for immense efforts to be spent mining the waters around Greece, and for a *Panzer* Division to be diverted from France to Greece.

Nonetheless, both Hitler and Italy's Marshall Ambrosio were confident that the first landings would be in Sardinia, and were later certain that the Allies had failed to take full advantage of their position by invading Sicily. They believed that an invasion of Sardinia would have enabled the Allies to sever the Axis forces in the South from those in the North – and in fact feared just this eventuality as the Allied build-up to the landings continued.

For these and other reasons, Italy was not in a happy condition. Most of those who had formerly been close to Mussolini now believed not only that Italy had lost the war, but that Germany would never be able to win it. A powerful group led by Count Ciano and two other ministers, and by Marshals Badoglio and Caviglia, was pressing either for Mussolini to break with Hitler and sue for peace, or for the arrest of Mussolini so that others could end Italy's association with Germany.

Against this background, Eisenhower and Alexander planned 'Operation Husky', with broadly the same command structure as had so recently been successful in Tunisia. The American 7th Army under General Patton was made up of II Corps, commanded by General Omar Bradley, and the autonomous 3rd Division under the command of the immensely tough General Truscott. Their role was to establish a beach-head in the Gulf of Gela, between Licata and Scoglitti, west of Sicily's southernmost tip, and then penetrate inland to the North. The British 8th Army under General Montgomery, consisting of XIII Corps under Lieutenant-General Miles Dempsey and XXX Corps commanded by Lieutenant-General Oliver Leese had the task of taking the coastline to the East of that Southernmost point, between Pachino and Avola.

As an essential first step, the Allies began on June 1st a major bombing offensive against Italian targets, starting with a round the clock bombardment from the air of the island of Pantelleria, midway between Tunisia and Sicily. This tremendous air attack on the island, which brought down some 6,500 tons of bombs on the 12,000 defenders (and the 10,000 civilians they were supposed to be defending), culminated in a landing on June 11th, and surrender by the Italian commander Admiral Pavesi on June 12th. On the same day, a hapless Sergeant pilot in the Royal Air Force, Sergeant Cohen, earned his place in history by capturing an enemy garrison single-handed. He made a forced landing on Lampedusa, a small island off Sicily, and the Italian defenders, seeing the arrival of the dreaded Allies of whom they had heard so much, surrendered without enquiring the reason for his visit.

All through June, Allied aircraft attacked Italian airfields, Italian ships at anchor and military installations both in Sicily and throughout mainland Italy. By Dawn on 10th July, when the Allied invasion of Sicily began, the Axis air defences in the area had been virtually destroyed. Tedder's 4,000 aircraft found they had only 200 Italian and 320 German aircraft with which to contend. The invasion itself, planned by Admiral Ramsay, who had masterminded the evacuation of Dunkirk, went extremely well. For the first time, new LST (Landing Ship, Tank) and LCT (Landing Craft, Tank) vessels were used to put armour ashore with the first wave of infantry, and the invaders were rapidly established, capturing the coastline and driving inland. Eight divisions landed from a thousand ships along a front some 100 miles long. By evening on the 11th July, 80,000 troops and 8,000 vehicles were ashore, Montgomery's 8th Army had occupied the ports of Syracuse and Augusta without a shot being fired, the garrisons having taken themselves elsewhere, and the *Hermann Goering Panzer* division had been badly mauled by US Navy fire from the cruisers *Boise* and *Savannah* when they attempted to take the US 1st Division to task on the coast near Niscemi. This was probably the first occasion when sea power decided a tank battle.

Both the American and the British Armies were heading for Messina at the northern tip of Sicily, and nurtured hopes that they might get there before the German army, so preventing an evacuation of Axis troops to the mainland. Field Marshal Kesselring, one of whose considerable talents was a mastery of organisation, was too clever to allow that to happen. By a minor miracle of improvisation, Kesselring transported on to the island from mainland Italy two paratroop regiments and the 29th *Panzergrenadier* Division, and put General Hube of XIV *Panzer* Corps in command of all German fighting troops in Sicily. From that point onward, the standard of Axis resistance to the Allied advance on both sides of Mount Etna became very much tougher. Nonetheless, General Patton made the rapid progress that was soon to become his trademark. The 7th Army established contact with the British 8th Army on July 14th, and then, despite appallingly rough terrain in the West of Sicily, launched one division upon the major task of taking Palermo, in the North-West of the island, and two others under General Bradley on the problem of fighting directly northwards to the North coast. Incredibly, Patton arrived in Palermo, to the cheers of a mightily relieved populace, only a week later, on the 22nd July, having overcome the Italian 'Assietta' Division on the way. From Palermo Eastward to Messina was not so easy.

Montgomery, meanwhile, had been having a difficult time on the Eastern plains of Sicily. Having captured Syracuse and Augusta by default, the 8th Army faced the problem of attacking across an open coastal plain towards the larger port of Catania, and of taking the town, before the entirely different problem of the assault through the foothills of Etna to Messina could be overcome. Montgomery encountered fierce resistance all the way to Catania, and was not able to take the town until August 5th. Before that, however, he had detached the 1st Canadian Division to attack to the West of Mount Etna (which displeased the US Army), and had hemmed in General Hube's forces ever closer to the North-East of the island.

Substantial Allied reinforcements were arriving via Palermo and Syracuse in the shape of the US 9th Division in the North-West, and the British 78th Division in the South-East, and the US and British forces now had an enormous numerical advantage over Hube's German defence force. A massive German withdrawal to the mainland began, and on 17th August, shortly after Hube had left on the final assault craft for Calabria, Patton arrived in Messina, a few hours ahead of the furious Montgomery, who had in his own view reserved the right to take the key northern city.

The Allies now found that they had captured 132,000 prisoners, 260 tanks and 520 guns. Approximately 8,600 German and Italian troops have known graves on Sicily, and almost 8,400 Allied soldiers were killed or posted missing, with nearly 14,500 wounded.

Italy's Turning Point

While these events had been taking place in Sicily, the politics of the Axis had been reaching crisis point in Italy. The King, under pressure to remove Mussolini, in fact sought to remove the entire Fascist party from power. The Fascists, at a meeting in Feltre with Hitler and Keitel, had sought far greater military support from the Germans, which, to some extent, Hitler said he was prepared to give, on condition that Mussolini mobilised Italy's manhood to greater effort and restored flagging Italian morale. Mussolini, urged by Ambrosio and his colleagues to break with Hitler and broadcast to the Allies for terms of surrender, could not bring himself to accept defeat, and to believe that Hitler's boasts of new reprisal weapons capable of destroying London by the Autumn were exaggerated. The meeting broke up inconclusively, with Mussolini still relying upon his faith in Hitler, and the Fascist ministers and High Command fuming.

A Fascist Grand Council on July 24th, called by Mussolini to discuss the situation, became the scene of a plot to oust the Duce. A motion put by Count Grandi, by which the Council required Mussolini to hand over authority over the Italian armed forces to the King, was carried by a large majority. The motion also authorised the monarch to remove Mussolini from power. At 5pm on the 25th, the King informed Mussolini that he was accepting his (unsubmitted) resignation, and that Marshal Badoglio was to be appointed Head of the Government in his place. Mussolini was driven ignominiously in an ambulance to a military police barracks, and the Fascist conspirators were denied all complicity in the new government. Count Ciano left for Germany lured by an invitation to a non-existent meeting, a trap which was ultimately to cost him his life.

Badoglio issued as his first act a proclamation that 'the war goes on'. But Hitler was not enthusiastic about the intentions of the new Italian government, and decided to take action to ensure that Italy was not snatched from the Germans' grasp by a defection to the Allies. Field Marshal Rommel was given command of 'Operation Alarich', and instructions to move Army Group B to Bologna by mid-August. By the time the Allies' conquest of Sicily was complete, eight divisions of crack German troops including the 24th *Panzer* Division and the *Leibstandarte Adolf Hitler Waffen SS* 1st *Panzer* Division were in position North of the Appenines. Kesselring, still the supreme commander in the field in the Mediterranean theatre, was reinforced with the 2nd Parachute Division.

On August 15th, General Jodl and Field Marshal Rommel met General Roatta, the Italian Army Chief of Staff in Bologna, and attempted to assure themselves that the Italian Government was not in the process of seeking an armistice with the Allies. Three days previously, Generals Castellano and Montenari had secretly met Eisenhower's Chief of Staff in Lisbon and had discussed the text of an armistice, but the Italians succeeded in lying their way out of their meetings with the Germans. On August 27th, the Generals returned to Rome with secret radio equipment capable of contacting the Allies, and with the text of the surrender. After extensive and intensive negotiations by which the Italians sought to gain the maximum protection from German reprisals against the Italian population and cities, the armistice was signed at 5.15pm on September 3rd. On the 8th, the Armistice was announced by Badoglio to the Italian people.

The German reaction was immediate, devastating and brutal. Whole divisions of Italian troops serving alongside those of Germany in Italy were taken prisoner and given scant comfort as prisoners of war. In the small hours of September 9th, the morning after the announcement of the armistice, a convoy of Italian warships heading for Malta to surrender was bombed by the Germans, and the battleship *Roma* was sunk with the loss of more than 1,500 lives. Away from the Mediterranean theatre, the Italian troops fared no better. In the Balkans, 29 divisions were attacked and surprised by the German army and disarmed. Two divisions (the 'Acqui' and the 'Bergamo') that put up a fight were besieged into surrender – and then thousands of soldiers were murdered after they had capitulated. Those that escaped joined the partisans and fought Germany from the hills.

Mussolini was sent to a remote residence in the *Gran Sasso*, high in the mountains. Hitler, determined to hold the brotherhood of fascist dictatorship high, sent a daring commando unit under Otto Skorzeny to rescue him from his captors. They succeeded brilliantly, landing in the mountains with several light aircraft, and bearing him back to a Hitler who felt that honour had thus been satisfied. Under pressure from the Fuehrer, Mussolini proclaimed on September 18th the 'Italian Social Republic', but it was an empty gesture recognised only by the puppet Axis governments and Japan.

On 12th September, as confusion continued to reign in the former Axis, the Free French embarked on the liberation of Corsica, and by October 4th the Allies had gained an additional valuable base by Italy's side door. Despite tremendous efforts by the French and Moroccan troops of the invasion force, the Germans kept their escape route open, and were able to evacuate 28,000 valuable battle-trained troops to the mainland.

Salerno – the Allied Success that Almost Wasn't
Having taken Sicily and achieved a considerable victory, and then secured the capitulation of the Italian state, the Allied High Command planned hastily – perhaps too hastily – to capitalise on the advantage thus created by establishing a presence on the Italian mainland.

The plan for the Salerno invasion was a two-part exercise. A Corps of the British 8th Army was first to launch an attack across the Straits of Messina with the objective of drawing the German army into battle. This, it was hoped, would divert attention away from the major landing – the second phase, which was to bring the US 5th Army commanded by General Mark Clark ashore in the Gulf of Salerno. When the British force – XIII Corps under General Dempsey – made its landing on September 3rd, the fourth anniversary of the outbreak of Hitler's war, it met very little resistance. Kesselring, expecting a diversionary attack before a main landing (which he thought would be further North, near Rome), had instructed the German 76th *Panzer* Corps not to become involved in battle unless it was unavoidable. Dempsey was able to advance some miles inland and await developments, a situation for which the Allied plan of attack did not provide. Ready withdrawal to strong defensive positions in the MacArthur mould was not expected of the German army.

'Operation Avalanche' began in earnest on September 9th, when the US VI Corps and the British X Corps landed in the Gulf of Salerno between Paestum and Maiori along a front of 25 miles. Initially, the invasion went well, and by the end of the first day the US 36th Division had made five miles progress inland, and the British X Corps, although held up in and around Salerno, was established, and seemed likely not to be thrown back into the sea. But Kesselring had a surprise in store. For a start, Hitler had long regarded Salerno as potentially important, and had allocated the crack 16th *Panzer* Division to its defence. Secondly, having captured Rome following the Italian government's armistice with the Allies. Kesselring was able to divert from the area around the capital the 3rd *Panzergrenadier* Division, and by September 12th General von Vietinghoff's 10th Army was able to field four and a half divisions against the Allies' three. Over the next three days, the situation was touch and go. The Germans almost succeeded in surrounding the American 45th Division, which had advanced farther than the British 56th that should have been alongside it, and only desperate measures by the stubborn and determined General Mark Clark saved the day at the Battle of Ponte Bruciato. The story has it that Clark armed as infantry two artillery battalions, the regimental band, all the HQ orderlies and the cooks. In any event, the effort succeeded in stopping the German advance some five miles from the beach-head, where the tactic of using naval gunfire in support of the land army, so effective in Sicily, was used again with considerable success.

Now General Alexander called Montgomery's 8th Army in to attack the German forces from the side. Montgomery's 5th Division reached Agropoli on September 16th, just as the US 5th Army, at terrible expense of life, was beating back the attack. Later that day, faced with the additional strength of Montgomery's troops in a battle that was already lost, Kesselring pulled back the 10th Army, and admitted that the Allies had won the Battle of Salerno. Speedily, the British army occupied the important Italian ports of Brindisi and Taranto.

It is arguable that the Germans would not have lost the battle for Salerno had Rommel and Kesselring not been in violent disagreement on the strategy for the defence of Italy. Rommel thought Germany should abandon Rome and pull back to the North. Kesselring, in theory the senior commander, resolved to defend the German Southern positions, but could not, because of Hitler's ambiguous orders and duplicated command structure, pull enough weight to force Rommel to release his best *Panzer* troops for the battle in the South.

Now began the arduous and extremely wet advance up the southern part of Italy to Rome, during which the heavy armour of the British and American troops, unable to leave the roads because of the sea of mud on either side, became vulnerable and slow. At Termoli in early October, at Sangro at the end of November, at Monte Cassino – again and again General von Vietinghoff turned the bad weather and the confusion it caused to the maximum advantage, turning and making a determined, even heroic stand at every opportunity. It was clear that neither Kesselring nor his commanders had any intention of giving up Italy lightly – and that Hitler was firmly behind this policy was made clear by the recall of Rommel on November 21st. Kesselring was now in total charge in Italy.

How Kesselring tackled the subsequent stages of the Battle for Italy will be discussed in a later chapter. At this point this narrative must return to the war at sea.

THE U-BOAT BEATEN

ALLIED SUCCESSES AT SEA

The winning of the Battle of the Atlantic was seen in 1941 and 1942, by Allies and Axis alike, as vital to their winning of the war. Churchill and Roosevelt knew that, if there was one major hinge upon which defeat might swing, it was the ability of Germany to prevent both the convoys from USA reaching Britain, and the convoys from Britain and the USA reaching the USSR. Hitler, Grand-Admiral Raeder and Admiral Doenitz believed that, given the much-vaunted *Luftwaffe's* demonstrated inability to subjugate Britain, their principal hope of final victory over their one enemy left in the West was to win the submarine war before the USA came officially into the conflict.

By 1942, America, whose ships had already been on active convoy protection duty for months while the USA was still neutral, had been brought into the war by Japan – an event that was as much a surprise for Hitler as it was for the United States. The Royal Navy's anti-submarine radar and Asdic techniques were improving dramatically, and despite the successes of the German U-Boat building programme, the balance was shifting perceptibly in the favour of the Allies. Nonetheless, the U-Boat remained throughout 1942 and into 1943 one of the major threats to the Allies' hopes of winning the war. An important reason for this was the continued ability of Admiral Doenitz's code breakers to read the signals of British Western Approaches Command to the convoys. For some unknown reason, British Naval Intelligence never realised that this was happening, or, if they did, never did anything to improve their coding practices. As a result, the U-Boat controllers were able not only to establish the positions of the convoys from the signals sent by the ships, but also to decode the information on supposed U-Boat positions sent to the convoys, and the instructions for avoiding the 'Wolf Packs' that were given by Western Approaches Command.

By 1943, although the *Kriegsmarine* was becoming short of skilled U-Boat crews, and was having to keep U-boats in port at Lorient or La Pallice (and later at Brest, St Nazaire and Bordeaux) for longer between operational trips than hitherto, those boats that were at sea were hunting in larger packs with deadly efficiency. Although U-Boat losses were mounting, German production figures reached an average of between 23 and 24 submarines a month in 1943, despite heavy Allied bombing of the shipyards in which they were built. There seemed to Doenitz every prospect of sustaining the battle almost indefinitely – in fact, at the beginning of 1943, Germany had the formidable total of 212 operational submarines, more than double the number of a year previously.

Until 1943, the U-Boat arm of the *Kriegsmarine* had been largely spared the phenomenon of Hitler as Commander in Chief and tactician. But at the beginning of January 1943, a battle took place in the Barents Sea between the Royal Navy escort of Convoy JW 51B, commanded by Captain Robert St Vincent Sherbrooke (who was awarded the Victoria Cross for his outstanding bravery and devotion to duty) and a German force of surface raiders and submarines. This engagement, which involved *Hipper, Lutzow* and U-354 provoked a crisis between Hitler and the German Navy because Vice-Admiral Kummitz, in command of the German flotilla, broke off the engagement, which he might conceivably have won, before it was concluded. He did this because he was aware of Hitler's contradictory orders that Germany's prestige surface ships should not take unnecessary risks, and because, just as he knew that he might win the battle, he was also acutely aware that he might lose it.

Although it was because of his orders that the incident occurred, Hitler was furious, and vented his ire on Grand-Admiral Raeder, who promptly resigned. Doenitz, until now the Admiral that could do no wrong, was promoted Grand-Admiral in Raeder's place – but never again commanded without the baleful eye of Adolf Hitler on his every move. Thus the U-boats entered 1943 with a new commander, Rear-Admiral Godt, and without the moral support of the surface raiders, which were effectively retired from active service for the time being as a result of Hitler's outburst.

The year also saw the eclipse of the *Luftwaffe* as an effective strike and defensive force at sea, which enabled the Allied air forces to become ever more effective at anti-submarine operations. During 1943, the RAF sank 41 U-boats in the Bay of Biscay without significant response from the *Luftwaffe*, and the production of escort carriers, mainly in United States shipyards, was stepped up to provide much wider airborne protection for convoys at sea. By the end of 1943, aircraft from escort carriers had destroyed no fewer than 26 U-boats. Typically, these mass-produced American ships of around 10,000 to 12,000 tons were built from scratch in less than a year. Like the other rapidly produced products of the American shipyards, notably the 'Liberty' ships, they made a very significant contribution to the Allied war effort.

Losses of merchant ships from the convoys were also reduced by the application of research into the history of convoy losses. It was found that, contrary to popular belief, large convoys were safer than small ones. Although easier to find, the large convoys, it was observed, lost only the same number of ships as a smaller convoy, given constant numbers of attacking submarines. In other words, six submarines could be expected statistically to pick off roughly the same number of 'kills' from any convoy, almost regardless of its size. Since a large convoy required a smaller number of escort vessels as a proportion of the total number of ships in the convoy to achieve the same degree of safety, it followed that more large convoys could be escorted by the same number of warships with fewer losses overall.

All these developments tended to decrease Allied shipping losses and increase the sinkings of German submarines. But of the four decisive advances that turned the Battle of the Atlantic and gave the Allies the upper hand, two were electronic and two were major advances in maritime weapons systems.

The first was the advent of centimetric radar. Installed on board the convoy escort vessels, this form of short-wave radar could not be spotted by the U-boats' detection equipment, which was designed for the much lower frequencies until then in use. The U-Boats had come to rely extensively on their ability to track convoys and find them at night by the detection of their radar emissions. Suddenly this facility was denied them.

The second electronic development was 'Huff Duff', otherwise and more correctly known as H/F D/F or High Frequency Direction Finder. This goniometric radio equipment was able to provide a fix on any U-Boat transmitting radio signals. With this equipment installed, the convoy could be steered away from the U-Boat packs, and the 'Hunter-Killer' Allied submarines could be directed on to their kill.

The first of the weapons systems that helped to end the Battle of the Atlantic was the 'Hedgehog', a projector in the bows of an escort vessel capable of firing a pattern of 24 contact-fused bombs for 250 yards ahead. By making it unnecessary for the escort to pass directly over its target before succeeding with depth charges, and by providing a larger spread of fire and less chance for the submarine to detect the presence and position of the escort, the 'Hedgehog' greatly increased the success rate of escorts against U-boats.

The fourth contributor was the airborne rocket. Increasingly being brought into use as a tank-busting weapon by the Allies, the rocket was shown to be every bit as effective against submarines on the surface, and speedily contributed to U-Boat sinkings from the end of May 1943 onwards.

With all these new-found advantages, the Allies turned the tide of the Atlantic war dramatically. The decisive year began, in January 1943, with a relatively quiet month in the North Atlantic because of appalling weather – only 50 Allied merchant vessels were sunk – but Doenitz achieved a major success off North Africa by sinking seven of a convoy of nine tankers carrying vital fuel to the Allied armies closing in on General von Arnim's army in Tunisia. In the next month the weather improved and so also did the German score. A total of 73 ships went to the bottom. But so did 19 U-boats, and the much greater success of the escorts in defending the convoys, as well as in sinking the submarines, was causing great concern at *Kriegsmarine* headquarters.

March seemed almost to reverse the situation. The carnage of Allied ships was awe-inspiring. In the first twenty days of the month no less than 97 Allied ships were sunk, almost two-thirds of them in properly escorted convoys. By the end of the month the total had passed 100 and settled at 102. Only 15 German submarines were destroyed during the month. For a moment it seemed to the Allied seamen that all was lost. But their commanders knew of the new weapons; were certain the battle was about to turn. April saw only half the Allied losses for a further 15 U-boats sunk. May brought 47 U-Boat losses for fewer Allied ships sunk than in April. Doenitz recognised defeat when he saw it.

On May 24th, Doenitz withdrew the U-Boat fleet from the Atlantic for modification and improvement. In July, the German submarine fleet reappeared in the Atlantic fitted with quadruple cannon on the conning towers. But this expedient proved useless against the Allied aircraft with their rockets, bombs and depth-charges. During the month of July, 37 more U-boats went to the bottom. In August a further 23 were destroyed.

By December 31st 1943, despite the intensive construction rate of U-boats throughout the year, the German submarine fleet was down to 168 operational vessels, as compared with 212 a year earlier. U-boats were no longer able to attack, or even operate, on the surface, and were forced to observe radio silence or be detected. Gone were the days of German superiority in radio communications. Gone was Doenitz' ability to direct his wolf-packs on their target without also calling in the Allies to their kill. Germany had lost the Battle of the Atlantic.

THE CARDS STACK UP AGAINST JAPAN

NEW GUINEA AND THE SOLOMONS

After Japan's lightning success of the first two months of 1942, there had been a strong body of opinion in the Japanese High Command, particularly in the Navy, that Japan should press on and take Australia, partly for the resources it offered and the prestige of its capture, but more as a means of preventing its becoming the base for an Allied counterattack. Those who disagreed with the idea of conquering Australia did so largely on the grounds that its sheer size would make it impossibly expensive to hold and garrison. That view, as we know, prevailed.

Nonetheless, it was agreed that New Guinea – the second largest island in the world – should be taken for its strategic position. During May 1942, Japan's planned capture of Port Moresby in New Guinea from the sea had been thwarted by the Battle of the Coral Sea, but on July 21st Major-General Tomataro Horii's South Seas Detachment had landed east of Gona with the intention of taking Port Moresby from the landward side, across the Owen Stanley mountains, via the village of Kokoda. To US and European military planners, this would have seemed an impossible task, but the training and native skills of the Japanese soldiers made them as capable of marching through jungle and apparently impenetrable vegetation as the western armies were of marching along a highway. In fact, the Japanese believed from aerial reconnaissance that there was a road over the mountains; only later did they discover it to be a two feet wide path known as the Kokoda Track.

By July 28th, the advance party had taken all the initial territory between their beach-head and Kokoda with virtually no resistance, and had captured Kokoda itself with surprising ease, largely because the Allies had not so far taken the Japanese attack as a serious threat to New Guinea as a whole, or to Port Moresby in particular. On August 24th, General Horii arrived in Kokoda at the head of 8,500 troops that had been put ashore in the wake of the initial landing. He found that a force of Australians – some of them relatively raw militiamen, the rest battle veterans recently returned from North Africa – was putting up a determined stand in the mountains at Isurava. His bombardment of their positions marked the beginning of a bitter struggle; not only did the Australians hold that position for three hard days, inflicting massive casualties on the Japanese, but they made Horii's army fight for every inch of that mountain trail.

The Owen Stanley Mountains are a series of steep, jungle-clad ridges rising to 7,000 feet and more, interspersed with deep valleys. Rivers, disease, the local wildlife and the damp all contributed to making the battle a miserable one for the

Australians. Although they fought tenaciously and well, Japanese skill in jungle warfare enabled Horii's infantry to advance inexorably through the raw jungle by a series of the same outflanking movements that had defeated the British Army in Malaya earlier in the year. By mid-September, the Japanese were within thirty-two miles of their objective, Port Moresby, and Horii called a halt on Ioribaiwa Ridge because his supply lines were getting stretched and because, in any event, he had orders not so attempt to take Port Moresby until he was reinforced from the sea via nearby Milne Bay.

Japanese attempts to land those reinforcements went badly. First, the army units assigned to the landing were diverted to Guadalcanal because of the US Marine Corps landing there. Then, because the Japanese discovered that the Allies were building an airfield overlooking Milne Bay, the site for the landing was switched to a nearby obscure coconut growing area called Gili-Gili, which not even the Japanese knew well. When the landings took place on August 25th, most things that could go wrong did. One detachment of the Japanese Marines was attacked by Allied aircraft and stranded without its invasion barges miles from its proper landing place. Another Marine unit landed miles from its target and was faced with a long march over densely vegetated hills to rejoin the fight. But this second group, under Commander Hayashi, was made of tough stuff. Fighting only at night, and advancing with a psychologically devastating flame thrower, Hayashi advanced to the airfield that the US Engineers were building between Rabi and Gili-Gili. There he called up reinforcements and, once they had arrived, launched a ferocious attack on August 31st. To Hayashi's considerable surprise, the Japanese encountered effective, indeed, devastating resistance, and by morning were forced to withdraw, with the Australian defenders in hot pursuit. During the retreat, Hayashi lost his life and his deputy was wounded. Over 600 Japanese soldiers were killed, another 300 were wounded. The Japanese force asked for and were sent an evacuation force, and by September 6th all the survivors were on their way back to Rabaul. The attempt to reinforce Horii's Port Moresby assault had failed, after the great success of the most hazardous part of the endeavour – the actual crossing of the mountains. Only thirty miles or so from Port Moresby, the assault had seemed certain to succeed. What had gone wrong?

The simple answer was – Japanese Intelligence. Between the end of June and the end of August, 4,500 Australian infantry, 3,000 Australian engineers and 1,300 American engineers had been brought into the Milne Bay area. This the Japanese did not know, and did not calculate for, so based all their tactics on the assumption that their opposition was of less than half the strength they actually encountered on the day of the invasion. They were not usually so careless. Now Horii was obliged to pay the cost of that carelessness.

With studied calm, the Allied troops waited. The attack that Horii and the Japanese troops expected did not come, for the Australians knew that his army's supplies were running out and that sooner or later Horii would be obliged to retreat with a hungry army. Desperate attempts by the Japanese to get supplies in from the other side of the mountains failed. On September 24th, the Japanese High Command ordered Horii to withdraw back across the mountains to the coast at Buna. The order was a shattering, unimaginable blow to the pride not only of the officers of Horii's army, but also to the ordinary soldiers. They had been brought up to believe that under no circumstance could a Japanese soldier retreat. When they were ordered to do so, the psychological blow was such that their morale evaporated. Hungry and ashamed, they ran for their lives.

Two days after the retreat began, the Australians counter-attacked. In hot pursuit, they were stopped on October 21st in the mountains by a rearguard unit positioned by Horii to hold out as long as possible and delay the Australian advance. With suicidal intensity, this small Japanese force did its job well. Despite almost equal determination, the Australians did not manage to break through until October 28th, which gave Horii sufficient time to evacuate Kokoda and set up his final defensive positions at Oivi and Gorari, below the mountains near the Kumusi River.

The Australians reached Oivi first, on November 5th 1942, and heavy fighting ensued, with the attackers making little headway against well-organised Japanese defence. Five days later, Australian troops attacked Gorari, and quickly overcame resistance. Now the defenders of Oivi risked being cut off if they did not head for the sea. They retreated again, along the river towards the coast. In small units, the South Seas Detachment crossed the Kumusi and headed for Buna. When they reached the coast, those that survived were in appalling condition. Starvation, Allied bombing, malaria and infected wounds wrought havoc with Horii's army. Horii had himself been killed attempting to cross the Kumusi on a raft to rejoin his soldiers. But, somehow, having completed the retreat, and thereby discharged their orders under grave adversity, the surviving Japanese soldiers' morale recovered, and they set about a spirited defence of their position at Buna. Japanese reinforcements arrived from Rabaul, in New Britain, their Australian attackers themselves became bogged down by the same problems of disease as had afflicted the Japanese, and by the end of November, no further Allied progress was being made at Buna.

General Douglas MacArthur responded to this situation from his base in Australia by sending US General Robert L. Eichelberger and 15,000 fresh troops to take Buna. His orders to Eichelberger were direct and to the point. 'Take Buna, or don't come back alive'.

Eichelberger was one of those remarkable Generals – Rommel was another – who genuinely and without affectation lead from the front because they know no other way. He wore badges of rank within view of snipers despite the common practice of not doing so. He operated from command posts only yards from his enemy. His example revitalised the Australian troops' morale and determination and brought great spirit and bravery from the Americans. Early in December, a remarkable exploit by one Sergeant Bottcher and his platoon of eighteen US soldiers had resulted in the capture and holding of a vital position on the beach between the two halves of the Japanese force. This gave the subsequent major assault on December 18th, when tanks and infantry advanced on 150 Japanese bunkers in the face of deadly fire, a real chance of success. Despite enormous casualties – something like half of the Australians taking part were killed or wounded – the Allied force established itself in strength along the coast. Gradually the battle went the way of the Allies, but losses both to Japanese arms and to malaria and other diseases remained very high. Incredibly, General Eichelberger managed to go through the whole campaign without injury or illness, and, at the end of January, was able to report to General MacArthur that Buna was once more in the possession of the Allies.

For two more years, almost to the end of the Pacific war, the battle for New Guinea was to continue, as the American and Australian troops pushed the Japanese ever further northward in an endless battle of pocket and foxhole, sniper and ambush. The fight for New Guinea was hard on both sides. It was, in a sense, a microcosm of the Pacific war – yet it was unique. It was the island to end all islands in a war to reclaim islands.

The Solomons

The battle for Guadalcanal, which was taking place at the same time as the events in New Guinea, ended after a hard and bloody campaign with total victory for the US Marines in February 1943. Japanese and American commentators alike were to reflect with hindsight that Guadalcanal was the beginning of the end for Japan. After that first battle for the Solomons, Japan was never to achieve another advance. For the next two and a half years, she was to be in retreat.

For the time being, however, there was no sign of defeatism in the Japanese approach to their problems in the Solomon Islands. They were, quite simply, determined to hold on to them at all costs, and to surrender nothing without a major battle. Fresh Japanese infantry, aircraft and ships were rushed to the Solomons after the debacle of Guadalcanal, and a major air offensive was launched in April 1943 against Allied bases in the Solomon Islands and New Guinea, although it did not achieve anything very significant. Admiral Yamamoto, who had planned and executed the attack on Pearl Harbor, decided to visit the area in May for a factfinding and morale-boosting tour, and had coded messages sent to local commanders so that they knew when he was coming. Unfortunately for him, he still did not know that the American Navy was able to decode virtually all Japanese naval transmissions. The news of Yamamoto's travel arrangements was communicated to Admiral Halsey, and he in turn set up a reception committee.

Yamamoto was due to arrive on Bougainville, in the Northern Solomons, at 9.30am on April 18th. With split second timing, an American squadron of eighteen P-38 Lightnings that had flown at the very limit of their range from Henderson Field on Guadalcanal pounced on his aircraft as it landed, shot it up on the runway, and killed Japan's greatest leader. As a psychological blow, following the Japanese reverses in New Guinea and Guadalcanal, the killing of Yamamoto was unparalleled during Japan's war until the nuclear attacks on Hiroshima and Nagasaki.

The Allied campaign in the Solomon Islands was one half of the strategy agreed by the Allies in the summer of 1943 by which the attack that the Japanese were expecting on their heavily defended southern Pacific base at Rabaul should be abandoned. Instead, the Allies put General Douglas MacArthur in command of a two pronged pincer movement around the base in New Britain which would both recapture the Solomon Islands in the North-East and New Guinea to the South-West, while at the same time cutting off from reinforcement and supplies the Japanese forces in Rabaul. Thus the battles in New Guinea as the US forces fought their way slowly North-West after the capture of Buna from the Japanese, and the island-hopping forays along the chain of the Solomons, were part of one and the same campaign. Admiral Halsey, who commanded the US forces in the Solomons, was therefore under the overall command of General MacArthur. His objective was Bougainville, the northernmost island of the archipelago, but there was little chance of attacking Bougainville without first gaining the islands between as bases to provide fighter cover for the landings.

Halsey began with an assault on New Georgia, which offered an ideal base for fighters at Munda airfield, but which was almost unassailable by conventional amphibious landing techniques because of the coral reefs around the island and the narrowness of the channels through which landing craft would have to pass. Halsey therefore planned a preliminary series of landings on neighbouring islands from which to attack from the air before putting his ground forces at risk. After a few small unopposed landings at the southern end of New Georgia itself and on nearby Vangunu Island, 6,000 men of the US 43rd Infantry Division landed on the night of 29/30 June on Rendova Island, South-West of New Georgia and, without too many problems, secured the island. Two days later, the rest of Major-General John Hester's 43rd Infantry Division landed successfully at Zanana on the southern coast of New Georgia, and another smaller force landed on the northern coast.

Their joint attempt to capture Munda did not go well. The Japanese defenders were determined, well dug-in, armed to the teeth and well supplied. The heat and the jungle terrain were devastating to inexperienced troops. Despite reinforcements, the advance slowed to a halt within five days. Encouraged, the Japanese commander called up reinforcements from Rabaul. Despite a series of 'Tokyo Express' naval battles North of New Georgia as the US Navy attempted to stop the troop transports – a situation reminiscent of the earlier battles around Guadalcanal – some 2,000 Japanese soldiers were successfully put ashore to join Major-General Sasaki's defenders. The inexperienced American troops soon learned of the Japanese predilection for night attacks, and of their skill in jungle warfare. US losses were high, and their success minimal.

Six weeks after the initial landing, the American forces were only half way to their first objective at Munda, despite reinforcements. To inject new resolve into the campaign, Major-General Oscar Griswold, commander of XIV Corps, decided to take over in New Georgia and get some results. A major attack with additional artillery began on July 25th, but progress remained slow. Griswold reacted by replacing General Hester with Major-General John Hodge, who had been at Guadalcanal, and gradually the campaign gathered momentum. On August 4th, the 43rd finally took Munda, although at enormous cost, and Halsey had got his first island airfield North of Henderson Field. By August 14th it was in operation. By the end of August, all remaining Japanese troops on New Georgia had been flushed out.

The next target in the Solomon Islands was Kolombangara, which also had a useful airstrip, and therefore a force of Japanese defenders, commanded by that same General Sasaki who had recently been ejected from New Georgia. Sasaki had, in fact, 10,000 troops under his command, and was planning his counterattack on New Georgia to assuage the dishonour of his recent defeat. Reinforcements were being brought in from Rabaul to take part in this attack, and the transports and their escorts bringing them were being attacked by US PT boats from Rendova. One of those PT boats was commanded by Lieutenant John F. Kennedy. After his boat was run down by a Japanese destroyer, he managed first to get himself ashore, and then to carry out a one-man seaborne rescue operation which saved most of his crew. He swam miles despite injuries to his back. The future President was tough as well as charismatic.

Five days later three of a force of four Japanese warships attempting to reinforce Sasaki's army were torpedoed by American destroyers, and took to the bottom almost two whole battalions of Japanese soldiers. Nonetheless, some got through, and Admiral Halsey began to like less and less the idea of another grinding offensive against an even more suicidally determined Sasaki. So he decided instead to go around Kolombangara and take Vella Lavella, just North-West of his original target. There, he reasoned, he could build an airfield from scratch, then isolate Sasaki and bring him down gradually. Moreover, Vella Lavella was that much closer to Bougainville, the ultimate objective in the Solomons.

On August 15th, part of the 25th Division landed on Vella Lavella against some resistance from the air but comparatively little on the ground. This proved to be because there were few Japanese on the island. As military historian Lieutenant-Colonel Bauer put it, the Americans had more trouble finding them than defeating them. By the end of September, Vella Lavella was securely in Allied hands, and a detachment of New Zealanders had taken over its custody from the American troops that had captured it. At about the same time, General Sasaki was ordered to evacuate Kolombangara, and early in October some 9,000 Japanese troops were successfully pulled back to Bougainville despite the energetic efforts of the US Navy to stop them. Now there were some 40,000 Japanese troops on Bougainville, under the overall command of General Hyakutake, late of Guadalcanal, plus a further 20,000 Japanese Navy men. A tough nut for Halsey to crack.

He decided to employ again the strategy of bypassing the objective in order to isolate it, and resolved to attempt an amphibious landing at the relatively lightly defended Empress Augusta Bay region in the centre of the Western coast of Bougainville, where he could establish airfields and attack the supply convoys from Rabaul bringing reinforcements to the Japanese forces in the North and South of the island. To confuse the Japanese as to his objectives, two small diversionary landings were staged, on 27th October in the Treasury Islands to the South (by New Zealand troops) and later the same day on Choiseul to the East (US Marines). For a week, these assaults caused a lot of noise and confusion, and diverted attention from the Empress Augusta Bay landing, which, when it took place on November 1st, met very little opposition. The Japanese had believed that nobody would be mad enough to land on such open marshy land.

The commander of the Marines landing at Empress Augusta Bay was the formidable General Vandegrift, who had led the conquest of Guadalcanal. He quickly captured a substantial beach-head and organised effective defences against air attack. The Japanese attempted to counterattack against the beach-head both by air and by sea, but in both cases encountered stiff opposition and suffered severe losses – although the US Navy fared almost as badly as the Japanese in the Battle of Empress Augusta Bay overnight on August 1st/2nd. Halsey struck back with two carrier borne air strikes against the Japanese bases at Rabaul on November 5th and 11th, which pushed the Japanese Navy back to safer bases further North, and thereby reduced the pressure on Bougainville and the other Solomon Islands.

On November 8th, the 37th Infantry Division landed to reinforce Vandegrift's force, and he began to enlarge his beach-head. He never looked back. Gradually the Japanese were pushed further and further from the beach-head, although with no major American assault. In March 1944, Hyatuke made his last attempt to push the Americans off Bougainville but achieved nothing more than the loss of 6,000 troops. He had lost the battle, and never again attacked in force. During the first half of 1944, the US troops on Bougainville were replaced with Australians, and the Americans moved on to capture more islands on their relentless journey to Tokyo. Rabaul had, by the two successes of the campaigns in the Solomons and in New Guinea, been successfully isolated from the rest of the Japanese war effort, and could be disregarded as an effective war base.

Almost as important was the huge drain on Japanese human and arms resources caused by their losses in the twin campaigns of New Guinea and the Solomons. Their army, navy and air force could never recover from the slaughter, and their ability to counterattack was relentlessly reduced as each successive island campaign was won. The seal had been affixed to Japan's eventual defeat. It was a matter of time – and determination.

THE POLITICS OF WAR

QUEBEC, CAIRO AND TEHERAN

By mid 1943 it was clear to the leaders of the three senior Allied powers, indeed to most of the world, that Germany and Japan would lose the war, and that the combined forces of the Allies would win it. Each of those leaders – Roosevelt, Churchill and Stalin – began to speculate on the attitudes of the others to the postwar world. Each was prey to the prejudices about and fears of the others that had until now been suppressed in the common cause.

Roosevelt and the US advisers began once more to think as an isolationist government – and yet to see the potential for world power that the USA's coming of age in international politics had brought. Roosevelt had an underlying belief in seeking and finding good in everyone, even a Communist tyrant who had been liquidating his opponents since before Roosevelt was President. He did not see in the USSR's fearsome accumulation of armed might the threat to the future of Europe that Churchill had come to believe was inevitable.

With General Marshall, the keystone of Washington strategic planning, Roosevelt shared a deep mistrust of the extent to which Britain was committed to an invasion of Europe across the English Channel – to the operation that had been called 'Roundup' and was now rechristened 'Overlord'. Twice already, Britain had deferred a major landing in northern Europe when the USA was eager to fight Germany in France. Now, Roosevelt feared, Churchill and his adviser Sir Alan Brooke would do it again, and would seek to involve the USA in Southern Europe, bringing America into the Mediterranean theatre even more deeply than she was already. The American President and his advisers believed that the memory of Dunkirk, of Flanders, of the Somme and Passchendaele was too vivid for Britain's military leaders to commit themselves wholly to France. Therefore, they reasoned, 'Overlord' must have an American commander. In fact they went further, and sought to gain acceptance from Churchill of a US Supreme Commander for all operations against Germany.

Britain's military planners, for their part, had never lost their mistrust of US military methods; of what they regarded as slapdash planning, brash arrogance, and an insensitive attitude to European needs. To them, as to Britain's mothers guarding their daughters, the US forces were 'oversexed, overpaid and over here'. Churchill, despite his close personal relationship with Franklin D. Roosevelt, was aware of Roosevelt's leaning to acceptance of his military advisers' views, and he did not like it. Churchill and Brooke were doubtful of the wisdom of Roosevelt's continuing faith in and desire to help Chiang Kai-shek in China, and had no confidence in American acceptance in principle of demands by

Chiang for greatly increased commitment of US troops and aircraft that were desperately needed to win the war against Germany. Churchill believed deeply in the strategy of 'Germany First', and was (probably wrongly) doubtful of the extent of the Pentagon's belief in the strategy agreed and reaffirmed at each Allied conference.

Perhaps more important, Churchill saw clearly Stalin's intention that the USSR should dominate Europe after the war, but was obliged nonetheless, in order to preserve the alliance and the relationship with Roosevelt, to participate in strategic planning which pivoted on the basic and inaccurate assumption that the USSR was honest, trustworthy and prepared to honour its pledges. To Churchill, Roosevelt's trust of Stalin, and the ailing President's courtship of the tyrannical Soviet leader, were deeply disturbing.

Stalin, for his part, believed that Russia had been fighting the Germans virtually single-handed since June 1941 – a view to which statistics alone would lend credence. His perpetual impatience, rising to blazing anger, at the failure of Britain to support US plans for an invasion of Northern Europe in 1942, then again in 1943, caused him to accuse Churchill and the British people of cowardice, an unwillingness to fight and a lack of fellow feeling for Britain's allies. The probability is that he had hoped for a premature invasion of France so that the British and Americans would become bogged down in a stalemate battle that they could not win, and thereby weaken Germany in the East by causing her to fight on two major fronts. That weakening would have enabled Stalin to realise to an even greater degree than he eventually did his true objective – the subjugation of Europe. Had Churchill not held out against a cross-Channel invasion until the Allies could push the German Army back where it came from, West Germany as we knew it until recently would not have existed.

Quebec

All these conflicts, undercurrents, fears and doubts came to the surface when Churchill heard from Averill Harriman that Roosevelt was planning a US-Soviet meeting without Britain. Swiftly, Churchill proposed an alternative summit meeting in Canada, which Roosevelt accepted. On August 14th, after a sedate crossing of the Atlantic in the *Queen Mary*, the Allied Chiefs of Staff met in one place, while Churchill and Roosevelt met in private elsewhere. It soon became apparent that these and the subsequent meetings at Quebec turned on the fundamental issue of 'Overlord' versus the Mediterranean theatre – a disagreement that had already been settled once at Casablanca. The American planners were convinced (with some justice in the light of postwar evidence) that Churchill was still seeking either greater commitment in the Mediterranean, or an invasion in Norway, or an assault in the Balkans – anything rather than a head-on confrontation in France. The facts were that, although Churchill had been energetically pursuing alternatives in the belief that 'Overlord' was an intensely risky undertaking, he had been convinced by the immensely upright Sir Alan Brooke that the commitment to 'Overlord' was right, and must stand.

Nonetheless, the British position at the Quebec conference was that a full-scale invasion in Italy to capitalise on the confusion following Mussolini's departure was vital as a prelude to an invasion of France. Only by having bases in northern Italy, the British argued, could the Allies have the means to strike at vital aircraft and arms manufacture in Southern Germany. This view, subject to an acceptance by Britain that 'Overlord' should have over-riding priority, was accepted reluctantly by the US President and the Chiefs of Staff, but the slowness of the campaign in Italy was to show that General Marshall may well have been right, and Brooke and Churchill wrong. During its discussions of European strategy, the Quebec conference also concluded that the bombing offensive on Germany should be intensified, again as a necessary preliminary to an invasion of France.

When the conference discussed the Far Eastern war, it was the turn of the British to express doubts about American objectives and policies. Yet here there was an illogical and unrealistic contradiction in the British position, perhaps because Churchill knew that it was the intention of the US delegation to suggest and promote at a later date a large scale landing in Burma with the objective of reopening the Burma Road. On the face of it, all the Americans were proposing for the Far East at Quebec was a nebulous British commitment to a greater effort in Burma, possibly because they feared that Britain did not intend doing much to advance the defeat of Japan in the forseeable future. The British Chiefs of Staff, resenting the implication of inaction and unwillingness to do battle, were nonetheless unprepared to agree to a Burma commitment because they knew such a strategy would inevitably mean amphibious landings, which would drain the available resources of landing craft and support vessels needed for 'Overlord'.

The contradiction was that, despite this rejection of positive plans for Burma, Churchill was enthusiastic about the plans propounded by Brigadier Orde Wingate, who was also at Quebec, for Chindit operations on a huge scale as a means of retaking Burma. In alarm, it was pointed out that such a plan would cause an even greater drain on 'Overlord' than an amphibious landing.

After days of muddled discussion on the Far East issue, one of the few positive, far-reaching and successful decisions reached was the creation of an Allied South-East Asia Command, and the appointment to its command of Vice-Admiral Lord Louis Mountbatten, with General Stilwell as his deptuy. In addition, the conference endorsed the decision, already being acted upon, to advance in New Guinea and the Solomons as a two-prong pincer movement to bypass and isolate Rabaul, and set a target date for the defeat of Japan as twelve months after the defeat of Germany.

Cairo and Teheran

In November 1943, after Roosevelt had refused to meet Churchill privately in Malta for a preliminary discussion before a summit conference at which Stalin and Chiang Kai-shek (the latter at Roosevelt's insistence) were to be present, Churchill sailed for Cairo in the battlecruiser *Renown*. The two linked conferences at Cairo and Teheran that were to last three weeks through the second half of November and the first week of December would clearly decide Allied strategy for the conduct of the remainder of the Second World War, and Churchill was far from happy – and, incidentally, far from well, with a severe sore throat and the effects of his inoculations for the trip keeping him in bed for days.

The Cairo conference took place in the shadow of the Sphinx at Giza, with Chiang Kai-shek present, but without Stalin. Mountbatten and Stilwell, the latter still Chiang's Chief of Staff despite his additional appointment as Deputy Supreme Commander South-East Asia, were also there. To Churchill's intense irritation, South-East Asia strategic issues were moved to second place on the agenda, and the continuing debate about the relationship between 'Overlord' and the Mediterranean war was relegated to third spot on the bill. Chiang was determined to get more than his fair share of conference time, and, if he could, more than a sensible slice of Allied resources, with the result that the detailed debate about Europe that Churchill wanted in plenary session before the encounter with Stalin in Teheran was late coming, and limited in scope. Despite this, separate meetings on Europe and Asia took place between the Chiefs of Staff each day, and there was considerable overlap between the two groups. Chiang fought hard for an impossibly large airlift of supplies over 'The Hump' to China, and in fact gained a commitment to 8,900 tons of supplies per month for the next two months. He also pushed hard for an invasion of the Andaman Islands (Operation 'Buccaneer') as an essential precursor to driving the Japanese northwards across Burma and reopening the Burma Road, and had the support of Roosevelt and the American Chiefs of Staff for this plan. The British demurred, wanting the overall strategy in South East Asia agreed before detailed individual operations were planned, and presented their proposals for further operations in the Mediterranean.

The British proposal was neatly summed up by Churchill as 'Rome in January, Rhodes in February, supplies to the Yugoslavs, a settlement of the command arrangements and the opening of the Aegean, subject to the outcome of an approach to Turkey; all preparations for Overlord to go ahead full steam within the framework of the foregoing policy for the Mediterranean.' The American Chiefs of Staff saw in this plan some confirmation of their worst fears, but Roosevelt, with some reluctance, accepted it as the basis for discussion with Stalin.

On November 28th, the British and American leaders and their staffs having moved to Teheran to meet Josef Stalin, the first plenary session with all three Allied leaders present took place. From the outset, Stalin surprised the other delegations by leading the debate, and announcing quite unexpectedly that, once Germany was defeated, the USSR would join her two allies in defeating Japan. When Churchill put the British strategic proposals for 'Overlord' backed by the capture of bases in Italy, Stalin cross-examined him remorselessly on the proportion of the British and American commitment that would be devoted to the French and Italian campaigns, and on the size and nature of the force that Churchill envisaged for the Balkans assault. Having got his answers on these points, Stalin announced that he did not agree with the proposed Balkans campaign (presumably because it would have muddied the Eastern European position for his intended postwar colonisation), and that the major effort for 1944 should be devoted to 'Overlord'. All this was music to the ears of Roosevelt and the US Chiefs of Staff.

Next day, General Sir Alan Brooke was subjected by the Russians – by Marshal Voroshilov in particular – to the kind of mistrustful interrogation on Britain's belief in and commitment to the 'Overlord' concept that he had previously experienced at the hands of the Americans. Progressively, and ever more determinedly, Stalin and his staff pushed for greater and more definite agreement on the invasion of Europe across the Channel. Churchill in turn pushed Roosevelt to abandon the 'Buccaneer' operation in South-East Asia, without apparent effect. When finally the Conference minute of agreement was drawn up, it was with the unanimous approval of those taking part. The Allies had agreed their strategy for the remainder of the European War as follows:

'(a) That we should continue to advance in Italy to the Pisa-Rimini line. (This means that the 68 LSTs which are due to be sent from the Mediterranean to the United Kingdom for Overlord must be kept in the Mediterranean until 15th January).

(b) That an operation shall be mounted against the South of France on as big a scale as landing craft will permit. For planning purposes, D-Day to be the same as Overlord D-Day.

(c) That we will launch Overlord in May, in conjunction with a supporting operation against the South of France.'

On December 2nd 1943, Churchill and Roosevelt arrived back in Cairo. There they tackled the tactical considerations that the strategic decisions raised, and conferred with their Chiefs of Staff on the logistics of two major simultaneous landings in France. For three days, amid the detailed discussions, Churchill and the British delegation urged Roosevelt and his Chiefs of Staff to forget 'Buccaneer', the operation to invade the Andaman Islands, and the drain on resources that it would bring. The US Generals stood firm on their commitment to Chiang Kai-shek. But on December 5th Roosevelt overruled them and told Churchill that Buccaneer was off. Now only the vexed question of the choice between an American and a British commander for the 'Overlord' invasion remained.

Churchill had long held that the preoponderance of British and Empire troops in the fight against Germany made a British commander obligatory, and had an informal understanding with General Sir Alan Brooke that he (Brooke) would have the command. But the US President stood firm on the necessity for an American commander. Given that they were obliged to accept an American general, the British wanted General Marshall. However, Roosevelt demurred, feeling – probably rightly – that Marshall's presence in Washington was too important to the successful prosecution of the war for him to be given another task, even one as important as this. In looking for an alternative there was, to Roosevelt, only one candidate – General Dwight D. Eisenhower. Thus it was that Eisenhower gained the most prestigious command of the Second World War, and with it the awesome responsibility of bringing to reality the long-awaited Allied assault on Europe.

SOVIET ADVANCES
KURSK, THE COUNTERATTACK
AND THE UKRAINE

On the Eastern Front, the colossal build-up of Soviet armed might had continued following the defeat of the German 6th Army at Stalingrad. In this chapter, we deal with the events of summer and autumn 1943, and the only major German offensive of that year, but as background to the story it is worth noting just how greatly the Soviet Union had succeeded in mobilising its manhood to war. Between mid-1941, when Germany launched its ill-fated invasion of Russia, and the end of 1943, Russia's total infantry forces had been increased from 175 divisions to 513 divisions; her armoured and mechanised brigades had risen in number from 78 to 290, and even her somewhat anachronistic cavalry forces (which were, despite their quaint appearance, magnificent in the mud) had been expanded from 30 to 41 divisions. Some differences in the way the Russians worked out their brigade and divisional strengths make the apparent superiority of these figures over the comparable German numbers exaggerated, but nothing can alter the fact that Russian military strength had tripled in the two-and-a-half-year period, despite the enormous Soviet losses of men and armaments during the first German advance to the perimeter of Moscow.

Similarly, German commanders on the Eastern Front were surprised not only by the apparently endless supply of human reinforcements that the Russians could conjure as if from nowhere, but also by the number and superiority of the new Russian weapons that were appearing. Perhaps the most significant of these was the latest version of the famed T-34 tank, the T-34/85, which mounted an 85mm gun capable of knocking out any German tank at any likely range, and which was so effective a weapon that it stayed in production until 1958. But the emergence of the Soviet SU-152 self-propelled gun also proved important, countering as it did the German 'Ferdinand' self-propelled gun, which proved to have a major disadvantage in having no forward-firing machine gun.

Finally, the perseverance and suffering of the British and American sailors who operated the North Atlantic convoys despite the threat of the U-Boats was paying off in the form of a considerable arsenal of Western Allied weapons and aircraft in Soviet hands. Britain supplied Russia with over 4,000 tanks, more than 4,000 anti-aircraft guns and almost 6,000 aircraft under Lend Lease; the USA provided almost 4,000 tanks and over 6,000 aircraft; Canada supplied over 1,000 tanks. Nevertheless, Stalin's propaganda machine attempted to belittle the Allied contribution. However much it stressed victory over Nazism in the East as the totally Soviet creation that Russians still believe it to have been, the fact remains that the USSR would have found it impossible to have turned the tide against Germany without Allied support on a massive scale.

We have already seen in an earlier chapter how badly 1943 had begun for the Germans at Stalingrad and in the Caucasus. In the North, the Army Groups Centre and North had fared little better. In January, first the German defenders of Velikiye-Luki had been besieged for a fortnight before being defeated by the Russians under Marshal Voroshilov. Then the German 18th Army commanded by Colonel-General Lindemann had been defeated on the shores of Lake Ladoga, following which the 17 month siege of Leningrad had at last been lifted. Railway communications between the city of the Winter Palace and the world from which it had been cut off for so long were restored on February 6th.

In the face of these defeats, Hitler permitted at long last the withdrawals to more defensible positions for which his generals had been pressing, and 30 divisions of the 4th and 9th Armies were withdrawn approximately 100 miles over a period of some three weeks without undue losses of men or equipment. This strategic retreat straightened the line that the Germans held, reducing its length by half to 230 miles and releasing 14 divisions for other tasks.

In April, it became clear what 'other tasks' Hitler had in mind. His Operational Order No. 16 set out his plan for 'Operation *Zitadelle*', an offensive designed to surround and annihilate the Soviet forces holding Kursk. The tone of the Operational Order makes it quite clear that Hitler saw this offensive as the means by which the world was to be jolted into realising that the force of German arms was not yet spent. His generals saw it in a somewhat different light, their opinions varying from the open and positive support for the plan on military grounds offered by Kluge, to the open opposition of Colonel-General Heinz Guderian, Inspector-General of Armoured Troops, who believed that the tanks that would be lost in the attack would certainly be needed during 1944 to repel an Allied invasion in Northern Europe.

In the event, Hitler's plan was acted upon, but not until July 1943, when the first units of the new PzKpfw V (Panther) tanks had arrived on active service. No less than 41 German divisions were thrown into the attack on July 5th, including 18 armoured *Panzer* and *Panzer-grenadier* Divisions with a total of about 1,000 tanks and 376 self-propelled guns. Air support was provided by *Luftflotte IV*. Against this German strength, the Soviet armies in the Kursk salient numbered about 75 divisions and 3,600 tanks, plus an amazing figure of 20,000 guns, howitzers and mortars, including 6,000 anti-tank guns and almost a thousand rocket launchers. The Russians had amassed, as a deliberate policy, sufficient artillery to form specific Artillery Divisions, something no other army had attempted, and the policy was to pay off handsomely during the advance on Germany.

Almost as important as the Russians' superiority of sheer firepower was her intelligence success in gathering up-to-date and accurate information on the German troop dispositions and strengths, and the sheer luck of having on July 4th, the day before the German offensive began, a Czech *Wehrmacht* deserter come over to the Soviet side and give exact details of the timing of the attack. As a result of this good fortune, the Red Army was able to deliver a formidable psychological stroke against the German 9th Army when, only twenty minutes before the attack was to begin, a massive Soviet artillery barrage hit the German positions with pinpoint accuracy, throwing the units keyed up for a surprise attack into considerable confusion. Although the German formations quickly recovered themselves, and launched their assault on time, the 9th Army advanced only six miles against the Soviet 13th during that hard-fought first day. In the next two days, the leading German units advanced only another six miles. On July 7th, the 9th Army's advance stopped, outgunned and outnumbered.

Further South, the German 4th Army did better, but not well enough. Strong air support enabled them to make initial advances more or less to plan, and by July 11th two defensive lines had been broken and the advance units were in a position to breach Russian supply lines. The 2nd *Waffen SS Panzer* Corps had played a major part in Manstein's being able to report on July 13th that the 4th *Panzerarmee* had taken 24,000 prisoners. But trouble had by then been brewing for the Germans for days. Aware that the two German armies that were seeking to establish a pincer movement and cut off the Russian forces were still 75 miles apart, the Russian General Vatutin, in command of the Voronezh Front, decided to counterattack. From July 10th, he brought up the crack 5th Guards Tank Army (the 'Guards' title was awarded for achievement in the Red Army) and the 1st Tank Army, and on the 12th launched the greatest tank battle of the Second World War against the Germans defending the over-extended positions of the Orel Salient. Well over 5,000 armoured vehicles took part in the Battle of Kursk, the might of the new Russian armour being pitched against German *Panzer* Divisions that were greatly weakened both by losses of men (20,000 during the previous week alone) and by mechanical wear and unreliability after months or years of compaigning in often appalling conditions with only rudimentary field maintenance to keep them going.

The main assault by the Russians on Orel, with 3,000 guns and 400 rocket launchers, made rapid progress, covering 15 miles in the first 48 hours. All along the complex front, other Russian formations breached the German defences and pushed infantry and artillery through the gaps to harry the Germans and break up their command structures. By July 15th, the German armies were clearly getting the worst of the situation around them; by the 20th the Germans had no alternative but to throw large numbers of precious aircraft into the desperate struggle to hold their positions against the mighty tank and artillery assault. On July 29th, the German evacuation of the Orel Salient, approved by Hitler, began.

Field-Marshal Kluge had been gloomy in his prognosis when he had, the previous week, reported events to Hitler. The Fuehrer was, in any event, already plunged into depression by the Allied successes in Sicily and the Italians' manifest failure to defend their territory. Faced with the need to withdraw resources from Russia to defend the Italian mainland against imminent invasion, Hitler did exactly what Roosevelt and the American Generals had said he would not do – he gave the order to withdraw and abandon Operation *Zitadelle*, and thereby demonstrated that the Allied invasion in the Mediterranean had succeeded after all in taking the pressure off the Eastern Front.

As the German armies retreated they destroyed everything in their path, leaving local populations without food and shelter. To the South of the retreating 9th and 4th Armies, Manstein's 42 German divisions faced some 120 Russian divisions, and even these numbers were being rapidly increased – by September, he was outnumbered eight to one. On August 3rd 1943, Colonel-General Vatutin and his colleague Colonel-General Konev advanced a wedge into Manstein's army, dividing the 4th *Panzerarmee* from the *Gruppe* 'Kempf' and thereby breaking the front. Now the Russians were swiftly able to liberate Belgorod and Bogodukhov, and, crashing on through the Ukraine, recaptured the city of Kharkov, which the Germans lost on August 22nd. By September 7th, Manstein's army was reduced to 257 tanks and 220 assault guns. Clearly, he had little alternative but to withdraw.

Hitler, realising at last that he was about to lose the great mineral resources of the Donets basin, and that the 'divisions' he still moved on his map were no longer the full strength *Blitzkrieg* units of June 1941, decided to visit Manstein at Zaporozhye on the Dnieper. From September 9th to the 16th they argued about the situation that faced them, Manstein putting clearly the impossible position in which the German armies found themselves. Finally, Hitler agreed to the withdrawal. On the night of September 15/16th it began with the evacuation of the Taman peninsula, a huge amphibious operation under Vice-Admiral Schurlen bringing over 200,000 troops and 15,000 vehicles, to say nothing of over 54,000 horses and 1,200 guns, across the Kerch Strait on the Sea of Azov. Manstein's forces to the North of the Sea of Azov (the 1st and 4th *Panzerarmee* and the 8th Army) were brought back across the Dnieper between Zaporozhye to the South and Kiev to the North, destroying crops and villages as they went.

If the Germans believed that getting to the Western bank of the Dnieper would earn them a chance to regroup, they were disappointed. The Russians rapidly crossed the river and established bridgeheads to secure their support positions from artillery and tank attack. This time they were West of the Dnieper for good. By the beginning of November, the German 17th Army had been trapped in the Crimea by the headlong advance of the Russian armies, although, after taking Zaporozhye on October 14th, the Russians had been checked on most fronts for a week or two by determined German defensive fighting. At Krivoi Rog, particularly, the XL *Panzer* Corps, reinforced by the 24th *Panzer* Division, had on October 28th pushed General Rotmistrov's 5th Guards Tank Army back some 15 miles, with Russian losses of 10,000 dead and 5,000 taken prisoner. This check on the Russian advance gave Manstein the chance to retreat from the Dniepropetrovsk salient that had developed, but the comparative peace did not last long.

On November 3rd, Colonel-General Vatutin attacked the German VII Corps defending Kiev, the capital of the Ukraine. With 30 infantry divisions and 1,500 tanks levelled against them, the German defenders could do little. On November 6th, the Russians were once more in possession of a city that had become a symbol of eventual German defeat on Russian soil. Manstein, however, did not take such humiliation lightly, and fought back vigorously, coming during December within 25 miles of recapturing Kiev. But to do so he had drawn on the resources of the German 8th Army, which, thus weakened, lost Cherkassy to Colonel-General Konev.

Thus 1943 ended with the Germans in full retreat all along the Eastern Front, with severely depleted formations, and with a massively reinforced Red Army flushed with success pursuing it relentlessly towards Berlin. The Russians had a long way to go. But their objective was never in doubt.

THE BATTLES FOR THE ISLANDS

THE GILBERTS, MARSHALLS AND PHILIPPINE SEA

By September 1943, the Japanese were under severe pressure – indeed, it can be argued that they were already beaten. Although Tojo, Japan's warlike and dictatorial Premier, was talking of and planning for the great offensive that would win the Pacific war for Japan, the High Command knew that they were in trouble. Shipping losses to US submarines were mounting because of inadequate convoys and worse convoy protection. Vital raw materials and supplies were going down with the ships. Terrible losses of pilots were being met only by cutting the training programmes of the pilots that replaced them, which inevitably produced still higher losses of both aircraft and crews. New aircraft types were just not materialising, with the result that Allied aircraft design and technology had overtaken the once all-conquering speed and firepower of the Zero fighter and Mitsubishi bomber. Perhaps most important, the USA was building and putting into action not only faster and better aircraft carriers, but also faster and more manoeuvrable longer-range and better-armed aircraft to fly from them.

To face this threat, the Japanese established in September 1943 a 'New Operational Policy' by which the Japanese garrisons holding a defensive line from Timor through western New Guinea, Biak Island, the Caroline Islands and the Marianas were to be immoveable. To them fell the honour of fighting to the death. To the US Marines fell most of the task of providing that glorious end. The first target was, after some initial debate between Admiral Nimitz on the one hand, and Admiral King and General Marshall on the other, settled as the Gilbert Islands, sixteen tiny atolls in the Central Pacific lying astride the Equator. In particular, the tiny yet colossally defended Tarawa Atoll was singled out as the most important target, because of its potential as a Japanese base to combat the necessary US conquest of the Marshall Islands.

The US attack on Tarawa Atoll, and most notably on the fortress-like two-mile by 900 yard island of Betio, was launched on November 20th 1943, and was to prove disastrous for the force that undertook it, yet entirely successful in its objectives. Over 4,500 Japanese were on the little island; virtually every palm tree, every fold in the beach concealed an arsenal. In sand-covered concrete bunkers, the defenders survived a barrage of 3,000 tons of shells from three battleships, nine destroyers and four cruisers of the US Navy plus bombing from the air, an assault which set virtually the entire island afire. When the first of 16,798 Marines attempted to land, they were met by a hail of fire such as few had ever imagined. Tricky tides, about which the invasion force had been warned, caused the landing craft to run aground on the reef, well short of the beach, and as the

Marines waded ashore they were gunned down by the hundred. Despite calling up his reserve forces on the afternoon of the first day, Major-General Julian C. Smith finished his first day ashore less than 200 yards from the waterline.

Over the next two days, every inch of the tiny island had to be fought for with flame throwers, grenades and small arms against an opponent who was determined to die. And die he did. By the end of the battle on Betio Island, 5,500 men had met their end, including more than a thousand US Marines. Over 2,000 Marines were wounded. Of the Japanese, all were slain except for one officer, 16 other ranks and a party of Korean labourers.

Nobody, least of all Admiral Nimitz, had expected such murderous resistance from such a small and apparently insignificant target. The appalling US death toll on Tarawa served as a warning for future invasions in the island-hopping campaign that was to lead ultimately to Tokyo, and the complete re-think of the pre-invasion barrage technique that resulted from it undoubtedly saved many lives in subsequent operations.

Elsewhere in the Gilbert Islands, the pattern was variable and less dramatic. To take the Makin Atoll to the North-West of Tarawa, Major-General Ralph C. Smith's 27th Division lost 64 men killed and 150 wounded, a considerably higher death toll than he had been led to expect, whereas the Abemama Atoll was taken with no problem at all by just a company of US Marines. The next target was the Marshall Islands, a bigger problem altogether, and one for which the US 5th Fleet was greatly reinforced. Newly-commanded by Rear-Admiral Mitscher, the fleet's Task Force 58 embarked upon the Marshalls operation with no less than 12 aircraft carriers, bearing 715 fighters, dive-bombers and torpedo-bombers. Rear-Admiral Turner's amphibious force was made up of 300 warships and transport ships.

Against all advice, Admiral Nimitz decided to make the obvious principal target of Kwajalein the main objective for an amphibious landing. The other two targets that were to be overcome, Maloelap and Wotje, were presented as objectives to Task Force 58. The Japanese, correctly anticipating that Nimitz would be advised, after Tarawa, to land on the easier targets first, cunningly diverted a significant part of their defence force away from Kwajalein to the other islands – and thereby contributed unwittingly to the success of Nimitz' bold stroke. With the lessons of Tarawa ever in mind, the air offensive against Kwajalein, Maloelap and Wotje, launched between the end of January 1944 and February 11th, was heavy and unrelenting. Over 6,000 missions were flown and more than 1,100 tons of bombs were dropped. In the midst of the holocaust the US 5th Amphibious Force, including the newly arrived 4th Marine Division, which had never been in action before, went ashore on Kwajalein in force and without major losses. Some 42,000 men landed, and this time only 372 were killed. The Japanese lost almost 8,000 men – but, to a man, they preferred death to surrender.

On February 17th came the next assault, against Eniwetok, which was again successful with relatively small losses. Once again the Japanese defenders preferred death – of 2,741 on the island, 2,677 were killed. Viewing the success of the operations in the Gilbert and Marshall Islands, Nimitz decided once again, as he had before in the Solomon Islands, not to bother with invading targets that, although held by the Japanese, were tactically unimportant once they were isolated from their brethren. The proposed assaults on Wotje and Maloelap, and the possible invasions of other small Japanese held groups, were cancelled. The Japanese that held them were left to consider their positions until the war was over. Similarly, the great Japanese naval base at Truk in the Caroline Islands was attacked fiercely and successfully from the air from February 17th to 20th with the loss of 33 ships and 250 Japanese aircraft – and was then left to its own devices for the remainder of the war. Interestingly, the sunken ships in Truk lagoon have, since the war, become a major site for marine biological research. Before the attack on the Japanese fleet, the sandy floor of the lagoon had supported little marine life, and biologists are able to measure exactly the development of marine life in a controlled environment with a known timescale.

However, marine biological research was far in the future as Nimitz and Mac-Arthur, the latter having fought his way almost to the tip of New Guinea, looked to their next target – the islands of Saipan, Tinian and Guam in the Philippine Sea, and ultimately the reconquest of the Philippines. Not for nothing had Douglas MacArthur vowed that he would return.

The Philippine Sea

A rapid and successful island-hopping exercise carried out by MacArthur's troops up the coast of New Guinea between May and July 1944 gave the Allies the islands of Wakde, Biak, and Numfoor and positioned MacArthur's troops by the end of July in the region of the 'Vogelkop' at the tip of New Guinea. Landings in April 1944 by the US 24th Division (Tanahmerah Bay) and the 41st Division (Hollandia and Aitape) to take General Adachi and the Japanese 18th Army by surprise were successful and, although the Japanese counterattacked and fought fiercely through July, by the end of the month the pincer movement of the two American forces had over 120,000 Japanese neatly trapped in appalling tropical conditions.

Meanwhile, the plan to take the islands of Guam, Saipan and Tinian, which were to become the air bases from which the assault on the Philippines and, eventually, the nuclear attacks on mainland Japan were launched, had been put into action on June 11th when the first of a long series of devastating bombing raids took off for the Marianas. Vice-Admiral Ozawa of the Japanese Navy, as soon as the bombing began, was ordered to take his 1st Mobile Fleet into the attack, since simply to await developments, now that the US Navy had twice the carrier-borne air power of the Japanese, was certain to result ultimately in US recapture of the Philippines. The Japanese High Command believed by this time that they had little to lose by attempting the near-impossible, and on June 15th Ozawa's fleet came throught the San Bernadino Strait and into the Philippine Sea, there linking up with Ugaki's Attack Division. On the same day, the 2nd and 4th US Marine Divisions landed on Saipan against ferocious defence by 32,000 Japanese soldiers, and by evening V Amphibious Corps had 20,000 Americans on Saipan.

As Ozawa's fleet approached to do battle, Admiral Spruance recalled his carriers and their aircraft, redeployed his fleet, and awaited events. He could not sail out to meet the enemy in the classic manner, for to do so would have exposed the Marines on Saipan to attack. So he just waited. He did not have to wait for long, and was, in any event, well briefed by US Intelligence, who continued to be able to decode and read in full Japanese Navy signals.

On June 19th two Japanese naval forces approached. The first was a decoy fleet under Vice-Admiral Kurita, whose role was to attract Admiral Spruance's aircraft into battle. This was followed at a respectful distance of over 100 miles by a much larger force that was intended to pick off the American aircraft carriers while their aircraft were away attacking Kurita's ships.

On the face of it, this was an excellent plan. It failed because of the massive superiority of US aircraft, crews and training. The Japanese lost 243 aircraft in the operation, two thirds of those that took part, and achieved almost nothing – minor damage to American ships, and 30 US aircraft shot down. The Japanese ships fared little better. Admiral Ozawa's flagship, the 29,300 ton aircraft carrier *Taiho*, was torpedoed and sunk during the morning, and a few hours later, in the afternoon, the 25,675 ton carrier *Shokaku*, completed only in 1941, met the same fate. Vice-Admiral Lockwood's submarines had had a good day.

Ozawa had survived the loss of his ship, and was now commanding his fleet from *Haguro*, a 13,400 ton heavy cruiser. During the late afternoon of 20th June, another battle took place in fading light, some 200 miles from the first. Amid fierce aerial combat, the Japanese lost another carrier, the 24,000 ton *Hiyo*, and a further 40 aircraft. The American fleet lost a total of 49 planes, more than half of which crashed while trying to land on the carriers after dark – albeit with the benefit of full landing lights that Spruance had had switched on despite the submarine risk. This decision saved many lives and enabled the rescue crews to find ditched pilots in the water around the carriers.

Following this second Battle of the Philippine Sea, Ozawa had only 35 aircraft left of the 473 with which he embarked upon his attack. The battles marked the end of effective Japanese carrier-borne operations, and also the end of Tojo's reign of terror at the head of Japan's government. Desperately seeking someone to blame for the disaster, governmental opinion in Japan rounded upon Tojo, who resigned. He was succeeded by General Kuniaki Koiso.

Meanwhile, on Saipan the 27th Infantry Division and the 2nd and 4th Marine Divisions had been fighting a gruelling campaign across rocky and mountainous terrain in which small pockets of Japanese soldiers were able to dig themselves in using caves and rocky defiles for cover. As each unit of Japanese infantry was pinned down and surrounded, its remaining soldiers would suddenly launch a last desperate suicidal *Banzai* attack, taking with them as many of the US troops as they could. Despite this wearying and grisly way of taking an island inch by inch, the Marines made progress, and by July 1st the battle was entering its final stage. Almost a week later, on the 7th, the last 2,500 or so Japanese defenders swept down upon the Americans in a final suicide attack and were annihilated. Admiral Nagumo shot himself, and General Saito, rather more colourfully, ceremonially slit his own stomach with his sword, then had his adjutant shoot him in the head. Who shot the adjutant is not clear.

Guam

While the Japanese Navy had been losing its aircraft in the Philippine Sea and the US 2nd and 4th Marines plus the 27th Infantry Division had been clearing Saipan, the 3rd Amphibious Corps (the same troops that had taken Bougainville, but under a different organisational title) had embarked upon the recapture of the 28 mile long narrow island of Guam. This important base for future operations was held by 18,500 Japanese army and navy personnel, a large proportion of whom were clustered around the airfield at Orote, close to the main town of Agana. With the massacre of Tarawa still fresh in their minds, and rather more experience of Japanese techniques of war since, the US commanders took no risks. The bombardment of Guam that preceded the landing began on July 2nd, almost three weeks before the actual invasion on July 21st.

The landing, close to and south of Agana, went well, and the US forces advanced rapidly, despite fierce fighting, towards the airfield and the high ground beyond. Then, on 25th July, the Japanese counterattacked, and there was a night of ferocious battle during which the Japanese troops all but overwhelmed the US headquarters on the island, taking as they did so quite appalling losses. By morning their losses were such that they could do nothing but fall back, and the battle for Guam was almost over. Yet it was not until August 10th that General Obata and his troops had been pushed to the sea, and not until the 11th that he too killed himself as the battle finally came to an end.

The battle for Guam cost the Japanese 17,300 dead at the time, and quite a few later as Japanese soldiers surfaced from hideouts determined to have their own last stand, some of them months after the battle was over. The Americans lost just under 2,000 soldiers on the island.

Tinian

The last of Nimitz's three Mariana targets was Tinian, a smaller island only 12 miles long but, unlike the others, almost entirely flat and capable of providing an easily constructed airfield for operation of the new Boeing B29 Superfortress long range bomber. Less than three miles from Saipan, it was, as soon as Saipan had been invaded, within gunnery range of land batteries. On July 24th 1944, the 24th and 25th Marines went ashore across narrow beaches after heavy gunfire both from the sea and from Saipan had reduced the level of resistance, and managed to establish a sound beach-head by nightfall. The battle lasted for a little over a week, and followed a similar pattern to that of the other islands – stubborn resistance by small groups of Japanese, followed by *Banzai* attacks when it was clear that Japanese arms could not prevail.

By July 31st, the Marines had taken Tinian town, the principal objective on the island. On August 1st the last militarily organised Japanese action ended, but once again it took until August 12th to round up all the remaining soldiers and hostile civilians. A further 6,000 Japanese soldiers died on Tinian. Only 235 prisoners were taken. A total of 290 US Marines died in the assault.

Thus ended the conquest of the Marianas, a necessary prelude to the reconquest of the Philippines. All told, the Japanese deathroll amounted to about 40,000 men, with just over 2,000 Japanese taken prisoner. The Americans lost 4,596 dead, with 19,323 wounded or missing.

THE ADVANCE ON ROME

ANZIO, KESSELRING AND THE STRUGGLE IN ITALY

The advance from the toe of Italy after the landings at Salerno had been slow and beset by unseasonably cold, wet weather. By the late autumn of 1943, it had developed into a sluggish near-stalemate from which neither side was making significant progress. The topography of Italy's boot is mountainous and difficult for all but the best mountain troops. Field-Marshal Kesselring, having stabilised the military situation following Italy's surrender to the Allies and the blood-letting that followed, was defending positions along the Gustav Line to the South and West of Rome with divisions that were severely under-strength and short of artillery ammunition, but whose morale, given the worldwide decline in Axis fortunes, was surprisingly good. Every day, the Germans shelled from their vantage points in the hills Allied positions that were little more than a welter of mud. Modern weapons became useless and unmoveable with a choice only between the morass of the valley or the rocky heights of the hills. The Second World War in Europe, for the whole of that miserable winter, became an echo of the mud of Flanders.

The stalemate, and the underlying Allied conviction that Rome was the psychologically important target in Italy for both sides, brought forward a number of Allied proposals, but Winston Churchill's idea for 'Operation Shingle' emerged by the end of 1943 as the plan that Roosevelt and Stalin had both accepted. A major attack in the South by Lieutenant-General Mark Clark's US 5th Army and Britain's 8th Army would draw Germany's depleted forces away from the areas around Rome, and from the Colli Laziali (or Alban Hills) between Rome and the coast. This was to make possible a surprise landing by the US VI Corps under Major-General John P. Lucas in the Anzio/Nettuno area, and a rapid advance into the Alban Hills to cut German communications and 'threaten the rear of the XIV German Corps'.

Clearly, the fundamental principle of the plan depended on speed at Anzio, since it was realised that a breakout towards Rome through the Alban Hills was unlikely to be realistically possible unless Kesselring had diverted a substantial part of the German forces defending Rome to the South and South-West. It was also clear that, once he was aware that a beach-head had been created at Anzio, Kesselring, a master organiser, would not be slow in plugging the gap in his defences.

When the plan was put into action, in January 1944, things did not go as Churchill and Roosevelt had hoped, although the reasons were less than simple. Journalists at the time, and some historians, have tended to place all the odium for the failure of the breakout from Anzio on Major-General Lucas, but, while there is no doubt that his approach to the problems that faced him was not the fire-eating 'go gettem' approach of a General Patton, some of the blame must be ascribed to Lieutenant-General Mark Clark. For it is established that, instead of passing on Alexander's orders simply to seize the beach-head, and then cut the enemy's communications, Clark ordered Lucas to seize *and secure* the beach-head then advance on the Colli Laziali. In other words, Clark's order implied that, until the beach-head was secure, the breakout was not to be attempted. Furthermore, even when the breakout began, it was in order to 'advance' on the Alban Hills, not to rush them and cut the enemy off from Kesselring's main forces as the original plan had envisaged.

Anzio

On January 16th 1944, General Clark's 5th Army once more attacked the German positions on and around Monte Cassino. This hill – or mountain – topped by a beautiful 14th century Benedictine monastery filled with priceless art treasures had already become symbolic of the Italian stalemate. Over the next four months it was to renew fears of apparent Nazi invincibility, and to become the focus of allegations of Allied vandalism that roll on into the Eighties.

Now, just before the amphibious landing at Anzio that was to come just under a week later, Monte Cassino was defended by General von Vietinghoff-Scheel's XIV *Panzer* Corps of the German 10th Army. The assault on the Cassino defile was to be carried out by the US II Corps under Major-General Geoffrey Keyes, supported on its right by General Juin's French Expeditionary Corps, which included Moroccan and Algerian troops who were to distinguish themselves many times during the ensuing months, and on the left by Lieutenant-General Sir Richard McCreery's British X Corps. The intention was to get across the Rapido, some five miles South of Cassino, and bypass the mountains along the Liri Valley towards Anzio. However, the plan took insufficient account of the terrain. Although X Corps got across the river – at that point the Garigliano, formed by the confluence of the Liri and the Rapido – they could advance little further and were badly mauled. The US 36th Division, which started North of the Rapido, was even thrown back across it, with terrible casualties. Only the French, who, because of their colonial mountain troops, had been given the task of taking the high ground, had any measure of success. But even they, having captured the mountains above the Rapido, did not have the necessary strength to descend to the valley behind the German defenders.

Nonetheless, although the operation seemed to achieve little militarily, it did succeed in part in its primary objective. General von Vietinghoff called for reinforcements, and Kesselring transferred the 29th and 90th *Panzergrenadier* Divisions from Rome.

At 2am on January 22nd, General Lucas's US VI Corps began landing at Anzio and Nettuno, and by midnight the same day had put ashore over 36,000 men, more than 3,000 vehicles and virtually all the guns that were to take part in the operation. The Corps in fact included, in addition to the US 3rd Division, the British 1st Division, a regiment and a battalion of paratroops, a brigade of commandos and three battalions of US Rangers. The two battalions of Germans that were the only German forces in the area were quickly wiped out, and, on the face of it, Rome was 37 miles away, and there was virtually nobody in the way of a speedy advance to the objective. Had General Patton been in command, he would undoubtedly have set off at high speed to the Eternal City, revolvers gleaming and eyes glinting. But would he have been right? And would he have succeeded?

General Truscott, the commander of the US 3rd Division, who was something of a fire-eater himself, thought not, and defended his then superior, General Lucas, for following the orders General Clark had given him and 'securing the beach head'. In his view, Kesselring would have pulled back to the area between Rome and Anzio within days, regardless of how far VI Corps had pushed on to Rome, and would probably have been able to cut the communications of the over-extended Allied advance while at the same time shelling the under-defended beach-head and inhibiting the landing of reinforcements and supplies. Nonetheless, Churchill was furious that Lucas stayed put at Anzio landing the remainder of his Corps, building up an immense stock of vehicles – one report quoted 17,000 vehicles for 70,000 men – and preparing his armour, while Hitler was issuing his Directive for the Battle of Rome, and Kesselring was organising LXXVI *Panzer* Corps for a counterattack. In a famous comment, Churchill said 'I expected to see a wildcat roaring into the mountains – and what do I find? A whale wallowing on the beaches!'

In fact, on the day after the Anzio landing, General von Mackensen arrived to take command of the already prepared German plan for tackling the problem, but had at that stage only a small detachment of the *Hermann Goering Panzer* Division and a few guns. By the 28th, he had three divisions in the defensive line. By the 31st he had eight, and the landing was effectively, for the time being at least, contained.

Hitler was, however, not content with containing the situation. He had ordered a counterattack that was to drive the Allies back into the sea, and had altered the plan by which LXXVI Corps was to carry out the attack so that the luckless *Panzer* Corps was to attack on a front only four miles wide without adequate air cover – for Field-Marshal von Richtofen's *Luftflotte II* simply did not have the aircraft, the pilots or, most important of all, the fuel for a sustained aerial assault and cover operation.

The German attack on February 16th ran into trouble almost as soon as it began. The initial barrage was, because of lack of ammunition, simply not enough to deter effective resistance to the first advance, and the Allied air attacks were pressed home effectively against tanks which could not leave the roads because of the softness of the Pontine marshes on either side. Air strikes also limited the quantity of supplies that the Germans could bring forward; nonetheless Mackensen's Corps had by the end of the first day advanced a third of the twelve miles to the Anzio beaches. On the second and third days, the German troops fought hard to pursue their initial advantage, but the Allied artillery and air power was too great for any significant progress to be possible. The Allied commanders reinforced the beach-head by bringing in the British 5th and the US 34th Divisions, and a new stalemate developed. The German artillery in the Alban Hills maintained constant harassment on the Allied position, and the Allies' guns and aircraft responded in kind. Nonetheless, the initiative had gone, and Rome had not been taken. Now the emphasis had to be returned to the route via Cassino.

The Battles of Monte Cassino

The failure of the Anzio landing to secure an immediate advance on Rome became the reason for some of the fiercest fighting of the war as the 5th Army struggled to take Monte Cassino from a remarkably tenacious German Army.

The French Expeditionary Corps under General Juin had, as early as January 23rd/24th, been given the ultra-hazardous task of attempting to go round Cassino via Monte Belvedere and Colle Abate, with the objective of surrounding their enemy and attacking them from all sides, and, although the encirclement had not been achieved, they had succeeded brilliantly in diverting two thirds of the German defenders to the job of holding down the Algerians and Tunisians. Not for nothing did Kesselring feel uneasy whenever the French Expeditionary Corps was thrown in against his armies. Juin's force held their mountaintop positions, but the US 34th Division was bogged down in its beach-head on the Cassino side of the River Rapido.

To give new impetus, Alexander provided General Clark with General Freyberg's New Zealand Corps – but Freyberg, believing that the historic abbey of Monte Cassino was being used as a German headquarters and stronghold, demanded its destruction by bombing to give his force a chance in the forthcoming battle. Clark opposed this bombing, partly because he was far from sure it was necessary, partly because it was to him an act of vandalism. But Freyberg's view won the day. On February 15th, 229 Allied bombers in three waves dropped 453 tons of high explosive on the venerable building and reduced it to total ruin.

In fact, before the attack, there were no Germans in the monastery other than two military police whose sole function was to protect it from incursion by troops. The only occupants were the abbot and his monks. But, once the damage had been done, the Germans moved into the ruin in force, and used the magnificent vantage point it provided to drive back first the 4th Indian Division and then the 2nd New Zealand Division as they attempted to storm the mountain top. Worse was to follow. On March 15th, the Allied commanders attempted once again to use the same tactics to dislodge the Germans from Cassino by heavy bombing. A total of 775 aircraft dropped 1,250 tons of bombs on the town of Cassino and the country immediately around it. As the Allied troops attempted to capitalise on the effect of the bombing and take the town, the extent of the destruction and cratering made it impossible for the tanks to enter the town. The infantry were on their own, and the ferocity of the fighting was appalling. Anti-personnel mines inflicted terrible casualties, and little progress was made against the crack German parachute troops defending Cassino and the area around it.

An equal lack of success was experienced on the hill below the monastery. It was like Verdun all over again – mud, blood and frustration. On March 23rd, Freyberg recognised the obvious and called off the attack. The losses of the attempts to take Cassino were frighteningly high. Over 22,000 Americans, more than 22,000 British, almost 8,000 French and nearly 400 Italians were killed, wounded or missing for virtually no gain. Alexander now decided to reorganise his force. The British X Corps passed from the 5th Army to the British 8th Army, which had been since December 23rd under the command of General Sir Oliver Leese following Montgomery's recall to Britain for his part in 'Overlord'. Leese was given the sector of the Italian front between the Abruzzi heights and the Liri valley. Clark's 5th Army was responsible now only for the Anzio beach-head and the area between the Liri and the Tyrrhenian Sea.

Alexander's objective remained the smashing of the German 10th Army, and on May 11th he launched his newly reformed forces into the Battle of the Gustav Line. After a night of bombardment and surprise Allied attacks along a 25 mile front, neither the British nor the Americans had made significant progress, and even General Anders' fearless Polish II Corps had been repulsed on the slopes of

Monte Cassino. But, after enduring heavy attack, minefields, flame throwers and just about everything the German Army had, General Juin's tough French Expeditionary Corps took Monte Majo on May 13th, and then went on to capture Monte Petrella on the 15th. On the 17th, the Poles finally made it to the ruined monastery on Monte Cassino, only to find it deserted. By May 23rd, the US II Corps was approaching Terracina, and Kesselring, to stop the advance, took reinforcements from Colonel-General von Mackensen's forces that were restraining the US VI Corps at Anzio. As a result, VI Corps, now under the command of General Truscott, broke out, captured Cisterna and, on May 25th, II Corps and VI Corps joined forces.

The Advance on Rome

Now the Allied offensive against the regrouping German 10th and 14th Armies was stepped up, and Churchill began sending signals urging Alexander to cut off as many of the German divisions from retreat as possible. There is no doubt that General Clark had a magnificent opportunity to capture much of Kesselring's army in a pocket – but instead of turning North to Valmontone to achieve this, Clark headed for Rome, sending only a small detachment towards Valmontone. Kesselring meanwhile was endeavouring to hold a line from the Alban Hills to Monti Lepini, and looked like succeeding until May 31st, when the US VI Corps pierced the German defences, scaled the Alban Hills, and started to advance on Rome. Kesselring had little option but to withdraw and proclaim Rome an open city, to avoid its bombardment and the destruction of its ancient buildings and historic treasures. On June 4th, the American 88th Division was the first Allied force to enter the Eternal City, for which so many had fought for so long.

This was by no means the end of the war in Italy – it had almost a year yet to run before the Italian people could begin to clear up the turmoil into which Mussolini's Fascists had let them fall. But the attention of the world now switched to 'Overlord', the great amphibious invasion of Normandy, which began only two days after the entry into Rome. We too shall look at 'Overlord' – but let us first take a look at the great bomber offensive; the war in the air.

BOMBER OFFENSIVE

THE ASSAULT FROM THE AIR

In earlier chapters of this book the bombing of Warsaw, the London Blitz, the devastating German air raids on Coventry, Clydebank, Plymouth and other targets have been described in the context of their tactical use as part of campaigns to capture Poland and Britain. The Allies took a different view of air power from that adopted by the *Luftwaffe* in general, and by Goering and Hitler in particular. To the Allies, air power was a strategic weapon aimed almost totally at the destruction of the means of production on the one hand, and of enemy towns, cities and morale on the other.

From the beginning, the *Luftwaffe* was designed as a weapon to achieve massive conquest in the shortest possible time – it was a *Blitzkrieg* weapon. Hitler's burgeoning ambition and proliferation of active fighting fronts stretched the *Luftwaffe* badly, as did its severe losses in the Battle of Britain, with the result that, after the initial successes in Russia in 1941, German air power began to wane. One of Hitler's least far-sighted directives had, in 1940, ordered the abandonment of work on all new aircraft types that could not be in service by 1942 on the grounds that 'they would not be needed after the war', and, as a result, development of new aircraft types was 'too little and too late'.

The British had quite early in the war – in August 1940 in fact – proved false Goering's notorious boast that Berlin would never be bombed, and throughout 1941 had maintained constant harassment of Germany by night, albeit on a relatively small scale by comparison with later raids. By spring 1942, the British build-up of bombers, and the development of longer range aircraft, had reached the point where large scale raids could be mounted, and on May 30th 1942, the RAF delivered its first '1,000 bomber raid' on Cologne. In fact, although there were actually just over 1,000 aircraft, many of them were obsolete, and losses were quite high. Cologne was left ablaze and the propaganda effect on the populations of both Britain and Germany was substantial. There followed a rapid series of night carpet bombing raids against the major strategic cities of the Reich – Essen, Dortmund, Leipzig, Hamburg, Berlin – in which civilian populations were hit as hard as German industry. But the assault was not against cities alone.

As longer range four engined aircraft such as the Stirling, the Halifax and the Lancaster became available, more ambitious heavy raids on specifically industrial targets were undertaken. Important centres of production like the steelworks of the Ruhr were hit repeatedly, and in May 1943, Barnes Wallis' famous bouncing bomb was used effectively against the Moehne, Eder and Sorpe dams by 617 Squadron RAF, led by Wing Commander Guy Gibson – the raid portrayed in the British motion picture *The Dam Busters*, made early in the 1950s.

Once the USA was into the war, an argument developed between the US 8th Air Force, formed and led in Britain by General Carl Spaatz, and RAF Bomber Command, under the command of Air Chief Marshal Sir Arthur (Bomber) Harris. The US aerial bombardment strategy was based upon the assumption that heavy bombers carrying sufficient guns could defend themselves against attacking fighters in daylight, and that daylight bombing with pinpoint accuracy was therefore possible. If this were correct, there was obviously much to commend the US approach, as it would reduce to a minimum the impact upon civilian populations and increase the effectiveness of every bomb. Spaatz also rejected Harris's contention that carpet bombing of German cities would break German morale; he argued that if German bombing had failed to bring London to its knees, there was no justification for assuming that Berlin or Hamburg would give in any more easily.

Sir Arthur Harris believed that there was no way in which heavy, relatively slow and largely unmanoeuvrable bombers could defend themselves effectively without fighter cover – a point which to British eyes had been substantially proved by the *Luftwaffe's* failure in daylight raids over Britain – and that, since no fighters existed with long enough range to fly to Germany and back, the only practical approach to strategic bombing was large scale carpet bombing at night of the areas in which large production and military installations were known to exist. He was also confident that bombing of the cities would result in the civilian population of Germany bringing massive pressure to bear on Hitler for an end to the war.

Since neither side wanted to give, and because there was no way of knowing for sure who was right without testing the hypothesis, a compromise was reached in September 1942 by which the US 8th Air Force attacked by day, and the RAF flew by night.

The American crews flew B-17 Flying Fortresses and B-24 Liberators – each bristling with pairs of 0.5 calibre Browning machine guns from hydraulically controlled turrets pointing in almost every direction. The B-17, originally designed in 1934 and first flown in 1935, operated during the Second World War in three principal versions, the B-17E, the B-17F and the B-17G. The majority of operational aircraft by mid 1944 were of the last type, distinguished by its unusual 'chin' gun turret, of which 8,680 were built. The B-17 typically carried a crew of nine, could carry a 10,500lb bomb load, and was fitted with the remarkably accurate Norden bombsight. If it got through to the target, which a significant proportion did, it was able to do tremendous damage with its pinpoint bombing. But, in the early days of the daylight bombing offensive, before suitable fighters were available to provide long range escort, German Messerschmitt 109 and Focke-Wulf 190 fighters were able to shoot down large numbers of the close formations of American bombers. In 1943, the *Luftwaffe* fighters even used successfully the tactic of bombing the formations from above.

In August 1943, the US Eighth Air Force began the process of attacking the *Luftwaffe* production line as a means of reducing the available German air power to combat 'Overlord' when it came. On August 17th, 376 Eighth Air Force aircraft bombed the aircraft factory at Regensburg and the massive ball-bearing production plant at Schweinfurt. Ball-bearing production was a key to the entire war production programme, and Albert Speer, Germany's Minister of Armaments Production, was quoted after the war as saying that if the pressure on ball-bearing production had been maintained, the war production machine would have ground to a halt in only four months. But the raid on Schweinfurt was very expensive indeed in both men and machines. Sixty bombers did not return to their bases in England, and that meant that over five hundred highly-skilled aircrew were lost to the war, either killed or taken prisoner. Not until long-range Mustangs with drop-tanks were available could the massive raids on the more distant parts of Germany continue. In fact, in October 1943, the loss of 153 US bombers in one week caused the cancellation of all raids without fighter escort.

The US raids were not all based in England. Just over two weeks before the raid on Schweinfurt, a force of 178 Consolidated B-24 Liberators took off from Libya to raid the Rumanian oilfields at Ploesti, the principal source of *Wehrmacht* fuel. This raid was enormously hazardous, stretching the range of the Liberator to the absolute limit, and requiring the crews to fly most of the 1,500 mile mission over German occupied territory beset by attacking fighters. Many of the force did not reach their target, but those that did caused great damage to the German war effort. Of the 1,733 men who flew the mission, 446 were killed. Only 33 of the original 178 aircraft flew in action again – many of those that managed to get back to North Africa were not economically repairable.

After the end of 1943, the invention of drop tanks made long range escort of the US bomber formations by the new Mustang fighter entirely routine and bomber losses fell sharply as the damage inflicted on the *Luftwaffe* by the Mustangs rose. The Mustang, with a range of 850 miles, was the longest-range fighter of World War Two, and performed many roles successfully – Group Captain Leonard Cheshire, VC, of the RAF even using one in his pioneering of pathfinder marking of night targets for the RAF bomber forces.

The biggest problem that had afflicted RAF night bombing in the early part of the war was the difficulty of finding the target. In 1940, investigations had shown that two-thirds of the RAF crews on a raid had not bombed within five miles of the target. This was solved to a large extent first by a guidance device known as 'Gee', then, from March 5th 1943, by a more sophisticated radar installation codenamed 'Oboe'. A Pathfinder Force was formed of crack crews, usually flying Lancasters, which were fitted with an even more effective radar known as 'H2S'. Their task was to precede the main force to the target and bomb it accurately with coloured flares to show the bomb-aimers of later aircraft where to target their bombloads.

The techniques of carpet bombing by night became gradually more effective, and all pretence of seeking military targets alone was abandoned after the Casablanca conference sanctioned the use of all-out strategic bombing of Germany. The RAF, in four nights between July 24th and August 3rd 1943, killed an estimated 33,000 people in Hamburg by creating a firestorm, a phenomenon previously known only in theory. Most of the dead were suffocated by the lack of oxygen resulting from the colossal and unimaginably intense fires that engulfed the city. Known to the German population, understandably, as *Die Katastrophe*, the raids on Hamburg stirred fierce resentment against the RAF, whose crews were known as *terrorflieger* and were treated roughly by North German townspeople if they were forced to bale out over the cities. In the first eight months of 1943, 11,000 tons of bombs were dropped by the RAF on Hamburg, 8,000 tons on Essen, 6,000 tons each on Duisburg and Berlin, and 5,000 tons each on Dusseldorf and Nuremberg.

Against these raids, the Germans developed a guidance system for its night-fighters which was known as the *Wurzberg*, a radar which enabled the night fighter controller to talk his squadrons on to the British formations, and a low-frequency radar called *Freya*, which acted as an early warning system. To combat these radar devices, which were becoming progressively more effective, British scientists came up with a delightfully simple idea codenamed 'Window' – nothing more than thousands of strips of metal foil dropped from the formations of aircraft, which, as it fluttered thousands of feet towards the ground provided the German controllers with thousands of false echoes and obscured the real ones that represented the aircraft. By pursuing a non-committal course until after the 'Window' was dropped, the bomber formations were able to conceal their real target from the night fighters and flak gunners until ground reports of the attack gave their positions away.

As 1944, the year of 'Overlord' approached, the Allied air offensive was stepped up, partly to maintain the pressure on armaments production and civilian morale, more to cause the *Luftwaffe* to pull back such reserves as it had from the Atlantic Wall and the defence of the Channel coast to Germany and the defence of the cities. Between January 1st and June 5th 1944, the day before D-Day, the US daylight marauders and the RAF night bombers between them delivered 102 major attacks on German cities. Berlin was almost destroyed by 17 fierce raids; Braunschweig was next in the league of destruction with 13 raids; Frankfurt received eight raids and Hanover five. Many other cities were attacked – Leipzig, Magdeburg, Duisburg, Essen, the other cities of the Ruhr and North Germany. Even Vienna was raided in March.

By the spring of 1944, the *Luftwaffe* was severely depleted, its means of production were being attacked almost daily, and, most important of all, its fuel supplies were reaching crisis point. Much of the credit for this acute shortage of fuel was due to the success of a campaign launched at the beginning of April 1944 by General Spaatz against Germany's sources not only of natural fuels, but also of the synthetic fuels that her scientists had learned to manufacture. We have already described the previous year's assault by Liberators on the oilfield at Ploesti in Rumania. By April 1944, the US Army Air Force was established in Italy, at Foggia, and was in a much stronger position to attack the oil-producing area at shorter range and with far greater chances of success.

On April 4th, a raid from Foggia on Ploesti by 230 bombers did far more damage to oil-field installations than had the previous raid, and the US airmen followed it up with attacks on refineries and storage depots in Bucharest, Budapest and Vienna, and with raids on the Danube ports and on the convoys of barges that transported fuel along the Danube. Between February 1944 and the end of June 1944, the amount of Rumanian oil and refined petroleum reaching Germany was reduced by 80 per cent, from 200,000 tons a month to 40,000 tons per month.

German synthetic fuel sources were hit even harder. On May 12th 1944, just under 1,000 US bombers attacked synthetic fuel plants at five separate targets – Brux, Lutzkendorf, Zeitz, Bohlen and Leuna. Just over two weeks later, on May 28th and 29th, those same targets were attacked again, and, in addition, the US Army Air Force destroyed the vital coal hydrogenation plants at Politz in Pomerania. The effect was devastating to the German war effort. From producing 181,000 tons of aviation fuel in March 1944, slightly more than the severely rationed *Luftwaffe* actually used, the Germans were down to a production of 10,000 tons in September, when they used 60,000 tons, and never again managed to get fuel production up either above 49,000 tons in a month, or up to the rate of consumption. The attacks on the fuel supplies were the death knell of the *Luftwaffe*.

Thus, when General Eisenhower was briefing his troops for 'Overlord', the long-awaited Allied invasion of Normandy, he was able to tell them, with some truth, that if they saw a warplane overhead, they could regard it as friendly. That this was so was due to a large extent to the success of the air offensive.

OVERLORD

THE ATLANTIC WALL AND D-DAY

Since 1940, on Rommel's evidence, Hitler had predicted that an Anglo-American invasion of the Channel coast of France would one day come. Since he had failed, before tackling Russia in the East, to conquer Britain in the West, his forecast did not require great perception. But by the end of 1943 and the beginning of 1944, as the Allied bombing offensive bit deep into German sources of production, and as the Allies advanced slowly but inexorably in Italy, it was clear that the landings could not long be delayed. For years, Hitler had stubbornly, in considering where the Allies would strike, favoured the beaches of Normandy. His subordinates, particularly Field-Marshal Gerd von Rundstedt, now his Supreme Commander in the West, were convinced that he was wrong, and that the Allied attack would be made across the narrowest part of the English Channel to the Pas de Calais. Only in the summer of 1944 did Hitler change his mind, and come round to believing in the invasion via the Straits of Dover.

His change of heart was in part due to some inventive Allied deceptions. An Army Pay Corps officer who in civilian life was an actor, Clifton James, who looked remarkably like Bernard Law Montgomery, was sent to make a much publicised tour of the Mediterranean theatre to direct German attention to the possibility of increased activity in the South. A bogus British Army was deployed with rubber tanks around the South-East corner of England to give German reconnaissance aircraft evidence of a build up around the Straits of Dover. Fake radio traffic was assiduously inserted into the normal transmissions for German monitors to hear. It all pointed to the Pas de Calais, and while it would exaggerate the effect of these devices to claim that the Germans were totally deceived, they were sufficiently unsure of the Allies' intentions to maintain a significant part of their forces in the Calais area, far from the Normandy beaches where the assault would actually come.

To guard against the expected invasion, wherever it was launched, Germany had during her years of occupation of France and the Low Countries progressively built and armed fortifications along the coast which were known, somewhat inaccurately, as the 'Atlantic Wall'. These fortifications, which extended from Holland to the Bay of Biscay, were for most of their length only well-protected gun emplacements with quite modest armament – 3-inch guns were typical. But in the vicinity of the Pas de Calais the guns were bigger and the defences more formidable. The British coastal towns of Dover, Deal and Ramsgate knew to their cost the range and power of the fourteen guns of calibres from 16-inch to 11-inch at Cap Gris Nez. During the spring of 1944, the state of readiness of these and the other armaments along the Atlantic Wall was to be increased sharply, but von Rundstedt had little faith in the capacity of the Wall to contain an Allied invasion, and believed that his Army Groups 'A' and 'B', held with their armour to the rear of the front line, would have the task of destroying the beach-head. As ever in the German High Command, there was sharp disagreement as to the use and dispersal of forces.

Field-Marshal Erwin Rommel, now in command of Army Group B, had been given by Hitler at the end of 1943 the task of inspecting and improving the defences of the Atlantic Wall, and had not been impressed by what he found. Under his direction, half a million men of the *Todt* Organisation were put to work on a massive programme of improvement and additional fortification. Rommel, while agreeing with von Rundstedt that the invasion would not be repulsed by static defences alone, believed strongly that the combined effect of the Wall and a mobile *Panzer* force immediately behind it could destroy the invasion force during what he saw as the critical first twenty-four hours.

As Army Group B commander, Rommel had the 7th and 15th Armies plus LXXXVIII Corps at his disposal, and put to Hitler his conviction based on successful experience of tank warfare that the only potential for victory over an Allied landing lay in the swift and effective deployment of mobile armour to destroy the British, American and Canadian troops on the beaches before they had had the opportunity to develop and strengthen their beach-head. Impressed by this argument, Hitler had on March 20th given Rommel command of *Panzergruppe* West, which consisted of I *Waffen SS Panzer* Corps, plus six other *Panzer* Divisions including the *Leibstandarte Adolf Hitler*. But despite gaining this tactical command, Rommel remained subject to the strategic decisions of von Rundstedt, who still favoured the outmoded concept of holding *Panzer* divisions back to the rear as a means of containing the attempts of the Allies to break out from their beach-head. Thus, although Rommel pushed hard to have the tanks ready to conduct lightning attacks on the Allied soldiers as they landed, wherever that might prove to be, he was not to have his way. In the event, this proved a major factor in the Allies' success on D-Day.

Allied preparations for the greatest amphibious invasion of all time had, as we have seen, been in the melting pot for years. But, by the beginning of 1944, the approximate date had been set, General Dwight D. Eisenhower had been appointed to Supreme Command of the operation, General Montgomery had been recalled from Italy to command Allied land forces in Normandy, and S.H.A.E.F. – Supreme Headquarters Allied Expeditionary Forces – had established the team that would see the invasion through to success.

The technological problems set by the landings and by the logistics of supplying the vast army that was to break out from the beach-head and liberate France and the Low Countries before advancing on Germany were quite unprecedented. They inspired scientific invention on a scale that had never before been seen in such a short span of time, and brought forth from the Allied scientists called upon by a British planning group under Lieutenant-General Sir Frederick Morgan, and taken over by S.H.A.E.F., an abundance of ideas, some of which seemed to border on fantasy.

The Normandy coastline is rich in sandy beaches that are often pounded by surf, but has few ports capable of berthing ships of any size or in any numbers. Some means of docking and unloading ships over a period of weeks, maybe months, had to be found. The answer was towed across the Channel with the invasion fleet – prefabricated concrete 'Mulberry' harbours that were sunk into position and used with complete success. Their hulks can still be seen off the Normandy coast today.

The fuel requirements of the Allied armies were recognised as being too large to be supplied entirely by sea. Again the scientists came up with an answer, this time known as PLUTO – pipeline under the ocean. Revolutionary at the time, the trans-channel pipeline worked well and overcame the problem. 'Crabs', developed versions of the tanks equipped with flails to clear mines – similar to the Scorpions which had earlier assisted the Eighth Army in the Western Desert – were deployed in far larger numbers, and proved invaluable during the invasion to combat the large minefields that Rommel had had laid along the coast. Innovation and inventiveness were as much weapons of the Allied Assault as tanks and guns.

During the months immediately preceding D-Day, the build-up of Allied troops and equipment in the South of England was colossal, and the whole area South of London and East of Lyme Regis became one vast army camp. Airfield resources were strained to breaking point as the mighty force of aircraft was crammed as close to France as possible for the attack. Close on three million men were under arms in Southern England as the day approached. Amidst this organised chaos, the Generals finalised their plans.

Despite occasional friction between the British and American commanders, the principle suggested by Montgomery of landings on a broad front by separate US, Canadian and British forces on separate beaches had been accepted early in the planning process. Montgomery was convinced – rightly – that funnelling too many men through too small a front was an invitation to disaster. His plan to disperse the landings ensured that relatively few successive waves of troops would land over any one area of beach on the first and second days, and thereby limited the risk to men and materials until the beach-head was secured and the danger of large-scale enemy attack on the beaches had been reduced. Once that beach-head was firmly in Allied hands, Montgomery's plan called for a massive feint by the British and Canadian troops eastwards towards Caen to draw the German defenders into battle on the East of the beach-head, while General Omar Bradley and the US 1st Army made the actual breakout in a Southerly direction from the West, followed by a swing Eastward, and an advance up the Seine to Paris. By cutting between the beach-head and the German rearguard, the American army would thus cut off the troops on the coast from their supply-line, and also, assisted by the damage already wrought from the air against bridges, prevent reinforcements arriving to hinder further Allied landings.

The sheer scale of the invasion plan agreed by S.H.A.E.F. required a transport fleet of 4,126 vessels manned by almost 200,000 sailors. The fleet included no less than 1,173 ships of all sizes carrying tanks and other armoured vehicles – vital to the initial assault on the Atlantic Wall if the infantry was to survive the initial attack. The assault fleet itself was made up of a further 1,213 ships, including 300 warships, of which 79 were detailed to attack the German batteries between Villerville and Barfleur Cape, under the direction of RAF Spitfires acting as airborne observation posts.

Going ashore on D-Day from the sea were 57,500 American and over 75,000 British and Canadian troops, plus 900 armoured vehicles and 600 guns. A remarkable total of 13,743 aircraft took part, including those that landed the 27,000 airborne troops on the night of June 5th/6th by parachute and in the force of 867 towed gliders.

The first attack was to be by these three airborne divisions, landing from midnight onwards just inland from the coast to the West of the main landing area, and securing vital bridges and positions prior to the amphibious assault. From 6.30am onwards, the landings were scheduled for five major beaches – the US 1st Army on Utah and Omaha Beaches, West and East of the Vire estuary; the British 2nd Army on Gold Beach at Arromanches, and on Sword Beach between Lion-sur-Mer and Ouistrehem; and the Canadians, also part of the British 2nd Army, on Juno Beach between Bernieres and St Aubin.

As June 5th, the scheduled day for the invasion, approached, the weather began to look worse by the hour. On June 4th, confident that not even the British would be mad enough to launch themselves upon their greatest adventure in gales and torrential rain, Rommel left France and went to visit his family in Ulm. On the next day, the fleet was actually at sea in appalling conditions when it was ordered back. Finally, despite continuing bad weather, Eisenhower, quite literally, decided to chance going ahead. So much organisational and logistic effort had gone into getting the fleet to sea that to delay longer meant an almost greater risk than launching the invasion in unfavourable conditions. D-Day was on.

That Longest Day
As the invasion fleet massed in the Channel during the night of June 5th/6th 1944, the US 82nd and 101st Airborne Divisions were landed North of the Vire. Their task was to secure the right bank of the River Merderet and provide cover for the westmost force of those landing on Utah Beach – VII Corps, commanded by Lieutenant-General Collins. In the bad weather, the airborne divisions' gliders and parachutists were blown off course and scattered, and relatively few units of the two divisions were able to carry out their prescribed tasks. Only one regiment of the 82nd achieved success – and made Sainte Mere-Eglise, on the main road from Cherbourg to Carentan (and the rest of France) the first French town to be liberated by the Allies. Despite considerable losses, the US troops managed to hold the town and link up with the US 4th Division after its landing on Utah Beach in the morning.

As dawn broke, the invasion force came out of the mist over the sea, to the frank disbelief of virtually everybody the German troops along the Atlantic Wall tried to tell. The German commanders were so convinced both that any landing would come in the Pas de Calais, and that the weather was too bad even for the English to cross the Channel, that the state of readiness was universally low. At 6.30 am, the US 4th, 9th, 79th and 90th Infantry Divisions began to stream from their landing craft on the Utah beach, and were supported by a tremendous naval bombardment which was deadly, accurate and effective. The shellfire and rockets from the fleet – which in the American Sector (Utah and Omaha) was commanded by Rear-Admiral A.G. Kirk, US Navy – destroyed minefields, pulverised bunkers and eliminated many of the German defensive positions before they had had a chance to do much damage. The Allied firepower was overwhelmingly superior to anything the Germans could lay down.

As a result, the Utah Beach forces had a rapid and successful landing, with very few men killed. On Omaha Beach, the story was sadly different. Most things that could go wrong did, and the beach became known as 'Bloody Omaha' with good reason. The air strike that was intended to eliminate the German defensive positions before the American divisions came ashore missed its target and left the defenders largely unscathed. Unknown to the combat troops of the US 2nd, 29th and 1st Infantry Divisions as they streamed ashore, their beach was defended by a newly arrived and very tough German division – the 352nd. The landing craft were shelled by expertly handled artillery as they lumbered to the beach. Many of the Americans' amphibious tanks sank in the rough water. Those of the 1st Infantry Division that managed to get ashore and run up the beach to the sea wall (and many did not get even that far) were pinned down by accurate and well-directed small-arms fire. The US demolition teams had suffered severe casualties and had lost much of their equipment, so were slow to smash openings in the wall. The situation was desperate.

Once again, the Navy came to the rescue. Admiral Kirk brought the guns of his destroyers to bear on the German 352nd Division's positions, and shelled them remorselessly. By 1pm, the Germans' lack of *materiel* was making itself felt, as the defending artillery began to run out of ammunition. During the afternoon, the US divisions were able to get off the beach, capture the coastal defence positions, and get their armour past the anti-tank obstacles. By comaprison with Utah Beach, where 197 men had died, Omaha was frighteningly expensive, 3,881 men were dead, missing or wounded at the end of the day.

On Gold, Juno and Sword Beaches, the British 2nd Army, commanded by General Dempsey, was assigned a formidable programme of operations and objectives. They were to capture Bayeux, Caen and Troarn and to extend its reconnaissance to Villers-Bocage and Evrecy – some 18 miles of Calvados coastline. In the light of later events, that the British Army did not quite succeed in all those objectives is less surprising than that they almost achieved most of them. The British sector, like the American, also had its crucial Airborne Division landings, which were blessed with better luck and appreciably greater success than those of the US Airborne Divisions. The objectives of the British 6th Airborne Division, who were, like the Americans to the West, entrusted with protecting their Army's flank, were:

1. To capture intact the bridges across the Orne and its canal between Benouville and Ranville.
2. To destroy the German coastal battery at Merville, close to the mouth of the Orne.
3. To destroy the Dives bridges between Troarn and the coast.

Only half an hour after midnight, the British Airborne had taken the Benouville bridges and by 4am the Merville guns had been silenced at considerable cost of life. As dawn came up, the British invasion swept ashore, their zero hour an hour later than that on the American beaches to the West. At 7.30am, as the British began to wade ashore from their landing craft, the Germans were no longer surprised and were only too well aware of what was going on. Here, as on Utah Beach, the role played by the fleet offshore in subduing the defences and lessening the casualties inflicted on the invaders was incalculable. Rear-Admiral Vian's British warships began shelling the Atlantic Wall defences in the British Sector at dawn, and succeeded in breaching the defences in several places.

The British troops had better luck with their amphibious tanks, being able to put them into the water nearer the beach with fewer underwater obstructions. Few were lost, and most were able to break out from the beach within the first hour or two of landing. The inventive flair of the British again proved useful – not only were the 'Crabs' able to detonate mines without harming personnel, but a new device called the A.V.R.E. carried a nine-inch mortar on an unarmoured tank chassis into close encounters with concrete gun emplacements and proved effective in dealing with them. Also in evidence on the British beaches was 'Crocodile', a tank with a long-range flame-thrower built into it and towing its own fuel tanker behind it.

Despite these wondrous devices, good generalship and the remarkably adept support of the Royal Navy, the British 2nd Army did not and could not meet its objectives. However, by the end of that first day, Major-General Rennie's British 3rd Division had got off Sword Beach, had joined up with the 6th Airborne, had crossed the Benouville bridge and had reached a point only three miles from Caen after a brisk battle with the German 21st *Panzer* Division. The Canadian 3rd Division had had a more difficult time on Juno Beach, again because of natural obstacles and sheer bad luck, but had overcome its problems sufficiently to be close to taking the Carpiquet airfield. Major-General Graham's 50th Division, which had landed on Gold Beach, was almost at Bayeaux. All this had been achieved with the loss of less than 3,000 men killed, wounded or missing.

The comparative slowness of the German response to this substantial success on the first day of the Allies' long-awaited Second Front was due in part to their sheer surprise that an invasion could be mounted in such terrible weather, and rather more to the fact that the German armour was not near the coast (although the effects of sea-power on tanks had been demonstrated convincingly at Anzio, and might have been demonstrated again if Rommel had had his way). A major factor in slowing the German chain of command was the simple fact that Hitler was asleep when the invasion started and nobody dared to wake him. But by far the largest influence upon German ability to react to the threat was Allied air supremacy.

Throughout the day, the Allied Air Forces gave support to every movement that the ground forces made to break out from their beaches, and attacked German columns, tanks, defensive gun emplacements, every obstacle that the Armies encountered. Some 4,600 air sorties were flown by Allied aircraft during that first day, most of them in the ground-attack role. The recently introduced Hawker Typhoon, resplendent, like other Allied aircraft over Normandy, in its black and white striped invasion markings, demonstrated convincingly, with the eight 60-pounder rockets that it carried beneath its wings, that it was the heir to the Stuka in its ability to destroy equipment on the ground. The American P-47 Thunderbolts, with their 10 five-inch anti-tank rockets, did tremendous damage to German armour. And the Mustangs, Hurricanes, Spitfires and Mosquitoes were everywhere.

Perhaps the greatest superiority of the Allies over the German forces on D-Day, apart from the sheer firepower that they could muster, was the success of the integrated Allied command structure. There was no one commander other than Hitler himself who could co-ordinate the activities of the German Army, the *Luftwaffe* and the *Waffen-SS*. Jealousies and duplicated command structures meant that few senior commanders in the German services had a clear idea of who could and who could not tell him what to do next. Everybody was afraid to act. Hence effective orders came only from the top, and delays were inevitable. In contrast, the careful planning of S.H.A.E.F., and the detailed briefing of every fighting man in the Allied forces resulted in complete harmony and cohesion of action at virtually every level in the Allied land, sea and air forces. Not for the first time did the Allied commanders reflect on how differently the war might have gone if the three Axis powers had co-operated as effectively from 1941 onwards.

The Week After D-Day

Having been caught with the entire eighteen divisions of their 15th Army in the Pas de Calais, the Germans might have been expected to move the lot southwestwards to Normandy as soon as the invasion had landed. But Hitler, incredibly, persisted in his belief that the Normandy attack was a diversionary exercise for another landing in the Pas de Calais, even after the Allied battle orders had been captured. He seemed to have convinced himself even that the orders captured from an abandoned American battle barge were forged and designed to mislead him. Rommel was therefore forbidden to use the reinforcements of the 15th Army to contain the Allied beach-head, and was thereby constantly at a greater disadvantage than was actually necessary.

The German counter-attacks began on the day following the initial invasion, as the Allied 'floating reserves' were beginning to land to build up the size of the Allied Armies for the breakout into Normandy. On June 7th and 8th, the formidable 12th *SS Hitlerjugend Panzer* Division, aided and abetted by the *Panzer Lehr* Division, attacked the British 2nd Army formation near Caen with the avowed intention of thrusting them back into the sea. Despite severe Canadian casualties, the Allied line held.

On D-Day+2, June 8th, the US 1st Army and the British 2nd Army linked up at Bayeux. The German 7th Army, constantly harried by Allied air attacks, was set to counterattack when its commander, General Geyr von Schweppenburg, was seriously injured in an air attack on his headquarters, and the attack was called off by his successor, General Sepp Dietrich. Four days later, on the 12th, now reinforced by the arrival of the 2nd *Panzer* Division, Dietrich successfully contained an attempt by XXX Corps to break out, but on the American front, the US 29th Division and the 101st Airborne jointly took Carentan. Thus, by the 12th, the Allied front extended from the Dives to Saint Marcouf. During the six days since the initial landing, five more infantry and three more airborne divisions had jonied the Allied armies from the sea. The Germans – mainly because Hitler had refused to use the 15th Army – had on paper brought up seven divisions, but all were under strength, and there was no doubt on either side that the Allies were succeeding in bringing up reinforcements more quickly and more effectively than were the Germans.

Now the world waited for the breakout from the beach-head – and the beginning of the true liberation of France.

THE BREAKOUT FROM NORMANDY
AND THE LIBERATION OF FRANCE

Everything that Rommel had tried with his beleaguered and depleted 7th Army during the week following the landings to contain the Allied beach-head and drive the invasion back to the sea had failed. The superiority of Allied air power was overwhelming. Everything that moved, it seemed, was attacked by the rockets and bombs of the Typhoons and Thunderbolts of the RAF and the US Army Air Force. Experienced field commander that he was, Rommel knew he was beaten; that Germany had little prospect of anything but defeat. Covertly, he was deep in the ill-destined plot to overthrow Hitler that was to cost him, Count von Stauffenberg and many other prominent Germans their lives – but still he knew his duty and his job, and fought tenaciously and well for the country he had served so brilliantly. The appalling mortality of senior German commanders in Normandy was already making itself felt – General Marcks of LXXXIV Panzer Corps had been killed, and more were soon to follow – and the German troops desperately needed success to boost their morale.

That success, albeit on a limited scale, almost came as Lieutenant-General Collins' VII Corps began its attempt to take first the West coast of the Cotentin, and then the port of Cherbourg. Montgomery's whole strategy for the initial battle of Normandy was aimed at drawing the firepower and the strength of Rommel's force to the Eastern sector of the beach-head, around Caen, so as to reduce the German defences in the West and give VII Corps an opportunity to take the vital port facilities that the Allies needed to control if their armies were to be supplied. The much criticised failure of the British 2nd Army to take Caen quickly achieved this secret objective fully, although the world's press did not realise the fact, and levelled many harsh words at Montgomery. Despite the weakening of German strength along the Western side of the beach-head, the first attempt by a US division to break out was unsuccessful. The 90th Division failed to get across the River Douve in the face of fierce opposition, and had to be withdrawn.

But now one of those rare commanders of vision and spirit made his appearance – Major-General Eddy, in command of the US 9th Division. Starting on June 14th, he led his division in a remarkable advance that earned him praise at all levels of the Allied armies, sweeping across the Cotentin in less than 24 hours, cutting off the remnants of three Divisions of General von Choltitz' LXXXIV Corps and wheeling smartly round to join the other two divisions of VII Corps in the attack on Cherbourg. As reinforcements poured in via the beaches before the great four-day storm that began on June 19th wrecked the Mulberry harbour on Omaha Beach, the American XIX and V Corps joined the front facing General Schlieben's Cherbourg defence. Nonetheless, a combination of spirited defence and prevarication about surrender ensured that it was not until July 3rd that the port fell to the American troops. The capture of Cherbourg provided the landfall, in August, for PLUTO, the undersea pipeline that was to supply a quarter of a million gallons of fuel per day to the Allied armies.

Now General Bradley, in command of the US 1st Army, who had arrived in Normandy on June 12th, regrouped his forces rapidly for an all-out attack on the German 7th Army between Coutances and St Lo, which began on June 24th. Appallingly wet weather had made the marshy ground soft and almost impassable to tanks, and the Normandy woodlands provided in any case a natural obstacle, so the armour had little options but to use the roads. This made the Churchill and Sherman tanks easy targets for the redoubtable German 88mm gun, and for the mighty 52 ton Mark VI Tiger tank, whose gun, also of 88mm, was capable of 'brewing up' a Sherman almost instantaneously. In one remarkable incident at Villers-Bocage in the British sector, *SS-Obersturmfuhrer* Wittman destroyed the whole of a column of 25 assorted tanks and armoured vehicles with his one tiger tank. Not surprisingly, US Army progress was slow and fearsomely expensive of life. During the four weeks between June 19th and July 22nd, American casualties went from 3,012 dead since D-day to 10,641, and from 15,362 wounded to 51,387.

Meanwhile, in the East of the beach-head, Dempsey's British 2nd Army had been fighting against mounting German odds to take Caen. On June 25th, General Sir Richard O'Connor, back from captivity after the Italian armistice, took his new command, VIII Corps, into action and by the 27th had captured a bridge over the River Odon on his way to positions near Villers Bocage, South of Caen. But there he was held, under increasing pressure, while the Battle for Caen raged on. Not until July 9th were the ancient town (now virtually in ruins), and the nearby Carpiquet airfield, finally taken.

To keep the German *Panzer* Divisions busy for a little longer until Bradley's great thrust to break out of the beach-head was ready to go, the British 2nd Army was now given the task of fighting their way out of Caen southwards towards Falaise against German opposition that was well prepared and ready to fight for every inch. Initial progress on July 18th was rapid, aided by an effective bombardment of the German 21st *Panzer* Division's positions from the air, but by the afternoon of the 18th the advance had slowed to a stop, and the British 11th Armoured Division was badly hit by a late night counterattack. The real success came the next day, not militarily, for O'Connor's force remained (literally) bogged down, but strategically, as Montgomery's main objective was realised. Believing that the British were about to take Falaise, Field Marshal von Kluge, who had just taken over from von Rundstedt, ordered the 2nd *Panzer* Division from St Lo in the West, to the area of Caen in the East, and committed (at long last) the German 15th Army to the fight against the British. Getting this far had cost the British 2nd Army 34,700 wounded, killed and missing. But there were now three times as many tanks defending Falaise against the British as there were facing the Americans.

On the German side, the casualties were mounting and, unlike the Allies, they were unable to bring up reinforcements at a rate sufficient to maintain strength. In the six weeks after D-Day, the German Army had lost 97,000 men killed, wounded or missing, including 28 Generals and the remarkable figure of 354 Lieutenant-Generals. Perhaps most portentous of all, Field-Marshal Rommel had been seriously injured when his car was strafed on July 17th, and had left the front for what was to prove to be the last time.

The US Army Breaks Out

On July 24th, the German LXXXIV Corps to the west of the Normandy beach-head experienced Allied air power at its most formidable, as 4,000 tons of bombs were dropped on its positions. Next morning, 2,410 aircraft poured more than 4,000 more tons of high explosive and napalm on to the German positions along the River Vire, opposite the US VII Corps – although some of that explosive was dropped on the Allied positions by mistake, and killed 111 men including a Lieutenant-General. The carnage on the German side was horrifying; all along the front up to half the men and much of the equipment of the defending units were put out of action. As a 'softening-up' exercise, the attacks were both successful and thorough. On July 26th, General Collins was able to break through the German line, and advance to Marigny and Saint Gilles.

Now Field Marshal von Kluge began to realise what Montgomery had succeeded in doing around Caen and Falaise. Hastily, he attempted to withdraw two *Panzer* Divisions back to the west, but they were two days getting to the Marigny area, and by then the breach in the line was permanent. General von Choltitz, in command of LXXXIV Corps, could do nothing but pull back and try to keep his battle-scarred forces together and in fighting order. The US VIII Corps under General Middleton was making the retreat more difficult for von Choltitz in the region of Periers, and Field Marshal von Kluge issued, against von Choltitz' wishes, the order to withdraw in a South-Easterly direction rather than to the South-West. Unwillingly, von Choltitz did just that, and thereby provided the Allies with the opportunity to send the US VIII Corps into Brittany, which, as we shall see, was captured in less than a week.

July 28th had seen the US 4th Armoured Division take Coutance and, only one day later, the 6th Armoured Division captured Avranches. The pace of the advance threw the German army into confusion, and von Kluge demanded reinforcements from Hitler, who reluctantly decided at long last that the invasion in Normandy was the real thing, and that there was not to be a further bigger landing in the Pas de Calais. Too late to achieve any real effect, a Corps and two divisions were ordered from the 15th Army to von Kluge's line, and a further Corps and two divisions were ordered up from the South of France to join the 7th Army. But large scale troop and tank movements take time. The US VIII Corps was now commanded by General George C. Patton, and on July 31st, hearing that the US 4th Armoured Division was at Pontaubault and had captured a bridge intact, he decided to push ahead and break out of Normandy once and for all.

Two US divisions, the 6th Armoured and the 79th Infantry set out across Brittany for the port of Brest, and two more made for Rennes. Patton, who had once had General Omar Bradley under his command in Italy, was now subordinate to Bradley, who had recently been confirmed in his appointment as C in C 12th Army Group. That this arrangement worked well most of the time is a tribute to both men. Nonetheless, during the first week of August, as Patton thrust on towards Brest, and Bradley issued orders to hold the advance until intermediate objectives were taken, there were moments of considerable discord and confusion. By August 5th, the 6th Armoured Division was tackling the German 265th defending Lorient, the 4th Armoured was attempting to flush the German 2nd Parachute Division out of Brest – and Patton was eyeing with interest a 65 mile gap in the line between Rennes and Nantes caused by the rapid advance of the US armour. When Eisenhower ordered that Brittany should not be allowed to occupy more than the minimum Allied forces, Patton seized his chance for a lightning advance which excited the world.

With three Corps, Patton headed South and South-East. By August 7th, XII Corps had liberated Nantes and Angers, and XV Corps had taken Chateau-Gontier and Laval. Now Patton was all set to drive South and East with his newly constituted US 3rd Army from Laval to take Le Mans, a move which would create the potential for a pincer movement carried out with the British 2nd Army, now almost due North of the Americans, to encircle von Kluge's German Army Group B, part of which was positioned between them.

Unknown to the Allied commanders, a substantial disagreement had been taking place between von Kluge and Hitler following von Kluge's request a week earlier to be allowed to withdraw and regroup in better defensive positions. Hitler had, after initially agreeing with Colonel-General Jodl that von Kluge should be permitted to retreat, changed his mind and issued an order for a counterattack that was sheer fantasy. Von Kluge was ordered to advance on Avranches and cut off the American troops in Brittany as a prelude to advancing on St Lo, overthrowing the US 1st Army and throwing the Allies back to the sea. To do this he was to use the *Panzer* units of the 7th Army. In vain, von Kluge pointed out that the *Panzer* Divisions were now desperately under strength, that his losses of troops were into six figures with almost nil reinforcements, and that those German soliders who were nominally still fit to fight were exhausted. The attack was set for August 7th.

Thus, as Patton was taking Chateau-Gontier and Laval, and beginning his push to Le Mans, heading Eastwards, the German 7th Army to its North began its thrust Westwards towards Avranche, increasing its danger of being encircled as it went. The counterattack was mounted by four *Panzer* divisions – the 2nd and 116th, plus two SS divisions, the 1st *Leibstandarte* and the 2nd *Das Reich*. Their thrust, which went well for the first eight hours, was countered by the US VII Corps (Major-General Collins) and the US 30th Division (Major-General Hobbs), both of which stood their ground well. As the weather and visibility improved after mid-day, the RAF Typhoons launched rocket attacks against the *Panzer* units, unhindered by the *Luftwaffe* aircraft that had been promised as air support because these had been attacked by Allied aircraft as they left their bases.

Once more, von Kluge recommended retreat. Once more it was refused, and, despite the obvious risk of the British 2nd Army attacking southwards from Caen, von Kluge was ordered to reinforce the attack on Avranches at the expense of the defence of Falaise. As General Bittrich's II SS *Panzer* Corps was detached from Falaise, Montgomery attacked from the North at midnight with two infantry and two armoured divisions. By morning, the headquarters of I SS *Panzer* Corps had been overrun, the 89th *Panzer* Division was in desperate trouble, and the 272nd was clearly losing ground. But, not for the first time, the redoubtable Brigadeführer Kurt Meyer and his 12th SS *Hitlerjugend Panzer* Division fought the attack to a standstill. Two days after it had begun, and only ten miles from Falaise, the Anglo-Canadian offensive ground to a halt. On the same day, Patton arrived in Le Mans and turned North towards the British 2nd Army, hoping to join up with them and encircle Kluge's Army Group as it tried to attack Westwards.

By August 13th, the US XV Corps was only 15 miles from Falaise, and seemed likely to get to the British and Canadian forces before the German Army, now beginning to retreat, could escape through the Falaise gap. But Bradley, on still-controversial orders from Eisenhower, ordered Patton to stop, and not to close the gap, whereupon the German Army Group, whether Hitler liked it or not (which he did not), went into headlong retreat in an attempt to escape the pocket. SS General Sepp Dietrich, now C in C 5th *Panzerarmee*, succeeded in extracting what was left of I SS *Panzer* Corps, and, adding to it a motley collection of German troops of every imaginable unit, broke through to the East of the gap, just as the Canadians took Falaise and joined up with the US V Corps to close the ring on August 17th.

For those German troops left within the pocket, the next few days were hell. A US 90th Division artillery barrage killed thousands. In full-scale panic, thousands more deserted their equipment and attempted to break out on foot. In the Argentan/Chambois area the Allies took 50,000 prisoners and burried 10,000 German dead. The 90th Armoured Division captured 380 armoured vehicles, 700 guns and 5,000 trucks. The French 2nd Armoured Division took a further 100 guns and 700 vehicles.

Von Kluge, dismissed and disgraced by Hitler, replaced by Field Marshal Model and totally disillusioned, took cyanide on August 18th. Model had taken over a chaotic situation on August 17th, with rampant Allied advances in Normandy all set to head for Paris, and his depleted Army Group B being ordered to withdraw to positions along the Seine by the same Commander in Chief who had so recently forbidden Kluge the withdrawal that would have saved half an army. Two days before, on August 15th, the overall situation in France had been further confused for the Germans by the Allies' embarking on their long-projected landing in the South of France. This was the next step in the elimination of the German occupation, and another nail in the coffin of the Third Reich.

Operation Dragoon, Nee Anvil

At successive Allied conferences, Roosevelt and Churchill had discussed at length the potential value and the risks of a landing on the Mediterranean coast of France either simultaneously with or shortly after the 'Overlord' landing in Normandy. As a result, 'Operation Anvil' had been a part of Allied strategy since the Casablanca conference, but, as late as August 6th 1944, Churchill was expressing doubts about the validity of the operation and propounding his oft-asserted belief in the potential benefit of an invasion in the Balkans. By now, the Mediterranean invasion was known as 'Operation Dragoon', and the Americans, correctly, believed that it could in part provide the coup de grace against German occupation in France.

The third major amphibious landing in Europe of 1944 took place on August 15th between St Raphael and le Lavandou, close to Monaco and the Italian border on the French Riviera. A fleet of a thousand ships and landing vessels, including five battleships, nine escort carriers with 216 aircraft, and 146 other warships brought the US 7th Army under the command of Lieutenant-General Patch to land under the guns of the German 19th Army, part of Colonel-General von Blaskowitz' Army Group G. The 19th Army, after losing some of its strength to the Normandy battles, consisted of six divisions – three each side of the Rhone, commanded by General Neuling.

Before the landing itself, following what was by now the established practice, the Allies launched on August 13th and 14th an air offensive all along the Mediterranean coastline from Genoa in the East to Port Vendre in the West, attacking communications, gun emplacements and coastal defences. On the day of the landing, the fleet, under the command of Admiral H. Kent Hewitt, fired some 50,000 shells in a prolonged barrage on enemy positions, while the Air Forces flew a total of 4,250 sorties opposed by only a token appearance by the once-powerful *Luftwaffe*. As the US VI Corps landed, supported by part of the French 1st Armoured Division, they met relatively little resistance by comparison with that of the Normandy beaches. By the end of the first day, the Allies had safely put ashore 60,000 men, 6,000 vehicles and 50,000 tons of supplies for the loss of 320 men.

Progress from the beach-head was rapid. Just twenty-four hours after the first toehold, the Americans had taken Le Luc (and with it the German commander, General Neuling), Draguignan and Frejus, and had spread out along the coast on a broad front. The second wave arrived on the 16th, and brought four divisions of French colonial troops, whom the Germans had learned in Italy to dread, plus the French 1st Armoured Division, all under the command of the immensely capable and much respected General de Lattre de Tassigny. The German *Panzer* units who were to do battle with the French 1st Armoured were to discover just how effective and spirited the French commanders were, and to comment many times after the war that these were some of the finest soldiers of the Second World War.

Enthusiastically, the Frenchman set about liberating their homeland, taking in rapid succession Salerne, Brignoles and Cuers. The US VI Corps, followed by the US 36th Division, set off from Digne, in the Basses Alpes, towards Sisteron, intending to cut off the German 19th Army at Montelimar, the US 45th Division set out for Aix en Provence, and the Germans decided that the time had come to fall back. In fact, Hitler had issued the initial order for the evacuation of South and South-East France on the day after the landing, August 16th, and it was decided that Army Group G would retreat to join up with Model's similarly retreating Army Group B at or near Sens. The ports of Toulon and Marseille were, however, to be defended to the last, and the 11th *Panzer* Division was ordered to cover the retreat.

As the Germans fell back from the South, hotly pursued by the Americans and French, Hitler issued a new directive on August 20th instructing Field-Marshal Model's Army Group B to hold a line around Paris and South to Switzerland – but it was already, like so many of Hitler's directives in the last year of the war, far too late. General Patton was already almost at Sens and Montereau, and was about to order XV Corps across the Seine at Mantes. The US XX Corps had reached Chartres as early as August 16th, 20 days ahead of schedule. The *Wehrmacht* in France had lost almost 300,000 officers and men since June 6th, and much of its equipment. To stop the headlong advance of Patton's US 3rd Army and the hardly more sedate push of Bradley's and Montgomery's troops further North was simply impracticable.

General de Gaule had arrived back in France on August 21st, and made representations to Eisenhower about the liberation of Paris. Eisenhower had intended simply to go around the French capital, but de Gaulle was aware of the grave risk of Communist uprising in Paris, fuelled by the acute lack of food in the capital for the population. Since August 16th, the Paris police had been on strike, and the danger was imminent. Reluctantly, Eisenhower agreed to allow the French troops to launch themselves upon the liberation of the city. General von Choltitz, who had since August 7th been Military Governor of Paris, had received on August 21st instructions from Hitler (whom he now regarded, according to his memoirs, as being mad) to defend Paris as a bridgehead against the approaching Americans. The order ended with the instruction 'Paris must only fall into enemy hands as a heap of rubble'.

Von Choltitz was both a realistic and a reasonable man. He saw no virtue in destroying a fine city in a spirit of revenge, so conducted clandestine negotiations with the Swedish Consul-General Raoul Nordling and the potential leaders of the uprising in Paris. He gained agreement to a compromise by which, if the uprising did not take place, the Germans would not destroy the city. Thus, the French 2nd Armoured Division was able to fight its way towards the city in two Combat Commands, losing over 300 men and more than 40 tanks to the German anti-tank guns as they went. By the morning of August 25th, the French tanks were in the suburbs of Paris. On the 26th, amid considerable rejoicing, Paris was freed. Hitler, in a bloodthirsty rage, ordered that the city be destroyed by the German Army's huge siege mortars. To his everlasting credit, General Speidel ignored the order, and Paris survived.

Meanwhile, in the South of France, General de Lattre de Tassigny had launched his French divisions on the daunting task of taking the fortresses of Toulon and Marseilles, the German defenders of both of which had been ordered to defend their positions to the last, an instruction taken literally in both cases. The fighting for Toulon on August 21st and 22nd was so fierce, so unrelenting, that heroes and acts of outstanding bravery were commonplace. The French commandos of Colonel Bouvet's famous unit distinguished themselves by climbing into Fort Coudon on ropes in the best Beau Geste fashion and hunting down the German occupants one by one, and on the 22nd earned equal distinction in the battle for the Toulon magazine from which few emerged alive. Toulon finally fell on August 27th after some of the bloodiest fighting of the European war. Over 2,700 French soldiers died, but they took more than 17,000 prisoners.

While the Battle for Toulon was raging, General de Lattre de Tassigny had ordered the French 1st Armoured Division with the 3rd Algerian Division and the Moroccan mountain troops into Marseilles. The battle was almost as fierce as that in Toulon, and culminated on the same day. On August 27th, the German commander asked for terms to end the fighting, and on the 28th an armistice was signed. Although the equipment and installations of the ports of Toulon and Marseilles were blown up by the Germans before their capitulation, the success of the French troops can be measured by the fact that their ending of the war in Provence and the South was a full month ahead of the Allies' schedule, and by the fact that the two ports, once brought into use, were key factors in the landing of Allied supplies for the remainder of the war.

In the northern sector of the battle for France, town after town fell to the remorseless advance of the American, Canadian and British troops until, on September 10th, only the three coastal bastions of Boulogne, Calais and Dunkirk remained substantially defended by German troops, and the British and American troops had advanced into Belgium and Luxembourg. Field-Marshal Montgomery (as he now was) had occupied Antwerp, Bruges and Ghent, and the US 12th Army Group was in Liege, Bastogne and Luxembourg. By the 15th September, further South, General Patton had taken Nancy and could see the way ahead into Germany, through Metz, if only he had the fuel. Desperately he appealed to Eisenhower, who remained unmoved. Patton must advance at the more considered pace of his colleagues in arms.

The logistic crisis brought about by the sensationally fast advance through France to Belgium was in fact now affecting all Allied land forces decisions. It was to be the underlying cause of the much-published dispute between

Montgomery and Patton as to who was to assault Germany and how. It was to make the next phase of the European war just a little less dazzling than the past three months. For France, give or take the coastal fortresses and a few isolated pockets of German resistance, was free of the German invader for the first time since May 1940. It had been a long four and a half years for the French.

RUSSIA'S INDOMITABLE ADVANCE

POLAND AND THE APPROACH TO GERMANY

June 1944 saw not only the Allied assault on Normandy and successes for the Americans in the Far East, but also the resumption of the war between Finland and Russia. Following breakdown of negotiations to settle the position resulting from the Winter War of 1940, some 20 divisions of Russian troops attacked the Finns and made rapid progress, taking Viipuri on June 20th. By mid-July, the Soviet Army had retaken the Karelian Isthmus and its advance had slowed to a stop. The Finns had little option but to accept the situation imposed on them, although their counterattacks went on for months.

For the Russians had weightier matters afoot. Three years to the day after Hitler had launched 'Barbarossa' against an unsuspecting Soviet Union, the Red Army and Air Force began on June 22nd 1944 the summer offensive that was to end all summer offensives, at least in this war. The objective was the annihilation of the German Army Group Centre, which was in a dangerously exposed salient in Belorussia following the retreats during the winter of Army Groups North and South, and which had recently been deprived of six infantry divisions and two *Panzer* Divisions by the need to reinforce Field-Marshal Model's Army Group B in France. Army Group Centre, commanded by Field-Marshal Busch, thus had only 37 divisions, all of which were well below strength and none of which stood any real chance of being reinforced.

Against these Germans forces were hurled 166 Soviet divisions, each of 10,000 men, and a total of 4,500 tanks against which the Germans could muster only some 400 tanks. The ratios of Soviet to German guns and aircraft were little different. The Germans were outgunned and outnumbered, but were nonetheless as willing as ever to fight bravely for their country. They were, however, fighting not one enemy but two. Like the armies in Normandy, the men of Army Group Centre were given by Hitler impossible orders based on erroneous hunches and irrational assessments. The obligation to carry out Hitler's Directive of the moment was almost a greater obstacle than the might of the Red Army.

Hitler had decided, on the basis of his own assumption that the Russians would seek next to take the Rumanian oilfields, that the Summer offensive would be directed against Army Group South. Despite compelling and ever growing intelligence based on factual reconnaissance that Soviet troop movements in early and mid-June were all directed at the area between Pripet and the Dvina, Hitler obstinately dismissed the possibility of an attack in Belorussia and a subsequent advance into Poland. He refused totally to consider moving troops to the threatened area from Army Group South, or to go back on an earlier and equally irrational decision to make certain important German strongholds 'fortified areas' in which the defenders would fight to the last after deliberately allowing themselves to become encircled. In vain did the experienced and senior Generals of Army Group Centre remonstrate about the loss of men, weapons and supplies. Hitler was beginning to apply his Gothic Wagnerian fantasy of the nobility of war to every decision.

The attack, when it came on 22nd June, was directed at Army Group Centre on a front totalling some 435 miles, with a primary first objective of encircling and taking the prestige target of Vitebsk, one of the cities that Hitler had nominated a fortified area. In only 48 hours, the German 3rd *Panzerarmee* was overrun on either side of the city, and the circle began to close. Colonel-General Reinhardt, in command of the 3rd Army, whose LIII Corps held Vitebsk, appealed to be allowed to withdraw, knowing from experience and from the evidence of his commanders in the field that there was no hope of holding the city. Hitler's reply, through his chief of Staff, Zeitzler, was that Vitebsk 'would be held'. Five hours later he countermanded his instruction and gave Reinhardt's LIII Corps permission to withdraw leaving only a token defending force. But it was already too late, and the Russians virtually annihilated the retreating force, which surrendered on June 27th leaving a gap nearly thirty miles wide in the German line.

The same story was repeated all along the line at each of the 'fortified areas'. Not until June 28th did Hitler accept that the attack in Belorussia was the actual assault rather than a feint. By then the brilliant and resourceful General Chernyakhovsy and his commanders had pushed forward and broken the line at countless points, destroying German communications and tactical command. As he did so, General Rokossovsky and his 1st Belorussian Front had bypassed the fortified areas, and had thrust through gaps to encircle the German forces beyond. By June 29th, he had destroyed two German Corps, had taken 16,000 prisoners and had killed 18,000 more.

All through July, the Soviet armies pushed relentlessly forward on six major fronts towards Poland and East Prussia, taking Vilnyus on the 13th, Pinsk on the 14th, Grodno on the 15th. July 18th saw Rokossovsky cross the arbitrary Russo-Polish frontier that had been fixed at the Teheran conference; without a backward glance he pushed on to Lublin by the 23rd, Brest-Litovsk by the 28th and Praga, in the suburbs of Warsaw, by the 31st. An idea of the pace of the advance can be gained by looking at the distance between Brest-Litovsk and Warsaw – 120 miles in less than three days. Vast Russian reinforcements had been brought into the battle during the month, and the ratio of fire-power and manpower against the German Army became ever more disadvantageous. So headlong was the German retreat at times that experienced and able commanders took desperate risks. The 8th *Panzer* Division was caught by Russian aircraft on the move in broad daylight along the main road to Brody, breaking every rule of tank warfare, and paid dearly with the total destruction of a large proportion of its tanks in one attack. In the same area, General Hauffe and 17,000 men of XIII Corps were taken prisoner. Another 30,000, either the lucky or the unlucky ones, depending on your view of Russian prison camps, were killed.

Having crossed the Vistula and reached Praga, within a few miles of the centre of Warsaw, Rokossovsky's Soviet advance came to a sudden and exhausted halt. That his troops were greatly fatigued, and that his lines of supply were extended and not at their best is beyond doubt. Nonetheless there was a strong political motive for the halt. Knowing that the Russians were close, an uprising of the non-Communist Polish Home Army, sparked by a broadcast by Radio

Moscow, was under way in Warsaw. Stalin had every reason for wanting as many non-Communist Poles as possible to be killed before his Communist 'Polish Army' 'liberated' their homeland. He knew that the Germans were massing what force they could to retake Praga, and that they would put down any insurrection, whatever its motives, without a thought. Throughout the first two weeks of August 1944, Stalin studiously ignored Churchill's calls either for Russian help for the Warsaw insurgents against the Germans, or for permission to land and refuel on Soviet-held territory Allied aircraft airlifting supplies to the beleaguered city.

The Germans counterattacked the Russians and drove them back from Praga – then turned their tanks and guns on the lightly armed Poles who held the centre of the city of Warsaw. A motley collection of ex-convicts and Russian prisoners in German uniforms under *Waffen-SS* control were turned loose on the gallant Polish patriots under General Bor-Komorowski, who were gradually hemmed in and either killed or captured. Appalling atrocities were committed in the name of order in the city before Bor-Komorowski finally surrendered on October 2nd, with 22,000 of his 40,000 fighters dead. Estimates put civilian deaths in the capital as high as 200,000.

By the end of September, the whole of the vast Russian front had caught up with the high-speed advance that had singled out Rokossovsky's advance on Warsaw, and the front stabilised along the line of the Rivers Narew and Vistula. The Russians had now advanced almost 400 miles since June 23rd, and had virtually annihilated 25 of the 37 divisions of the Germany Army Group Centre. As winter came on, the pace quietened, and the Red Army in Poland and on the border of East Prussia prepared its supply lines, brought up its new tanks and equipment, and trained yet more reinforcements for the final push that would clearly bring to Germany the peril it had dreaded more than any other – the Bolshevik invasion.

In Germany, the immense losses of men and equipment brought desperate measures. On October 5th it was announced that all 16-year old youths were to be conscripted for military service and that all hospitals were to be under military control. The *Volkssturm* or People's Militia was formed to defend the homeland, and all night clubs that had remained open after the disaster of Stalingrad, together with other places of entertainment were closed. To add to the gloom, Goebbels announced that Erwin Rommel had 'died of his wounds'. In fact, he had committed suicide, aged 52, when it was made plain to him that this was the only permitted alternative to trial, humiliation and execution for his part in the July 20th plot. Thus did Hitler serve those of ability.

The anguish of the German civilian population could only get worse, and get worse it assuredly did as the Allied air offensive maintained the pressure on German cities and sources of production, and the armies of the USA, Britain and Canada advanced on Germany's cities from the West. But it was in the East that terror lay, and the vast exodus of German refugees Westward caused by the Russian advance early in 1945 was to see no equal in the West. The Germans had had their fill of tyranny, and had no wish to exchange one tyrant for another.

BACK IN THE PHILIPPINES

AMERICA'S TRIUMPH WON WITH BLOOD

As the Allies in Europe advanced on Germany, the Americans in the Pacific were torn between General MacArthur's sworn intention to liberate the Philippines at the earliest possible opportunity, and the preference of the Admirals for bypassing the Philippines to take Formosa. By the end of September 1944, after some powerful argument by MacArthur, they had made their decision in favour of the Philippines, and had set a date for an invasion of the island of Leyte in the Central Philippines by the combined forces of Nimitz' and MacArthur's until now separate offensives. The date was October 20th.

Meanwhile, Admiral Halsey had successfully landed the US 1st Marine Division on the island of Peleliu in mid-September, an action that was to continue, with reinforcements by the US 85th Infantry Division, until November 25th before the last of the Japanese under Lieutenant-General Inouye had surrendered. MacArthur captured the island of Morotai to isolate the Japanese bases in the Moluccas, and at the beginning of October, Admiral Halsey's Task Force 38 attacked Japanese positions on the Ryukyu Islands to prevent them being used as bases for attacks on the forthcoming invasion of Leyte. Rear-Admiral Marc Mitscher's 1,100 carrier-borne fighters and fighter-bombers engaged almost as many Japanese aircraft during the attack on the Ryukyus, and scored a clear victory by destroying more than 500 of them for the loss of only 110 US aircraft, although two US cruisers were also torpedoed.

Leyte and the Battle of Leyte Gulf

With the Japanese ability to respond to a landing in the Philippines thus reduced, Vice-Admiral Thomas Kinkaid's 7th Fleet arrived in the Gulf of Leyte on October 17th with 174,000 men of the US 6th Army, and began a two day bombardment of the island to 'soften up' the defence, which consisted of just one Japanese division under Lieutenant-General Makino. The Japanese had in fact realised the extent to which the island was under-defended, and General Yamashita, the Japanese C in C in the Philippines had been ordered to reinforce Leyte with another of his seven divisions. Fortunately for the Americans, the US Army got there first.

All through the day on October 20th the US 6th Army poured men and equipment ashore on the island and by evening a substantial bridgehead had been established on a seventeen mile front. MacArthur had himself landed during the day – Yamashita later said that he would have launched a suicide attack against the island if he had known that the hated MacArthur was there in person.

As the bridgehead was strengthened and supplied the Japanese were not idle, and put into action a complex plan which was potentially brilliant in the short term if it succeeded, and failed almost as completely to provide for the long term if it failed.

The greatest single shortage from which the Japanese suffered was that of aircraft and the trained crews to fly them. We noted in an earlier chapter the failure of Japanese aircraft design and technology to keep pace with that of the Americans, and the consequent progressively greater outclassing of Japanese aircraft in combat. This had led by 1943 to the disproportionate losses of Japanese aircraft by comparison with US planes that characterised every battle from the Solomon Islands onwards – and, because virtually all these aerial engagements were fought over the sea, the loss of an aircraft usually meant the loss of a pilot.

Thus, by the time the Japanese came to respond to the invasion of Leyte Gulf in 1944, they were desperately short of aircraft and crews, and had aircraft carriers at sea that were down to less than half strength. The Japanese plan for the Battle of Leyte Gulf used this fact alongside the concept, alien to Western cultures, of willing acceptance of suicide as a glorious death for a warrior. Vice-Admiral Ozawa was ordered to take his task force of carriers, only four of which actually had operational aircraft, supported by two battleship-carriers, three light cruisers and eight destroyers, to the East of Luzon as a gigantic decoy. This, it was planned, would lure Vice-Admiral Mitscher's aircraft carrier force out to a battle that was virtually certain to result in the destruction of Ozawa's fleet, but which would cause the invasion force on Leyte to be virtually unprotected. Then, the plan went, Vice-Admirals Kurita and Nishimura would launch a pincer attack against Leyte with their fleets from North-East and South-West.

In the event, although it resulted in the greatest naval battle the world has ever seen, the Japanese scheme did not go entirely to plan. Kurita's 1st Striking Force, the more northerly of the two, ran into two American submarines, *Dace* and *Darter*, on October 23rd. In a short sharp engagement, Kurita lost the 13,200 ton heavy cruiser *Maya*, which blew up, her sister ship *Takao*, which had to retire from the operation for repairs, and his own flagship, also a 13,200 ton sister ship of *Maya* called the *Atago*, which sank. Nonetheless, bloody but unbowed, Kurita arrived off Mindoro, a Philippine island North-West of Leyte, on the 24th. On hearing of the exploits of the two submarines, Admiral Halsey, who had been tracking the movements of Rear-Admiral Shima's force coming from the North, and of Nishimura's fleet South-West of Leyte, decided that he could leave Vice-Admiral Kinkaid to cope with anything that Shima and Nishimura might offer, and set out with Task Force 38 to deal with Kurita.

During the afternoon of October 24th, Admiral Halsey's aircraft flew more than 250 sorties against Kurita's force, sinking the 64,000 ton battleship *Musashi* and damaging several other smaller warships against heavy anti-aircraft fire, but without significant opposition from Japanese aircraft which were elsewhere attacking the US 3rd Fleet, resulting in the loss on that same day of the 11,000 ton light carrier USS *Princeton*. Believing that he had effectively removed the danger from Kurita's fleet, and still under the impression that Admiral Kinkaid could handle any Japanese activity around Leyte, Halsey now did exactly what the Japanese High Command had hoped he would do – he set off Northwards to intercept what seemed on the face of it to be the main Japanese fleet. This was in fact Admiral Ozawa's half-empty fleet of carriers.

By sailing North, Halsey left the San Bernadino Straight unguarded – apparently because he over-estimated appreciably the extent to which his force had neutralised the potential for attack of Vice-Admiral Kurita's fleet. Although he knew soon afterwards that Kurita had turned back East, he pushed on, believing that Ozawa's fleet represented the more important objective. Vice-Admiral Kinkaid was therefore on his own with his fleet of 42 ships, divided as two Attack Groups, when he first encountered Nishimura's fleet on October 25th. This initial engagement went well for the Americans, the Japanese losing in rapid succession a battleship and three destroyers, and suffering severe damage to the 1917 vintage 35,000 ton battleship *Yamashiro* that was Nishimura's flagship. Despite this setback, *Yamashiro* pushed on with the 12,500 ton cruiser *Mogami* into Leyte Gulf. There they met Rear-Admiral Weyler's six battleships, which sank *Yamashiro*, killing Admiral Nishimura.

Vice-Admiral Shima's force, which had been a few miles behind Nishimura, ran into the same US Navy trap, and was attacked relentlessly by the torpedos of the PT boats and the aircraft of Kinkaid's carriers. By dawn on October 25th, only 2 of his 19 ships had survived.

On the face of it, the Americans had achieved at Surigao overnight a major victory, but they had reckoned without the presence of Kurita and the absence of Halsey. For Kurita was now hell bent on the destruction of the US Navy in Leyte Gulf, and by 7am that same morning Kurita's modern, fast and heavily armed fleet was off Samar Island shelling the nearest ships of the much slower and more lightly-armed American fleet in Leyte Gulf – Rear-Admiral Sprague's Task Force 77.4. Despite the Americans' situation being apparently hopeless, the US Navy fought hard and well against an adversary which, fortunately for them, seemed to lack a cohesive plan of attack or any direction. The American commanders created as much confusion as possible by laying smoke, and thereby heightened the misdirection of effort of the Japanese fleet. Nonetheless, the Japanese advantage was colossal, and the escort carrier *Gambier Bay*, the destroyer *Samuel B. Roberts*, the *Johnston* and the *Hoel* were lost. Remarkably, however, the Japanese did not have it all their own way, for they lost the cruisers *Chokai* and *Chikuma* and the *Kumano*. But it seemed that the Japanese could not fail to defeat the US Task Force in the end, so severely outnumbered were the US ships.

Then, at almost 9.30am, the Japanese ships turned tail and retreated, apparently because they were sufficiently confused to believe that they were in battle with Halsey's Task Force 38 after all. Whether they were actually confused, or whether there were other reasons that have never come to light, we shall probably never know, but by retreating from the Battle of Leyte Gulf, Vice-Admiral Kurita cost the Japanese their best chance of a victory in 1944. Later that same day, October 25th, Admiral Kinkaid's fleet had to contend with a new menace – the infamous *Kamikaze* attacks. Fanatical pilots flew suicide missions in aircraft loaded with explosive and converted, in effect, into piloted bombs. Dived directly at the deck and superstructure of an Allied ship, the *Kamikaze* aircraft was a formidable weapon. During the 25th, one such attack hit and sank the escort carrier *Saint Lo*, and five other suicide attacks caused substantial damage to a further five ships. *Kamikaze*, incidentally, literally translated as 'Divine Wind', was the name given in the Middle Ages to a storm that saved Japan from invasion by blowing away enemy ships. The symbolism was apposite.

The battle off Samar Island cost the US Navy five ships, 23 aircraft and 2,043 men killed or wounded. Far to the North, Admiral Halsey was about to do battle with what was left of Ozawa's fleet, and early in the morning on October 26th the first of six attacks totalling 527 sorties took off. By mid-day, the Japanese fleet had lost four carriers either sunk or put out of commission, including the 25,675 ton

Zuikaku, completed in 1941, the last remaining carrier of those that had launched the attack on Pearl Harbor. During the afternoon another Japanese carrier went to the bottom.

Taking all the engagements of the Battle of Leyte Gulf together, it was undoubtedly the greatest naval battle in history by tonnage (just over two million tons of warship employed), although the Battle of Jutland brought together ten more ships than the 244 at Leyte Gulf. The Japanese lost an incredible 306,000 tons to the US Navy's losses of 37,000 tons. The way to the final re-conquest of the Philippines was open.

MacArthur's Promise Finally Fulfilled

The efforts of the US Navy in Leyte Gulf had ensured that the Japanese fleet's original objective of being able to attack the US invasion of Leyte in force could not be fulfilled. As a result, the initial American landing was successful, the Marines' stores and vehicles were put ashore without serious losses, and the beachhead was established on a broad front by nightfall on the first day ashore. General MacArthur made a (justifiably) emotional broadcast to the people of the Philippines announcing his return, and asked the population of the islands to rise against the Japanese and assist the Americans with the reconquest of their homeland.

General Makino's 16th Division was ordered by General Yamashita to hold the airfields at all costs so that two more divisions and a brigade could be flown in from Luzon, to the North. Makino's orders were to hold a line well back from the coast and, by November 2nd, MacArthur's 6th Army of 183,000 men had advanced well inland and had captured all of the available coastal airstrips. During November, heavy USAAF and US Navy attacks on Japanese convoys bringing men and equipment to Leyte succeeded in reducing the effectiveness of the Japanese High Command's attempt to reinforce the island, but did not prevent them quadrupling the number of defenders to 60,000 – still less than a third of the strength of the US 6th Army. Yamashita decided to counterattack, and to launch his assault by destroying the airfields that the Americans were using to supply the army.

A series of misadventures made several attempts by army demolition engineers and parachutists to land and destroy the installations almost farcical, and not until December 7th did the Japanese Army manage to put down a paratroop attack in any force. Even that fizzled out after two nights of fighting. The situation began to look like a stalemate, and with MacArthur's original optimistic date of December 20th for the invasion of Luzon already deferred, delay could not be tolerated. General Walter Krueger, commanding the 6th Army, decided to make a second landing at Ormoc with the objective of dividing the enemy force and weakening its resistance. When the US 77th Division came ashore on December 7th they met virtually no resistance, and by December 10th they had taken Ormoc, the principal Japanese base on Leyte, before General Suzuki could reach and reinforce it from his former position opposing the original landing.

By December 20th the two American forces had joined up, and on December 25th they took Palompon, the last significant port on the island. Although organised Japanese army resistance was over, Yamashita had ordered his countrymen to fight to the death while he concentrated on the defence of Luzon. Thus isolated skirmishes continued on Leyte until the end of March. The capture of the island had cost the US Army over 15,500 casualties, including more than 3,500 killed.

The Assault on Luzon

On December 15th, while the battles on Leyte were still being fought to their close, the small US 'Western Visayan Task Force' under Brigadier-General Dunckel had landed on and taken unopposed the small island of Mindoro to build two airstrips for the assault on Luzon. By Christmas, they were in use, building up the aircraft that were to support the January landing on the principal island of the Philippines.

On Luzon itself, General Yamashita had 250,000 men of the 14th Area Army, but only 150 aircraft. Although his force seemed adequate for the defence of the island at first sight, it must be remembered that the great damage inflicted upon the Japanese fleet during the recent Battle of Leyte Gulf and in earlier encounters had removed virtually all possibility of reinforcement from the sea. Like Hitler's Germany, thousands of miles away in Europe, Japan was, and was looking, a spent force. Nonetheless, MacArthur's army faced the prospect of defeating a quarter of a million Japanese soldiers whose culture and commander alike demanded that they die for their country rather than surrender.

To achieve that defeat, the US 6th Army under General Walter Krueger had almost 200,000 men, with plenty in reserve, and the resources of Admiral Kinkaid's 7th Fleet of over 850 ships. The plan for the invasion required that the 6th Army land on the broad open beaches of Lingayen Gulf and then establish rapidly a large beach-head on the central plain of Luzon. This opens immediately beyond the beaches, and leads directly to Manila, the capital of the Philippines. General Yamashita, a veteran of amphibious landings, decided not to attempt to repel the Americans on the beaches, but to position his entire army in the high ground surrounding the central plain of the island, and thereby fence the invaders into their beach-head. He also issued orders that the new *Kamikaze* weapon was to be used to the greatest possible extent against the US Fleet that brought the invasion.

Thus, when Vice-Admiral Jessie Oldendorf's battle-fleet sailed for Luzon on January 2nd to begin the bombardment prior to the landing, the *Kamikaze* attacks were vicious, frequent and damaging. On January 4th, the escort carrier *Ommaney Bay* was lost. On the 5th, eleven American and Australian ships including two escort carriers, two cruisers and two destroyers were hit and damaged. On the 6th, as Oldendorf's ships reached Lingayen, the *Kamikaze* attacks reached a shattering climax as two battleships, three cruisers, three destroyers and several other ships were damaged. Fortunately, the next day saw successful attacks by Halsey's carrier-borne aircraft against the airfields of Luzon, which were so badly hit that all the Japanese aircraft left on the island were withdrawn.

Now Oldendorf's bombardment, for which the men of his fleet had endured so much, could begin. For three days the guns roared and the bombs dropped on the invasion zone. On January 9th the troops of the 6th Army went in expecting their toughest reception yet – but, because Yamashita had chosen not to fight on the beaches, there was not a Japanese in sight. Quickly, the army capitalised on its good fortune, got its supplies ashore and established its beach-head. By nightfall the 6th Army had secured an area seventeen miles wide and, in some places, four miles deep. General MacArthur had landed too – this was one day he had no intention of missing.

Now the 6th Army was to fight as two Corps, one (I Corps) under Major-General Swift with the task of securing the left flank of the proposed path of advance, the other under Major-General Griswold to advance to and take Manila. Krueger's orders to Griswold were to bide his time until Swift had tackled the immediate opposition in the high hinterland beyond the plain – the 'Shobu' Group, made up of 152,000 of Yamashita's men well dug-in along a 25 mile line. Swift found the battle tough going, but made gradual progress, and by the end of Janaury had pushed Yamashita's troops back into the mountains, had cut across the land to the Eastern shore, and had thereby cut Yamashita's communications with a large part of his army. Meanwhile, Griswold had begun to advance in the wake of Swift's gradual success, with little trouble or opposition in the early stages.

The Liberation of Manila

By January 17th MacArthur was pressing for faster progress towards Manila, partly to be able to take over and use Clark Field for air operations, partly to liberate the ill-treated prisoners of the Japanese. As Griswold attempted to comply he ran into another smaller group of Yamashita's troops, the 'Kembu' Group, made up of 30,000 men, whose task was specifically to prevent the Americans gaining access to Clark Field. The fighting was bitter, but by January 31st the 'Kembu' Group was beaten back into the mountains, American troops were cleaning up Clark Field, and Griswold had resumed his drive on Manila.

Meanwhile more troops had landed on Luzon at fresh invasion points – XI Corps on the West coast above Bataan Peninsula, part of the 11th Airborne at Nasugu Bay, 50 miles South-West of Manila, and the rest of the 11th Airborne on February 3rd at Tagaytay Ridge, well inland and South-West of the capital. As the combined strengths of the American forces now on the island converged on the capital the Japanese resistance strengthened to the point where it was all the Americans could do not to retreat. No further progress was being made from the southerly side of the city.

Realising the position even before it had fully developed, MacArthur had therefore given the 37th US Infantry and the 1st US Cavalry the unenviable task of taking Manila from the North. By February 3rd, real progress was being made, as the 1st Cavalry liberated the Santo Tomas civilian internment camp, and the 37th Infantry opened up another prison and freed 1,300 civilians and prisoners of war. But at that point progress stopped. Detachments of naval troops had been ordered to defend Manila to the last, regardless of the damage this would do to its ancient buildings, and, after a week's reluctance to embark on shelling and street fighting, the Americans began what was to prove to be the only street battle of the Pacific War.

The fighting was fierce and bloody, and took a terrible toll of civilians, whom the Japanese refused to allow to leave the city. Not until March 3rd was Manila finally taken, and by then it was a city in ruins, with over 100,000 of its civilian population dead. Over 6,500 Americans were killed or wounded in taking the city. Virtually every one of the 17,000 Japanese Navy men defending it died.

By the third week of March 1945, the Bataan Peninsula had been cleared of Japanese troops, the Japanese defenders on the island of Corregidor having capitulated on the 28th of February after two weeks of bitter fighting. Not until mid-April was the centre of Luzon and Manila Bay officially clear of enemy influence, but even then there were still almost 200,000 Japanese troops on the island, still commanded by Yamashita, and holding the North and South-East of Luzon.

General Krueger's first target was the 'Shimbu' Group, which had given General Swift so much trouble, and which was now dug in East of Manila. The battle to dislodge General Yokohama's 80,000 troops was to prove long and arduous.

By the end of March, General Griswold's troops had managed to penetrate Yokahama's army and divide it into two groups, but not until the end of May was the 'Shimbu' Group finally annihilated. During the same period, three other Groups of Japanese had been wearisomely attacked, worn down and defeated, and the South of Luzon was clear by the end of May. But still there remained the largest and most fearsome Group of all – that commanded by Yamahsita himself, and consisting of 110,000 dedicted troops in the North of the island. After a month of unremitting fighting through June, an Airborne Division landing and many men's lives lost, Yamashita still had 65,000 men under his command in his mountain stronghold. There they stayed for the remaining weeks of the war, the only Japanese to succeed in holding any part of the Philippines until their Emperor bade them leave.

THE GERMAN RETREAT

FROM THE BALTIC AND THE BALKANS

The last four months of 1944 in Eastern Europe were increasingly disastrous for the Third Reich and its armies, as Russian fire and air power became progressively more dominant over a diminished, tired and ill-equipped German *Wehrmacht*, and as Hitler's orders, directives and responses to events became ever more irrational, dangerous and bizarre. In telling the story of such a confused period affecting the futures of several countries and millions of people, one must inevitably generalise, but to retain some measure of clarity the text of this chapter is divided into sections, with one section per country.

Finland

The passionately fought Winter War of 1940, in which Finland had faced the Russian aggressor with such determination and had then been obliged to accept armistice terms requiring the loss of a significant part of her country to Russia, had left the Finns with little option but to accept German overtures to ally themselves with Germany for the assault on Russia. The alliance was, as we have seen, shaky and incomplete, and the Finns flatly refused to take part in the siege of Leningrad and other punitive operations. As the Soviet forces gained the upper hand over the *Wehrmacht* and drove it back Westwards, Finland looked likely once more to be the subject of the unwelcome attentions of the Soviet Union.

During the summer of 1944, war came once more to the Isthmus of Karelia, and once again the Finns put up fierce resistance to Russian incursion. In an effort to acquire the arms to sustain the fight against the Soviet Union, President Ryti allowed himself to be blackmailed by Ribbentrop into signing a document confirming Finland's unconditional alliance with Germany. By the end of July it was clear that Finland's best hope lay in the betrayal of this document, which had in any case been signed under duress, and President Ryti was replaced by the 77 year old Marshal Mannerheim, who negotiated an armistice with the Soviet Union. The ceasefire came on September 5th.

One of the conditions of the armistice was the removal of all *Wehrmacht* troops from Finland by September 14th, or their internment by Finland thereafter. Because General Vogel's XXXVI Mountain Corps, part of Colonel-General Rendulic's 20th Army, was over 600 miles from the nearest Finnish border, it was clearly not possible to get them out of Finland by the deadline. As Mannerheim sought means of interning them, Hitler, true to form, ordered the *Kriegsmarine* to attack the Finnish island of Sur Sari in the Gulf of Finland in an attempt to provide a temporary haven for German troops. The assault took place on September

14th and 15th, and was a disaster for the Germans. Over 300 men were killed or wounded, and 1,000 were forced to surrender.

Over the next month, there was fierce fighting in several parts of Finland. Mannerheim's troops attempted to prevent the Germans escaping from the area around the Gulf of Bothnia into occupied Norway, but eventually had to allow them to retreat into safety in mid-October, leaving a trail of devastated villages and destroyed bridges behind them. In Finnish Lapland, Colonel-General Rendulic attempted to retain the base at Petsamo and the nickel mines at Kolosjoki for Germany, but was attacked on October 7th by the Russian Karelian Front under General Meretskov. By October 15th, the Russians had captured Petsamo, and had also carried on into Norway and captured Lyngenfjord. By the armistice between Finland and Russia, signed on 19th September, and by the force of subsequent events, Finland had now lost her access to the Atlantic, via Petsamo, and the valuable nickel mines of the region.

Lithuania and Estonia

The advance of the Soviet armies towards East Prussia during the summer of 1944 had cut off from Germany and her other armies the unfortunate Colonel-General Schorner and his Army Group North, now retreated to the Baltic States that had been occupied by Germany immediately before the war. In mid-August, Colonel-General Raus and the 3rd *Panzerarmee* managed to counterattack from the South of General Bagramyan's 1st Baltic Front, and re-established contact with Army Group North near Tukums. Desperately, Colonel-General Guderian, in his recently acquired role of Chief of Staff at OKH, tried to persuade Hitler to permit a withdrawal by Schorner's army while there was a gap through which they could retreat. Hitler refused, his grounds being that a retreat might cause Finland to withdraw from alliance with Germany! Since this had virtually happened anyway, the Führer's reason made little sense.

A month later, on September 24th, Marshal Govarov had captured almost the whole of Estonia, and launched six divisions in an amphibious invasion of the islands of the Gulf of Riga, held by two German divisions. After a spirited and hopelessly outnumbered defence lasting almost two months, the German divisions were successfully evacuated by the *Kriegsmarine* under cover of fire from the *Lutzow*, *Scheer* and several cruisers. Six weeks earlier, soldiers of General Eremenko's 3rd Baltic Front had taken Riga, the capital of Latvia, on October 13th. As long before as August 21st, Guderian had instructed Schorner to reinforce the port of Memel because he was certain that the Russians would attempt to take it and isolate Army Group North again. Schorner did not accept Guderian's reasoning, and disobeyed the order. On October 5th, he had cause to regret it.

General Bagramyan attacked the weak defences along the road to Memel with 500 tanks and, meeting inadequate resistance, averaged 15 miles per day to reach the Baltic at Palanga in just six days. The 26 Divisions of Army Group North were largely cut off from German supplies and were isolated. Defeat was inevitable.

Hungary, Bulgaria and Czechoslovakia

Throughout the second half of 1944, Soviet troops of the 2nd and 3rd Ukrainian Fronts fought their way through the Balkan states. From August 20th, when the 2nd Ukrainian Front attacked Iasi, capital of Moldavia, through to the siege of Budapest at Christmas, the German Army was gradually pushed back. As the

Russian conquests moved Westwards, the Bulgarian government announced on August 26th that it was withdrawing from the war, and set about disarming German garrisons. On August 29th, a German move to take over the puppet state of Slovakia to prevent similar action sparked off a Slovak national uprising that kept significant numbers of crack German troops busy for almost two months until the insurgents were driven into the Low Tatra mountains in October.

On September 8th, following a declaration of war against Bulgaria on September 5th, the Russians entered Bulgaria and took the port of Varna. On the same day, the 8th, the Bulgarian government declared war on Germany in an effort to counter the Russian attack, and launched its 5th Army, commanded by General Stanchev, against Germany. This army was well equipped with German weapons, including the 88mm anti-aircraft and anti-tank gun, and had 88 German Pzkpfw 4 tanks. It became the left wing of Marshal Tolbukhin's army, and was given the task of cutting the retreat of the German army as it made its way from the Balkans.

Rumania

But the major interest in this area of the Balkans centred on Rumania. After Russia's defeat of German troops at Stalingrad, the Rumanian opposition forces had secretly contacted Great Britain and the United States, and a revolutionary plan had been formulated against the day when it could be put into effect. Now, as Marshal Antonescu, who had taken Rumania into active participation in the Axis war, organised with Hitler's staff the defence of Rumania against the Russian advance, King Michael I of Rumania and the leader of the National Peasants' Party, Julius Maniu, planned to unseat Antonescu and turn the tide of Rumanian action against Germany.

This was potentially much more significant for Germany's ability to resist the Soviet advance than similar events in other Balkan countries simply because of the level of commitment and integration of Rumanian troops into the German armies. Of the four Armies making up the two sections of the German Army Group South Ukraine and defending Rumania, two were Rumanian, and had sworn an oath to their king. Although it might be argued that for some considerable time they had not been discharging that oath effectively, King Michael was confident that the loyalty of the Rumanian rank and file to Germany was less than their loyalty to him.

So, on August 23rd, Michael called Antonescu and his Minister for Foreign Affairs to his palace and ordered them to conclude an immediate armistice with the Allies. They did not agree, and were immediately arrested. That evening, Radio Bucharest broadcast an order to all Rumanian troops to cease fire, which caused Colonel-General Friessner, in command of Army Group South Ukraine, to telephone Generals Dumitrescu and Steflea, who commanded the two Rumanian Armies in the German line. Both refused to disobey their king's orders.

Because of this turn of events, Hitler took characteristically rash and ill-considered action, and ordered the bombing of Bucharest. This gave the new Prime Minister of Rumania, General Sanatescu, good reason to declare war on Germany, which he did on August 25th. Rumanian troops occupied the bridges over the Danube, the Prut and the Siretul and opened them to the advancing Russians, who speedily cut off the German 6th Army in a gigantic pincer movement. Fourteen German divisions were annihilated, and only two of the divisional commanders escaped without being killed or captured. The German 8th

Army fared little better, for its IV Corps was forced to surrender. Colonel-General Friessner had lost 16 of his 24 divisions in just two weeks.

Albania and Greece

The change of loyalties of the Rumanian Army brought a speedy order to Army Group E in Greece at the end of August to begin an evacuation of the Aegean and Ionian islands and of the mainland, but Bulgaria's declaration of war on Germany early in September caused a further change of plan. Now Hitler's instruction to Colonel-General Lohr was to retreat to what had in 1939 been the frontier between Bulgaria and Yugoslavia. There he was to join up with General de Angelis' 2nd *Panzerarmee* and the tail of Army Group F to protect a corridor through which German troops could retreat, and by which the Danube plain could be defended against the Bulgarian 5th Army, now on the attack.

Some 40,000 of the 60,000 German soldiers on the Greek islands were evacuated, the remainder staying in considerable comfort until the war was over. The unlucky ones were pulled back first to Athens, which was handed over to its Mayor on October 4th, and then to Yugoslavia. The smooth and relatively untroubled nature of the withdrawal was helped by an undercover agreement between the Germans and the ELAS Communist partisans, by which ELAS undertook not to obstruct the retreat if the Germans left them large quantities of weapons and ammunition.

Back in Greece itself, a British Airborne force had, on October 4th, helped Greek patriots to liberate Patras, and on October 14th a naval squadron made up of both Greek and British ships and commanded by Rear-Admiral Troubridge arrived in Piraeus. There it disembarked Lieutenant-General Scobie and III Corps of the British Army, with specific instructions from the British Government to prevent the overthrow of the Greek regime by communist insurrection. In fact, Scobie was unable to prevent a revolution that was, after an initial success that brought near-peace in February 1945, to drag on for almost four years. Even as he arrived in Greece, the Communist ELAS was straggling across country into Athens bearing the arms that they had so recently acquired by their deal with the Germans. The best that Scobie's British troops could do was to overcome the initial surge to arms, then provide a policing presence – a procedure to which the British Army was to become accustomed during the coming decades.

Yugoslavia

In Yugoslavia, unlike the other Balkan countries, war against the occupying Axis army had been conducted with considerable success for more than three years by Tito and his Partisan Army, despite the British government's politically expedient but misguided belief in, and support of, Mihailović's much smaller and virtually inactive non-communist Četnik army until early in 1944. Tito's Partisan Army had withstood seven major offensives by vastly better equipped and numerically superior German forces, and had aroused the admiration of the world. Nonetheless, Britain, committed to support of the Royal Yugoslav government in exile under King Peter, could not support fully Tito's fight against the Axis until there was some form of agreement between Tito and the government in exile on the form of government in postwar Yugoslavia.

In June 1944, Tito somewhat unwillingly met the leader of the government in exile at the Partisan Army's new headquarters on the island of Vis, off the Dalmation coast. The government in exile agreed to full support of the Partisan Army, and both agreed to allow the Yugoslav people to determine the question of whether there should continue to be a monarchy after the war. Mihailović was dismissed from his nominal post as Minister for War in the Royalist government, and the way was open for Churchill to meet Tito and provide full support for the closing stages of the Partisan campaign. The meeting took place on 12th August in Naples, to which Tito was flown by the RAF. Two weeks later, as the Red Army entered Rumania, Tito suggested that he should visit Stalin, and on 21st September he was flown in a Soviet aircraft to Moscow, where he startled the Soviet leader, not for the last time, by making it quite clear that Yugoslavia was not to become simply a Soviet satellite state, as Stalin expected, and that the Red Army had only the right to fight through Yugoslavia, if need be, not the right of occupation.

As we have seen, General von Löhr's Army Group E, retreating from Greece, sought to establish a defensive line north of Yugoslavia to prevent encirclement by the advancing Red Army. Von Löhr's withdrawal started at the beginning of September 1944, and the Partisan Army, supported by the RAF and the United States Air Force, launched attacks against Axis communications. The Bulgarian army, now fighting against the Axis, had taken Nis, and had thereby barred the German columns' most practical route to the Danube, so the Germans had little choice but to retreat through the length of Yugoslavia. By the end of September, Partisan armies were converging on Belgrade under two of Tito's most successful commanders, Popovic and Dapćević, and two strong Red Army forces advanced from other directions, joining with the Partisans as they approached the city. Desperate to retain their communications southwards until the German retreat was complete, the Germans reinforced the Belgrade garrison with every soldier available, and the battle that followed was as savage as any in Eastern Europe. Not until 20th October did Tito's First Proletarian Division, the elite formation of the Partisan Army, finally drive the Germans from their capital city so that Tito could enter in triumph as his country's liberator.

From Belgrade, the Germans continued their withdrawal as best they could, and within only a few weeks most of the country was free of the Axis presence. Tito's National Committee ruled in Belgrade as the effective government, soon to be ratified as the official government by the Allies and, in March 1945, by King Peter. What remained of the German army of occupation was trapped in Croatia and Slovenia until the German capitulation, and lost almost 100,000 killed and 200,000 wounded during the last two months of the war under furious attacks from the Partisans. On 7th May 1945, General von Löhr was forced to surrender to the Partisans. He expected death at their hands, and was duly executed.

Hungary

The battle to push the German Army Group South out of Hungary rolled on throughout the autumn and winter of 1944 and into the New Year. Once again the unique brand of bizarre incompetence that Hitler had espoused as his own was to play a major part in events, and from the actions he took to defend Budapest were to spring the successes of the Soviet Army in East Prussia and Eastern Germany. When, on October 6th, Marshal Malinovsky's 2nd Ukrainian Front launched its offensive westwards into Hungary, it was opposing nine corps and 26 divisions of Army Group South. But 14 of those divisions were Hungarian, and Colonel-General Friessner, commanding Army Group South, had grave reservations about their battle-worthiness, doubts that were fully to be realised when they went into action.

Manoeuvring on the vast Hungarian plain, the *Panzer* corps of Friessner's Group were able to use their North African desert experience to the full, and did in fact frequently outmanoeuvre the Russian armour. But so outnumbered were the German troops that no amount of skill could produce a victory. By October 20th, Malinovsky had taken Debrecen. Ten days later, the German High Command announced, with some exaggeration, that Malinovsky had lost over 18,500 men killed or captured, 1,000 tanks and over 900 guns, as a result of an excursion by General Pliev into the Tokay vineyards along the River Tisza and a successful pincer trap pulled on his force. Victory for the German 6th Army though this was, it had been won at an enormous price, for the 6th Army now had only 67 tanks. Nonetheless, it had saved the German 8th Army from being trapped by the Russians.

Now the weight of the offensive shifted away from the German 6th and 8th Armies to the Hungarian 3rd Army, which stood in the way of Malinovsky's 6th Guards Tank Army's approach to Budapest. The offensive began on October 29th, and rapidly overcame the Hungarian Axis defenders. Within days, they were within 40 miles of Budapest itself. The German defence rapidly regrouped, but were desperately short of men and equipment. Hitler decided to reinforce Army Group South for the defence of Budapest, and sent three new *Panzer* divisions and three additional battalions of tanks. But the Soviet Army was also able to call up major reinforcements in the shape of the 3rd Ukrainian Front following the fall of Belgrade. On November 27th, the Russians went on the offensive again.

From both sides of Budapest, the two Russian Armies, the 2nd and 3rd Ukrainian Fronts, converged on the capital. Throughout the first three weeks of December, the German armies were pushed remorselessly back on two fronts. Just before Christmas, the Germans lost 12,000 dead, over 5,000 prisoners, over 300 tanks and almost 250 guns in a last ditch defence of the small town of Szekesfehervar. Three days later, on December 27th, the two Russian armies met and joined for the final assault that would finally clear the Germans from Hungary. Four days earlier, Colonel-General Friessner and his colleague General Fretter-Pico had been dismissed and disgraced for allowing the Russian armies to triumph, and Friessner was replaced by General Woehler. On Christmas Day, Hitler issued a fateful order that was to have grave consequences for his defence of East Prussia. Because he had designated Budapest a 'fortress', and it could not therefore be allowed to be lost, he transferred two *Panzer* Divisions and a *Panzer* Corps from Army Group Centre's defence of East Prussia, and brought them South to Hungary. In vain did his Generals protest at the danger this presented to Germany. To delay the inevitable in Budapest for just a few weeks, Hitler opened the way for the Russians into the Fatherland.

REVENGE
HITLER'S V-WEAPON TURNED ON BRITAIN

From 1942 onwards, Hitler frequently told those who dared to express doubt in the eventual German victory that the war would be decided by Germany's secret weapons, against which there would be no defence. In fact, among his Staff, the constant assertions about secret weapons that never seemed to materialise became something of a joke. Yet, in strictest secrecy, research was well advanced, and the German Minister for Armaments, Albert Speer, recalled after the war in his book *Inside the Third Reich* that the first experimental firing of a V2 rocket had taken place on June 13th 1942 – and had almost killed him and the armaments chiefs of all three armed forces in one fell swoop when it went out of control and crashed back to earth half a mile from where they stood. On October 14th 1942, Speer told Hitler that the second test firing had gone perfectly, and on December 22nd 1942, Hitler signed an order for their mass production.

Rumours and fragments of information about German research into new and terrible means of creating death and destruction were, by the beginning of 1943, reaching Allied intelligence through Resistance and espionage sources so frequently that it was clear that something was afoot. In the spring of 1943, the Polish Home Army obtained information about a secret establishment at Peenemunde, on an island named Usedom at the mouth of the River Oder. A Polish engineer studied the evidence and decided that it could mean only that Germany was experimenting with rockets and techniques of jet propulsion. The Poles, at enormous risk to themselves, sent the information through to London. At about the same time, British Intelligence received from occupied Denmark a photograph taken by a Danish officer of a small pilotless monoplane with what seemed to be a jet engine mounted above the fuselage – the shape that was to become known to millions of long-suffering British and Belgian civilians as the flying bomb, nicknamed by Londoners the doodlebug, and correctly designated the VI.

The VI that had crashed without exploding on the island of Bornholm had been photographed, and the picture provided British Intelligence with confirmation that the Poles were on to something. A hazardous reconnaissance sortie photographed the Peenemunde site from the air, and the results made it clear that action was needed. On 17th July 1943, 600 bombers launched a major raid on Peenemunde, doing damage that postwar evidence confirmed had set back German rocket development substantially. Later that summer, an experimental launching ramp for the VI was built in Poland near Blizna, and test launchings of the VI went ahead in profusion. The ever-vigilant Polish Resistance rapidly discovered the site, and by studying it and the missile launchings guessed that the device could have a range of some 200 miles. The Home Army collected fragments of flying bombs that had exploded, and were able to determine where they had been built – information which was passed to London and became the basis for targetting raids of the mounting Allied bomber offensive. But the Poles' greatest coup came when an unexploded VI settled in the mud of the River Bug.

At enormous risk, the intrepid Poles removed its wings (which had been showing above the water) so that the Germans could not find their lost secret weapon. At a suitable moment, Polish engineers recovered most of the bomb (although sadly not the warhead) and smuggled it in small pieces to Warsaw, from where the results of detailed examination were sent to the Polish government in exile in London. This excited the British and American scientists enough for them to decide to collect the prize from occupied Poland. In an extraordinarily risky and yet sucessful operation, a Douglas DC3 'Dakota' was flown from Italy and landed in a muddy Polish field. Several days later, the crew and the Polish resistance men together managed to ungum the Dakota from the mud, and Germany's secret weapon was flown to England.

As a result of this acquisition, the Allied scientists and defence chiefs knew with considerable accuracy, by the time the Flying Bombs came to be used in earnest, what the weapon could do and how it worked. They knew its range. But they did not know Hitler's plans, or when the weapon would be ready.

The Battle of London

A combination of Allied raids on the 96 original VI launching ramps and the natural delays that all new technologies are heir to had made Hitler's new revenge weapons late. Not until a week after the D-Day invasion in Normandy were the first VI Flying Bombs launched against London. On June 13th 1944, three VI weapons reached Britain's capital. One landed in the East London area of Bethnal Green, killing six and injuring nine people. The other two, by sheer good fortune, caused no casualties. But this was no more than a foretaste. Two days later, on June 15th, the Germans began their second great campaign to smash London and the Londoners' morale – christened some weeks later 'The Battle of London'. No less than 244 VI Flying Bombs were launched in that one twenty-four hour period, of which 144 crossed the English coast and 72 exploded in Greater London.

The Commander of 12 Group RAF, Air Marshal Roderic Hill, now faced a major task, quite unlike any that Fighter Command RAF had faced previously. He put into action Operation Overlord/Diver, an extensively planned defence exercise designed to combat pilotless bombs with RAF fighter aircraft in close cooperation with Anti-Aircraft Command and Balloon Command. Eight day-fighter squadrons – flying Spitfires, Tempests and Typhoons – and four Mosquito night fighter squadrons were allotted to the task of destroying the Flying Bombs. To them, in August 1944, would be added the first of the Gloster Meteor I jet fighters, the Allies' first operational jet aircraft.

On Sunday June 18th, a VI scored a direct hit on the Guards Chapel at Wellington Barracks, close to Buckingham Palace, Westminster Abbey and the Houses of Parliament. Nearly two hundred Guardsmen and many civilians were killed or wounded. As the weeks of June wore on, every part of London was hit, but the areas South of the Thames and in direct line between the German launch ramps in the Pas de Calais and Tower Bridge, upon which all the bombs were theoretically aimed, took the brunt of the attack. The aiming of the VI was inherently crude, and a fifteen mile radius of error was normal, with undershooting of the target more common than overshooting. Thus the suburban boroughs within 10 miles or so of the river to the South were badly hit.

Worst hit of all was Croydon, some twelve miles from central London, where the author lived as a child at the time. Some idea of the concentration of the attack can be gained from the map of the Croydon area – 141 fell on the borough, destroying totally 1,400 houses, and damaging 54,000 more (75 per cent of all the houses in the borough). Most explosions killed or maimed a considerable number of civilians; in Croydon, 211 people were killed, 697 were seriously injured and 1,277 slightly injured by VI attacks.

London's anti-aircraft defences fought back strongly, but shooting a bomb down over London merely served to fulfil German intentions, so other means were sought. It was soon found that the VI, with a speed of slightly more than 400mph, outpaced all available fighter aircraft except the newly introduced Hawker Tempest V, which, with its 2,180hp Napier Sabre engine had a maximum speed in level flight of 436mph. Roderic Hill's 12 Group, which attempted initially to attack the VI Bombs with Spitfires and Typhoons as well as the Tempest, found that attempting to shoot down the VI was both unreliable and hazardous – at 400 yds the VI, with a wingspan of only 17.5 feet, presented too small a target; at 200 yds the attacking aircraft was likely to be destroyed along with its target as the 1,870 lb of high explosive in the VI blew up. Nonetheless, many were detonated in the air by cannon fire. However, the RAF pilots devised a precision flying technique by which the airflow over the upper surface of a Tempest's wing, positioned only inches below the wing of the Flying Bomb, disturbed the aerodynamic performance of the VI's wings sufficiently to tip the bomb over and send it crashing into the sea. In one way or the other, RAF fighters, mainly Tempests, accounted for more than a third of the VIs that were destroyed before they reached London and its suburbs.

But before that technique could be developed, urgent means had to be found to reduce the number of VIs reaching their London targets. Allied bombers were remorselessly bombing the underground storage caverns in Northern France in which the bombs were kept until launching, and were achieving significant reductions in the number launched. Nonetheless, large numbers were still crossing the Channel. By June 21st, all the central London anti-aircraft defences had been moved to the North Downs, some twenty miles South of the capital. Barrage balloons floated over the Southern edges of London, and succeeded in trapping 232 VIs during the course of the Battle. By July 6th, Winston Churchill was reporting to Parliament that 2,754 bombs had so far been launched against London, that 'a very large proportion of these have either failed to cross the Channel or have been shot down and destroyed by various methods' and that 2,752 fatal casualties had been sustained.

In mid-July, it was clear that something more was needed. Duncan Sandys, Winston Churchill's son-in-law, had been given the task of co-ordinating defences against the V-bomb attack, and his 'Crossbow' committee recommended the bold step of moving the anti-aircraft defences to the coast, where the newly available American proximity-fused shells could safely be used against Flying Bombs approaching from the sea. These shells exploded only if close to their target, so fell back to earth unexploded if badly aimed. As a result, they could not safely be used over land. In only four days, four hundred heavy anti-aircraft guns and six hundred Bofors guns were moved and re-sited. Three thousand miles of telephone cable were laid, and 23,000 personnel were relocated.

By the end of August only one VI in seven was getting through to London, and on August 28th ninety of ninety-four bombs crossing the Channel were destroyed. Of those, the coastal guns shot down sixty-five. In the first week of September, the rapid advance of the Allied armies Eastwards through France reached the launch sites, and the V1 attack came virtually to an end, although isolated long-range versions of the weapon continued to be launched from Holland almost until the end of the war, the last arriving over London in March 1945. A total of 6,184 civilians had been killed, 17,981 had been seriously injured, and countless people had sustained minor injuries without hospital treatment. The total number of Flying Bombs launched against the southern part of England is not clear – in his *The Second World War*, Winston Churchill quoted a grand total of 8,564 Flying Bombs launched, of which 1,006 crashed soon after launching and never crossed the Channel. Other writers since have quoted varying figures, their information differing according to its source. The highest figure the author has seen is one of 10,492 launched against England, with 3,000 not getting across the Channel – which, in terms of Flying Bombs arriving in England, more or less agrees with Churchill's figure.

The V2 Rockets

While wrestling with the problems of the V1 attack, the British scientists and defence planners were also faced with a potentially more serious threat from the V2 rocket, the brainchild of Wernher von Braun, later to achieve further fame at NASA. By late July 1944, as a result of a remarkable error on June 13th, gleefully reported by Winston Churchill in his *The Second World War*, the Allied scientists had sufficient fragments of a V2 that had exploded in neutral Sweden after a test flight to know most of its specification and performance. What they had learned was not encouraging. The V2 weighed about 12 tons, carried a ton of high explosive – slightly more than the V1 – and had a range of approximately 200 miles. This distance it traversed in a huge parabola at speeds of up to 4,000 mph, completing its journey from launch to detonation in only three to four minutes, and giving the recipients of its destruction no warning whatever.

By May 1944 (postwar captured records showed), the Germans were manufacturing 300 of these formidable weapons per month, and had a stockpile of some 1,800. Between September 1944 and March 1945, they were building an average of 618 per month. Massive German resistance to Allied attempts to capture the V2 launch sites around The Hague in Holland lasted until March 1945, and until then rocket attacks were a regular feature of life not only in London but also in Antwerp, attacked once it had been taken by the Allies because of its crucial importance as a source of supply to the advancing Allied armies.

The first two V2 rockets to land in London arrived within sixteen seconds of each other, the first in Chiswick, to the West of London, the second in Epping, just north of the capital. A total of 1,359 rockets were fired against London during the ensuing autumn and winter, of which 1,190 actually succeeded in leaving the launch pad. More than half of those fell short of England's capital, but the five hundred that did get to London killed 2,724 people and injured 6,476 more.

By comparison, Antwerp received 8,696 V1 Flying Bombs and 1,610 V2 rockets, of which 5,960 of the combined total fell within eight miles of the city centre. Another 3,141 flying bombs were launched against Liege, and a further 151 V2 rockets against Brussels. The attacks on Antwerp alone killed 3,470 Belgian civilians and 682 Allied servicemen.

An Even Bigger Bang

But for the successful Allied Commando raids earlier in the war on the German heavy water plant in Norway, Germany would probably have succeeded in having available a nuclear bomb before the date of the actual end of the war. Since this weapon would have become available in the very last stages of the conflict, when Hitler's decisions were irrational and unbalanced, the effects of his having had the nuclear bomb available are almost unimaginable.

Nearer to actual realisation was his V3 revenge weapon, which was horrific on paper, but which simply failed to work in practice. A fifty-barrelled long-range gun installation was buried in a fortified emplacement near the village of Mimoyecques in the Pas de Calais. Each of the smooth-bored barrels was about four hundred feet long, and had successive small explosive charges in side-tubes at frequent intervals along the barrel. These charges were fired in rapid succession as a shell of approximately six inches diameter with fins at the back end passed up the barrel. The idea was that the fins would stabilise the shell, and that the range would be sufficient for the device to hit London continuously at a rate of one shell every few minutes. In the event, the shells from the weapon simply toppled in the air, and turned end over end, thereby losing speed and range. London, when it heard about that particular failure, was suitably grateful.

In truth, Hitler's revenge weapons were less than successful and, although they killed many people, they did little to alter the course of the war against Germany and used huge resources that could have turned out thousands of tanks and fighters which would have directly contributed to Germany's success against the Allies. The Normandy invasion might not have succeeded at all if the *Luftwaffe* had been as strong in 1944 as it had been in 1941. In his lust for revenge, and in his misdirection of resources to unattainable objectives, Hitler made yet another of his personal contributions to the loss of a war that Germany might just have won.

ARNHEM

THE AUTUMN OF 1944 IN THE WEST

L ike the Normandy invasion that preceded it, and the Battle of the Bulge in the Ardennes that was to follow it, the Arnhem adventure has been made part of British and American folk history by the books that have been written and the films that have been made about it. The Arnhem airborne landing had and has all the ingredients of a ripping yarn – daring, risk, imagination, the secret enemy that nobody allowed for in the planning, even commanders on the same side in disagreement with each other. And yet it was so much more than a film scenario in the making. Given a great deal of good luck, which the plan almost presupposed, it could have worked. Given a great deal more good luck in the couple of months immediately following its successful conclusion, it could have brought an end to the war in 1944. And that in turn would have called a halt to Russian advances outside East Germany, and might have changed the face of postwar politics.

However, the plain fact is that Operation Market Garden, as it was curiously named, was a sad failure that nonetheless inspired the Dutch people and earned for Britain a lasting tie of friendship in that part of Holland. The scheme was conceived by Field-Marshal Montgomery, who, like General Patton, was frustrated. He had come so far through France and Belgium so quickly since D-Day, and yet was unable to push on through Holland and into Germany. The sluggishness that had overcome the campaign was due to the appalling weather, to the acute shortage of fuel and ammunition from which the Allied army was suffering, and to the fact that the Allies were now facing the first thoroughly prepared defensive positions that they had encountered since Normandy. Everything was having to be brought from Normandy by road along the 'Red Ball Highways' until the vital Belgian port of Antwerp could be put to use to supply the Allied armies. Until then, there was not enough fuel for an advance on a broad front. General Eisenhower, who had always favoured the broad front concept, with each of the armies advancing at roughly the same pace, had earlier ordered Field-Marshal Montgomery to concentrate first on the capture of Antwerp itself (which was achieved on September 4th), and then on the positions along the Scheldt estuary that would enable the Allies to open and use the port. Despite these orders, Montgomery argued persuasively that the Germans had a long front to defend, had few fixed defences at the northern end of their front in Holland, and that a concentrated thrust on the left of the front would cause those relatively light defences to crumble. If, he reasoned, an airborne landing in the vicinity of Arnhem could capture roads and bridges to form a 'carpet' along which an armoured thrust could advance quickly around the northern end of the Siegfried Line and into Germany's industrial heartland in the Ruhr, the Reich's armaments production programme would be strangled, and the war could be brought to an early end. Eisenhower was persuaded by the sheer imaginativeness of the Arnhem scheme, and gave it his approval.

General Bradley was amazed, not only that the 'pious, teetotalling Montgomery', known for the caution of his actions, should have come up with what he regarded as a harebrained plan, but also that his commander, Dwight Eisenhower, should have allowed it to go ahead. Nonetheless, he conceded after the war the potential of the idea, and regretted deeply its failure.

Eisenhower gave Montgomery for the Arnhem operation the 1st Airborne Army, commanded by the US Lieutenant-General Brereton. The brunt of the airborne assault was to be borne by Lieutenant-General 'Boy' Browning's I Airborne Corps, made up of the US 82nd Airborne Division, the US 101st Airborne Division and the British 1st Airborne Division. Of those, the British 1st Airborne under Major-General Urquhart was to take the bridges over the Neder Rijn at Arnhem, establish a bridgehead around the town, and await reinforcement by the Polish 1st Parachute Brigade and the British 52nd (Airportable) Division. The US 101st Airborne was to surprise the garrison at Eindhoven and capture the bridges over the Wilhelmina Canal, the Dommel and the Willems Canal. The US 82nd Airborne was given the task of taking the Grave bridge over the Maas and the bridge over the Waal at Nijmegen.

To land these three divisions, General Browning had available only 2,800 aircraft and 1,600 gliders, clearly not enough to land the entire force in the first wave. Three waves were therefore required, which introduced the first major hazard to the plan – the need for accuracy to ensure that the second and third waves were dropped in such a position as to be able to reinforce the first wave. The three Airborne Divisions, by meeting their objectives, would open up a corridor along which General Horrocks' XXX Corps, made up of the Guards Armoured Division, the 50th Division and the 43rd Division, could advance swiftly to Arnhem, then on to the Zuider Zee, 37 miles further towards Germany.

The airborne landing took place on schedule on Sunday September 17th 1944, under the cover of 1,200 Allied fighter aircraft. The initial landings by the American Divisions achieved a considerable degree of surprise. The 82nd Airborne successfully took the Grave bridge, only to be baulked at their first attempt on the bridge at Nijmegen several hours after they had landed, the Germans having by this time recovered from the initial shock of unexpected company. The 101st Airborne achieved their initial objectives with the exception of taking the Son bridge over the Wilhelmina Canal, which was blown before they reached it.

The first wave of the British 1st Airborne had a less auspicious start. The plan decreed that, because of stiff anti-aircraft defences around Arnhem, their landing would take place in open scrubland over seven miles from the bridges that were their principal objective. Soon after their arrival, as they began to advance on Arnhem, the British division's radio communications proved unsuitable for the terrain and conditions, and General Urquhart found himself completely unable to control his division. He therefore went up to the front line himself, which in the event made his communications problem worse rather than better. By evening, the 2nd Battalion of the 1st Parachute Brigade under Lt Col John Frost had reached the Arnhem road bridge, but was pinned down and virtually surrounded.

Montgomery's plan had envisaged General Horrocks and XXX Corps being at Arnhem within two days. Lieutenant-General Browning had guessed that the forward units of his 1st Airborne would with luck be able to hold the bridges, if necessary, for four days. Nonetheless, he observed to Montgomery, as though providing the title for a film, that he thought they might be going 'a bridge too far'. What neither he nor General Horrocks had been told by Field-Marshal Montgomery was that there were two *Panzer* Divisions resting and refitting just North of Arnhem, one of them the crack 10th SS *Frundsberg Panzer* Division. Montgomery had evidently discounted these divisions from his calculations because they were out of service, but this was to prove a sad error of judgement. By coincidence, Field Marshal Model and his headquarters staff of Army Group B were just along the road at Oosterbeck when the landing began. Having watched the British troops land, Model moved smartly back to avoid capture, set General Bittrich's II SS *Panzer* Corps on the alert, and despatched the two *Panzer* divisions towards Arnhem, one on each side of the river.

Thus, as XXX Corps began its armoured thrust at 2.35pm on the 17th, preceded by the rocket firing Typhoon fighter-bombers of Air Marshal Broadhurst's 83 group, TAF, its approach up the narrow corridor was awaited by a far stiffer force of defenders than Montgomery's planners had envisaged. To make matters worse, the entire Allied plan for the whole Market-Garden operation had been captured from an American troop-carrying glider that had been shot down over German held territory. General Kurt Student, Germany's leading expert on airborne operations, was already co-ordinating defence operations based on exact knowledge of Allied intentions by the evening of the first day.

By the end of the 17th, the column had reached Valkenswaard. By the 19th, the Guards Armoured Division had reached, repaired and crossed the Son bridge. That evening, having joined up with the 82nd Airborne Division, XXX Corps reached Nijmegen with the Americans, but it took another day of fierce fighting to get across the Waal. By now, Colonel Frost and his stalwarts of the Paras had held the bridge at Arnhem for three days. On the 21st, Urquhart was forced to pull back from Arnhem to Oosterbeck, leaving Frost and his men defending the bridge alone. That evening, Colonel Frost was seriously wounded. He had only 100 men left, and they were overrun and captured.

Too late, having been delayed for days by the terrible weather, Major-General Sosabowski's fearsome Polish 1st Parachute Brigade landed opposite Oosterbeck to reinforce the British 1st Airborne. The Guards Armoured Division and the 43rd Division, battling to cover the ten miles to Arnhem from the Waal, were trapped by the 10th SS *Panzer* Division and could not advance further. It seemed certain that the Allied armoured column of XXX Corps would be divided and encircled at any time. Accepting the inevitable, Browning ordered the survivors of the British 1st Airborne to retreat back across the Neder Rijn. Of the almost 9,000 officers and men, plus 1,100 glider pilots, that had been holding the II SS *Panzer* Corps at bay for almost ten days, only 2,163 got back across the river on September 26th.

Over 3,700 American Airborne personnel and a total of around 11,000 men of all units were killed, wounded or posted missing at Arnhem. It was one of those operations which brought out the best among soldiers.

Antwerp and the Scheldt Estuary
The capture of the vital Belgian city of Antwerp on September 4th had been achieved relatively painlessly by British tanks largely because of the guile and planning of a lone Belgian resistance worker named Vekemans, who was also an engineer with experience of demolitions before the Belgian surrender in 1940.

Vekemans had reconnoitred the German positions along the Scheldt South of the port, and had used his specialised knowledge as an engineer to assess the size, number and positions of demolition charges on the bridges. On the 4th September, Vekemans waited beside the road for the advancing British tanks and succeeded both in flagging down the first squadron to come along and in convincing its commander to accept his plan. Taking a small lane off the main road, and skirting around the German defences, Vekemans enabled the tank squadron not only to cross the Scheldt without having to fight for the privilege, but also to capture the bridges intact.

The frustrating sequel to this story was that, although the city and port of Antwerp was in British hands, the estuary, and with it the vital access to the North Sea, was not. In this vital strategic point lay the reason for General Omar Bradley's opposition to Montgomery's plan to take Arnhem and its bridges. If the same Allied effort that was devoted to Arnhem had been applied to the capture of the Scheldt estuary in September, the Germans would have been overcome, and the port of Antwerp opened, within the month. With Antwerp open at the beginning of October 1944, the war would have been shortened by at least a month or two. As it was, by the time the Arnhem adventure was over, and the more mundane operations to capture the islands and positions along the Scheldt estuary had begun, the German 15th Army had had plenty of time to take up strong defensive positions.

The first three weeks of October 1944 were spent by the British I Corps and the Canadian II Corps in fighting their way slowly northwards from the city, and in eliminating pockets of German resistance from the area around Antwerp. The one German 64th Division put up a brave and effective defence against the three British and Canadian divisions, and it was not until October 22nd that Breskens was captured. Between the 22nd and the 31st, the British and Canadians fought a successful pincer operation, so that, by November 1st, General Eberding, commanding the German 64th Division, had been captured and Zuid-Beveland had been taken by the Allies.

Now began the fight to take the island of Walcheren. The sea-dyke around the island had been breached by bombing, so that the centre of the island, which lay below sea level, was flooded. The German 70th Division under Lieutenant-General Daser was therefore obliged to defend the narrow perimeter. On November 1st, under covering fire from three warships, a brigade of Royal Marines went ashore on the island at Westkapelle, and were joined by the British 52nd Division crossing from Breskens (opposite Flushing across the estuary). Fierce fighting lasted until November 3rd, and the mopping-up operations went on until the 9th, when General Daser was captured.

Thus, by mid-November Antwerp was open and, after the clearance of mines laid by the Germans, in use to provide the Allies with the vital port facilities that were needed to keep supplied the 60 divisions that Eisenhower had in Europe. Clearing the estuary had cost almost 13,000 Allied casualties, the majority Canadian, and had resulted in the taking of over 40,000 German prisoners.

The Assault on the *Westwall*
References to the Autumn 1944 battle for the *Westwall*, or Siegfried Line, Germany's fortified defensive line along her western border, are usually limited to General Bradley's US 1st Army assault along a five-mile front of the Dutch/ German frontier near Maastricht, which began on October 8th, and undoubtedly faced the most heavily defended section of the wall, guarding as it did the

natural approach to the Ruhr. The US XIX Corps under Major-General Corlett advanced slowly and painfully with the support of almost 400 fighter-bombers and with frequent attacks by four-engined bombers on the railway marshalling yards at Cologne, Kassell and Hamm that were the basis of the German supply line. In five days, Corlett advanced five miles, but as he did so his colleague General Hodges was able to encircle Aachen by October 17th and take it on the 21st – the first German city to be captured by the Allies.

Meanwhile, the endlessly frustrated General Patton fumed with his station-ary US 3rd Army at Metz, starved of fuel by the shortages, and by Eisenhower's decision to give the 1st Army priority. A top-level command conference at Montgomery's Brussels headquarters in late October decided that the next offen-sive should be a two-pronged attack to break the *Westwall* and thrust into Ger-many. The US 9th Army was to advance on Cologne, the US 3rd Army further South was to advance on Mannheim and Frankfurt.

The 9th Army's Northern attack began on November 16th, and made slow progress against the 5th *Panzerarmee*, but by December 10th the Americans were within 25 miles of Cologne, albeit with the considerable problem of the capture of the dams on the Roer to be overcome before they could safely advance further. Patton's 3rd Army was not ready to launch its advance to strike at the *Westwall* until November 8th, when the Americans were able to field 250,000 men against approximately 90,000 German defenders in Lorraine. The extremely wet weather of the second half of 1944 continued, and the terrain was so sodden that the German defenders believed an attack was impossible. Thus, when Patton's army went over to the offensive despite the rain, the surprise was a significant factor in Patton's success, and the 90th Infantry Division reached the German frontier on November 20th. On December 3rd, General Walker's XX Corps took a bridge over the River Saar near Saarlouis, securing the right bank, and by the 18th, joined by the 5th and 90th Infantry Divisions, the 3rd Army had a substantial bridgehead in the Saar.

All down the line of the *Westwall* and the German frontier to Switzerland, the Allied forces wore down the defences of the once-great German nation, yet the morale of the German troops remained high, and the *Wehrmacht* formations and garrisons continued to fight bravely. The French Generals – de Lattre de Tassigny and Leclerc – fought magnificent actions in the Vosges, on the Swiss border, and throughout the Southern sector. General Leclerc succeeded by a series of daring attacks in capturing Strasbourg, and in securing the surrender of Lieutenant-General Vaterrodt and his defending force. In Alsace, General Patch and the US 7th Army fought hard against considerable frustrations, and by December was attacking the *Westwall* with his VI and XV Corps in support of the 3rd Army. His objective was to break through between the Rhine and the Saar. Then, a SHAEF order removed his objectives and gave them instead to the French 1st Army, leaving Patch frustrated once more. Such are the political hazards of command. But the French went on to advance on the German border and thrust one more finger of defeat in the direction of Hitler's Thousand Year Reich.

It seemed that the Allies were about to eliminate Germany as a military power for ever. Then, just as over-confidence might have begun to establish itself at SHAEF, Hitler sprang the last great offensive of his career, a brilliantly ex-ecuted counterattack that set the Allies reeling. This was the Battle of the Bulge – and it is the subject of the next chapter of this book.

THE BATTLE OF THE BULGE

HITLER'S LAST OFFENSIVE

As Christmas 1944 approached, it seemed that Germany's final collapse could only be a matter of time and continued Allied determination. The Allies had been on the offensive, with varying degrees of success, for so long that the notion of the German High Command having the will, the equipment or the manpower to achieve a new offensive in any strength seemed absurd. To Eisenhower, to Bradley and even to Montgomery, by now perpetually at odds with his American colleagues in arms, the only questions to be answered were where, when and how the assault on the Rhine was to be launched.

They reckoned without the last flush of Adolf Hitler's considerable talent for major strategic vision and tactical bravura. For Hitler, always one to be mindful of historical precedent, had observed that history was repeating itself, and saw in that phenomenon an opportunity. Four years earlier, a plan that had itself seen its origins in a First World War strategy had enabled General Guderian to surprise the French and British armies with a lightning advance to the Meuse through Belgium's Ardennes forests which had, to traditional military eyes, seemed impassable to tanks, and was therefore only lightly defended. Despite that salutary lesson in *Blitzkrieg*, the Allies had once again made the assumption, Hitler observed, that an offensive through the Ardennes forest was not a practical option for either side. Like General Gamelin in 1940, Bradley had not allowed for the possibility of an armoured thrust. Only four divisions of General Middleton's VIII Corps were holding a front of fully eighty miles.

Because the German armies had now been pushed back almost to Germany, and were in some areas already fighting on German soil, major troop movements and concentrations of armour necessarily took place in Germany. Thus the Allies had now lost the important intelligence advantage of constantly updated information on troop movements that the French and Belgian Resistance had provided. As a result, Hitler was able to assemble the twenty-one divisions for which his plan called without the Allied commanders knowing anything of it from a hostile civilian population. Nonetheless, it has never been explained satisfactorily why Allied intelligence ignored information from captured German soldiers almost two weeks before the German push began which clearly indicated a major build-up.

Although the plan for the Ardennes offensive has often been credited to Field-Marshal von Rundstedt, now reappointed at the age of seventy to be Commander-in-Chief in the West, Rundstedt in fact opposed the whole concept bitterly. The entire plan was the work of Hitler and his immediate staff, prepared in total secrecy without even von Rundstedt's or Model's assistance. The orders to Army Group B for the attack were complete down to the last detail. Attempts by Field-Marshal Model and the youthful General Hasso von Manteuffel, who at 47 had been put in command of the 5th *Panzerarmee*, to impose alterations met only with limited success, and changed only the times of attack and the sequence of events during the initial assault. The plan itself, declared Hitler, was irrevocable.

The scheme was magnificent in its simplicity, and, had Germany in fact had the equipment, the men and the resources of fuel and supplies that Hitler's plan required for success, it could have succeeded and given Germany a major victory in the West. Nothing less would satisfy the Führer. Three armies were to take part in the offensive: the newly-formed 6th SS *Panzerarmee* under Colonel-General Sepp Dietrich, the 5th *Panzerarmee* under Colonel-General Sepp Dietrich, the 5th *Panzerarmee* commanded by General von Manteuffel, and the 7th Army under General Brandenburger. The 5th and 6th were to push in one massive breakout through the Ardennes forests to the Meuse, and were given by the plan just 48 hours to reach their goal. There they would fan out, Dietrich's 6th crossing the Meuse North of Liege and driving forward to re-capture Antwerp, and von Manteuffel's 5th heading for Namur and Brussels. To the 7th Army fell the task of covering the whole exercise against outside Allied interference from the South. Once the 5th and 6th reached Brussels and Antwerp, the communications and supply lines of the entire Allied 21st Army Group and most of the Allied 12th Army Group could be attacked from two sides and put out of action. More than half of Eisenhower's army would be destroyed.

Fortunately for the Allies, Hitler's fantasising about the manpower, the availability of equipment and the logistics of his armies had reached an advanced stage, and his plan took no account either of the fact that the three German *Panzer* Divisions of 5th *Panzerarmee* were already down to about 100 tanks per division, roughly half the divisional strength of the American armoured divisions, nor of their desperate shortage of fuel, despite Albert Speer's Armaments Ministry's considerable success in maintaining production throughout the Allied bomber offensive. Only the four divisions of Sepp Dietrich's 6th *Waffen SS Panzerarmee* had been brought up to full strength with a total of 640 tanks.

At 5.30 in the morning on December 16th 1944, Hitler's greatest gamble began. With the benefit of fog and cloud which kept the Allied air forces on the ground, twenty-one German divisions attacked the American line between Monschau and Echternach along a 90-mile front, with high morale but minimal fuel. The 6th *Panzerarmee* launched their assault between Saint Vith and Malmedy in the Northern sector; the 5th under von Manteuffel pushed straight into the Ardennes forests in the direction of Celles and Dinant – the point on the Meuse where the German victory of 1940 had been accomplished. To the South of the 5th *Panzerarmee*, and North of Trier, General Brandenberger's 7th Army guarded the flank of von Manteuffel's thrust against the expected move Northward by General Patton's US 3rd Army.

A feature of the attack was the activities of the so-called 150th *Panzer* Brigade, a unit of some 2,000 English-speaking German commandos who knew American service slang and customs. Under Colonel Otto Skortzeny, using captured American Jeeps, and wearing American combat jackets over their German uniforms, the Germans advanced far ahead of the main force, cutting telephone wires, turning signposts, setting up false red minefield indicators and creating as much confusion as possible. Each was under orders, if captured, to tell their captors that thousands of Germans were loose in American uniforms, driving Jeeps. The success of the first group was outstanding – forty Jeeps got through the American lines to commit their sabotage, and all but eight got back again. Those that were captured duly carried out their orders and spread rumours of a vast force of Germans in US uniform – with the result that huge traffic jams developed on the narrow roads through the forest as Jeeps were stopped and checked. Hundreds of American soldiers who failed to prove their American origin by answering check questions correctly were arrested. Many a GI had cause to reflect in the cooler that a little more attention to schoolday lessons about the height of the Empire State Building and the content of the Gettysburg Address might have saved him a lot of bother.

Later groups of Skorzeny's saboteurs were less successful, although one man captured on the 19th launched a fresh rumour of an attempt on Eisenhower's life which caused a rash of extra security precautions that did much to slow the Supreme Commander's progress for days. Since the activities of the 150th *Panzer* Brigade were entirely contrary to the Geneva Convention, the Americans began summarily to try and shoot the men captured in US uniform, and this ended their incursions. The whole idea had been Hitler's – unbalanced he may have been, but a measure of originality still characterised his military solutions.

Less palatable were the appalling and unnecessary atrocities committed by the leading column of the elite 1st SS *Panzer* Division, known as 'Battle Group Peiper', after its commander *SS Standartenführer Peiper*. This unit captured the important communications centre of Stavelot (only to lose it again later the same day), but in the meantime discovered a group of civilians, mainly women and children, huddled in a cellar. Despite the fact that there was no evidence whatever of their complicity in any military activity, they were all taken out and shot in cold blood, with exception of one woman and her two children. Unarmed American prisoners were also murdered in contravention of the Geneva Convention.

The 'Battle Group Peiper' was the first thrust of the 6th *Panzerarmee* in the northern sector, which encountered far stronger resistance than it had expected at the hands of the US 99th Infantry Division, the southernmost of General Gerow's V Corps. The men of V Corps held their positions until reinforcements arrived, and prevented Peiper from proceeeding towards his objectives. Incredibly, while Peiper was held up at Stavelot he was within a mile of a vast and lightly guarded US fuel dump containing over 2.5 million gallons of gasoline – but he did not know it was there, and made no attempt to capture fuel which might have transformed the offensive for Hitler. By contrast, von Manteuffel's 5th broke through strongly in the Schnee Eifel sector (just to the South of Dietrich's positions) against the newly arrived US 106th Division and the 14th Cavalry Group. By the following day, the 17th December, the 5th *Panzerarmee* had surrounded the 106th and forced the surrender of some 7,000 men – the worst reverse suffered by the American Army during the whole of 1944 and 1945 in Europe.

Further South again in von Manteuffel's sector, the 58th and 47th *Panzer* Corps made strong progress. The 58th crossed the River Our and pushed on towards Houffalize to attempt to secure a bridgehead over the Meuse between Ardenne and Namur. The 47th was to cross the Our and capture Bastogne, a key town positioned at the junction of vital roads. By the night of the 17th December, both Corps were close to their objectives at Houffalize and Bastogne.

Only now did the Allied High Command take the offensive seriously and realise just how vigorously the German High Command was bidding for an eleventh hour victory. The 6th *Panzerarmee* had come perilously close to the US First Army HQ at Spa, which had been pulled hastily back. By December 18th, the US 7th Armoured Division had been equally hastily moved to counter German pressure on the important road centre of St Vith, but were failing to hold the assault of the 6th *Panzerarmee*, which was outflanking St Vith on both sides. So hard pressed were they that no help could be detached for the trapped regiments of the 106th Divison at Bastogne. As the German 47th *Panzer* Corps closed in, combat command and engineer reinforcements from the US 9th Armoured Division reached Bastogne and slowed the German advance. This was crucial, since, on the 19th, the US 101st Airborne Division arrived at Bastogne (after delays caused by being sent to the wrong place), just before the town was bypassed by von Manteuffel's tanks and cut off from all other American forces on the 20th.

On the 19th December, General Bradley ordered the 10th Armoured Division to move North to reinforce the American line against the advancing *Panzers*. This brought 60,000 more US troops into the endangered area; a further 180,000 would be moved up over the next eight days. The US 30th Division was sent to Malmedy from rest positions near Aachen, and was then moved further West to push *SS Standartenführer* Peiper's Battle Group out of Stavelot with the help of fighter-bomber attacks. Peiper was now himself cut off from the rest of the 6th *Panzerarmee*, and was running desperately short of fuel. By the 24th he had no gasoline at all, and his Group abandoned their tanks and walked back through the forest.

Further South, von Manteuffel had forced the US defending troops out of St Vith, and was pressing hard against the US 7th Armoured and 106th Divisions, which were obliged to retreat to safer positions. The Allied line was now burst wide open, and Eisenhower decided that rapid action was needed. In a major change of the command structure, he put Montgomery in charge of all land forces North of the breach, and Bradley in command of those South of it. Montgomery insisted of having Major-General J. Lawton Collins, commander of the US 7th Corps, for the task of commanding the two armoured and two infantry divisions that were to be given the task of stopping von Manteuffel reaching the Meuse. To 'Lightning Joe' Collins were given the 2nd and 3rd Armoured Divisions and the 75th and 84th Infantry Divisions. His orders were to mount a counterattack.

South of the breach, General Bradley gave General Patton the formidable task of wheeling and repositioning two Corps (III and XII) from the Saar front to the counterattack to relieve Bastogne, where the position was, and remained for days, critical. The commander at Bastogne was Brigadier-General McAuliffe, who earned his place in history not only with his inspirational leadership of the defenders of the town, but also by his one-word answer to General Luttwitz' offer of surrender terms. McAuliffe instructed his staff officer to tell the German white flag party 'Nuts!'. The Germans, with Teutonic thoroughness, queried the meaning of this answer. The young American officer thought for a moment then offered the translation 'Go to Hell!'. The Germans went, although their final destination is unrecorded.

December 23rd at last brought a break in the unremitting low cloud and bad weather of the previous week, and the Allied Air Forces were unleashed in earnest, flying 2,000 sorties on the 23rd, and a total of 15,000 over the next three days. More American reinforcements were moved up to the Southern side of the German bulge, and von Rundstedt renewed his requests to Hitler that the whole offensive should be called off. Once more, Hitler refused. By the 24th, Christmas

Eve, the defenders of Bastogne were nearer than ever before to being defeated, but still they held on with great heroism. On Christmas Day, the German tanks made an all-out effort to break into the town, but, remarkably, General McAuliffe's defenders still held out. At 4.45pm on the 26th, their persistence and bravery was at last rewarded. The US 4th Armoured Division under Major-General Gaffey broke through and made contact with the beleaguered and exhausted garrison of Bastogne.

By the 24th, Patton's advance from the South was pushing back the German 7th Army, and was coming closer to von Manteuffel's flank as the 5th *Panzerarmee* continued its push for the Meuse despite heightened Allied opposition. Hitler had now released from reserve the 9th *Panzer* and 15th *Panzergrenadier* Divisions to reinforce von Manteuffel's army, but General Collins' relentless push was too strong even for the reinforced *Panzer* force, and on Christmas Day, he re-took Celles, just five miles from the Meuse. This marked the turning point of the Battle of the Bulge. Hitler's dream was to come no coser to the Meuse than this.

By the 26th December, the 5th *Panzerarmee* was beginning to retreat, and von Manteuffel was fuming at the fact that only now was he given the reinforcements he needed – but without the fuel to use them. The Battle of the Bulge was over, and Germany's last great offensive had failed. The losses had been serious on both sides, but whereas the Allies could replace arms and equipment destroyed, the Germans could not. All told, the Americans lost 76,890 killed and wounded, the Germans 81,834. Over 700 US tanks were destroyed to 324 German, over 590 aircraft to just 320 German. However, it should be remembered that these losses were approximately equal as proportions of the total of each type of equipment employed in the battle by each side.

Incredibly, Hitler now began to fantasise about a great offensive to destroy the Allies in Alsace and Lorraine, apparently oblivious to the tremendous Soviet build-up on the Vistula which heralded Stalin's final push to destroy the Reich and dominate Eastern Europe. His Generals were in despair. It was now clear that Germany as they knew it had but months to live.

THE BATTLE FOR THE RHINE

THE LAND WAR REACHES GERMANY IN THE WEST

Although the German armies had been conclusively beaten in the Ardennes, and began 1945 at great disadvantage both psychologically and logistically, Hitler did not see the German situation in that light. As always, he viewed any notion of strategic withdrawal as an admission of failure and defeat, and therefore, against all advice, ordered that Germany should stand and fight West of the Rhine rather than follow the course of withdrawal and regrouping to its East that common sense and most of his General Staff urged upon him.

Recognising that continued German resistance without withdrawal was to characterise the next part of the drive to crush Germany in the West, General Eisenhower planned the final phase of the Allied assault that had brought him from Normandy to Germany in three stages. Always in favour of the 'broad front' approach to Allied planning, he ordered that, as phase one, the Allied armies must first destroy the German hold on all positions West of the Rhine, and then (and only then) launch phase two by crossing the river to establish bridgeheads. Phase three was to consist of two simultaneous thrusts. The first, by Field Marshal Montgomery's 21st Army Group, which now, it should be remembered, included the US 9th Army, would drive North from Duisberg to skirt North of the Ruhr industrial region and capture the North German plain. This was to be the principal assault, and would occupy 35 of the available 85 divisions. The second thrust, using the 25 divisions of Bradley's 12th Army Group, was to push South of the Ruhr from the Mainz/Frankfurt area North-East to Kassel. The overall objective was to effect 'a massive double envelopment of the Ruhr to be followed by a great thrust to join up with the Russians'. The remaining 25 divisions of the Allied western armies were to hold the Southern Karlsruhe/ Basle and Bonn/Bingen areas of the Rhine which offered minimal opportunities for large scale assault crossings.

There was considerable British disagreement with this plan, despite the fact that it gave Montgomery and the British and Canadian Armies the major opportunity to shine, and relegated Bradley's command to that of supporting the success of a commander whom he had come to loathe. The British General Staff believed that Eisenhower did not have the strength to mount more than one successful and crushing attack across the Rhine, and contended that that assault should properly be in the North and against the Ruhr. Perhaps, when Brooke had floated this criticism at the end of 1944, it was justified, but by the time the dispute came to be decided, in January 1945, events had proved Eisenhower to be right. The Russians were about to advance to the River Oder; Hitler, believing that he had 'regained the initiative' in the Ardennes, and could afford to relax a little in the West, had transferred the ten divisions of the 6th *Panzerarmee* to the Hungarian front; and the desperate fuel shortage that afflicted every aspect of German planning had virtually grounded the *Luftwaffe*. The defences on the Rhine were a pale shadow of what they had formerly been.

The Colmar Pocket

While this argument was being fought out, the 21st and 12th Army Groups were almost stationary, mopping up the last vestiges of the Ardennes offensive, counting the cost and preparing for the next stage of the battle. The 6th Army Group, made up of the 1st French Army and the US 7th Army, was far to the south and was fighting fiercely to eliminate a German push to recapture Strasbourg and the plain of Alsace. Overnight on New Year's Eve, Heinrich Himmler, as commander of Army Group *'Oberrhein'* had made his bid for military fame by launching Operation *Nordwind* with the objective of reaching the Saverne Gap and cutting General Patch's US 7th Army in two. Patch was in a difficult position, having been obliged in December to extend his line to cover the gap caused by General Patton having to head North for the Ardennes. When the German attack came, the 7th Army had only its seven divisions to defend a 90-mile front against eight German divisions including the 21st *Panzer* and an *SS Panzergrenadier* Division. SHAEF was inclined to order strategic withdrawal, abandoning Strasbourg and the Alsace plain until General Devers 6th Army Group could be adequately reinforced for a counterattack. But General Juin, and General de Lattre de Tassigny of the French 1st Army, thought otherwise. They refused to contemplate a French Army withdrawing under any conditions to surrender newly liberated French territory back to the Germans, and earned the support of General de Gaulle for their stand.

On the night of January 2nd/3rd, General de Lattre moved his redoubtable 3rd Algerian Division up to hold Strasbourg. On the 6th, the German 19th Army suddenly launched an offensive from the Colmar bridgehead that they had stubbornly held on the West bank of the Rhine, and pushed to within 13 miles of Strasbourg on the Erstein Heights. The battle around Strasbourg raged for two weeks in a series of largely fruitless attacks and counterattacks that served to prove only the determination of the French Army and the inability of Himmler to control operations from the far side of the Rhine. By January 26th, the German Army had accepted that it had failed to retake Strasbourg; General Wiese was relieved of his command, thereby 'carrying the can' for the incompetence of his superior, who had earlier failed even as a chicken farmer, and Himmler's disaster was rewarded in true Hitlerian style with a promotion for the *Reichsführer SS* to command the crucial Army Group *'Vistula'*.

In the latter days of the battle around Strasbourg, the French had set about the literal interpretation of General de Lattre's order of January 15th by which he had instructed his army to 'Leave the Germans no chance of escape ... Free Colmar undamaged ... strangle the pocket alongside the Rhine where it receives its supplies ... around Brisach.' Substantial reinforcements were provided by SHAEF for the French operation to strangle the Colmar pocket. In addition to the US 3rd Division, the French were given the US 28th Division and the US 12th Armoured Division, plus the French 2nd Armoured Division under General Leclerc which was also moved down from Strasbourg for the operation. All these reinforcements brought General de Lattre's command up to twelve strong, well-equipped divisions, of which the 3rd Algerian, being fully occupied around Strasbourg, was to take no part in the Colmar action. Thus the Allied forces at Colmar actually amounted to eleven divisions.

Facing them were seven German divisions of the 19th Army, stretched along a bridgehead of 100 miles West of the Rhine. But they were divisions in little more than name, with between 4,500 and 7,000 men per division, and a serious shortage of ammunition. The Germans did, however, have superior armour, and much greater artillery firepower, being blessed with the formidable 88mm anti-tank gun. The weather was also on the side of static defence – first it snowed, then it thawed, and the Allied forces were obliged to advance first in bitterly cold conditions, then through a quagmire of mud.

From January 20th, when the attack began, until January 27th, when the US 3rd Division finally reached the Colmar Canal, the offensive was one of the slowest and most bitterly fought of the European campaign. On the 27th, General Rasp, commanding the 19th Army, was authorised by OKW to pull his badly battered army back over the Rhine, but, newly reinforced again with the US 75th Division and US XXI Corps (whose commander, Major-General Milburn, now took command of all US troops engaged in the Colmar offensive) the French 1st Army set about occupying Colmar itself and encircling the German defenders in the pocket. On February 5th, the French and American troops joined up, and by so doing trapped approximately a quarter of the 19th Army. When, on February 9th, the 19th escaped back across the Rhine, they left behind over 22,000 prisoners, 80 guns and 70 tanks. Nonetheless, although more than a quarter of his manpower was left in Allied hands, General Rasp had managed to take back to the Fatherland 1,500 guns, 60 armoured troop carriers and tanks and 7,000 other motor vehicles, in itself a considerable military achievement.

The February Offensive

With the Colmar pocket cleared, the political hot potato of Strasbourg safely removed from the German oven, and the Allied front as tidy as could be expected, even by Eisenhower, the stage was set for the great advance from the *Westwall* – the Siegfried Line – to and beyond the Rhine. Although the German frontier had been crossed already by the Allies at several points, it remained broadly true that, at the beginning of February 1945 the Allied armies were ranged along the Reich's borders with (from North to South) Holland, Belgium, Luxembourg and France. Only in the vicinity of Aachen (Aix-la-Chappelle) had the *Westwall* been significantly and permanently breached.

Early on the morning of February 8th 1945, before first light, the offensive opened in the North of the line with a bombardment by 1,400 guns of the Canadian 1st Army. On the receiving end of this crippling fire was the German 84th Division, which had been reassured repeatedly by General von Blaskowitz, the commander of Army Group H, that the Allies in general, and the reputedly cautious Montgomery in particular, would not be foolhardy enough to attack in this sector. Both von Blaskowitz and OKH, reputedly all the way up to Hitler himself, had decided that Montgomery would decline a fight across marshy ground, between a flood on one side and the Reichswald Forest on the other. Just how wrong they were was proved at 10.30am, when, on a front of only seven miles between the Maas and the Waal, near the Dutch/German border, the augmented British XXX Corps attacked. Lieutenant-General Brian Horrocks put five divisions into the first wave of the attack and retained two, including the Guards Armoured Division, in reserve. By the end of the first day, the Germans had lost 1,300 men captured and were collapsing.

By February 13th, after days of fierce and bloody fighting, the Canadian 1st Army had moved on to Kleve, on the German side of the border, having finished the mopping up of the Reichswald. At Gennep, as reinforcements for the Canadians arrived in the form of the British 52nd Division and the 11th Armoured Division, General Schlemm, the commander of the German 1st Parachute Army, stepped up German resistance to the developing Allied pressure. He moved two infantry divisions and a *Panzer* division from further South, thereby balancing the Allied reinforcements. The advance came almost to a stop, some 15 miles from its jumping-off point.

It would, however, be quite wrong to assume that it had in any way failed. For Montgomery had once again played the card that had been so successful in Normandy, when the British 2nd Army at Caen had drawn the enemy's reinforcements in advance of the American attack on the western side of the beach-head. By forcing Schlemm to concentrate the German forces against the Canadians, he had reduced the resistance to Operation 'Grenade', the attack by which the US 9th Army would cross the Roer and advance to the Rhine at Dusseldorf. 'Grenade' was now due for February 23rd after being postponed from February 10th because of the massive flooding of the Eifel area caused by the German engineers opening the valves on the Roer dams as they retreated. On February 22nd, as a prelude to the American attack, one of the largest air bombing offensives ever mounted was launched against Germany's communications network to reduce the German army's ability to bring up supplies and reinforcements, and to increase the confusion that was already evident in the German command structure.

Operation 'Grenade'

Next day, in the small hours of the morning, the US artillery opened its bombardment of the German positions on the Roer, defended by the German 15th Army. Quickly, the Americans took Duren and Julich, and, despite frantic German movement of the reinforcements just sent to Schlemm back southwards, the US push continued indomitably to positions near Erkolenz on February 27th, and to Rheydt on March 1st. On the US 9th Army's left, Major-General Anderson's XVI Corps made similarly rapid advances towards Roermond and Venlo, and on the right XIX Corps approached Neuss, just across the Rhine from Dusseldorf. The pressure on General Schlemm was tremendous, and he was ordered by OKH to pull back across the Rhine – itself no mean feat in the circumstances. It is a tribute to his skill and generalship that he managed successfully to set up rearguard actions at Xanten and Rheinberg which caused sufficient delay to enable his engineers to demolish the bridges after most of his army had crossed the river.

Now the US 9th Army and the Canadian 1st Army were able to turn North and South respectively, to link up at Wesel and form a continuous front along the Rhine. The whole operation since February 8th in the 21st Army Group sector had lost the Germans 53,000 prisoners, but the Canadians and British alone had in the same time suffered losses of over 15,500 killed and wounded. The Americans fared rather better.

On March 6th came another major landmark in the defeat of Hitler's Germany as the US VII Corps entered Cologne, thereby completing the Allied chain from Nijmegen in Holland to Cologne, some 100 miles further upstream. South of Cologne, the German 5th *Panzerarmee* was facing both the US 1st and the US 3rd Armies, and was losing ground fast. General Patton's presence in the battle had not been intended by SHAEF, and was due entirely to Patton's own hotheaded and impetuous way of defeating enemies before he had been told to –

he had pushed forward contrary to orders during January and February. Nonetheless, his presence hastened the defeat of Colonel-General Harpe's *Panzerarmee* significantly.

Having taken Cologne, the US Army did not rest on its laurels, for the successes against the German 15th Army made it possible for some more rapid advances to be snatched before the German army regrouped, insofar as it was now able to do so. From Cologne on March 7th, VII Corps set off to take Bonn, and III Corps set out to capture the crossings over the Ahr. At noon on that day, the intrepid Brigadier-General Hoge, commanding Combat Group B of the US 9th Armoured Division within III Corps, heard the remarkable news that the Ludendorff Bridge over the Rhine at Remagen had not been blown. Recognising the enormous opportunity that capturing this bridge intact would present to the Allies, he went against his orders, and raced to Remagen. At 4pm that day, as his US troops attempted to cross the bridge, the German defenders attempted to explode the charges that were set along it, but failed. The Americans were across the Rhine, and Sergeant Alex Drabik became the first US serviceman to set foot East of the river. The German Major who had been supposed to blow the bridge, and two of his subordinates, were shot on Hitler's personal orders.

The Americans were more forgiving of General Hoge's temporary insubordination, and within twenty-four hours had capitalised on his magnificent stroke by putting 8,000 US troops into the bridge-head East of the Rhine. Hitler vented his wrath by launching air attacks, sending the 11th *Panzer* Division from Bonn, ordering artillery bombardments and even by commanding that a V2 rocket strike be launched against the bridge, but did not manage to knock it down until March 17th, by which time the Americans had not only built another bridge nearby, but had also got four divisions including one armoured division dug in on the eastern side. The 11th *Panzer* had been unable to rectify the situation mainly because it had only 60 tanks, 5,000 men, 30 guns and almost no gasoline.

Further South, General Patton's 3rd Army, having lost III Corps by its transfer to the US 1st Army, was still made up of 12 divisions (three of them armoured) organised as three Corps. By the end of February, these forces had eliminated most of the centre of the Siegfried line, and had moved forward to take Saarburg against the extremely determined resistance of the German 7th Army of General Brandenberger, which, on March 1st, collapsed for lack of supplies. Two days later on the 3rd, the 5th Division reached Kyllburg and crossed the River Kyll. This enabled the 4th Division, on March 4th, to rush forward to Daun, and finding the route relatively lightly defended, to push on to reach the Rhine near Koblenz on March 6th. On March 11th, the US 11th Armoured Division became the first unit of the US 3rd Army to join up with the US 1st Army on the Rhine. Patton's 3rd Army had once more reinforced its reputation for speed, and had achieved its additional kudos with losses of only 3,650 killed and 1,374 missing between January 29th and March 12th.

During the following week the action shifted to the US XII Corps under Major-General Eddy and to XX Corps commanded by Major-General Walker. On March 14th, the 4th and 11th Armoured Divisions of XII Corps were set on their way from Treis towards the Rhine, the 4th advancing 32 miles in its first 48 hours and becoming involved in a major pitched battle with the 2nd *Panzer* Division. After some reinforcement, Major-General Gaffey overcame that problem, and by March 19th was between Mainz and Worms. On the 21st, the 4th occupied Worms, the 90th Division had taken Mainz and XX Corps was pushing headlong for Ludwigshafen.

Further South, the US 7th Army faced an uphill struggle against the German 1st Army. Between March 15th when their assault began, and March 19th, progress was slow, and Major-General Brooks, commanding VI Corps had great difficulty in breaking through a remorselessly defended part of the *Westwall*. On March 18th the French General de Monsabert was given command of a task force to head for and take Speyer. By March 24th he had reached Maximiliansau, across the Rhine from Karlsruhe, and General Patch had taken Landau.

Two nights previously, General Patton, this time with General Bradley's full approval, had crossed the Rhine near Oppenheim during the night of March 22/23rd, and by daybreak had almost 5,000 men on the East bank of the Rhine for the loss of only eight men killed. To Bradley's immense satisfaction, the Americans were, after all, across the Rhine before Montgomery's British and Canadian troops, but Montgomery was not to be far behind, and, when he crossed, he crossed in style.

That great crossing of the Rhine, under the eye of Winston Churchill, will in this book be the prologue to the last act of the German tragedy. Until then, we must leave the Rhine and return to the Eastern Front.

THE RUSSIANS SWEEP INTO GERMANY

THE STRIKE AT THE THIRD REICH'S HEART

On the colossal and complex front to the East of the Third Reich, the Soviet armies had been since the end of their massive drive into Poland regrouping, refitting and improving their formidably long supply lines. In December, Major-General Gehlen, in command of German Military Intelligence on the Eastern Front, had warned OKH in general, and Hitler in particular, of the tremendous build-up of Russian strength, particularly on the Vistula, which threatened East Prussia and, through it, Prussia, Berlin and the heart of the Reich. Gehlen was a reliable and experienced staff officer, not given (as the postwar facts proved) to exaggeration. Colonel-General Heinz Guderian, OKH Chief of Staff, supported Gehlen's conclusion that the greatest threat to the security of Germany lay in the might of the 1st, 2nd and 3rd Belorussian Fronts, and 1st and 4th Ukrainian Fronts, the five great Soviet armies poised to sweep West from Poland into Germany. Hitler disagreed, believing against all the evidence that the Soviet build-up was no more than mere propaganda, and that his armies had regained the initiative in the West as a result of the Ardennes offensive. As we have seen in an earlier chapter, Hitler even detached without reference to Guderian the IV SS *Panzer* Corps from German Army Group Centre for what was essentially a hopeless errand to relieve Budapest. By so doing he reduced the strength of the Group's reserves from 14 to 12 divisions.

The colossal foolhardiness of this action can be appreciated only by comparing the enormous strength of the Russian forces massed ready for the attack with those of the German defending armies. On paper, OKH could muster 164 divisions to defend a front extending from Hungary to Lithuania, of which 99 were effectively in the area that mattered to Prussia – Army Groups A and Centre. But all those divisions were grossly undermanned and most were seriously underequipped. All were short of fuel and some lacked normal supplies of ammunition. Against them, according to Gehlen's calculations, were massed at least 231 infantry divisions, 22 tank corps, 29 independent tank brigades and three cavalry corps, to say nothing of a mighty and effective air force. All these units were well-equipped and to a greater or lesser extent fully-manned.

Russian sources calculated that the Soviet/German ratios were 5.5:1 in men, 7.8:1 in guns, 5.7:1 in armour and a massive 17.7:1 in aircraft. The Russians had no fewer than 13,400 armoured vehicles, mainly tanks and self-propelled assault guns, and some 5,300,000 men on the Eastern Front. In addition to the famous T-34 tank, the Soviet army now had the JS-3, the best-armed tank of the war, with its 122mm gun, a top speed of 25 mph (despite its 45 tons weight), and a range of

120 miles. Russian aircraft had improved enormously, as had the quality of the Soviet pilots' training.

Despite his earlier rebuff from Hitler when the subject of Soviet strength and the imminent danger of a Russian attack was mentioned, Guderian broached to Hitler on January 9th a detailed plan for a structured withdrawal to more defensible positions, and for transfer of a significant number of divisions from the western front to the East. Hitler responded with a furious rage, once again refusing to accept the possibility of a threat from a race whom he had regarded as subhuman. In his fury, he demanded Gehlen's committal to a lunatic asylum, which Guderian countered by saying that if Gehlen went, he went too. It seemed to the desperate Guderian, one of the most successful soldiers of the Second World War, that nothing could be done to forestall the military disaster that was about to befall the once-proud German Army.

The Soviet High Command, *Stavka*, had planned its new offensive for January 20th, along a 750 mile front extending from Tilsit on the Niemen, on the borders of Lithuania and close to the Baltic, southwards to Baranow on the Lower Vistula. Because of urgent appeals from Churchill to Stalin to launch an offensive in the East as soon as possible to take the heat off the western front, the Russian's first attack was brought forward to January 12th, and was far to the South of the line. It came from the 1st Ukrainian Front, which was facing the German XLVIII Corps of the 4th *Panzerarmee* across the lower Vistula at Baranow. The German Corps was thinly spread along its front, with only three weak infantry divisions, each of which was down to six battalions. At Hitler's insistence, and against all advice from Colonel-General Harpe, the reserves were only 12 miles to the rear. Despite firm evidence of new Soviet high-speed tanks whose armament and armour made them virtually unstoppable, Hitler refused to believe that a Russian armoured column would be capable of covering 12 miles in one day. Furthermore, Hitler issued a firm order that the reserves were not to be thrown into action without his express permission – but nonetheless continued to lie abed until 11am.

The attack began at 3am with an artillery barrage, followed by a brief diversionary attack to cause the *Panzer* units to reveal their positions in the darkness. The Soviet army, commanded by Marshal Konev, swiftly demonstrated what Major-General Gehlen had meant by superiority of fire power. Along the line of attack at Baranow, Konev launched against the German defences no less than 34 infantry divisions and 1,000 tanks, and hammered the German positions with guns 320 to the mile – virtually wheel to wheel. In one day on January 12th, the 1st Ukrainian Front completely overran the 4th *Panzerarmee* and advanced up to 15 miles; so rapid was the advance that by the time Hitler was available to make decisions about the reserves, the decisions were no longer necessary. As darkness fell, the Russians pushed right on without stopping.

On January 14th, the next Soviet army to the North, Marshal Zhukov's 1st Belorussian Front, broke out of the Pulawy and Magnuszew bridgeheads on the Vistula and, more by chance than planning, encountered German *Panzer* formations that were well separated from each other and thereby incapable of putting up a united front. General Berzarin's 5th Shock Army and Chuikov's 8th Guards Army virtually annihilated three German divisions that were absurdly outnumbered, and the Soviet 33rd and 69th Armies overran two luckless German divisions whose soldiers must have wondered what hit them. The tidal wave of Russian power almost destroyed the German 9th Army, sweeping across the Vistula and carrying all before it.

Further North again, the Russians encountered firmer German resistance. On January 13th and 14th, the 2nd and 3rd Belorussian Fronts and their respective Air Armies went into action against German Army Group Centre and achieved little headway until January 16th, despite outnumbering the German defenders locally by at least 3:1. Soviet intelligence had failed to note that the crack *Grossdeutschland Panzer* Corps was in the sector it had attacked, and the experienced and skilful German tank commanders made the most of foggy conditions and the surprise their presence had created. On January 14th, the German *Panzer* units, despite their numerical disadvantage, had launched 37 counterattacks in one day.

Clearly, the *Grossdeustchland Panzer* Corps had become a key factor in keeping the Soviet 3rd Army at bay. Hitler therefore made, and obstinately refused to alter despite the obvious facts and the outspoken criticism of his Chief of Staff, a decision that even he rarely exceeded in its sheer madness. He ordered that the *Grossdeutschland Panzer* Corps should be immediately transferred from its present location in Army Group Centre to Army Group A, where it was to attack the Russian forces advancing on Poznan, despite the fact that it would almost certainly be too late arriving there to be any use, and that its removal from its current location would assuredly cause the collapse of the German line.

The *Grossdeutschland* Corps was duly pulled out of the line, and, on the 16th of January, the Soviet armies began to break through the greatly weakened German 2nd Army. By the 20th January, Marshal Rokossovsky had reached the border of East Prussia and had crossed it, launching his 5th Tank Army towards Elbing. Meanwhile the *Grossdeutschland Panzer* Corps arrived at Lodz just in time to retreat under heavy fire in an impossible situation and only just made cover in Prussia without being encircled. Hitler's decision precipitated the destruction of no less than 28 German divisions.

To the North, the 3rd Belorussian Front under Chernyakhovsky had pressed forward, overcoming and destroying the 3rd *Panzerarmee* and approaching, as January drew to a close, within 30 miles of Konigsberg. Colonel-General Reinhardt's 4th Army had, on January 17th, been in what was clearly a dangerously exposed position, and liable to encirclement as the 2nd Belorussian Front pushed forward. Despite urgent appeals from Reinhardt, Hitler refused permission to withdraw. The inevitable happened. On January 21st, 350,000 men of the German 4th Army were encircled and trapped at Lotzen. With considerable ingenuity and great bravery, General Hossbach broke out Southwards and attempted by forced marches over five days through biting snowstorms to get to Elbing before the 5th Guards Tank Army. He failed. The Russian tanks had reached Elbing on January 27th.

Further South, Marshals Zhukov and Konev crashed on towards their goal. The German 2nd Army was shattered and unable to do anything constructive to stop the Russian advance. Between January 19th and January 23rd, Marshal Konev fought 90 miles towards Berlin in just three days. Colonel-General Schoerner, who had replaced Harpe following the latter's disgrace at Hitler's hands following the collapse of Army Group Centre, was a competent general, and a capable administrator, but there was nothing he could do to slow the Russian advance. By the end of January the forward troops of the 1st Ukrainian Front had reached the River Oder above Oppeln and either side of Breslau. At two points they were on the West bank of the Oder. Further South, Zhukov's tank armies had, by the end of the first week of February, reached Frankfurt on Oder, and were only some 50 miles from Hitler's bunker.

At the end of January, Hitler made his last disastrous attempt at reorganising the smashed German armies into some semblance of resistance to the Russian onslaught. Instead of giving the experienced Colonel-General Weichs command of the new Army Group Vistula, as Guderian had wanted, Hitler gave it to his uniquely incompetent and twisted *Reichsführer SS* Heinrich Himmler, who had already proved with Operation *Nordwind* the massive extent of his inability to achieve military success. Himmler compounded Hitler's stupidity by appointing his commanders on a basis of party purity rather than military competence. The scene was set for total and unmitigated disaster.

After February 6th, when the Soviet front line extended almost to the border of Prussia, the Soviet advance slowed. Throughout February 1945 and into March, the Russian armies continued the task of isolating and annihilating Germany's remaining forces in Silesia and East Prussia. By mid-April, East Prussia had been taken, and the Soviet line extended from Stettin on the Baltic coast, southwards to Frankfurt on Oder, Forst and Bunzlau, then South-Eastwards around the borders of Czechoslovakia. The victory was almost, but not quite complete. The final act remained to be played, in the West as in the East.

DIVIDING THE SPOILS

THE ALLIES CONFER AT QUEBEC, MOSCOW AND YALTA

A s the purely military aspects of the war became increasingly clear cut following the Allied successes in 1944, the political considerations of victory began to have increasing significance in the minds of the Allied leaders. Roosevelt had become increasingly trustful and admiring of Marshal Stalin, a trait that Winston Churchill did not find to his liking but which may have had some of its origins in the pro-Soviet sympathies of the President's long-time confidant and adviser Harry Hopkins. Churchill, for his part, was deeply worried about Stalin's intentions in Eastern Europe, and, while confident of a successful and friendly relationship with the Russian leader for as long as Hitler's Germany remained their common enemy, was aware that divergent interests would almost certainly prevail once Germany was defeated.

A further factor in the equation was the imminence of the US Presidential elections of November 1944, and the President's failing health. Despite his obviously being sick and in a state of decline, President Roosevelt clearly felt it to be his duty to see America through the closing stages of the war he had done so much to bring to a successful conclusion for the Allies. He therefore ran for a fourth term of office, and, no doubt feeling that a lame horse was better than an unknown mount at this crucial stage of the war, the American people duly elected him for a further term on November 7th 1944. However, there is no doubt that his faculties were less acute than they had been, particularly by the time of the all-important Yalta Conference in the Crimea in February 1945, and that Stalin used this factor to his own and Russia's advantage, and to the disadvantage of the whole of Eastern Europe.

The development of the Allied agreements on the partition of Europe that emerged from the series of three conferences began when Churchill and Roosevelt met in Quebec on September 11th 1944. Called principally to discuss the role of Britain's armed forces in the defeat of Japan after the victory in Germany had been concluded, the Quebec conference tackled the partition of Europe almost as an afterthought – but the discussions were crucial. On the Japanese war, the decisions reached were all made on the assumption, then current in US Staff circles, that the defeat of Japan would take a further eighteen months after Germany had been conquered. The US Chiefs of Staff had hoped that substantial elements of the British Army would be sent as reinforcements to the Australian and New Zealand troops that had long been under General MacArthur's command, but Churchill was opposed to this. In a lengthy minute quoted in full in 'Triumph and Tragedy', Volume 6 of his *The Second World*

War, Churchill pronounced himself in favour of 'British diversionary exercises on a major scale calculated to wear down the enemy forces by land and air, and also to regain British possessions conquered by the Japanese'. He proposed to the Quebec Conference '... a direct thrust across the Bay of Bengal aimed at "Dracula" (Rangoon), "Culverin" (Sumatra) or other attainable preliminary objectives'.

According to Churchill, the British delegation at Quebec carried the Americans with it on the Rangoon plan, which he saw as having many advantages as a strategy. Churchill pointed out that six months' fighting in the hills and jungles of Burma and on the frontier of India was estimated to have cost the British and Empire forces 288,000 losses from sickness alone, but that a seaborne strike against Rangoon and a northward advance would cut the enemy's communications and divide his forces at minimum cost. Churchill in fact went so far as to suggest that the USA might care to lend Britain a couple of divisions to fight in Burma, but his suggestion was, he says, 'not adopted'.

Thus the final verdict at Quebec on the Far Eastern War was that Britain should 'give naval assistance on the largest scale to the main American operations' but should 'keep our own thrust for Rangoon as a preliminary operation ... to a major attack upon Singapore'.

The Morgenthau Plan

The strangest and most controversial decision taken at Quebec was the adoption of the infamous Morgenthau Plan as Allied policy. With hindsight, it seems incredible that such a plan should have been suggested, let alone supported by Roosevelt and accepted by Churchill. That it was thus accepted, and that we find its acceptance so strange, is a measure of the extent to which attitudes to Germany and the German wars, and thought on issues of the rights of nations and peoples have changed in almost forty-five years.

Henry Morgenthau Junior was the Secretary of the Treasury in Roosevelt's administration. He became aware in August 1944 that there was discussion between General Eisenhower and the US War Department to formulate policies for the treatment of Germany and its population, industry and institutions once Germany had been defeated. Being in the President's confidence, he formulated his own proposals for the Allied treatment of Germany, and took them, behind the War Department's back, to Roosevelt. Roosevelt concurred in Morgenthau's proposals, despite the opposition of Henry Stimson, the Secretary of War, and the Morgenthau Plan therefore went to Quebec as a firm American proposal.

The Plan proposed that Germany would not only have all factories, steel production plants and industrial enterprises destroyed, but would also be forbidden the production of industrial raw materials. The coal and iron mines were to be flooded and destroyed, and the entire population was to be forced to return to an entirely agricultural and peasant way of life, dependent totally on the growing of crops and the breeding of animals.

Nobody seems to have made at the time the point that seems so obvious now – that the plan was, in all but the crucial aspect of mass murder, not unlike the SS ideals of the manipulation of populations and racial supremacy. The plan was both impractical and inhuman. On September 13th, Churchill is reported by his doctor, Lord Moran, as having said at a dinner in Quebec 'I'm all for disarming Germany, but we ought not to prevent her living decently. There are bonds between the working classes of all countries, and the English people will not stand for the policy you are advocating'. Yet by September 15th he had apparently been convinced by Professor Lindemann (Lord Cherwell) that the plan had the advantage of eliminating a postwar trade competitor, and should therefore be adopted. In all events, Churchill signed. Anthony Eden, then Britain's Foreign Secretary, remarked in his memoirs that its proposals for the Ruhr were like deciding to turn the Black Country into Devonshire.

Resistance to the Morgenthau Plan mounted once it was known that it had been signed. To Henry Stimson's side came Secretary of State Cordell Hull, Deputy Secretary of War John McCloy and General Eisenhower. Finally Harry Hopkins joined the protest movement – and at that point Roosevelt convinced Morgenthau that the plan must be shelved. It never saw the light of day again.

The Moscow Meeting

Churchill now turned his attention to his increasing fears that Stalin's political motives underlying the massive Soviet war effort were not entirely unblemished. It was by now clear that the Soviet Union had every intention of sweeping Europe on a massive front from the Baltic in the North, and (apparently) to the Adriatic in the South. Although Churchill was not over concerned about Rumania and Hungary, he was deeply interested to see that Poland and Austria were treated justly, and to ensure that Greece was not enslaved unwillingly (or even willingly) to Communism.

At the end of September 1944, Churchill therefore broached to Stalin the idea of a meeting in Moscow, and flew to see the Russian leader on October 9th. Roosevelt had declined to attend the conference on the grounds that the Presidential elections were close at hand, and delegated Averell Harriman as his observer, but with no power to negotiate on behalf of the United States. Furthermore, to Churchill's considerable chagrin, Roosevelt made it quite clear in a letter to Stalin that the would not be bound by any decision taken at Moscow, and that he regarded any discussions merely as a preliminary to a further conference of all three leaders. Churchill took this (correctly) as a lack of trust on Roosevelt's part in the conservatism of his (Churchill's) strategic thinking, but coming so soon after the Morgenthau episode, one might be forgiven for thinking that Roosevelt was being high-handed, to say the least.

Late in the evening of October 9th, immediately after their tiring trip to Moscow, Churchill and Eden met Stalin and the Soviet Foreign Minister, Molotov, for initial discussions. Harriman had yet to arrive, so there was no US presence. As if from a hat, Churchill produced immediately proposals for the possible division of Europe into spheres of influence after the end of the war. While the translators were explaining to Stalin and Molotov the Churchill plans, Churchill wrote down on a scrap of paper the world-changing proposal that influence in the Balkans and Eastern Europe should be apportioned as:

Rumania.
Russia 90 per cent
The others 10 per cent

Greece
Great Britain
(in accord with USA) 90 per cent
Russia 10 per cent

Yugoslavia 50–50 per cent

Hungary 50–50 per cent

Bulgaria
Russia 75 per cent
The others 25 per cent

According to Eden, Stalin simply ticked the piece of paper and returned it to Churchill, who subsequently wrote 'it was all settled in no more time than it takes to write down'.

The scene is unmistakably redolent of the meeting between Chamberlain and Hitler in 1938 when Hitler almost absent-mindedly signed Chamberlain's scrap of paper. Churchill was not sufficiently naive to claim 'peace in our time' – but subsequent experience showed that his fundamental instincts about Stalin and the Soviet government were correct and that the Soviet Union had no intention of honouring any agreement in respect of Eastern Europe unless it operated to its advantage.

On October 13th, delegates of the Polish government in exile, who were naturally deeply concerned at the existence of a Russian-backed communist Lublin 'National Committee', met Stalin, Molotov, Churchill, Eden and Harriman. Their mission was to discuss two issues – the formation of a unified Polish government after the ejection of Germany from their country, and the troubled question of the postwar Polish eastern frontier. The unfortunate Poles, led by their Prime Minister Stanislas Mikolajczyk, discovered for the first time at this meeting that the Allies had already decided at Teheran that the Curzon Line was to become their postwar frontier – which meant the loss to Russia of 48 per cent of the territory Poland had had in 1939, including the cities of Lvov and Vilnyus. Expecting support from the British delegation against this plan – after all, Britain had gone to war in 1939 over a much smaller part of Poland – the Polish government team found that Churchill was vehement in his support for it. In this, Churchill was doing no more than recognising the inevitable, but to the Poles it looked like, and possibly was, a sell-out.

And so to Yalta

During the winter of 1944/45, much occurred which altered the world stage and the dispositions of the politicians upon it. Roosevelt, re-elected on November 7th, had a new and effective Vice-President to replace the professional nonentity, Henry Wallace, who had been his understudy almost since America's war had begun. Harry S. Truman, though inexperienced in government, rose well to the occasion when catapulted into one of the most powerful positions on earth in April 1945, and was an able and worthy man.

During that same winter, the President had become visibly more frail and ill, and Lord Moran, when he saw him in February at Yalta, diagnosed at a distance advanced atherosclerosis and gave as his unofficial opinon that he had only months to live. On the military front, as we have seen, the Ardennes offensive had come and gone, and the Allies in the West were poised for the assault on the Rhine. In Eastern Europe, the Russians had swept into Poland and were about to stabilise their front on the Oder. Germany was demonstrably defeated. The matter of final decisions on territorial rights and the administration of Germany after the war had become urgent.

On February 2nd 1945, Roosevelt and Churchill arrived in Malta to confer with the Combined Chiefs of Staff Committee, who had been finalising over the previous few days the plans for the final sweep into the centre of Germany from the West. Having agreed the plans, the two leaders flew to the Crimea for the Yalta Conference, the first meeting of which took place on the following day, February 4th. From the start, Stalin had the conference under control. He proposed that the ailing Roosevelt should be in the chair, and thereby effectively reduced the influence of Churchill's ally in the discussions. Of the other US delegates to whom Churchill might have turned, Harry Hopkins was very pro-Russian and, by now, somewhat out of favour with Roosevelt, and the US team even included a diplomat called Alger Hiss, who in 1950 was convicted in the USA for perjury in respect of his communist party membership. Clearly, the pro-socialist camp was in the ascendant.

The troubled conference came to final decisions on three major areas of concern – Poland, Germany and the Far East. Let us look at the conclusions on each in turn.

Poland   It was agreed that the Oder and the Neisse were to become the Western boundary of Poland, although Stalin took the opportunity to claim that he had referred all along to the Western Neisse, when everybody else had been referring to the Eastern Neisse, which actually passes through the town of Neisse. Stalin's winning of this point meant the uprooting of eight million Germans. The Soviet leader made some modest concessions on the location of the Eastern frontier, but they were of relatively little significance. The Polish Government was to be created from both the communist Lublin Committee and from the London government in exile, but nobody specified how many members of the government were to be allotted from each. Since Molotov was to chair the steering commission, the outcome was never in doubt.

Germany   After some difficulty, the British delegation persuaded Stalin to accept that France should be a member of the Allied Control Commission that would administer Germany after the surrender. The borders of the Allied occupation zones were decided, and the principle of dividing Germany permanently was agreed, although without any detailed proposals being settled. Instead, a commission was set up under the chairmanship of Britain's Anthony Eden to study the problem. Roosevelt and Stalin agreed between them that Germany should pay '20,000 million dollars in reparations, half of it to be paid in kind to the Soviet Union by the transfer of industrial equipment, annual deliveries of goods and the use of German manpower'.

The Far East   In return for the return to the USSR of the Southern part of the island of Sakhalin, the port of Dairen, the Manchuria Railway and its lease on Port Arthur, all lost to Japan after the war of 1905, plus the Kurile Islands, Russia undertook in a secret agreement to lend forces to the defeat of Japan after the defeat of Germany.

Thus did a tyrant, a dying President, and a great Prime Minister with few cards to play settle the fate of a large part of Europe and the Far East in the sapce of a few days. Meanwhile, far from their remote meeting-place in the Crimea the war raged on.

THE END IN ITALY
THE NET CLOSES

The late summer and autumn of 1944 in Italy had seen a protracted defensive campaign by a somewhat heterogeneous German army, supported by large concentrations of forced labour units of the Todt Organisation. The German defence had been masterfully organised by Field-Marshal Kesselring to delay and hold General (later Field-Marshal) Alexander's attempts to cross the Appenines and advance to a line running from Venice to Brescia, and also to fend off an amphibious invasion that the Germans were (wrongly) convinced would come from the Bay of Venice. Such an invasion was in fact almost impossible because of the sandbanks offshore, but Kesselring appeared not to be aware of this, a fact that worked appreciably to the Allies' advantage by keeping six German divisions tied down to the defence of the coastline.

Hitler was of course aware that a successful advance to the Alps would present the Allies with not only the option of an assault on Austria and Germany from the South, but also a greatly-improved ability to bomb the Rumanian oilfields and the important aircraft factories in the South of Germany. He had made substantial resources available to Kesselring for the fortification of the 'Gothic Line', a defensive position running coast to coast across the mountains for 200 miles from a point near La Spezia on the Gulf of Genoa to Pesaro on the Adriatic. Every mountain route that Alexander and General Mark Clark could reasonably take to the Po valley was protected by heavily defended strongpoints, and when the battle for the Gothic Line began in earnest in August 1944, the Germans had installed 2,376 machine gun nests, 479 anti-tank and assault gun positions and four of the formidable 75mm Panther gun turrets. Had Alexander waited longer before attacking, there would have been 30 of these Panther installations, and the course of the battle would have been harder for the Allies.

In August, Kesselring had been able to field 26 divisions, including six armoured *Panzer* and *Panzergrenadier* divisions and six Italian divisions loyal to Mussolini's German-supported 'government in exile'. The Allies had only 20 divisions, following Alexander's having to give up seven divisions for 'Dragoon', the Allied amphibious landing in the South of France, but, as in every other theatre by this stage of the war, Allied air superiority was total. Alexander was able to call on the service of no less than 75 bomber and fighter-bomber squadrons, plus plenty of air transport and supply aircraft. Kesselring had only 170 aircraft of all types. Given that Kesselring had detached substantial forces to defend the Bay of Venice, the balance of power was in the Allies' favour, but not to a sufficient degree to make a rapid victory likely or predictable. In this context it should not be forgotten that the Italian partisans were now constantly and effectively active against the German army's depots and military installations behind German lines, and were directly beneficial to the Allies.

The Allies' originally-planned direct frontal assault against the Gothic Line in the mountains was re-planned early in August as a 'two-handed punch' towards both Ravenna and Bologna. The bulk of the British 8th Army under General Sir Oliver Leese – two Corps – was to attack towards Ravenna along the East coast via Route 16, and through the nearby hills to Route 9, the only available routes that did not cross the mountains. The other British Corps, XIII Corps, was to join II Corps of the US 5th Army for the assault on Bologna, and two more US Corps, plus the 6th South African Armoured Division, were to hold the remainder of the 5th Army line while the assault took place.

The snag, early in August, was that the entire 8th Army was in the mountains, positioned for the attack as originally planned. A massive secret operation was mounted to move the two Corps to the plain without the Germans finding out, and it succeeded brilliantly. When the attack on the coast came on August 25th, Kesselring did not take it seriously, believing that all the Allies' strength was far away in the mountains. By the time he discovered the truth it was too late, and the Polish, Canadian and British troops of the 8th Army were through the Gothic Line on a narrow front. By August 31st they held the heavily defended town of Montegridolfo, and on September 1st took Tavoleto. The Canadians suffered a great many casualties in fierce fighting, but succeeded in getting across the River Conca and establishing a bridgehead.

In the mountains, the 5th Army found the assault far more difficult and costly. Rough mountainous terrain made the advance slow, and gave the advantage to the defenders. Kesselring managed to get substantial reinforcements up to the front, and, during the first week of September, the Italian autumn once more provided the unremitting rain that had bedevilled the Allied campaign of a year before. The Air Forces could no longer guarantee the all-important 'aerial artillery' function, and the Allied advance ground to a halt. General Clark reviewed the situation, and regrouped for a set-piece attack against the German positions at their most vulnerable points. On September 12th, with better weather permitting air support once more, the attack began again, this time with two corps on a narrow front against the Gothic Line fortifications near the Il Giogo pass. By September 18th, Clark's army held seven miles of the Gothic Line defences, and the Americans began to fight their way towards Route 9 at Imola, where it was hoped that they would join up with the 8th Army.

Kesselring threw in almost all the reinforcements he had available in the area to prevent the US 88th Division reaching Imola, and although on September 27th the US troops were ten miles from the town, they were still no closer a week later after fierce fighting against four entire German divisions. The weather was now closing in, and the worsening conditions favoured the defenders. So General Clark abandoned his attempt on Imola for the time being, and pursued his major objective of reaching Bologna. On the plains of the Romagna, near the Adriatic coast to the East, the New Zealand, Greek and Canadian troops of the 8th Army had pushed both North and towards Route 9 from the other side, but the New Zealanders had become bogged down by the heavy rain on the banks of the River Fiumicino.

Clark's progress through the mountains towards Bologna was punctuated with heavy casualties in terrible conditions. Kesselring had reinforced the German 10th Army with five additional divisions, including the redoubtable 16th SS

Panzer Division, and the Americans had to fight for every inch of the rocky terrain. Monte Grande fell to the US 88th Division on October 20th, but by the 25th conditions were so bad, and so little progress was being made that General Clark gave the order to dig in. Both in the mountains and on the plain the intensity of the deluge was so great that bridges were swept away and rapid advances were virtually impossible. Not until just before Christmas could the offensive be resumed, and then it was only for a matter of days before Field-Marshal Alexander gave the order to return to the defensive as the bitterly cold winter weather closed in on the armies of both sides.

The Last Push into 1945 and Victory

During the lull of the winter, the Allied armies in Italy were substantially reinforced with new weapons; new better-armed tanks, armoured vehicles with wider tracks to cope with the soft ground, and tracked landing vehicles for use in the marshy areas around Lake Comacchio. Alexander had been appointed Supreme Commander in the Mediterranean in succession to Maitland Wilson, and as the winter began to recede, Allied morale was high. The Germans set to work with their huge forced labour organisation building yet more defences on every river line in the path of the Allied advance, and remorselessly trained the heavily reinforced 10th Army, now commanded by General Herr, for the struggle to come. Kesselring's Armies were now probably the best equipped facing the Allies anywhere in the European war, and the 10th Army, defending the Eastern (Adriatic) sector had had a whole Parachute Corps of 30,000 men under General Heidrich newly added to it. General Senger, commanding the German 14th Army in the Western sector, defending the approach to Bologna, had the 51st Mountain Corps holding the line towards Genoa and the Mediterranean, and the 14th *Panzer* Corps providing the defence of Bologna itself.

By comparison, the strength of the Allied 15th Army had been reduced, it having lost three divisions to the quelling of civil war in Greece, and the Canadian I Corps to the Allied push in Holland. Alexander was down to 17 divisions in the field, but remained totally in command of the air, and with it, in the end, the battle. Between February and April 1945, the strategic bombing force in Italy was progressively increased, and by the time the April offensive began, there were some 4,000 Allied aircraft taking part. As early as February 6th the bombers had begun attacking the German fuel dumps. By April, every railway line North of the River Po had been cut in several places, and the German armies were doing battle with their supply problems to an increasing degree every day. As the weather improved, the Allied bombing intensified and the Germans became more aware that the date of the new Allied offensive could not be far off, Field Marshal Kesselring was suddenly recalled to Germany on March 8th to become Commander-in-Chief in the West, in succession to Field Marshal Gerd von Rundstedt, and Colonel-General Heinrich von Vietinghoff-Scheel was appointed to succeed him as German Commander-in-Chief in the Mediterranean.

The plan for the Allied spring offensive was again based upon Alexander's favoured approach of the two-fisted thrust, but this time with two twists. A diversionary (and yet nonetheless necessary) attack was mounted by the Commandos before the main offensive to clear the nearer shore and the islands of Lake Comacchio of German troops. The actual objective of this operation was to clear the way for the main advance by the 8th Army, almost the whole of which had been moved secretly to a position just North of Route 9, but the intention was that it should also deceive the German commanders into believing that the expected major landing in the vicinity of Venice was at last imminent. The second twist was to follow as the 5th Army began its attack towards Bologna, when elements of the 8th Army, instead of pushing ahead on the Eastern sector front, would cross Lake Comacchio in 'Fantail' tracked amphibious landing vehicles (the 56th Division) and break out from the newly-won Santerno bridgeheads (78th Division) in a push to take Bastia. This, it was hoped, would cut the German line of withdrawal to the East.

But, between the two twists, it was necessary to win the Santerno bridgeheads. To do that, the 8th Army would first have to cross the Senio river, fight its way North-West to the Santerno, then cross that river in turn. In the evening of April 9th, after three hours of ceaseless bombing by Allied aircraft (one account says that 125,000 fragmentation bombs were dropped on German defenders along the Senio that afternoon), followed by four hours of mortar bombardment, the two divisions of V Corps, the 2nd New Zealand and the 8th Indian, plus the Polish II Corps, crossed the first river. That night, under fearsome conditions of fire, and under constant flame thrower attack, the Allied engineers built the bridges upon which the Allied armour was to cross. On the 10th, the Allied air assault began again, with 1,600 heavy bombers dropping thousands more bombs on the German positions, and opening the way to the Santerno. The carnage was appalling, and the Allied army began to win the battle by sheer attrition of manpower. The next day, the 11th April, the New Zealanders crossed the Santerno, thereby gaining their bridge-head, and more than 2,000 German prisoners.

Bad weather grounded the Allied aircraft temporarily, and delayed the next stage of the attack, but by the 14th April conditions were again good enough for the campaign to be resumed in earnest. On that day, the Poles took the heavily-defended town of Imola, the New Zealand Division pushed forward over the River Sillaro and the 78th Division, which had been steadily moving towards Bastia managed to take the bridge in the town, join up with the 56th Division and mount a joint attack on the road to the crucial gap in the terrain at Argenta.

Now General Truscott, who, since General Clark's promotion to command the 15th Army Group, was the commander of the 5th Army, launched his army into the attack in the Western sector from positions West of the road from Pistoia to Bologna. During the next four days, the Allied air forces flew more than 4,000 sorties in support of the assault, and it was reported that during the first half-hour of the attack more than 75,000 shells fell on the German mountain positions. Despite this intensity of fire-power, the 5th Army advanced scarcely more than two miles in three days, and it took a week of tough fighting before they managed to break out, by-passing Bologna to the West, as had been agreed under Alexander's plan, and advancing North.

General von Vietinghoff was now acutely aware that Hitler's standard form of order to any defensive force, by which he had been forbidden under any conditions to retreat, was about to cost him his army, as the 5th Army wheeled around him to the South-West, and the 8th Army did the same from the North-East. Unless he could retreat beyond the jaws of the pincer, his army was trapped. On April 20th, von Vietinghoff, in total defiance of Hitler, ordered a retreat to the already prepared defensive positions along the River Po, but his order was already too late. Argenta had been taken by the Allies, and the British 6th Armoured Division was moving at high speed towards Ferrara. The bridges across the Po were all either destroyed by the Allied air attack, or totally blocked by burning or burnt-out German vehicles. German positions defended by Heidrich's I Parachute Corps in Bologna, heavily threatened by the US 34th Division from the South, and by the Poles from the East, fell on the 21st April. The 5th Army, preceded by tactical air strikes every mile of the way, advanced amid the increasing ruins of the German armies towards the Po, and by the 23rd the first US soldiers were over the river – the 10th US Mountain Division claiming the honour of being first on the other side.

Now the right flank of the 5th Army, the 6th South African Division, was able to join up with the left flank of the 8th Army, and the pincer was complete. Behind them were 67,000 German casualties and 35,000 German prisoners. General von Senger succeeded, as did many of his troops, in retreating across the Po, but there was little left to fight for, even less to fight with, and overwhelming Allied superiority in every aspect of the battle. On April 25th, an Allied signal to the Italian partisans brought forth a major rising against the remaining German defenders, now little organised and unable to fight in a coherent way. Individual garrisons began to surrender – Churchill tells of the surrender of the 4,000 men of the Genoa garrison to one British liaison officer. On the 27th April, the 8th Army crossed the Adige on its way to Venice, and the 5th, which had already captured Verona, headed for Vicenza and Trento.

The Allied victory in Italy was complete. On May 2nd, recognising the situation and the many individual surrenders that had already taken place, the remaining German and Italian troops of Army Group C surrendered unconditionally. Almost a million men joined the ranks of the prisoners in Allied care.

VICTORY IN EUROPE

THE END OF HITLER'S GERMANY

As we noted in the previous chapter, Field-Marshal Kesselring had been re-called by Hitler early in March to take over as Commander-in-Chief in the West, and found himself heir to a situation in which Hitler and the commanders of OKW had devoted most of the remaining strength of the *Wehrmacht* to the defence of the Eastern frontier of Greater Germany, and to the fortification of Berlin. With some measure of credibility, although nonetheless with tremendous optimism, Hitler and Guderian hoped to hold and defeat the Soviet armies on the Oder, and thereby to be able in time to transfer reinforcements from the East to the West. Kesselring's task, he was assured by Hitler, was to stabilise the pres-ent position, mop up the Allied bridgehead at Remagen, and then, when the reinforcements were available, to launch a counter-offensive to repel the invaders from the Reich.

Kesselring was nothing if not a realist, and soon realised that Hitler's require-ment of him to hold the position along the Rhine was simply not practicable unless entirely unforeseen circumstances worked in his favour. The total comple-ment of the *Wehrmacht* armies in the West amounted to 55 divisions, all of which were seriously under strength, and most of which were 'padded' with troops who were inadequately trained. Although the concentration of the German troops in and around Germany had largely resolved the supplies problem, and there was sufficient ammunition for defensive operations, the ammunition stocks were nowhere near enough for the scale of offensive that would be re-quired to recapture the bridge-head at Remagen. There was also a desperate shortage of fuel which made reliance upon armoured strength risky in the ex-treme. With only some 63 armed fighting men per mile of the long Western Front, Kesselring was facing 85 Allied Divisions, all at full strength, all with plenty of fuel and all with high morale.

Yet, despite this depressing situation, Kesselring remained loyal to his leader to the extent of refusing to conspire against him. When the *Waffen SS* officer, Karl Wolff, who had been secretly negotiating with Allen Dullen of the O.S.S. (Office of Strategic Services) for an armistice in Italy, approached Kesselring in March suggesting that the whole German Western Front should be included in the offer of a surrender, Kesselring refused – but he nonetheless approved of Wolff's efforts to secure the end to fighting in Italy. When, on March 19th, Hitler issued his notorious Order instructing the German armies to destroy everything in their path as they retreated across Germany, regardless of the needs of the German population, Kesselring secretly connived at Albert Speer's plan to frustrate the transmission and execution of this order, a sensible disloyalty that was made easier for the ever-correct Kesselring to justify to himself by the sheer speed of the Allied advance, and hence the German retreat, and by the acute lack of explosives to destroy anything in their path.

Montgomery Crosses the Rhine

Although, when Kesselring took over his new command, the Americans were already well established in some force East of the Rhine in the Remagen bridgehead, Montgomery's 21st Army Group, made up from North to South of the Canadian 1st Army Group, the British 2nd Army and the US 9th Army, was still on the West bank. Field-Marshal Montgomery, its commander, was engrossed in what seemed to the less detail-conscious Americans to be apparently endless preparations for his crossing in force. By the third week of March, all was prepared. A Royal Navy detachment under Vice-Admiral Sir Harold Burrough had ferried 45 landing craft and a formation of Buffalo amphibious tanks from Antwerp through the canals of Belgium, Holland and Germany to the ten crossing areas along the 21st Army Group's 20-mile Rhine front, where the river is almost a quarter of a mile wide. Between March 20th and 22nd, RAF Bomber Command and the US 8th and 9th Air Forces flew some 16,000 sorties over the area selected for the assault and the supply lines beyond it, dropping almost 50,000 tons of bombs. Huge quantities of ammunition and fuel had been accumulated in dumps before the attack – the quantities gave the US generals cause for derision, although it should be pointed out that Montgomery's assaults rarely ran short of supplies, whereas those of the US forces were more troubled. For the mammoth bridge-building tasks that lay ahead once the river had been crossed, 30,000 tons of bridge-building equipment and almost 60,000 engineers had been moved up to the assault zone. Finally, before the initial assault of 80,000 men made the first crossing and opened the way for almost a million more, a smoke-screen was laid along 75 miles of the Rhine from dawn on March 21st until early evening on the 23rd to conceal troop movements and final preparations.

Through the night of March 23rd/24th, the formidable artillery resources of the British 2nd Army and the US 9th Army pounded the German positions across the river with over 3,000 guns, as the British 15th and 51st Divisions and the US 30th and 79th poured across the river in the Buffalo swimming tanks. By dawn, the Allied armies had bridge-heads and were expanding them, and the 1st British Commando Brigade was in Wesel clearing the German defenders. Under the watching eye of Winston Churchill in a command post on the Allied side of the river, the next stage of the drama unfolded as an armada of more than 2,000 aircraft, including the fighter escort, carried the British 6th Airborne Division and the US 17th Airborne Division to a parachute and glider attack around Hamminkeln, only some five miles inland from the river bank. More than 1,300 gliders took part in this landing, which was a considerable success and enabled the Allied army to silence the German artillery that might otherwise have greatly slowed the vital bridge building operations on the Rhine. By evening on the 24th, the 17th Airborne had made contact with the British XII Corps, and had also taken intact vital bridges over the Ijssel which helped to make possible the subsequent rapid expansion of the bridge-head. The German 84th Division, caught between the Airborne troops in the rear, and the infantry in the front, had been virtually wiped out, with almost 4,000 prisoners being taken by the Allies. The heaviest resistance to the crossing was encountered at Rees, where a battalion of German parachutists held out bravely for three days before being forced to surrender.

Advances into Germany

By March 26th, in an incredible feat of engineering and endurance, the engineers of the 21st Army Group had opened seven 40-ton bridges to traffic across the Rhine. The German 1st Parachute Army was cut off by US and British troops advancing on both banks of the River Lippe, a tributary of the Rhine, and by the 28th March the 8th Armoured Division was 25 miles east of the Rhine, the Guards Armoured Division was approaching Munster, and the Canadian II Corps with XXX Corps reached the Dutch frontier. Now, as the US 3rd Armoured approached the 8th Armoured, it became clear that their throwing back on to German Army Group B of the five threadbare *Panzer* divisions that had opposed their advance could mean the encirclement of the whole of Army Group B. On April 2nd, the two Allied Armoured Divisions joined up. The remains of the 5th *Panzerarmee*, plus the 19 divisions of the German 15th Army were encircled in what Hitler quickly and opportunistically named the 'Fortified Area of the Ruhr'.

General Bradley allotted the task of reducing and destroying the German 15th Army, and of capturing the Ruhr, to a new 15th Army under the command of Lieutenant-General Grerow, consisting of 18 divisions taken from the US 9th and 1st Armies and organised as five corps. By April 12th, after attacking South across the Ruhr and West across the Sieg, Grerow had occupied the entire coal-producing area, and by the 14th the two converging US forces had cut the German defences in two. By now, Field Marshal Model, who was nominally in command of Army Group B had vanished, and Colonel-General Harpe, the commander of the 5th *Panzerarmee* assumed command and ordered the whole of German Army Group B to cease fire. His surrender added a further 325,000 prisoners, including 29 Generals, to the Allied bag. Field Marshal Model committed suicide on April 21st.

Advances into Germany on the Western front continued apace, and the average number of prisoners taken per day rose by mid April to an incredible 50,000. The US 9th Army took Hanover on April 10th and reached the Elbe on April 13th, crossing to take Barby and establish the first Allied bridge-head East of the river. Now the US Army was only 75 miles from Berlin, and advancing at such a pace that, had Eisenhower been prepared to recognise the political desirability, as urged upon him by Churchill repeatedly over the preceding months, of reaching Berlin either ahead of or at the same time as the Russians, the history of Europe, despite the decisions of Yalta, might have been dramatically altered. Eisenhower, however, chose to view his task only in military terms, and saw, quite correctly, that the Soviet armies were better able to capture Berlin than those of the Allies. He continued to take the view that to advance to Berlin would cost the Allies unnecessary casualties, and that the occupation of Southern Germany was also of pressing importance. In this his conviction was fuelled by the Intelligence Department of SHAEF, who had convinced him that Hitler and the central figures of the Nazi regime intended to take themselves and several crack SS divisions into the mountains of Southern Germany and create there a remote 'Southern Redoubt' which could be defended almost indefinitely. Postwar evidence showed conclusively that such a plan simply did not exist, and that the Nazi hierarchy were by this time far too fragmented for the plan ever to have been practicable. This raises the interesting possibility, for which, as far as is known, there is no shred of evidence, that the whole 'Last Redoubt' notion was planted at SHAEF by Russian agents intent on ensuring that the US Army turned South, and left Berlin to the Russians.

The US 1st Army crossed the Weser at Munden on April 8th, and pushed on at high speed across Thuringia, covering some 75 miles in five days. Its left flank joined up with the right of the US 9th Army, and thereby cut off the German 11th Army in the Harz Mountains. The *'Clausewitz' Panzer* Division, sent to rescue the 11th Army, was encircled before it arrived, and both it and the 11th Army were wiped out. On April 14th, the US VII Corps took Halle and Leipzig, joining at Leipzig the 9th Armoured Division from General Patton's 3rd Army.

General Patton had, since March 30th, pushed eastwards to Jena and on to Muhlhausen. By the 21st, his XX Corps had reached Chemnitz in Saxony, and XII Corps had moved South-East to Bavaria and was well beyond Bayreuth. By the day of the final German surrender, Patton's troops were in Linz, where Hitler had gone to school, and his 13th Armoured Division had, on May 2nd, crossed the River Inn at Braunau, where Hitler had been born. Once again, Eisenhower's misplaced trust in the Russians played Europe false. Patton was all set to push on and take Prague, but after some argument, Eisenhower ordered him on May 6th not to do so. The outcome we know.

The North German Plain and Holland

In the North, Montgomery's 21st Army Group faced the task of cutting across the North German plain to Lubeck, thereby securing the entrance to the Baltic and cutting off the German armies in Denmark and Norway. Montgomery, being more politically inclined than Eisenhower, also saw his manoeuvre in terms of preventing the Soviet armies from adding Denmark to their gains in Europe. The 16 divisions of the British 2nd Army and the Canadian 1st Army, of which six were armoured, faced the German 25th Army under General von Blumentritt plus the remnants of the 1st Parachute Army, responsible for the 'Northern Defence Zone' made up of the Netherlands, Denmark, Norway and North-West Germany.

By April 29th, the British VIII Corps of the 2nd Army, reinforced at Montgomery's request by the XVIII Airborne Corps (five divisions) had reached the Elbe on its way to Lubeck. Over two days, reinforced by the formidable support of the newly operational British Gloster Meteor jet fighters, Montgomery's force fought its way across the Elbe and by May 2nd the spearhead of VIII Corps was in Lubeck. Just 28 miles further East, on May 2nd, the 6th Airborne Division entered and took Wismar only six hours before Marshal Rokossovsy's troops arrived.

Bremen had fallen on April 26th to General Sir Brian Horrocks and XXX Corps, and on May 2nd, Hamburg was surrendered to the Allies by Lieutenant-General Wolz. On the 4th, the 7th Armoured Division took intact a bridge over the Kiel Canal, and on the same day the Guards Armoured Division took Cuxhaven. Thus did the Baltic coast and the great German naval base at Kiel fall into British rather than Russian hands.

In Holland, General Crerar had begun April with the dual tasks of driving up between the Weser and the Zuider Zee alongside XXX Corps in the general direction of Wilhelmshaven and Emden, and also of freeing those areas of Holland that were still occupied by German troops. The push to Wilhelmshaven and Emden was allotted to the Canadian II Corps, and progress through Holland towards Germany was brisk, Zutphen and Almelo falling to the Canadians on April 6th, and Groningen and Leeuwarden on April 10th. Once in Germany, the defenders' resistance was extremely fierce, and Lieutenant-General Simonds, in command of II Corps, called for reinforcements to deal with the German II Parachute Corps. With the help of the Canadian 5th Armoured Division, the Polish

1st Armoured Division and the British 3rd Division, General Straube's parachutists were pushed back. By the time the German army surrendered in the North, the Canadians were almost in Emden, and the Poles were a few miles short of Wilhelmshaven.

In Holland, Arnhem had been captured by the Canadian I Corps, who then pushed on to the Zuider Zee at Harderwijk. The Germans, as the Allied armies approached, opened the sea dykes and thereby threatened the lowlands of the reclaimed areas with flooding that would have cost thousands of civilian lives and great damage to property and homes. To prevent this disaster in Holland, General Crerar agreed to a cease-fire with General Blumentritt provided that Allied aircraft bringing supplies of food and medicines to the Dutch civilian population were not molested. This arrangement worked well for the remaining few days of the war.

Southern Germany and Austria
In yet another change of command in the closing days of the war, Field-Marshal Kesselring was obliged, in addition to his role as C-in-C West, to undertake the direct command of the 'Southern Defence Zone', the counterpart in the South of Field-Marshal Busch's command in North Germany and Holland. Thus, Kesselring found himself once more in command of a motley assortment of German formations of varying degrees of competence, facing General Devers' 6th Army Group.

On March 26th, the American 7th Army had crossed the Rhine at Gernsheim, and had gone on rapidly to take Mannheim and Heidelberg on March 30th. Despite quite firm resistance from the German defenders, Wurzburg fell on April 5th, and General Patch, commanding the 7th Army, launched a determined thrust to capture the heavily defended areas of Schweinfurt and Nuremberg. The American troops met determined resistance, but by the end of April were across the Danube, had captured Munich and had taken the remains of the German XIII Corps as prisoners. On May 4th, the French 2nd Armoured Division captured Hitler's mountain retreat, the Berghof, on the Obersalzberg mountain.

Meanwhile, the French II Corps had been fighting hard throughout April after an improvised but brilliantly successful crossing of the Rhine at Speyer. Against powerful and effective resistance from the German 19th Army, the French took Karlsruhe on April 4th and, in a constantly changing battle reminiscent of greater days of the German army, captured Pforzheim on April 8th. On April 20th, again after fierce battles, the French captured Tubingen and took 28,000 prisoners. Five days later, General de Lattre's formidable French Colonial Army took another 40,000 German prisoners when General Keppler's XVIII SS Corps was cut off and encircled on the Swiss border.

At the end of April, General de Lattre ordered his I Corps to attack the German 24th Army, whose defined role was to prevent the French entering Austria. They lost no time. On April 30th, the 4th Moroccan Mountain Division and the French 5th Armoured Division took Bregenz, and from there on made a flower-decked progress through Austria as the populace welcomed them as liberators. On May 7th Kesselring capitulated to General Devers and a cease-fire was declared in Austria, thus preventing any further damage to a beautiful country.

The Soviet Advance to Berlin
To reinforce Eisenhower's known disposition not to advance on Berlin, and to allow the Soviet armies to handle the assault on the German capital, Stalin had

sent him a telegram assuring him that only 'secondary forces' were being sent against the capital. Those secondary forces proved to consist of 20 armies, 6,300 tanks, 41,000 mortars and almost 8,500 aircraft. The Russian leaders were clearly determined that their final assault on Hitler's citadel, which began early in the morning of April 16th 1945, should succeed.

The southernmost of the three Fronts of Army Groups attacking the German defenders was Marshal Konev's 1st Ukrainian Front, with seven armies plus an Air Army. He was to advance across the Neisse and towards Dresden, wheeling towards Berlin if Marshal Zhukov's 1st Belorussian proved to need his support. Zhukov's Front was in the centre, facing the German 9th Army, and had ten armies and an Air Army. His task was to encircle and capture Berlin. To Zhukov's North was the 2nd Belorussian Front of Marshal Rokossovsky, with five armies and an Air Army. The Russians had on the Eastern front, as the British, French and Americans had on the Western, total air superiority, and used it to the full.

Initially, the attacks along the Oder were repelled by the German defenders, although Marshal Konev's forces made some slow progress. Counterattacks followed every attack, and, had the Germans had the reinforcements to match their losses, which the Russians clearly did, the battle would have gone on for far longer. There was no lack of determination or morale on the German side in this last great defence against the hated Bolshevik invader. But in a war of attrition, the Soviet armies could not fail to win, and the beginning of the end for the Germans came on April 19th, when the German 9th Army collapsed. Suddenly, Zhukov was through a breach in the line and in Strausberg, only 22 miles from Hitler's bunker. Konev, meanwhile had crossed the Spree at Spremberg and was in Saxony, receiving orders to turn North to support Zhukov.

On April 22nd, the two Soviet armies met at Konigs Wusterhausen, to the South-East of Berlin, and the German 9th Army was encircled. Two days later, Berlin itself was totally surrounded. Hitler, personally in charge of the defence of the city, but by now living in a world of fantasy, had despatched Field-Marshal Keitel and Colonel-General Jodl to command the counterattacks that were totally to annihilate the Soviet invaders. Meanwhile he and Dr Josef Goebbels, in the latter's capacity as Gauleiter of Berlin, would organise the 90,000 boys and old men of the *Volkssturm* and hold off the Russian armies indefinitely.

In response to an extraordinary order requiring him to come to the defence of Berlin, General Wenck and the 12th Army gave way to the Western Allies on the Elbe, and headed for Berlin. At Potsdam, it acquired the remains of the 9th Army that had escaped the Russians, and, on 29th April, approached the city as Zhukov's armies began the last great push to break the city's defenders. Some 25,000 guns rained over 25,000 tons of shells on the besieged capital in one week. Wenck and the 12th Army could do nothing, and were soundly defeated. The Russians had Berlin.

The End of Hitler

Adolf Hitler, now a prematurely aged sick man whose appearance shocked all who saw him, had no intention of allowing himself to be captured by the Soviet troops whom he loathed, and to whose nation he had brought such dreadful suffering and losses. He had come in six years from a zenith of conquest, the equal of which Europe had never before seen, to total disaster and the destruction of his adopted land. His Thousand Year Reich, born of the Germanic myths, of the injustices of Versailles, of the desires of the German people for the greatness that they believed themselves heir to, had been grossly perverted to the service of hideously inhuman ideas and practices. Hitler's philosophy, so clearly set out in *Mein Kampf* in 1924 and 1927, and yet totally ignored by those who had allowed his rise to European power to go unchecked, had been directly respons- ible for the deaths of six million Jews, 20 million Russians, and millions more Allied civilians and soldiers. To Adolf Hitler must go the distinction of having caused more human deaths and suffering than any other man in history.

Now, after marrying his mistress and confidante Eva Braun on April 29th, the one time ruler of Europe and his wife of a few hours mutually committed suicide on April 30th, 1945. Their bodies were taken to the garden of the Chancel- lery by those still loyal to them in the bunker and burned. Josef Goebbels, Reich Propaganda Minister and his wife Magda, who were also in the Führer's bunker, poisoned their children and then committed suicide, he by the bullet, she by poison. Martin Bormann, Hitler's secretary and aide, disappeared, believed killed by a Soviet tank attempting to escape from Berlin. Grand Admiral Doenitz, in Flensburg, learned that he had been named in Hitler's will as the new Führer of Germany. Goering, Keitel, Jodl, Kesselring, Speer and the rest of the Nazi hierarchy were progressively over the following few weeks captured and sent to await either trial for war crimes, or their interrogation and appearance as witnesses at the Nuremberg War Crimes Tribunal.

The Surrender

But, before the leaders passed into captivity, the very last act of the war that the German Reich had begun with such bravura and style, and which had changed permanently the face of Europe, remained to be played out. On May 3rd, a depu- tation led by General E. Kinzel, Chief of Staff to Field-Marshal Busch, and Admi- ral von Friedeburg, the new head of the *Kriegsmarine* following Doenitz' elevation to his role as Head of State, presented themselves at the caravan that had been Field-Marshal Montgomery's travelling headquarters since 1943, and which was now on Luneburg Heath on the North German plain. They offered Montgomery the surrender of the German forces in the North of Germany, in- cluding those in retreat from Marshal Rokossovsky on the Eastern front. Rather disconcertingly, Montgomery dismissed them as he might have done an applica- tion for compassionate leave from his batman.

The next day, they were invited back, and were obliged to accede to terms of total and abject surrender, but only in respect of the forces facing Montgomery's 21st Army Group. The Allied Command in the West was resolved not to provide refuge from the advancing Soviet armies, something that Doenitz was anxious to achieve for as many as possible of his countrymen.

The final surrender ending the European war totally was signed on May 7th 1945 in a schoolroom at Rheims. Lieutenant-General Walter Bedell Smith of the US Army, deputising for General Eisenhower, read to the German representat- ives, Colonel-General Jodl, Admiral von Friedeburg and Major-General Oxenius of the *Luftwaffe* the full document, which ordered the simultaneous cessation of hostilities on all fronts on May 8th at 11.01pm. The surrender document, con- firmed the total defeat of the armed forces of the Third Reich, and settled the terms of their yielding their arms and accepting Allied orders.

Colonel-General Jodl and his colleagues each signed on behalf of Germany, then General Bedell Smith added his signature. Next was Lieutenant-General Sir Frederick Morgan for Great Britain, General Sevez for France, and Major- General Susloporov for the USSR. Next day, a further act of surrender took place in Berlin, when Field-Marshal Keitel, Admiral von Friedeburg and Colonel-

General Stumpf signed a further document of unconditional surrender in the presence of Marshal Zhukov, General de Lattre de Tassigny, Air Chief Marshal Sir Arthur Tedder and General Spaatz.

The war in Europe was at last really over. To rejoicing not only in Britain, where the population of London danced in the streets all night on 'VE night', May 8th 1945, but also in the USA and in France was added total joy in tens of countries around the world. But there was another war to finish. Hardly had the excitement of the surrender passed before the Allies' near-total attention was focused on the Far East, where the war still raged on. This book will look at the immediate post-war events in Germany in the last chapter. Let us now return to the defeat of Japan.

THE FINAL PUSH IN BURMA

THE END OF JAPANESE DOMINATION

The Burma war had, since May 1942, when the British Army had been driven out of Burma, been remote both from the European War, which it resembled so little as to be almost incomprehensible to the soldiers fighting in Europe, and from the American war against Japan, nearer at hand but totally different in character. The Japanese, having captured Burma and the road to Chiang Kai-shek's Nationalist China, were content to stay on the defensive. The successive British and Allied commanders felt on the one hand an obligation and a duty to attack, and on the other a sense of the futility of repeated offensives and counteroffensives that achieved little and could be predicted to do little more than cost lives.

The frustration of Churchill and the Allied political leaders with the moving stalemate of Burma had been echoed in repeated changes in command at all levels. These had culminated, after the Allies' disastrous performance during 1942 and 1943 in the Arakan coastal region of North-West Burma, in the total restructuring of the Allied command. General Wavell had, in 1943, become Viceroy of India, General Sir Claude Auchinleck had become Commander-in-Chief in India, and Admiral Lord Louis Mountbatten had been appointed Allied Supreme Commander, South-East Asia Command, based in Ceylon (now Sri Lanka). An 11th Army Group commanded by General Sir George Giffard had included a new 14th Army commanded by Lieutenant-General (as he·then was) William Slim.

The new organisation had prospered, and the structure of the military organisation in India and Burma was overhauled from top to bottom. When the third Arakan offensive had been launched after the monsoon at the end of 1943, it had been a much tougher and better equipped Allied army that advanced down the Mayu peninsula to the heavily-fortified Maungdaw-Buthidaung line to join battle with the Japanese at the beginning of 1944. The Japanese 55th Division under Lieutenant-General Hanaya had attacked the strung-out Allied army by their well-tried techniques of jungle infiltration and outflanking movements, mainly as a diversionary tactic to draw as much Allied strength as possible into the Arakan, and away from the other side of Burma. For it was there, the Japanese High Command had decided, that their main strategy for 1944 was to be concentrated in an attack west across the Chindwin hills towards Imphal.

The so-called 'Ha-Go' offensive by the Japanese had lasted three weeks in February 1944 before General Hanaya, recognising that XV Corps intended to hold out indefinitely, called it off as a battle he could not win. For the first time in the Burma war, the British and Commonwealth army had used air support, proved by the Chindits to be an effective and practical supply system, to maintain a full-scale siege and eliminate the need to withdraw in the face of attack. General Slim's new Army had shown that the Japanese were not, after all, invincible. As for Hanaya, although he had lost the battle, he had achieved his greater objective. One Japanese division had succeeded in tying down more than six Allied divisions while the parallel 'U-Go' offensive against the British stronghold at Imphal was mounted. The new administrative and organisational structure of the 14th Army had, however, been shown to be the hinge of successful defence; now it was to become the thin end of the wedge of victory.

The Japanese attack on Imphal began in earnest on March 8th 1944, forestalling the Allies' own intended advance to the Chindwin River. Lieutenant-General Yanagida's 33rd Japanese division crossed the Chindwin and advanced against the British IV Corps under General Scoones. Rather than attempt to fight the Japanese on their own ground, in the jungles through which they had proved themselves the superior soldiers, Slim instructed Scoones to withdraw to the plain, and bring the Japanese out into the open terrain in which they were least effective. In doing this, the Allied commanders knew that if the Japanese succeeded in cutting the road to the railhead at Dimapur, the defenders of Imphal would be totally dependent on supply from the air. The Japanese in fact intended not only to cut the road but also to capture the railway, and thereby to block the supply route by which Chiang Kai-shek's arms and supplies reached General Stilwell's air force, which in turn ferried them 'over the hump' to China.

The Japanese commanders now made the same mistake, born of overconfidence nurtured by years of success, that they had made in the recent Arakan campaign. They gambled on the availability of the supplies at Imphal to feed their own army. They thus made an assumption of rapid victory that was not to be justified in the event. By the end of March 1944, the Japanese had succeeded in cutting the road to Dimapur, and were advancing on to the plain of Imphal from three sides. Allied air power now began to tell in purely military terms, as the 5th Indian Division was flown into Imphal from the Arakan, and the 7th Indian Division was brought by air to Dimapur.

Meanwhile, to the North, the parallel Japanese attack against the town of Kohima, which was the key to a pass to the Assam Valley, had been stemmed by the defenders. They were a lean, hungry, small but determined force made up of a battalion of the Royal West Kent Regiment, a Nepalese battalion, a battalion of the Assam Rifles and every walking wounded and convalescent from the military hospital capable of firing a rifle. On April 4th, the Japanese 31st Division attacked viciously, driving them into an even tighter perimeter, and eventually on to one hill. There, supported by bombing attacks from Allied aircraft, they held on tenaciously and stubbornly, supplied entirely from the air and denying the Japanese army passage through the pass to Assam, until they were relieved on April 20th.

Even after the relief of Kohima by the 161st Indian Brigade, there were still 60,000 British and Indian troops encircled at Imphal requiring all their supplies and food and ammunition to be dropped from the air. Mountbatten was desperately short of transport aircraft, and clung firmly to twenty American aircraft that he had 'borrowed' from Stilwell's 'Hump' air force, and had neglected to return, despite every encouragement from the Americans to do so. But to supply Imphal effectively, and starve the Japanese army into retreat, he needed seventy more transport aircraft quickly. Appeals to the Americans for yet more aircraft were unsuccessful – perhaps they suspected they might not get those back either – and it eventually fell to Churchill to pull strings and deprive Field Marshal Sir Harold Alexander of seventy of his transport aircraft from the Mediterranean.

As May ended and June began, the siege of Imphal continued unremittingly. The Japanese overall commander in the Sector, Lieutenant-General Mutaguchi, secure in a distant hill station, instructed the commanders of his 15th and 33rd Japanese Divisions to fight on and not under any circumstances to retreat. In fact, the Japanese divisions were now desperately short of food and equipment, as a result of the Chindits having cut their supply lines, and were attacking fanatically as their strength ebbed. General Scoones, commanding IV Corps in the defence of Imphal, had been ordered to break out, but the effort of maintaining his line against suicide attacks aimed at capturing his food supplies was tying down a substantial part of the Corps. By the third week of June, the Monsoon was in full spate, the Japanese had lost ground and were being squeezed by the British 2nd Division coming from Kohima, and it seemed that the end of the battle was in sight. But the monsoon conditions effectively prevented Allied air power from dominating the battle. Not until June 22nd did the British 2nd Division and the Indian 5th Division meet and open the road to Imphal. With some justification, Lord Louis Mountbatten predicted that the first major British victory in Burma was in sight.

General Slim ordered IV Corps and the divisions that had lifted the siege to pursue the two Japanese divisions, who, despite their privations – the 33rd were in far less difficulty with disease and starvation than the 15th Division – were fighting grimly on the roads to the South. But Allied air superiority, the increasing ravages of the monsoon and the devastation wrought by disease completed the Japanese defeat. Of the 88,000 Japanese soldiers who had crossed the Irawaddy to begin the attack, over 53,000 were dead, sick or wounded. Allied casualties at Imphal and Kohima totalled 16,700.

The victory at Imphal began the advance by Lieutenant-General Slim's 14th Army back to the Chindwin, which was crossed in December 1944. At the same time, the British 36th Division, a part of General Stilwell's Northern Combat Area Command, had fought its way South down the railway from Mogaung and was, at the turn of the year only 100 miles North of Mandalay. The 36th Division played a major role in limiting the options of the Japanese 15th Army by turning its flank as the 14th Army advanced. Now the final push to victory in Burma could begin.

The Road to Mandalay

As the 19th Indian Division made the 14th Army's first crossing of the Chindwin River early in December 1944, Lieutenant-General Slim, who had planned a campaign West of the Chindwin to eliminate the expected Japanese resistance in that area, suddenly found he had to revise his plans. Major-General Rees' 19th Indian Division made contact so quickly with the British 36th Division from the Northern Combat Area Command that it was apparent the Japanese had little intention of making a major stand East of the Chindwin river. Slim therefore decided to push for Mandalay, East of the Irawaddy, the great river that flows South to the strategically vital port of Rangoon, and which stood between the 14th Army and the regaining of Lashio and the Burma Road.

General Stopford's XXXIII Corps was to push as two columns from Kalewa via Yeu to the Irawaddy North of Mandalay, and via Monywa to the South of the city. The 19th Indian Division, already East of the river well North of Mandalay, would advance down the East bank to the objective, and IV Corps under Lieutenant-General Messervy would cross the Irawaddy well South-West of the city and strike East to take Meiktila, the most important road, rail and communications centre of the region. The advance went well. As February began, Stopford's XXXIII Corps was across the Irawaddy, and two weeks later IV Corps was in position for its Southern crossing. While the 14th Army was pushing forward, Commando units captured the island of Akyab and Ramree to provide sites for airfields necessary if the armies were to be supplied from the air in sufficient quantity.

To the North, General Stilwell's 140,000 troops of the Northern Combat Area Command were advancing southwards against stiff opposition from Lieutenant-General Honda's Japanese 33rd Army. On the Burmese coast, General Christison's XV Corps was fighting the Japanese 28th Army for an opportunity to get through the An and Taungup passes and hammer the Japanese communications to the rear of the army facing the other fronts. But for the Japanese Army's jungle experience and training, their position would have been precarious in the extreme. As it was, they were outnumbered, unable to call up any reserves, and constantly threatened by massive Allied air superiority.

As General Stopford's 20th Division of XXXIII Corps crossed the Irawaddy, the Japanese counterattacked in force on February 12th, and although the division established a bridge-head, the battle raged for two weeks before the 20th could break out and continue the advance. During that time, the 2nd Division also crossed, some miles further North, and had a similarly difficult time, but between the two of them the 20th and the 2nd Divisions kept the much-depleted 15th Army busy while General Messervy's 7th Division crossed with only limited resistance on its way to take Meiktila. By February 20th, Messervy's IV Corps had consolidated its bridge-head sufficiently to make its move towards the target, 80 miles away. By the end of February, Major-General Cowan's 17th Division of IV Corps had reached Meiktila, and on March 1st, without wasting any time, they attacked. By March 3rd, Cowan had both the town and the airfield, which was absolutely vital for the Allied airborne supply operation. Despite many Japanese counter-attacks, Major-General Cowan, reinforced with an extra brigade, not only held on to Meiktila, but also launched a number of successful local forays that mopped up Japanese opposition.

While all this was happening in Meiktila, Stopford's divisions were advancing on Mandalay, and although the 19th Division ran into stiff opposition around Mandalay Hill, and the 2nd Division found the old town of Ava more difficult to take than expected, Slim found that overall the defence of Mandalay was lighter than had been anticipated. So he ordered a column of the 20th Division to bypass Mandalay and head South to Meiktila, and gave the 2nd Division the job of capturing the city. By March 20th Mandalay had fallen, and the Allies at last knew they were beating the Japanese at their own game.

In the North, General Stilwell's troops had been similarly successful, and had taken Hsenwi on March 1st, and the vital target of Lashio on March 6th. On March 24th, the Burma Road from Lashio to Mandalay was once again open to Allied traffic. The success of the campaign for Mandalay and Lashio was the swansong of the Northern Combat Area Command. On March 19th it was disbanded, and its Chinese divisions returned to the liberation of China's rice-growing areas from the Japanese.

The 14th Army had, since crossing the Irawaddy, lost some 10,600 killed, wounded and missing in the fighting. But they had gained a considerable prize. Now all eyes turned on Rangoon, the great port to the South.

The Sweep to Rangoon – and the End of the War in Burma

The 14th Army had come a long way since Imphal. But Rangoon was a long hard fight ahead of them at the end of March 1945. One of the earliest and bloodiest actions of the campaign had come at Kangaw, two months earlier, while the campaign for Mandalay was in its early stages. Holding the An and Taungup passes, Lieutenant-General Miyazaki and his 54th Division sent a covering force to delay the advancing 81st and 82nd West African Divisions for as long as possible, and set about establishing full-scale defensive positions in two crucial areas. The principal defence was in the region of Kangaw, 40 miles East of Akyab, and only 10 miles East of the Myebon peninsula. The secondary force was in the town of Taungup. Since January 1945, the Allied navies had been in total control once more of the Bay of Bengal, and furthermore Akyab itself had been recaptured. It was decided that the 3rd Commando Brigade would take Myebon with an amphibious landing, and open the way for the 74th Brigade to advance inland and cut the Japanese division's communications at Kangaw.

On January 12th, 42 Commando, Royal Marines, went ashore in style on the beaches of Myebon, closely followed by 5 Commando, who were supposed to be there, and by 1 and 44 Commandos who were supposed to be on quite a different beach but landed anyway. The next day, Myebon itself was taken, and by the 17th the whole peninsula was in Allied hands. The 74th Brigade set out for Kangaw, and the Commandos were withdrawn for their assault role. The plan at Kangaw was for the Commando Brigade to seize a bridge-head on the East bank of the River Diangbon Chaung two miles South-West of the town of Kangaw, and for the 51st Brigade to go through the bridgehead and join up with the 74th after their march overland from Myebon. This would hem the Japanese force in on three sides. But surprise was vital.

On January 21st, a Royal Navy force of 50 assorted ships and craft anchored off the mouth of the Diangbon Chaung and bombarded the beaches, while aircraft of the RAF bombed Japanese positions. The Japanese did not see the attack coming, and were thrown completely off balance. Over two days, first 5 Commando, then Nos. 42 and 44 Royal Marine Commandos went ashore and established positions under heavy fire. The Japanese fought back fiercely, bombarding the invaders with artillery and repelling attempts to take Kangaw. On the 26th January, the 51st and 53rd Brigades landed, bringing tanks to reinforce the Commandos.

General Miyazaki responded by bringing up his own reinforcements in the shape of three infantry battalions and an artillery battalion under Major-General Koga. On January 31st, they attacked the Commando positions with everything they could muster, and for almost two days a fierce battle continued without respite, and without the Japanese taking the British positions. By the time the 74th Brigade arrived, the Commandos had killed more than 300 Japanese, had lost 66 killed and 259 wounded, and had won a posthumous Victoria Cross – that of Lieutenant Knowland of No. 1 Commando. By mid February, the Japanese had withdrawn to the An pass, and Kangaw was won – a vital step in the campaign that began one month later to capture Rangoon.

Since November 1944, the 11th Army Group had been disbanded, and Lieutenant-General Slim and the 14th Army came under Lieutenant-General Sir Oliver Leese, in his new role as Commander, Allied Land Forces, South-East Asia. After the capture of Mandalay on March 20th, Mountbatten and Leese were anxious to complete the clearance of Japanese forces in Burma by advancing to Rangoon before the monsoon. General Slim was therefore instructed to drive southwards, again as a two-corps thrust. General Stopford's XXXIII Corps was to move down the Irawaddy valley to Prome and on to Rangoon; General Messervy and IV Corps were to follow the road through Pyabwe, Pyinmana, Toungoo and Pegu. The two Corps would, it was decided, move from airfield to airfield, being resupplied at each as it was captured. More than 3,000 local fighters, the Karens, were organised as a defence force in the Hills to protect the flanks of the advancing Corps, which each had 350 miles to advance before reaching their goal.

The advance went smoothly, with only occasional serious hold-ups due to determined Japanese resistance. General Stopford captured Chauk on April 18th; Magwe and Yenangyaung on April 21st. His Corps reached Prome on May 3rd. General Messervy and IV Corps took Pyinmana on April 19th, Toungoo on the 22nd and Pegu on May 1st. Messervy was now only 50 miles from Rangoon.

Meanwhile, Mountbatten, alarmed at the imminence of the rains of the monsoon, and its potential for delaying the end of the war in Burma, had decided to go ahead with an amphibious invasion of Rangoon. On april 27th, two naval forces set sail to support the operation. One, consisting of two battleships (one of them the French *Richelieu*), four cruisers and two escort carriers, bombarded targets in the Nicobar and Andaman Islands to prevent intervention from Japanese forces based on them. The other was made up of three destroyers and succeeded in sinking most of a small Japanese convoy carrying reinforcements and stores. Early in the morning of May 1st, a battalion of the 50th Gurkha Parachute Brigade was dropped at Elephant Point, where they overcame a small force of Japanese defenders, and cleared the way for landing craft to come up the river to Rangoon itself. During that day, an RAF Mosquito twin-engined fighter-bomber, flying over Rangoon jail, saw the immortal words 'Japs gone. Extract digit' painted on the roof. Knowing that only those with a sound grasp of RAF slang could have painted such words, the pilot, Wing-Commander Saunders, landed at a nearby airfield, which was deserted, made contact with the prisoners, and then, because his aircraft had been damaged while landing, took to the river in a motor boat to alert the landing troops that the Japanese had left. As he did so, the 26th Division came up the river and took the city.

Thus was the victory in Burma finally won. To be sure, there were many small engagements between May and August, mainly in the appalling conditions of an unusually severe monsoon flood, but organised resistance by the Japanese had been broken, and they held no further major strategic Burmese locations. Lieutenant-General Slim, promoted full General, became Commander Allied Land Forces South-East Asia in succession to Leese, and, his reputation made, was set for a distinguished postwar career.

Only the final assault on the Japanese islands, and on Japan itself remained before the Second World War would finally be concluded.

THE LAST OF THE ISLANDS

IWO JIMA AND OKINAWA

As the US forces advanced across the Pacific, drawing closer to Japan with each successive island and archipelago, the resistance from the Japanese armies that they encountered became stronger rather than weaker. As the hopelessness of their military position became more apparent, so the Japanse commanders and their men relied more upon the ancient tenets of their culture and less upon the Western military wisdom that their nation had learned so quickly since the latter part of the nineteenth century. Instead of making rational decisions to retreat, or surrender, as any Western army would have done – and indeed did in Germany – when hopelessly outnumbered, outgunned and surrounded, the Japanese fought relentlessly to the point of starvation or the last bullet, and even then launched themselves into last bids for suicidal glory, desperately seeking to take as many as possible of their enemy with them to a certain death. The most difficult part of beating the Japanese was that they could not honourably acknowledge themselves to be beaten.

By the end of 1944, the US commanders had recognised this fact, and the horrifying potential for bloodshed that the Japanese attitude to war and defeat promised should America ever attempt an invasion of mainland Japan. It was clear that Japan must be bombed into submission, but even this presented major obstacles. Although the capture of the Marianas brought Japan within effective range of the new US Boeing B-29 Superfortress bombers, the presence of substantial Japanese air bases on islands closer to Japan meant that the bombers could be intercepted and damaged en route. Without bases or emergency airstrips nearer to their target than their home base, damaged aircraft were likely to have to ditch in the vastness of the Pacific, which in turn usually meant the total loss of the aircraft and the death of the crew.

Thus it was primarily to secure vital airfields, both to prevent their use against US aircraft, and to make them available as emergency landing facilities, that the US Chiefs of Staff reluctantly ordered the assault in February 1945 on the tiny island of Iow Jima– just over four and a half miles long by two and a half miles wide, but with two operational Japanese-built airfields, and a third airfield under construction. Not surprisingly, the commander of the Japanese troops on the island, Lieutenant-General Kuribayashi, was aware of its importance to the defence of Japan, and of its potential value to the US forces. He had been given orders as early as 1942 to prepare to defend Iow Jima to the last, and had set his men to work on what became probably the most comprehensive and best-planned defensive system in the Pacific theatre of war. The island's eight square miles had 800 pillboxes and an incredible three miles of tunnels connecting them and the deep concrete shelters designed to protect the troops from an expected pre-invasion bombardment. Not only were the beaches fully protected by guns with overlapping fields of fire, but there was a series of further defence lines with saturation coverage of the ground before them at carefully chosen intervals inland from the beaches. There were almost a thousand field guns, howitzers, anti-aircraft guns, rocket launchers and mortars. There were 20,000 light guns and machine-guns, with 22 million rounds of ammunition. Almost 21,000 Japanese troops were on the island by the time the American assault began. There were even 22 tanks – and all within less than five miles by three.

Of course, Allied intelligence knew quite a bit about this and was aware that the island was exceptionally heavily defended. Throughout the second half of 1944, from June through to January 1945, a constant air offensive was maintained in preparation for an assault that, in mid-1944, was probably going to be necessary and, by the end of the year was positively planned. What the American Intelligence men had not discovered or appreciated was the extent to which the defenders were protected by tunnels and deep shelters. Thus, the erroneous assumption was made that, by the time the three-day bombardment by the US Navy that preceded the invasion was completed, the Japanese defence would have been reduced to a fraction of its former power.

In fact, when the 4th and 5th Divisions of the US Marine Corps under General Holland Smith swarmed up the beaches of Iwo Jima just after 9 am on February 19th 1945, the ferocity of their reception was unprecedented. Withering machine-gun fire from emplacements in a wide arc before them mingled with mortar fire, and many Marines died there and then on the beaches. Using flame-throwers and explosives, tanks brought ashore in the second wave and every assault weapon available to them, the Marines managed by the end of the first day to isolate the Japanese troops defending Mount Suribachi, a 550ft extinct volcano that dominates the topography of the little island, and thereby secure a beach-head.

Under any normal conditions, the US Marines might then have expected to mop up the defence of the hill and move on to other matters within a few hours, but the defensive positions around Mount Suribachi were so strong, and the Japanese defenders were so determined, that it was not until late on February 21st, two days later, that the hill was totally surrounded, and not until the 23rd that a patrol under Lieutenant Harold Shrier managed to take the summit and plant the Stars and Stripes.

On February 24th, the battle to take the airfields of Iow Jima began. Despite an air strike, a naval bombardment lasting more than an hour and constant artillery fire, the deep, thick concrete emplacements that protected the Japanese defenders held up, and the advancing tanks of the 4th and 5th Divisions of the Marines, moving down the two side of the airfield, were once again extremely hard put to it to achieve any gains. The 4th Division advance was stopped by mines and guns; the 5th was just 500 yards nearer the Japanese positions after a day of fierce fighting. Next day, the newly-landed 3rd Division began their attempt to capture the plateau at the northern end of Iow Jima. It took three days of determined fighting, culminating in the use of tanks with flame throwers to incinerate the Japanese in their bunkers, to break through the Japanese line.

By the 28th, the three divisions of the US Marines had captured all three airfields and were mopping up, but there remained a major fight ahead. Two hills, each honeycombed with tunnels built by the Japanese defenders, became the centre of costly battles, as the Japanese army fought fiercely and, as always, to the death. One of them, known as Hill 382, had an associated rocky outcrop christened by the Marines 'Turkey Knob'. Nearby was a natural hollow, filled with defence emplacements and hull-down Japanese tanks, which became known as 'The Amphitheatre'. It took ten days, and hundreds of American casualties, just to capture those features, and it was not until March 10th that they were in American hands. Almost as long a time elapsed before the Marines captured Hill 362A, whose tunnels and surrounding rough ground gave the defenders a tremendous advantage. But on March 8th, that hill fell too. Even then the Japanese kept attacking, but their artillery was gone, and their last major effort was more in the nature of a mediaeval charge than a modern battle.

After March 10th, organised resistance on Iwo Jama was finished, but each isolated defensive position fought on to the bitter end, most of them to the death. Not until March 25th was the Battle for Iwo Jima finally over. It had taken more than a month, and the lives of almost 6,000 Marines – with more than 17,000 wounded – to capture the tiny island. Of the 21,000 Japanese on the island, only 216 were captured. The remainder died in accordance with their ancient code.

To put the Marine losses in perspective, the battle for Iwo Jima proved subsequently, by providing emergency airfields for American aircraft, to have saved nearly 25,000 aircrew from almost certain death. The Marines did not die in vain.

Okinawa

The next target was Okinawa, a much larger island some 60 miles long, and, although 18 miles wide at one point, a mere two miles wide at its narrowest. US Intelligence once again underestimated the enemy, this time as a result of being unable, because of the extreme range of Okinawa from any available US air base during the planning phase, to get adequate aerial reconnaissance pictures. The Intelligence estimate of Japanese army strength on the island was 65,000. In fact there were well over 100,000 defenders, including locally recruited soldiers and a force of auxiliaries whose function it was to transport ammunition and supplies and thereby relieve the front line troops of support duties and keep them in the fighting line. Lieutenant-General Ushijima, in command of the defenders, accepted from the outset that there would be no victory. His objective was simply to hold out for as long as he could, kill as many Americans as he could and delay an American advance on the Japanese mainland, only 350 miles away. He therefore decided to concentrate the bulk of his 32nd Army in the Southern part of the island, with its four important airfields, and put up only a token defence in the northern part.

The newly designated US 10th Army that put 154,000 men into the struggle for Okinawa that began on April 1st 1945 was in fact made up of seven of the toughest and most battle-hardened divisions in the Pacific war – XIV Corps under General Hodge included the 7th and 96th Infantry Divisions, III Amphibious (Marine) Corps under Major-General Geiger was made up of the 1st and 6th Marine Divisions, and the reserve included the 27th and 77th Infantry Divisions and the 2nd Marine Division. The two Corps that made the initial landing totalled about 116,000 men. Just before the main Okinawa landing, the nearby islands of the Kerama Retto group were captured by the 77th Division under Major-General Bruce between March 26th and March 29th to prevent their being used as bases for counter-attacks.

Air attacks were made by carrier-borne US bombers on the airfields on Kyushu from which the Japanese might (if they had had sufficient fuel, which was doubtful) have launched fighter bomber raids on the invasion force. Vice-Admiral Blandy's Task Force 52 spent a week before the invasion both clearing the dense minefield off the Okinawa beaches and bombarding them with over 13,000 shells. More than 3,000 sorties were flown by fighter bombers from Blandy's Task Force against targets on Okinawa. In fact, it subsequently proved that much of this fire power had been wasted on areas North of the centre of the island in which there were relatively few Japanese defenders.

The bombardment from the sea continued right up to the time when the invasion fleet landed – only to find that the landing itself was virtually unopposed. More than 60,000 American troops were ashore at the end of the first day. At the same time as the first wave had landed in the morning, a dummy assault mounted by the 2nd Marine Division had diverted Japanese attention from the main landing by seeming to approach for an amphibious landing in the South, only to turn away again. This ruse was repeated on the second day, and helped to tie down the Japanese forces in the South while the beach-head was established.

Quickly, the Americans crossed the island, isolating the North from the South, still without significant Japanese opposition. Not until the 7th and 96th Infantry Divisions were sent South after learning from local inhabitants that the Japanese had concentrated in that area did the real battle for Okinawa begin. And what a battle it proved to be.

On April 5th, the US troops ran into determined opposition, but were still able to advance, although with difficulty. By the 9th, the resistance was so fierce that both divisions were brought to a standstill before a heavily defended position on Kakazu Ridge. For days the Americans attacked the ridge and were driven back. The Japanese took appalling casualties. By April 12th, more than 5,500 Japanese had died, against 451 Americans, and on that sad day when President Roosevelt died (to the joy of Adolf Hitler in far-away Germany) the two infantry divisions were still stuck in front of Kakazu Ridge. Suddenly the Japanese counterattacked, and for two fearsome days the American troops found themselves defending their hard-won positions against desperately determined Japanese soldiers. Each successive Japanese attack was held, and by the 14th April the front had settled down, with little change since the 12th. The Battle of Okinawa was beginning to assume something of the character of the Battles of the Somme.

Meanwhile, the 6th Marine Division had been sent to clear the Northern part of the island, a task which proved extremely difficult in the highly defensible narrow-necked Motobu Peninsula. General Geiger's troops spent twelve days in bloody battle before the peninsula was cleared, and even after it was declared secure parties of Japanese soldiers turned guerillas were harrying the US positions.

In the South, General Hodge had decided to try to bypass the Kakazu Ridge and thrust deep into the Japanese positions with an attack that began on April 19th and was a costly and bloody failure. Over 700 Americans died, and XXIV Corps was no further forward. Next day they tried again, pushing towards Machinato airfield, and again the attack failed. For a week they strove to take the airfield, and a terrible week it was. Not until April 27th was 'Item Pocket', as the area had become known, declared secure. During the preceding three days, Kakazu Ridge had at last fallen, but every day's fighting was gaining only yards, and still the Japanese seemed able to hold the Shuri region for ever.

On May 4th, after another week's desperate and largely fruitless battle, General Ushijima launched a Japanese counterattack, attempting to split the US 10th

Army in half with an amphibious landing to capture Tanabaru Ridge at the centre of the American army. By the 7th, his attack had failed totally, and the American commanders decided to attempt to 'wrong foot' the Japanese by attacking before they had time to regroup. This time the American attack succeeded, although slowly, and by the third week of May several important hills had been taken and the Americans seemed poised to begin the encirclement of Japanese positions. But the weather suddenly turned against the attackers. Huge rainstorms made the island a quagmire and rendered the American attack many times more difficult. Nonetheless, the American troops persevered and gradually advanced on either side of the Japanese army. Recognising the probability of encirclement, General Ushijima now decided to evacuate the Shuri region altogether, and withdraw for a last stand in the extreme South of the island. Overnight on May 23rd/24th, the 32nd Army began to pull back under cover of a rearguard action, and by the end of the month, most of the Japanese forces were well South of their front line in the Shuri, which was still holding against the American offensive. When, on May 31st, the Shuri line collapsed, the Americans were disappointed to find that they had not, after all, encircled an army. The bird had flown.

Now began the last phase in Okinawa. Between June 12th and June 17th the Americans fought, against an enemy who seemed to be more ferocious than ever, to capture what was identified as the Yaeju-Dake position. Every machine-gun nest, every foxhole, had to be blasted with unimaginable force before the defenders gave up – usually because they were dead. By the 17th, the survivors were in a pocket only eight miles by eight. After refusing an appeal to surrender and save his men's lives, Ushijima committed *hara-kiri* on the 21st June, and on the same day the last major Japanese position was taken. Isolated resistance continued until July 2nd 1945, when Okinawa was finally declared secure after one of the worst battles of the war for the Americans. Over 49,000 Americans had been killed or wounded, and 763 US aircraft had been lost. The Navy had lost 36 ships, and had had 368 damaged.

But the terrible toll of American life was as nothing to that of the lives of Japanese soldiers. Over 110,000 had died; only 7,400 prisoners were taken. In ten large-scale *kamikaze* suicide air attacks, 1,465 Japanese aricraft and pilots had been hurled at US ships. A reputed 7,800 Japanese aircraft had been destroyed, and the Japanese Navy had lost 16 ships, including the giant battleship *Yamato*, sent on a useless and ineffective suicide mission and sunk by US aircraft before even coming within sight of Okinawa.

There remained only the homeland of Japan to defend. As the wearisome battle for Okinawa had ground to its close, the bomber offensive against mainland Japan was reaching its climax. The chilling horrors of nuclear war were, unknown to all but a select few, about to be unleashed for the first time in the Earth's history. It was an awe-inspiring moment.

FINAL SURRENDER
THE AIR OFFENSIVE – HIROSHIMA & NAGASAKI

Since October 1944, when the B-29 bombers of the US 21st Bomber Command had been moved up to bases in the Marianas from China and India, the bomber fleet had been able, albeit hazardously, to strike at targets in mainland Japan. The first large-scale raid on Tokyo was launched on November 24th 1944, but, because the Japanese were able to put up fighter intercepter forces from their bases on Iwo Jima and Okinawa, and because bombers had such a long trip home, losses were high. Moreover, the actual effectiveness of the raids was not great. The B-29s were using the high-level precision daylight bombing techniques that had always been favoured by the American Air Staff, and were doing relatively little damage. This was partly because the combination of high altitude and extreme range rendered the aircraft unable to carry more than a fraction of their maximum bomb load.

The final capture of Iwo Jima in March 1945, and the arrival of the innovative and adventurously inclined Major-General Curtis LeMay as commander of the 21st Bomber Command, changed things dramatically. It was clear that the final assault on mainland Japan had to be from the air, and LeMay set about finding ways to maximise the effectiveness of the B-29 raids. Perhaps benefiting (at long last) from the experience of RAF Bomber Command over Germany during the previous two years, LeMay decided to try low-level night bombing with a mixture of incendiary and high explosive bombs. The technique was, if anything, more capable of bringing about destruction on a massive scale in Japan than it had been in Germany, since most Japanese houses were of relatively flimsy timber construction. After small-scale test raids on Nagoya in January and Kobe in February, the first full-scale night raid of the offensive was scheduled for the night of March 9th/10th. The target was Tokyo.

To prevent possible mayhem caused by crews unaccustomed to night raids firing at each other in the dark, the B-29s flew without ammunition for their machine-guns. The weight saving made it possible for each aircraft to carry an additional 3,200 pounds of bombs to the target, a significant addition which brought the average load per bomber for the low-level raid to about six tons. Between them that night, the 334 B-29 aircraft delivered about 2,000 tons of bombs from between 4,900 and 9,200 feet. The effect on Tokyo was awful and awe-inspiring. More than a quarter of a million buildings were destroyed; over a million people were made homeless; 83,000 people died; almost 41,000 were injured. Nearly 16 square miles of the city were burnt out in the fire storm that the raid raised, which had been visible to the crews of the returning bombers for more than 150 miles. Many of the crucial industrial plants supplying the Japanese war effort were destroyed beyond repair. Against this raid, the Japanese had been unable to put up fighters, and had found their anti-aircraft fire to be almost totally ineffective. Only 14 American bombers were lost; 42 more were damaged.

It seemed that LeMay had found the answer to crushing Japan. But when this success for the American bomber fleet was followed on March 11th with a similar raid on Nagoya, the centre of Japan's aircraft industry, the results were less devastating by far. Although more bombs were dropped, there was no firestorm, no general devastation, and no total destruction of industrial plants. In part, this was due to the still air of the night, but far more of the credit for saving a large part of the city went to the efficiency of the fire fighters, and the fact that their water supply continued to work through and after the raid. The American bombers all returned, with the exception of one that ditched at take-off.

Two days later, after the American ground-crews had worked ceaselessly to repair the 20 aircraft damaged over Nagoya and the 42 that had limped back from Tokyo, the B-29s struck again, this time against the port and shipbuilding centre of Osaka. A total of 301 B-29s, each with six tons of bombs, left the Marianas; 274 found the target and dropped over 1,700 tons of bombs on it. Once again, they started a firestorm, although, because the Japanese people were far better prepared, many fewer inhabitants of Osaka died than had met their end in the Tokyo raid. Nearly 4,000 civilians were killed, and another 8,400 were injured. Over eight square miles of the city were burnt out, with the loss of 119 major factories and almost 135,000 houses. On March 16th, the bombers hit Kobe, another port, and Japan's sixth largest city, destroying 500 industrial buildings and almost 66,000 houses, disabling Japan's submarine-building yard and killing nearly 3,000 people. Three days later, Nagoya was bombed again, this time with more than 1,800 tons of bombs including a significantly greater proportion of high explosive than had been used in the earlier raid. As a result, the fire-fighting on the ground was less effective, and a firestorm burned out three square miles.

The March raids had proved that strategic night bombing at low altitudes achieved dramatic results with relatively light losses. During April 1945, the wearisome and bloody campaign in Okinawa needed all the support the bombers could give, and the attacks on Japan ceased, giving the devastated cities a breathing space in which to begin the major task of clearing up. The last bodies of people killed in the first Tokyo raid of March 9th/10th were not found and removed until the second week of April, and the immensity of the task of restoring some semblance of civic order was daunting. But the experience of the American Army and Marine Corps in Okinawa was sufficient to convince both Curtis LeMay and his superiors that an amphibious invasion of mainland Japan should be considered only as a last resort. During April, the cities and industrial centres of Japan had been graded as targets according to their strategic significance, and in May the remorseless assault from the air began again with yet another raid on Nagoya, home of the Mitsubishi engineering and aircraft factories. LeMay now had more aircraft at his disposal, and was able to send 472 B-29s to deliver more than 2,500 tons of bombs – but he sent them by day to bomb from a height of between 12,000 and 20,500 feet, carrying an average of 5.3 tons apiece. The force lost ten aircraft, and achieved less damage than had the earlier night raids. Two days later, the 21st Bomber Command attacked by night at low level again, once more against Nagoya. This time the aircraft carried 8 tons each, and finally managed virtually to destroy the Mitsubishi aircraft works, with the loss of only three aircraft, all of which suffered mechanical failure rather than the effects of enemy action.

Through May and June the night attacks continued, raining destruction on the major cities and industrial centres of Japan. On May 25th, only two nights after a further raid on Tokyo had burned out over five square miles, the worst non-nuclear raid of the war on Japan totally destroyed 16.8 square miles of the city. By the end of June, 105.6 square miles of the total 257.2 square miles area of Japan's six largest cities had been burned out. More than half of Tokyo was in total ruins. Even so, in excess of sixty attacks were made between June 17th and August 14th. Yet still the spirit of Japan prevailed. Absolute devotion to the Emperor could only be overcome by the Emperor himself accepting surrender. How, the Allies asked themselves, does one persuade a god to accept defeat?

The Nuclear Holocaust

In the strictest secrecy, the 'Manhattan' project had, as the conventional war progressed, created in America the world's first practical nuclear weapons. Two separate lines of weapons research had resulted in the USA having, by the spring of 1945, two entirely different types of atomic bomb. The first, a gun-assembly weapon known as 'Little Boy', was an oblong, parallel sided bomb containing, at one end of the casing, a quantity of Uranium 235 fissionable material that was just short of the critical mass, and, at the other, a gun 'loaded' with a segment of the same material. When the gun was fired, and the smaller piece of ratio-active uranium was propelled into the larger, the total mass became critical and a massive explosion ensued. This was the bomb that was to create the devastation of Hiroshima.

The other weapon, 'Fat Boy', used plutonium as its fissionable material, and relied upon the implosion principle for its detonation. A core made up of several separate units of plutonium was contained within a casing of TNT. When the conventional explosive was detonated, the plutonium was collapsed into one larger critical mass to create the nuclear blast. America's second bomb, dropped over Nagasaki, was of this type.

In June 1945, knowing that 'Little Boy' could be ready late in July, and that 'Fat Boy' could be operational at about the same time if tests in July proved that it worked, a meeting between President Truman and the US Chiefs of Staff discussed the disturbing question of whether the new weapon should or should not be used. The problem was not quite as straightforward as it has sometimes been made to seem. General George C. Marshall had calculated that, if mainland Japan was to be invaded as the means of ending war, it would have to be tackled in two major campaigns, the first against the island of Kyushu, the second some months later against Honshu. He had worked out from Okinawa experience of the Japanese army's fanatical preparedness to die that the first of these attacks alone would cost the USA as many as 69,000 killed and wounded out of a proposed force of 190,000. What the losses arising from the final attack on Honshu would have been, once the Japanese army had reached the zenith of its suicidal zeal, nobody seems to have dared to calculate. Despite these figures, Marshall favoured holding back the atomic weapons, and the June meeting did in fact agree that the invasion of Kyushu would begin on November 1st 1945, and that the invasion of Honsho would be scheduled for March 1946.

A further school of thought held that there was no need either to use the nuclear weapons or to invade. Since Japan could shortly be totally surrounded and blockaded, it was argued, her own inability to feed her population without imports would ensure her defeat. But this argument did not gain ground, and by the time the Potsdam Conference issued its considered view, on July 26th, that Japan must either surrender unconditionally or accept 'prompt and utter destruction', the weapons were ready, and the Allies clearly intended that the Potsdam ultimatum was to be taken seriously. Despite appeals to the military government of Japan by Emperor Hirohito to accept surrender if the terms could be negotiated to include the continued existence of the Imperial Throne, Prime Minister Suzuki declined to consider the acceptance of defeat. The die was cast.

The 509th Composite Group of the USAAF, which had been based at North Field on Tinian Island in the Marianas since May, was put on readiness to deliver the new secret weapon on or after August 3rd. The uranium 235 necessary for the 'Little Boy' bomb had arrived on Tinian on July 26th. The crews of the 509th had been training for months, dropping large high explosive bombs with similar characteristics to the atomic weapons in raids over Japan. Now they waited for the clear weather that was obligatory for the dropping of the most terrible weapon man had yet devised.

On August 6th, the weather cleared, and Colonel Paul Tibbets, commander of the 509th Group, rostered himself to fly the 'Enola Gay', the long-range B-29 that he had named after his mother. Two other B-29 aircraft flew with him as observers. The target was Hiroshima. The 'Little Boy' bomb, armed during the flight to avoid dangers to Tinian Island should an accident occur at take-off, weighed 9,000 lbs, and the 'Enola Gay' was, at 65 tons take-off weight, fully eight tons over the normal operational bombing weight for a B-29. Despite this, the take-off was uneventful, the flight to the Japanese mainland passed without incident, and when the lone B-29 whose task it was to check on weather conditions over the target signalled at 7.15am that it was clear, the three aircraft bringing the bomb began their approach to the target. By the time they arrived over the city at 8.06am, the earlier air raid warning triggered by the weather aircraft had been cancelled. People were on the streets, and the city continued to go about its business, undeterred by the three aircraft far above at over 31,000 feet. Survivors reported noticing that the two aircraft either side of the leading B-29 turned away unusually tightly and made off at speed after an object on a parachute was dropped.

Just 17 seconds after 8.15am, a mighty flash, followed by searing heat and an explosion like a hundred claps of thunder rolled together, followed by blast that lifted and disintegrated buildings, tramcars, people, virtually everything in its path, burst open the stricken city, as 'Little Boy' detonated about 2,000 ft above a bridge that was the target marker. A huge mushroom cloud of debris and dust rose boiling into the atmosphere, higher than the aircraft that had brought the devastation. A blast equal to 170,000 tons of TNT and the firestorm that it raised completely flattened almost everything for 4.7 miles around the point directly below the explosion. Two thirds – 60,000 out of 90,000 – of the buildings within 9.5 square miles were either destroyed or seriously damaged. Between 60,000 and 80,000 people died, either immediately or in the weeks immediately following the bomb being dropped. Another 70,000 suffered terrible injuries. Over 20,000 children died in the blast.

On August 9th, another group of three B-29 bombers carried 'Fat Boy' to Nagasaki. Although this attack was a chapter of minor difficulties, and the aircraft delivering the bomb had subsequently to make an emergency landing on Okinawa with almost empty fuel tanks, the raid itself achieved its objective. The blast from the plutonium bomb was greater than that of the uranium bomb dropped at Hiroshima, but its equivalent explosive force to 20,000 tons of TNT in fact did rather less damage, mainly because of the more hilly topography of Nagasaki. Some 35,000 people were killed or injured in the attack and its immediate aftermath, but it should not be forgotten that the real total of killed and injured for both nuclear attacks was very much higher than the figures for immediate casualties suggest. The subsequent radiation sickness, and high incidence of cancers, congenitally abnormal births, cataract, spontaneous abortion and other conditions greatly increased the total casualties over a period of twenty and thirty years, and even as this book is written, the final genetic effects cannot be fully known. Not for nothing has the attack on Hiroshima become a symbol of the nuclear age.

Russia Claims the Pickings – and Japan Surrenders

On August 8th, after the nuclear attack on Hiroshima and before the second bomb fell on Nagasaki, Russia honoured her undertaking to enter the war against Japan once the war in Europe had been won. At midnight on the 8th, the Japanese ambassador in Moscow received the Soviet declaration of war. Ten minutes later, 1,500,000 Russian troops, 5,500 armoured vehicles and almost 4,000 aircraft embarked on a high-speed campaign against the 1,040,000-strong Japanese army in Manchuria. This was to be the last offensive of the Second World War, and it demonstrated to a watching world just how effective the Soviet war machine had become since 1941. Until the August 1945 offensive, both Japan and Russia had observed carefully, even stringently, the Neutrality Pact of April 1941. Now, after three and a half months of transporting the Russian army across a continent – 750,000 were moved on the Trans-Siberian railway alone, and 136,000 truckloads of equipment were driven to the Easternmost extremity of the USSR – the Soviet army was ready. The principal push into Manchuria was to come from Marshal Malinovsky's Transbaikal Front, made up of five armies plus the 12th Air Army, which would enter Manchuria from the West and thrust Eastwards to Mukden and Chang-chun. Far to the East, in the Maritime province North of Vladivostock, where the Japanese expected the offensive, the 1st Far Eastern Front under Marshal Meretskov, made up of the 1st, 5th, 25th, and 35th Armies faced formidable fortifications built by the Japanese against this day.

On Marshal Malinovsky's front, the 6th Guards Tank Army, despite problems of supply of fuel and water, attacked the Japanese across what most regarded as an impossible barrier – the Gobi Desert in August; hot, arid and inhospitable. For four days, the Russians advanced without opposition, for no attack had been expected on that front. As fuel and water were dropped from the air in a spectacular airlift operation, the advancing Russian Tank Army overcame the Japanese 80th Brigade, then the 107th Division, who fought on oblivious to Japan's total surrender on August 15th. The Russian 17th Army made similar progress, and by August 20th was over the Chinese border. All along the front, the armies of Soviet Russia rushed forward, overcoming all in their path. After 15th August, news of Japan's surrender gradually reached the Japanese armies in the field, many units of which simply failed to believe what they heard and fought on. But the progressive surrender of Japanese units speeded the Russian advance all along the Transbaikal Front, and by the 24th August, the Russian forces were in Mukden, Dairen and Port Arthur, and had avenged Russia's defeat by Japan in 1905. More to the point, Stalin had successfully grabbed some more territory before the war finally ended.

On the Far Eastern Front, the Japanese armies were better defended and more concentrated, and fought fiercely. Only the final surrender of Japan saved the

Soviet troops from a protracted and bloody campaign of the sort the Americans had suffered throughout the long haul back across the Pacific. This was particularly true of the Russian landing on Sakhalin and in the Kurile Islands. Now Russia was able to support with arms captured from the Japanese the Communist forces fighting the civil war in China against the Nationalist army of Chiang Kai-shek. Faced with this new peril, Chiang's future was bleak.

The Final Surrender

The devastation of the two atomic bombs, and the Russian declaration of war and offensive against Manchuria, convinced Emperor Hirohito of Japan that the time had come for a little rational Western thinking, and for his nation to surrender. For almost ten years, he had been effectively a puppet Emperor, unable to do more than accept the dictates of his 'advisers' and acquiesce in the rule of the military government. Now, when the military dictatorship had demonstrably failed, and Japan had been brought to her knees, he convened a meeting in the air-raid shelter of the Imperial Palace at midnight on August 9th 1945. There was a heated discussion. All agreed that any surrender must permit the Emperor to retain his throne and his sovereignty, but the military members of the government wanted also to ensure that there was no Allied occupation, and that Japanese war criminals would be tried by Japanese in Japan. When everyone had had their say, Hirohito, for the first time since the Thirties, took a decision. Japan would offer surrender on only the one condition – that the sovereign power of the Emperor would be retained.

The decision was cabled to the Allies. The US Secretary of State, James Byrnes, responded swiftly – only unconditional surrender was acceptable, and the Emperor was to be 'subject to' the Supreme Allied Commander. More heated discussion ensued in the Japanese Cabinet, and on August 14th a further meeting with the Emperor again elicited a decision made by him alone without deference to his government. Japan would accept the Allied conditions. Radio messages were sent forthwith to all Japanese armies and troops in the field telling them of the surrender and instructing them to lay down their arms. Most did. Some fought on. Many officers committed ritual *Hara kiri* rather than dishonour themselves by surrender.

To convince the Japanese population that the unthinkable had happened, Emperor Hirohito, for the first time in a reign spanning (since 1926) almost two decades, recorded a radio broadcast, and at noon on August 15th the Japanese population heard the voice of their Emperor, still officially a god, telling them that the war was at an end and that Japan was to be occupied.

On August 30th, the first of the occupation forces, a contingent of American and British troops, landed at Yokosuka. Three days later, on September 2nd, just one day and three hours short of six years after the first Allied declaration of war against Hitler by Britain in 1939, the Second World War came officially to an end when the formal surrender was signed aboard the battleship USS *Missouri* in Tokyo harbour. The newly appointed Foreign Minister of Japan, Mamoru Shigemitsu, and representatives of the Japanese armed services signed on behalf of their country. General Douglas MacArthur, and generals and admirals of the USA, Great Britain, China, Russia, the Netherlands, New Zealand, Canada, France and Australia signed on behalf of the Allies. There remained now only the rebuilding of a peacetime world.

THE LEGACY OF WAR

AND ITS POST WAR IMPACT

The end of the Second World War ushered in a period of world-wide political change. The invasions and counter-invasions of the aggressors and those who sought to liberate had brought forth from nations the world over an increased awareness of the meaning of freedom; of human rights; of the horrors of war. The bursting forth of Soviet socialism across Europe and Asia swept up in its wake proud nations whose history was as individual and as deserving of preservation as any on earth, and substituted a new tyranny for that which had so recently been defeated.

In the USA, the death in April of President Roosevelt, who had for so long believed that Stalin would not deceive him, brought to the Presidency Harry S. Truman, who recognised that the West had already been deceived, and that the USSR could be checked only by the nuclear deterrent. Truman dismissed Henry Morgenthau Jr, the Secretary of the Treasury whose extraordinary plan to pastoralise Germany into a purely agricultural community had come so close to being Allied policy. Under Truman, the USA took a more realistic view of Germay's future and sought to rebuild the economy of the new Federal Republic.

In Britain, Winston Churchill, having inspired and led Britain tirelessly through her most desperate hours, was remorselessly sacked and sent home to the country by a swing to Socialism apparently boosted by the votes of the returning servicemen. Just when Britain needed that leadership again, it got instead Clement Attlee; a worthy Prime Minister, an excellent administrator, but lacking in inspirational quality.

In India, General Wavell was replaced as Viceroy almost as soon as Attlee came to power, and it was to Admiral Lord Louis Mountbatten that the task of guiding India to independence fell, a task completed in 1947.

In Japan, General Douglas MacArthur administered the Allied occupation wisely and well, guiding the Japanese nation to a new alliance of traditional values and Western attitudes. MacArthur proved himself a considerable politician, pushing through radical changes in the Japanese constitution that outlawed war entirely, guaranteed political freedom and created a democratic state. The Emperor was stripped of all but his symbolic status, and formally renounced his divinity. The major Japanese war leaders were tried for their crimes. Seven, including General Yamashita, General Tojo and General Homma, the perpetrator of the infamous 'Death March' in the Philippines, were hanged. Two – Prince Funimaro Konoye and General Honjo – beat the hangman and committed suicide.

In Germany – the part of that country the world was now obliged to become accustomed to calling West Germany – a War Crimes Tribunal was convened on a much larger scale. Under four-power jurisdiction, the Tribunal was to try the former leaders of Nazi Germany for having committed crimes against humanity. On October 18th 1945, the prosecutors issued indictments against twenty-one Nazis. Thirty days later, on November 20th, the accused faced their accusers in one of the few intact buildings left in Nuremberg. As in Japan, some of the war criminals beat the hangman. Hitler, Goebbels and Himmler were all dead long before their crimes were heard.

Two observers of those hearings in Nuremberg have described their overwhelming impression to me in exactly the same words – 'they looked so ordinary'. For the men of Nuremberg were by now crumpled, exhausted, beaten, and, in most cases, quite old. For ten months the hearings continued, bringing forth daily in evidence the indescribable sufferings of the six million Jews murdered in pursuit of Himmler's 'Final Solution'; the atrocities against civilian populations in reprisal for incidents against the German Army; the callousness and brutality with which Hitler's Reich rightly became identified.

When it was all over, twelve of the accused were sentenced to death. Hermann Goering, Martin Bormann (in his absence) and Foreign Minister Joachim von Ribbentrop; Ernst Kaltenbrunner, who had succeeded 'Hangman Heydrich' as Protector of Bohemia and Moravia after Heydrich's assassination; Rosenberg, the party 'philosopher'; Hans Frank, the Nazi inquisitor in Poland; Julius Streicher, the Jew baiter of Nuremberg, probably the most unpleasant and sadistic of the Nazi hierarchy; The curiously colourless Frick, Plenipotenary for Administration in Hitler's cabinet; Fritz Sauckel, the organiser of slave labour; Dr Arthur Seyss-Inquart, the quisling Governor of Austria; Keitel and Jodl. All were hanged in the early morning of October 16th 1946 – except for Goering, who succeeded in taking poison an hour before he was due to die, and Bormann, who has never been located and was probably already dead.

Three of the accused were acquitted – Hjalmar Schacht, who had attempted as Hitler's Economics Minister and President of the Reichsbank to keep the Führer in touch with reality; Franz von Papen, once Chancellor of Germany; and Hans Fritsche. The remainder, including Albert Speer, Hitler's Armaments Minister, Rudolf Hess, who had flown to Britain in May 1941 to seek peace, and Grand Admiral Karl Doenitz, nominated by Hitler as his successor, were imprisoned for varying terms. Most were released in the Fifties. Only Hess remained in captivity, the lone prisoner in Berlin's Spandau Prison, until his controversial death by strangulation in 1987.

With the conclusion of the Nuremberg trials, it was as though the past ended and the future began. The Soviet Union, constantly aware of the enormous strategic advantage gained by the USA as a result of having the nuclear bomb, had begun in 1945 a campaign of espionage to obtain the necessary secrets. On July 10th 1949, Russia proved the effectiveness of both her espionage and her scientists by conducting a successful nuclear test. The age of the rival deterrents had arrived, years before Washington believed it possible.

Little more than a year earlier the USSR had reacted sharply and quite indefensibly to US action to revitalise the West German economy by abolishing Hitler's Reichsmark and introducing a new Deutschmark. Recognising that Berlin, then as now, was isolated within Soviet dominated East Germany, Russia callously attempted to starve the population of West Berlin into submission to Russian domination by closing all land routes from West Germany to the former capital. The Allies could do nothing to reopen the roads and canals thus closed short of going to war with Russia, for there were 17 Red Army divisions between Berlin and the Western Zones of Occupation. But Russia had not and could not close the air lanes.

Thus began the Berlin Airlift, by which two and a quarter million Berliners were supplied with their every essential for almost a year before the Russians gave in, admitted defeat and reopened the land routes. By the time the airlift finished, the pilots and controllers had become so efficient that every day saw lifted into Berlin three times more supplies than the city needed for a day. The Russians learned from this a great lesson – the value of strategic military transport aircraft. One has only to reflect on the efficiency of their invasion of Afghanistan at Christmas 1979 to recognise how well the lesson was learned.

Even in the years immediately after the war, Russian influence extended far beyond Berlin, Germany or indeed Europe. As soon as the Japanese were defeated by the advancing Red Army in Manchuria, the captured arms began to be ferried to Mao-Tse-Tung's communist revolutionaries in China. Although the USA tried repeatedly to find diplomatic means to reconcile Chiang Kai-Shek and Mao, and did achieve, through a mission by General George C. Marshall, a truce between the two in 1946, by the end of 1949 Mao had smashed the Kuomintang, Chiang Kai-shek had retreated to his Formosan Nationalist stronghold (now Taiwan), and Mao was in control of what became known as Red China.

There next emerged what is now a familiar Soviet tactic designed to extend Russian domination – the supply of arms to a guerilla force. Many of those same captured Japanese arms, and many more of the genuine Russian article, found their way into North Korea, where the communists were seeking to overrun the (genuinely) democratic South. The Americans intervened forcefully and successfully to contain the Communist attack, and prevented the loss of South Korea to the free world – but, when the stalemate armistice was signed at Panmunjom, it was the United Nations that enforced it.

Born of an idea hatched between Roosevelt and Churchill, christened by Roosevelt, and brought to maturity by a series of conferences at Dumbarton Oaks, Washington DC, during 1944, and at a meeting in San Francisco in April 1945, the United Nations had been already in existence by the end of the war. Because it was genuinely an organisation seeking to avoid unnecessary conflict, it was and, to a lesser extent is, a more successful policing body than the League of Nations, which had failed in so many crises during the Thirties. In the early years after the war, before its original political polarisation and intent was clouded and put out of balance by the procession of newly independent emergent countries of the Sixties and Seventies, the United Nations was an effective balance in the Cold War, and several times prevented the Cold War becoming hot. But, as the Fifties succeeded the Forties, it was the balance of power rather than idealistic concepts that once more determined whether the peace was preserved. That balance, by 1949, was polarised as being between, on the one hand, the Soviet Union itself with the Soviet dominated countries that the USSR had overrun in the closing stages of the war, which now became known collectively as the Warsaw Pact nations, and, on the other, the North Atlantic Treaty Orgnisation, known as NATO. The Treaty was ratified on 4th April 1949, and brought together with the USA and Canada under a common umbrella of defence spending and planning eleven nations of Western Europe, to which were later added Greece and Turkey, which joined in 1952, and West Germany, which joined in 1955.

The emergence of NATO was perhaps the most significant single example of the mighty change in the position of the USA that the war had wrought. Before the Second World War, Britain had been a great imperial power, still wielding the influence and through it much of the wealth of the Victorian era. The USA was a determinedly neutral, isolationist nation. When America threw its means of production heart and soul into the war, it actually did the nation good. The standard of living in the United States rose sharply during the war; in other combatant countries it fell. British and British Commonwealth shipping losses reduced the size of their fleet from 40,000,000 tons to only 19,500,000 tons. The US merchant fleet quadrupled to 50,000,000 tons. Britain lost as a result of the war 35 times as much foreign invested capital as did the USA. The USA ended the war rich. Britain ended it poor.

Recognising this situation, the USA put its new-found wealth to the defence of the free world; and in particular to the defence of Western Europe. From being an isolationist power observing the doings of the British Empire with intererst, America had become the most significant financial and international diplomatic force on earth. From that again sprang the space programme. For, as General Patton's 3rd Army had rushed through Southern Germany in the closing stages of the war, they had discovered a stockpile of complete and near complete V2 rockets. The US Army had also secured the services of Wernher von Braun, the brilliant chief scientist of Hitler's rocket programme. After a discreet interval, von Braun and his rockets were reunited in the USA, and from his continued work were developed the 'Gemini', 'Mercury' and 'Apollo' programmes which put Neil Armstrong and his successors on the moon.

When he set out to conquer Europe and subjugate Russia, Hitler sought to change the face of the world. He and his allies drew a large part of the world into war. He conquered; he over-reached himself; he was totally defeated. The evils of his regime were so great that almost any result was to be preferred to his success. But although his plans for the world were not to be, the pattern of political and military power was altered for the remainder of the twentieth century, and probably for the twenty-first, by the perverted genius of the Austrian corporal. His impact upon history, and upon our lives, has been greater than that of any other man since the ancients.